BORDERLAND

JOHN R. STILGOE # BORDERLAND

ORIGINS OF THE AMERICAN SUBURB, 1820–1939

YALE UNIVERSITY PRESS   NEW HAVEN AND LONDON

Designed by Sally Harris and set in Kennerly type by
The Composing Room of Michigan.
Printed in the United States of America by Halliday
Lithograph, West Hanover, Massachusetts.

Library of Congress Cataloging-in-Publication Data

Stilgoe, John R.
    Borderland : origins of the American suburb,
1820–1939 / John R. Stilgoe.
        p.   cm.
    Bibliography: p.
    Includes index.
    ISBN 0–300–04257–4 (alk. paper)
    1. Suburbs—United States—History—19th
century.   2. Suburbs—United States—History—
20th century.   3. Landscape assessment—United
States—History—19th century.   4. Landscape
assessment—United States—History—20th century.
I. Title
HT351.S84   1988
307.7'4'0973—dc19   88–13981
                        CIP

The paper in this book meets the guidelines for
permanence and durability of the Committee on
Production Guidelines for Book Longevity of the
Council on Library Resources.

10 9 8 7 6 5 4 3 2 1

Title page illustration: "Monday Morning."
For a moment, perhaps two, suburban women felt
bereft as their commuter husbands left for work after
pleasant weekends. But then they remembered that all
day they would live in a land almost free of male
restriction, and as the face of this woman suggests, they
began to plan.

For John Brinckerhoff Jackson

We are the borderers of civilization in America, but borderers of the nineteenth century, when all distances are lessened, whether moral or physical.

Susan Cooper   1857

CONTENTS

PREFACE

Six years ago in the small attic seminar of
Sever Hall at Harvard University, I began teaching a new course on the post–
World War II suburban landscape. Two objectives shaped the content. On the one
hand, I wanted my students to scrutinize the built environment in which so many
have spent their childhoods, and particularly to grasp the visual changes of the last
fifty years, to know that once upon a time the "leafy" or "large-lot" suburbs now
characterized by modified houses, mature trees and other planting, private outdoor
space, and other created elements had not long ago been condemned as bare, scruffy
deserts of identical houses. On the other hand, I wanted to explore—as much for my
sake as for theirs—the transformation of the so-called suburban landscape into the
as-yet-unnamed environment sprawling around Princeton in New Jersey, Tyson's
Corners in Virginia, and elsewhere, a transformation about which I had already
published journal articles and which continues to intrigue me. And so with a hand-
picked group of graduate and undergraduate students already familiar with theories
and methods of analyzing the large-scale North American built environment, I
began with the "streetcar suburbs" of late-nineteenth-century cities and moved
with dispatch to the places so gratefully discovered by ex-GIs and their new
families.[1]

Yet always I caught the shadows of earlier suburban landscapes, shadows
something like the images caught in old glass-plate negatives twice exposed. Of
course my students caught the faint images too, and from the beginning asked about
the background of the 1950s suburbs. Commuting alone often preoccupied us, and
not only commuting in its modern and contemporary forms, but commuting as mid-
nineteenth-century commuters knew it. "The objection that too much time is thus
lost in traveling to and fro is not well founded," asserts Henry Hudson Holly in his
1863 *Country Seats,* "since it actually requires but little more to reach a country
place twenty miles from town than to go from an office in Wall Street to a residence
in the upper part of the city."[2] But what did long-distance commuting do to the
commuter's awareness of space, to his understanding of city, country, distance? Did
the commuter every day evaluate the visual environment of both city and suburb,

did commuting heighten appreciation, or disgust, with the worlds at opposite ends of the line? Such questions led me backward, beyond the era of electric streetcars, beyond even the era of railroad commuting, back to the time when *borderland* designated a novel and unique landscape.

Borderland: Origins of the American Suburb introduces a landscape over time, but a landscape that addressed curiously timeless concerns. It makes no attempt to unravel the great forces, economic, technological, religious, and otherwise, that comprise the "sociology of suburbia," but deals rather with the theater in which "suburbans" chose to live in the century after 1820. It probes and pokes at visual things, and in a time when urban form receives so much scrutiny, it focuses on a purely marginal place, "commuter country," the borderlands, the suburbs as Americans once knew them.[3]

ACKNOWLEDGMENTS

No one writes a book of this kind without the help of others, and I have been exceptionally fortunate in having colleagues and friends who provided much assistance.

Above all, however, John Brinckerhoff Jackson receives my deepst thanks. So many years ago he directed my attention at the nearly unknown territory of landscape history and urged me to explore. From that day to this, his example remains an inspiration and his friendship a rare gift. However far into the territory any of us venture, we encounter his blazings.

Next come my students. They are indeed a new generation, young men and women for whom "the suburban built environment" is as much a given as space travel and biotechnics. When they question, they question from points of view not only novel, but remarkably insightful. And while much of their interest focuses on suburbs after World War II, some of it focuses just as strongly on much earlier periods. My women students, having come of age in a time of feminist ideology and economic uncertainty, often wonder especially about a now-ignored landscape of reform shaped in large part by women concerned with the same issues that trouble contemporary women. All of my "suburbs seminar" students, women and men, here receive my thanks.

My colleagues and friends have urged me on. At Harvard, Louis Bakanowsky, Gerald M. McCue, Peter Rowe, Eduard Sekler, Carl Steinitz, Albert Szabo, Michael VanValkenburgh, and Francois Vigier all shared their understanding of contemporary suburban issues. James Hodgson, Librarian of the Loeb Library, and two of his associates, Christopher Hail and Katherine Poole, provided the wonderful help that only the finest of first-class librarians can provide. Colleagues and friends elsewhere helped too, particularly Robert Emlen, Judith Fryer, and Cecelia Tichi. As always, Judy Metro, my editor at Yale University Press, must receive much credit for whatever successes are found in this book. She and her associates Sally Harris, Stephanie Jones, John Ryden, and Tina Weiner comprise a unique and wonderful team, the sort few authors ever encounter.

I thank my friends and townsmen, too, for they did much to support my efforts.

Bob Belyea, Lee and Donna Clabots, Jeff Fitzgerald, Steve Forti, Sue Jevne, Phil Joseph, Bill Langone, Scott McClean, Joe McGuire, Gary Naylor, Eleanor Norris, and Harold and Sue Tuttle especially provided much critical insight and help at a time when I needed it most. And without the love of my sons, Adam and Nathaniel, and of my closest friend, Debra Reynolds, this book would not be.

INTRODUCTION

Suburbs deserve scrutiny. To wander purposefully in suburbs, to observe firsthand the complex artifact of space and structure, is to glimpse the rich diversity of a built form too often ignored or insulted by partisans of city or country.

Once *suburb* denoted inhabited land immediately below hilltop walled towns, the houses, gardens, workshops and other built forms literally beneath—and beyond—ramparts and gates. Always *suburban* connoted inferiority, for a suburb lay low, in the shadow of the municipality above it. Dependent, forlorn, prey to brigands and attacking armies, the ancient and medieval suburb existed fitfully, lacking any respectable identity. Not village. not town, not even hamlet, its inhabitants cringed under the scorn of burghers complacent behind stout walls. Suburbanites envied the uphill security, the order implicit in corporate charters and mercantile effort. They wanted little else than to join the walled-in fortunates, to achieve citizenship. As individuals, they aspired to owning real estate within the walls. As a group, they dreamed of annexation, of the municipality extending its walls and enfolding their chaos into order. *Suburb* is an old word, old even in English. "Where dwelle ye, if it to telle be?" asks one of Chaucer's pilgrims. " 'In the suburbes of a toun.' quod he" runs the following line, instantly describing the answerer. In 1386 no reader of *The Canterbury Tales* needed elaboration. After all, in the late fourteenth century, the suburbs of Canterbury greeted all pilgrims to the cathedral town.[1]

Medieval English suburbs grew haphazardly, stretching ribbonlike along the main roads leading to town gates. Consider Winchester and its poor hanger-on, the suburb of Soke. In the early fourteenth century, not one prosperous citizen lived in the ramshackle suburb huddled against the east gate of the town. Nearly two centuries later, both walled town and rickety suburb had grown in population, but still Soke housed not one wealthy family. All across England—indeed everywhere in Europe—suburbs like Soke nestled against town walls and grew by reaching away from the very walls they cherished, grew by reaching into orchards and wheat fields and meadows.[2] "London, what are thy Suburbes but licensed Stewes?"

mocked one commentator in 1593, enraged at prostitution, drunkenness, and other evil "next door to the Magistrates."[3] Prosperous, walled-in citizens profited from suburban stews, however. They owned the agricultural land across which suburbs inched, and they rented the land to the inhabitants of cottages and hovels, finding ground rents more lucrative than husbandry. And townsmen taxed suburbanites, especially when town walls needed repair, and scorned them as they taxed. "There's a trim rabble let in," jeers one character in Shakespeare's 1613 play, *Henry VIII:* "are all these Your faithful friends o' th' Suburbs?"[4] Craving security, order, urbanity, craving to be let in, suburbanites received only taxation, insult, and the privilege of living adjacent to fitful employment. From ancient times to the early eighteenth century, suburbs existed on the edge, in a marginal zone neither municipal nor rural. To pass from Soke to Winchester, to enter the gateway, meant leaving chaos for order, destitution for plenty. To pass from Soke into the rural landscape meant nearly the same.

Now in the United States, Canada, and Australia the situation is different, spun about in forms that vex visitors from Austria, Brazil, and Tokyo. Across the Republic, urban downtowns, industrial zones, and fringe residential districts screech in their shabbiness, their decrepitude, screech in a destitution of spirit and tax base almost unrelieved by a few blocks of glittering office towers or renovated row houses. Suburbs, and particularly the suburbs of the wealthy and the middle class, use and abuse the power wielded by American cities until the early 1920s. Suburbs control state and national elections, suburbs consume the bulk of manufactured goods, suburbs sprawl across vast areas that defy traditional political nomenclature or topographical analysis. If opinion polls prove accurate, suburbs represent the good life, the life of the dream, the dream of happiness in a single-family house in an attractive, congenial community that inspires so many urban apartment and condominium dwellers to work, to save, to get out of cities they perceive as chaotic, inimical to childhood joy, unnaturally paced, incredibly polluted, and just too crowded.[5] Suburbs now set standards—standards as simple as the "proper" sort and amount of domestic indoor space and as complex as the naturalness of a contrived forest—by which a majority of Americans judge cities and find them wanting.

Suburbs differ one from another, however, and lumping together the nearly incredible array of places identified by the slippery designation perpetuates the confusion that overwhelmed observers in the years just following World War II, when the reach of massive subdivision and building efforts struck home among intellectuals uncertain of their own values and social status.[6] In the years of treeless Levittowns and organization men, books like Erich Hodgins' *Mr. Blandings Builds His Dream House* and John Keats's *The Crack in the Picture Window,* television shows like *Leave It to Beaver* and *Ozzie and Harriet,* engine-driven lawnmowers and interstate highways, contemporaneous commentators almost without thinking reworked a vocabulary of the late 1920s and early 1930s. In the three decades following 1955, social critics, landscape planners, and historians, almost all resident

The Saturday Evening

POST

November 26, 1960 — 15¢

The Inside Story of
THE MAYO CLINIC

Adventures of the Mind:
HOW LIFE BEGAN

LYNDALE

BUS STOP
NO
PARKING

By 1960, as railroad commuting diminished in importance, humorists treated the trials of the "kiss-and-ride" in increasingly nostalgic ways, forgetting that the chauffeur-wife, for all her occasional difficulties, enjoyed the family car all day.

in the urban east, rediscovered the suburbs as the scruffy frontier known to their forebears a few decades earlier.

Consider "The Frontier and Literature," a 1931 *New Republic* review essay by Matthew Josephson, formerly one of the "lost generation" expatriates in Paris, an advisory editor of *Broom,* and, in the years just before his article, an editor of *transition.* Nothing sets apart the article from its genre. Its author scorns the cultureless frontier, condemns the pioneering experience as the national prelude to the business culture of the 1920s, and quotes approvingly H. L. Mencken on the "qualities of unsettled, lawless, transition." The frontier experience, concludes Josephson bluntly, "was inimical to artistic production" and seriously damaged the national spirit; in short, the pioneers sired a generation of small-town small minds.[7] Yet even as Josephson and so many of his fellow east-coast, urban, avant-garde colleagues wrote, scholars like Constance Rourke and Lucy Lockwood Hazard had begun flatly contradicting his "highbrow" assertions. Rourke's *American Humor: A Study of the National Character* slowly reshaped 1930s thinking; by 1941, when Hazard published *The Frontier in American Literature,* a massive revision had gathered steam. By the 1960s historians and the educated general public knew of many complex frontiers—urban, ranching, mining, farming, and others—and the biting sarcasm of Josephson had vanished. As I suggest in chapter 23, however, the anti-frontier school shifted its sarcasm to what it perceived as the new frontier of cultureless, small-minded people, the suburbs, and focused its attention particularly on the "leafy" outer suburbs—or *borderlands,* as early nineteenth-century intellectuals termed them—of the large eastern cities.[8]

Not until the 1920s did those suburbs substantially unnerve American intellectuals. Indeed until that time most intellectuals favored their creation. Only during and after the Great War, when Josephson and many other lost generation writers discovered in the outer suburbs an intellectual tradition slow to accept the European avant garde, did urban writers, especially in New York, turn on the suburbs as the home of a narrow-mindedness equal to anything Mencken found on the western frontier or on Main Street.[9] Perhaps Sinclair Lewis' *Babbitt* remains the best known of the attacks on the suburbs, and perhaps it best shows the subtle transition from the attack on western small towns, but it is only one of many works by the self-styled new thinkers who knew clearly that educated suburbanites accepted few of their premises. In the outer suburbs thrived a mindset, almost a philosophy, that challenged urban intellectuals profoundly smitten with European thinking. And in time, as urban thinkers discerned the financial and political power of the suburbanites, their attacks became as strident as Josephson's assault on the frontier and its small-town midwestern and western descendants. Architects entranced with the flat-roofed, cement apartment houses of 1930s Berlin reeled from steadfast suburban love of single-family, pitched roof houses; interior decorators announcing the wonders of tube-steel furniture found a burgeoning interest in American wooden antique; city planners championing great boulevards and public parks learned of gardeners anxious to shape their own private spaces; and social critics and historians struggling to interpret the great forces guiding the passage of the Republic found families making separate peace with urbanization, corporate employment, and high-paced political and social change.

This book examines outer suburbs from the early nineteenth century to the early 1930s, the time of the split, when most urban intellectuals began condemning the perceived conservatism, pettiness, and "tackiness" of the suburbs, establishing the lines of argument still evident today. By the late 1930s too, automobile transportation had reoriented lifestyle and built form, and after World War II, as Kenneth Jackson has shown in his *Crabgrass Frontier: The Suburbanization of the United States,* massive federal intervention fueled the exodus of middle-class Americans from troubled cities. The concatenation of space and structure away from large and small cities after World War II—the as-yet-undesignated concatenation so evident around Princeton in New Jersey, Tyson's Corners in Virginia, and south of San Diego, for example—transcends not only the landscape of the borderlands, but the postwar concept of the suburb, and it will form the core of another book, a sequel to this. Likewise, the landscape wrought by the twentieth-century "back-to-the-farm" movement, the subject of a work now in hand, usually lies literally beyond the borderlands and so beyond this book.[10] But the evolution of the borderland landscape throughout the nineteenth century illuminates not only something of the postwar automobile suburb in all its forms but also something of the relationship of educated Americans to the larger residential landscape. While the subject of this book is somewhat narrower than the "landscape of American suburbs," therefore, it is a broad subject nonetheless.

In the title of Part Three lie definitions peculiar to the argument. By *commuter* I mean much more than the person, in this period usually a man, who traveled by carriage, steamboat, or train between home and place of business, usually an office. *To commute* also means to mitigate or to lessen, and in my opinion the outer suburbs began and developed as a spatial means of grappling with and lessening the difficulties of urbanization and, especially, urbanization based on industrialization and corporate capitalism. By *country* I mean space visually dominated by trees and displaying vestiges of early nineteenth-century agricultural beauty, the landscape so accurately described by Frederick S. Cozzens in "The Sparrowgrass Papers, or Living in the Country" (a novel of borderland family adventure serialized in 1855 and 1856 in *Putnam's Magazine*) and by many other writers throughout the century. By no means does the term suggest a rural place dependent on farming. "No place can be rural, in all the *virtues* of the phrase, where a steamer will take the villager to the city between noon and night, and bring him back between midnight and morning," mused Nathaniel Parker Willis as early as 1840 in *American Scenery Illustrated.* "There is a suburban look and character about all the villages on the Hudson which seem out of place among such scenery. They are suburbs; in fact, steam has destroyed the distance between them and the city."[11] While his contemporaries wondered at the potential of railroad trains, Willis surveyed the passing steamboats and grasped the linked importance of the "come-outer" commuter and the countryside.

Underlying this study is one interpretation of the American come-outer tradition, a fragment of the American experience all too frequently ignored despite the continuing belief that the Republic is a nation of immigrants. All Americans, except those of direct African ancestry, descend from people who more or less willingly deserted homelands, who ventured forth for a hundred reasons out of England, Ireland, Russia, Poland, Italy, China.[12] Americans teach their children that the come-outers sought religious freedom, safety from tyranny, refuge from military conscription, and above all the opportunity to better themselves and their children economically, usually, but not invariably, by owning land. Of the other point of view, the one still presented around tavern and cantina tables across Europe, schoolbooks and national mythology speak nothing. Did the lazy, the cowardly, the quitters, the refuse emigrate to the Republic? Did they harm the people, the nations they left behind?

No immigrant group worried more about the question than the settlers of seventeenth-century New England. William Bradford's history of the Plymouth colony begins with an intricate catalogue of explanations for the Separatist removal from England to The Netherlands, and an even longer catalogue of reasons for the decision to cross the Atlantic. "Not out of any newfangledness or other such like giddy humor by which men are oftentimes transported to their great hurt and danger, but for sundry weighty and solid reasons" did the tiny group desert British, then Dutch rule.[13] John Winthrop, the first governor of the Massachusetts Bay Colony, worried that by deserting England his band of Puritans might weaken the struggle for religious reform, endanger likeminded worshipers unwilling to emigrate, and indeed harm the realm by removing hard-working people from it. One close friend told him that "the church and commonwelthe heere at home, hath more neede of your best abyllitie in these dangerous tymes, than any remote planta-tion."[14] But Bradford, Winthrop, and thousands of fellow Puritans chose to leave, and in so choosing not only aroused the anger and scorn of their countrymen but posed a continuing problem for shapers of national mythology.

Bradford, the first historian, clearly understood that the reasons for removal must be weighty indeed, lest the Plymouth settlers be forever condemned as giddy. His list, the prototypical list of almost all subsequent histories, enumerates financial hardship, children "drawn away by evil examples into extravagant and dangerous courses, getting the reins off their necks," and the burning desire to worship with-out restraint.[15] In his 1702 opus, *Magnalia Christi Americana; or, The Ecclesiastical History of New-England,* Cotton Mather included a far more detailed but similar list of "general considerations for the plantation of New-England," prefacing it with a blunt affirmation that the Holy Spirit moved the Puritans to leave.[16] Decade after decade, historians emphasized the wretched conditions that prompted the Puritans to abandon England. "Numbers of devout and brave men gave way to the convic-tion, that, for such as they, England was ceasing for ever to be a habitable place," concluded John Gorham Palfrey in 1858 in his *History of New England.*[17] As late as 1931, popular historians stressed the righteousness of emigration. "The American dream was beginning to take form in the hearts of men," remarked James Truslow

Adams in his best-selling *Epic of America.* "The economic motive was unquestion-
ably powerful, often dominant, in the minds of those who took part in the great
migration, but mixed with this was also frequently present the hope of a better and a
freer life, a life in which a man might think as he would and develop as he willed."
Adams, as had so many historians before him, argued that "the common man as well
as the leader was hoping for greater freedom and happiness for himself and his
children."[18] So accustomed are Americans to the litany of reasons for emigration, a
litany reinforced in late eighteenth- and early nineteenth-century religious awakenings, in twentieth-century evangelical preaching, a litany hammered home by grade
school and high school history texts, that the essential meaning vanishes in un-
critical conviction.

Puritans equated their colonizing attempt with the flight of the Jews from
Egypt, emphasizing their own "errand into the wilderness," their own wanderings
in the forest desert.[19] Over and over, Puritan clergymen and historians cited biblical
precedent and advice for abandoning England. "Come out of her, my people, lest
you take part in her sins," says the heavenly voice in Revelation 18:4. Abandon
Babylon, abandon England, go west.

Cotton Mather wondered at the emotions awakened by flight from native
shores, cherished firesides, the ground of parents' memories. As a third-generation
New Englander resident in the town of his grandfather, he perhaps marveled at the
willingness to remove. By the beginning of the eighteenth century, however, New
Englanders, Virginians, Pennsylvanians, and other colonists had learned to desert
coastal communities for backcountry enterprise, and Mather had glimpsed the
significance of that migration for coastal settlements. He and other observers usually saw the westward movement not as giddy desertion, but as movement *to*
something, as a grand course of empire; they kept to themselves vague doubts about
long-term impacts on regions left behind.[20] Only astute European observers now
and then grasped what troubled eastern Americans—the unwillingness of many
Americans to succeed in a difficult place, to improve unfavorable conditions rather
than flee them.

"They broke the ties of attachment to their native soil long ago, and have not
formed new ones since," wrote Tocqueville in 1848 of the families pushing west
from recently settled western states. The Frenchman wondered about the significance of geographic mobility, finally concluding that "a restless spirit, immoderate
desire for wealth, and an extreme love of independence," all passions Europeans
considered great social dangers, contributed to the strength and peacefulness of the
Republic. "Without such restless passions the population would be concentrated
around a few places and would soon experience, as we do, needs which are hard to
satisfy."[21] *Democracy in America* analyzes what citizens of the early Republic took
for granted, the lack of restriction on movement. Only rarely did Americans of the
early nineteenth century explicate the spatial mobility implicitly guaranteed in their
new Constitution, and then usually when writing for European audiences. James
Fenimore Cooper's 1828 *Notions of the Americans,* for example, juxtaposes the

unmarked New York–Connecticut border so casually crossed by wagon and stage-coach with the boundaries of European nations guarded by "agents of the police."[22] Americans descend from people who moved about, and they consider freedom of movement so precious—and commonplace—that they rarely think about it at all. "But I reckon I got to light out for the Territory" says Huckleberry Finn at the close of Mark Twain's 1885 novel.[23] West from Anglicanism, pogroms, and grinding agricultural poverty, west from rocky New England farms and worn-out Virginia soil, west from Ohio and Tennessee, from Nevada and New Mexico, Americans moved and move still.

And they move now ignorant of the mid-nineteenth-century connotation of *come-outer,* a connotation that intrigued John Russell Bartlett, the compiler of *Dictionary of Americanism,* and contemporaneous explicators of American religion. "They have not themselves assumed any distinctive organization," wrote one of these commentators in 1844 of the new come-outers. "They have no creed, believ-ing that every one should be left free to hold such *opinions* on religious subjects as he pleases, without being held accountable for the same to any human authority." The anonymous "American editor" of John Evans' *History of All Christian Sects* defined a new sort of American, one neither agnostic nor unchurched, but nondenomina-tional, one more secular and tolerant (except of slaveholding and war), perhaps, than his forebears, one perhaps more attuned to the ministrations of nature and fellowship, one perhaps as likely to avoid evil as contest it. The old come-outers are everywhere in American writing, of course, but after Tocqueville's time, and es-pecially after the 1850s, so also are the new, in works ranging from Thomas Chan-dler Haliburton's 1855 *Nature and Human Nature* to Joseph C. Lincoln's 1904 novel, *Cap'n Eri: A Story of the Coast.*[24] The new come-outers share with the old a predilection for separation, for small-group removal from onerous situations.

In *The Logic of Collective Action,* Mancur Olson offers a penetrating analysis of the come-outer predilection to separate from trouble, explaining the motivations and activities of small groups, especially those seeking to satisfy some want or commute some evil. A small group often succeeds in its efforts because any indi-vidual will obtain for the entire group a good that he wants for himself. Large groups often fail because enthusiastic individuals cannot secure a good for all their fellows. Consider an English Puritan in 1630. However much he might want a just govern-ment, he knows that he can do little to secure it. But if he chooses to emigrate with his family or a slightly larger group, his energy and efforts within the group count for a great deal. In order to reform his own situation, he abandons the large group and its space, and moves with a small group to a new territory. Such is the rationale, argues Sydney E. Mead in *The Lively Experiment: The Shaping of Christianity in America,* for sects, denominations, and individuals coming out of larger orders with "the idea of building anew in the American wilderness."[25] And just as most Americans immigrants bore the charge of cowardly desertion, so suburbanites bear it still. Fleeing the city for wilderness purity or rural virtue means abandoning the city, abandoning the large group; it has since biblical and classical times. Fleeing it for a life of modest comfort strikes many urbanites as even worse, and has seemed so, in English verse at least, certainly since 1700 when John Pomfret published "The Choice":

> *Near some fair Town, I'd have a private Seat,*
> *Built uniform; not little, nor too great:*
> *Better, if on a rising Ground it stood;*
> *On this Side Fields, on that a neighb'ring Wood.*[26]

To leave for comfort, for simplicity, means denying to the urban population, even that of a fair town, one more voice, one more vote, in favor of such goods within the city.

Such is the issue of commuting urban trouble. It is perhaps a key issue of American civilization, simply because it grows out of the national religious taproot, out of the great immigration and westering enterprises, and because it continues to haunt public discourse about contemporary urban problems. If the Irish were right to desert an island struck by famine and misrule rather than rebelling against the English, why should they not have begun deserting eastern American cities in the 1920s, when a number of complex issues seemingly defied solution? Certainly many nationally known writers never thought to ask the question. In 1935, for example, Philip Curtiss published a lengthy, especially thoughtful *Harper's Monthly* piece on migration to rural areas by professional and working-class New York families. The article insists that rural New Englanders and upstate New Yorkers are anything but backward; after all, they descend from the upright, hard-working stock who remained on nineteenth-century farms while "the ne'er-do-wells and the indolent went elsewhere, often to become mere factory fodder."[27] Yet it misses the very significance implicit in its praise of writers and carpenters deserting New York City. Who will be left behind in the city when the industrious and wise are all settled on "private seats" in the Berkshires? In his enthusiasm for individual and family salvation from urban travail, Curtiss fails even to glimpse the question.

At the same time, Curtiss uses *country* so loosely as to nearly strip the term of any meaning whatsoever. Yet in his era, when the far outer suburbs blended subtly into rural space, the word—and *countryside* too—often did not connote regions wholly dependent on agriculture.

In this book the word *country* means that region designated *borderlands* or *environs* by such mid-nineteenth-century writers as Alice Cary, Susan Cooper, and Nathaniel Parker Willis, who scrutinized a zone *between* rural space and urban residential rings. Contemporaneous writers now and then used *suburban* to designate places near towns—Hawthorne used the word in that way when writing about farmhouses within easy walking distance of Salem—but they usually chose that term as the best name for the scruffy, new, often poorly built zone of mixed residence and manufacturing that hung about the edges of large cities, not the outer landscape of "beautiful, well-built little houses, with their orchards and grounds, which lie like pearls set in the emerald green frame of the river," so lovingly described by Fredrika Bremer in her *Homes of the New World: Impressions of*

America in 1853.[28] Three forms combined to create country and distinguish it from suburbs: working farms with pastures and arable fields, mature trees on sloping land abandoned by farmers as unproductive, and "country residences," the seasonal or year-round private seats of families with urban business and social connections. In the literature of borderland living, fields suggest rural virtue and offer long, diverse views; trees and hilly ground—the mix Pomfret suggests in "The Choice"—offer privacy and vantage points; and the country residences announce the presence of sensitive, educated people who live in the region by choice. In the borderlands, from rising ground, artists after the 1790s painted the distant city and its suburbs, commanding the view and—perhaps—the subject.[29]

Census data and other quantitative information do little to describe and explicate the borderland landscape, for after all, the creators and users of borderland landscape understood things in essentially visual ways. Between the end of the eighteenth century and the 1930s, certain visual characteristics remain relatively constant in writing about borderland space, and few are susceptible to tabulation. Indeed much that *is* susceptible to tabulation—the seeming decline in the purchasing power of white-collar employees between 1890 and the present, the availability and variety of mortgage financing between 1840 and 1920, the proportion of Americans defined as middle class against those defined as middle income, the relative rates of inflation in food, transportation, and housing costs after 1880, the costs of "landscaping" versus those of carpentry, even businessmen's lengthening work day sometimes implicit in magazine articles and commuter train timetables—has been scarcely examined by social and economic historians, even by those intrigued with urban and metropolitan issues. In the end, however, analysis of borderland landscape involves firsthand observation, days spent judging the age of trees, calculating long grown-over vistas, remarking the longevity of appearance in places surrounded by more modern form. "There is great odds betwixt the knowledge of a traveler, that in his own person hath taken a view of many coasts, passed through many countries, and hath there taken up his abode some time, and by experience hath been an eyewitness of the extreme cold, and scorching heats, hath surveyed the glory and beauty of the one, the barrenness and meanness of the other," asserted Connecticut clergyman Thomas Hooker in his 1659 opus, *The Application of Redemption,* "and another that sits by his fireside, and happily reads the story of these in a book or views the proportion of these in a map, the odds is great, and the difference of their knowledge more than a little: the one saw the country really, the other only in the story; the one hath seen the very place. the other only in the paint of the map drawn." Hooker had been and seen. He had left a comfortable English fireside to come out into the ocean, to the Bay Colony, then he had left that for wilderness and the settling of Connecticut. The travels from which this book derives have been infinitely less jarring than his, but often they were just as far removed from written documents.[30] How else does one locate the borderlands, if one eschews census tracts and tax records and notes the absence of social and economic monographs?

One searches, one searches as precisely as possible, as precisely as men and women searched more than a century ago. Old distinguishing characteristics endure as solidly and persistently as attitudes endure through a century of borderland documents. In this book the borderlands are—or were—where houses are so far apart that even in winter they cast shadows only on their own lots; the borderlands are ordered about a horseback and carriage pace, not a pedestrian one: the borderlands are distant enough from cities to be free of pigeons; they have only one-armed utility poles, if the poles have arms at all. In the borderlands the smell of burning leaves marks autumn; their people enjoy the rain because they keep gardens; trees offer an illusion of privacy, of distance, of nature as the limit above which no structure, except church spires, may reach. In the borderlands houses boast many windows and even cupolas opening on vistas; in the borderlands seasonal rhythm contests the rule of mechanical timekeeping, and especially of alarm clocks; in the borderlands houselot size makes continual casual conversation between neighbors difficult. In the borderlands survives an uncommon landscape whose *appearance* has long comforted millions of Americans and fascinated a small but outspoken number of writers.

Novelists have long understood the borderlands as distinct from the sort of front-lawn suburbs I describe in *Metropolitan Corridor: Railroads and the American Scene*. Novelists writing largely for women seem to have understood them best. Faith Baldwin's 1938 *Station Wagon Set* introduces Little Oxford, a place "definitely gentry and definitely country," a place that "prides itself on not being suburban. Yet it is not completely rural, for it is only sixty miles from town." Little Oxford "harbors ancient houses complete with lawns and shade trees, set well back from the residential streets, and beyond the village with old farmhouses converted into modern dwellings and the usual quantity of renovated barns. It is famous for its many estates, ranging from five acres to a thousand."[31] Such description is far from casual, and in the late 1930s its components spoke precisely to readers who understood the connotations of sixty-mile commuting distances, ancient houses, renovated barns, and the mixture of large and small "estates." Indeed *Station Wagon Set* depends for its success on an audience well educated in the meaning of borderland space—for that space is the theater in which social and economic conflict occurs—and in borderland terminology. It depends on an audience knowing the commuter train countryside connotation of automobiles called *station* wagons.

Consequently this book focuses on the visual elements of the borderlands, not on the financial underpinnings, the religious denominationalism, the reordering of family life, the political changes, the sanitary awakening, and other great issues properly studied—as Robert H. Wiebe demonstrates so convincingly in *The Search for Order, 1877–1920*—in national frames. It deals with the broader borderland landscape, touching only on the history of domestic architecture, choosing borderland places like West Philadelphia and Shaker Heights only as illustrations, and hoping only to introduce the borderlands for further study, especially as the historical backdrop against which the post–World War II "suburban" movement occurred and the repeopling of rural America occurs. My choice of period is deliberate. As I suggest in my recent articles on contemporary American suburbs, after World

The Saturday Evening POST

Combined Issues
Dec. 24 – Dec. 31, 1960 – *15¢*

A Five-Nation Survey by the Gallup Poll:

Is European Education Better Than Ours?

COMPLETE IN THIS ISSUE

The commuter arriving home in the suburbs often confronts natural wilderness for the first time in his or her day; high heels and thin coats prove almost useless in the snow of the "country."

War II borderland landscape began to reflect massive change that deserves a mono-graph of its own.[32]

Underlying this study is a range of sources, stretching from such secondary classics as Peter Schmitt's *Back to Nature; The Arcadian Myth in Urban America*, Raymond Williams' *The Country and the City*, and Sam Bass Warner's *Streetcar Suburbs: The Process of Growth in Boston* to newer studies like Gwendolyn Wright's *Building the Dream: A Social History of Housing in America* and Alan Gowans' *The Comfortable House: North American Suburban Architecture, 1890–1930* to now almost forgotten nineteenth-century books like Willis' *Out-Doors at Idlewild* and Henry Cuyler Bunner's *Suburban Sage* to special-interest magazines like *National Real Estate Journal* to those nearly magical repositories of late eigh-teenth- and early nineteenth-century landscape musing, the Newark *Rural Maga-zine*, the Rutland *Rural Magazine or Vermont Repository*, and the Hartford *Rural Magazine and Farmer's Monthly Museum*. Also underlying it is the emerging liter-ature analyzing, among so many other things, changes in visual perception and painting against urbanization, a literature highlighted by Christopher Brown's *Dutch Landscape: The Early Years: Haarlem and Amsterdam, 1590–1650* and Michael Rosenthal's *Constable: The Painter and His Landscape*. Beneath it too is my own deciphering of early nineteenth-century American painting as expression of topographical values, begun as my contribution to Edward J. Nygren's *Views and Visions: American Landscape Before 1830*. I also draw upon the new historical scholarship focused on the uncertainties linked with early nineteenth-century ur-banization. Books like Paul S. Boyer's *Urban Masses and Moral Order in America, 1820–1920*, Amy Bridges' *A City in the Republic: Antebellum New York and the Origins of Machine Politics*, Karen Halttunen's *Confidence Men and Painted Wom-en: A Study of Middle-Class Culture in America, 1830–1870*, and Anne C. Rose's *Transcendentalism as a Social Movement, 1830–1850* have directed many of my inquiries, and John Mack Faragher's recent *Sugar Creek: Life on the Illinois Prairie* has reinforced my belief that the landscape of "open-country communities" de-serves continuing scrutiny. But this book began in the "rural" periodicals, during my reading for the volume that became *Common Landscape of America, 1580 to 1845*. Clearly the editors of those magazines understood, however vaguely, that by 1820 the agricultural press had begun attracting a nonfarming readership intrigued by rural residence, if only for the summer months. From there, beginning with their point of view, not that of city writers, I traced the creation of the uncommon landscape I describe in the following pages, rummaging through horticultural maga-zines and novels, real estate advertisements and diaries, women's gift books and urban booster guides, and always walking and driving through the places described so long ago—even if now a urban framework of elevated trains and high-rise apartment houses obscures nearly everything of country. I have tried to keep the notes as ballast, not barnacles to the text, and have so cited only a fragment of my reading, especially in the periodical press. And one sort of reading I have chosen to use only as uncited background.

In the late 1930s New Yorker cartoons emphasized the growing influence of readers in the far suburbs, and of novels directed to those readers, as more than hinted at in the caption to this cartoon: "Faith Baldwin is this way, and Lily Pons is that way."

"Faith Baldwin is this way, and Lily Pons is that way."

Faith Baldwin understood the social importance of the railroad station and station wagons in the life of Little Oxford, as the dust-jacket illustration of Station Wagon Set makes clear.

Borderland and suburban newspapers offer an astoundingly fertile field for the landscape historian, and for the social historian too. Often ill-collected and worse housed, they reveal much about the conscious thinking of men and women in places away from cities but no longer small towns. Consider as only one example *The Chronicle* of Cambridge, Massachusetts, a weekly newspaper used so effectively by Hency C. Binford in his recent study of Cambridge and Somerville, *The First Suburbs: Residential Communities on the Boston Periphery, 1815 to 1860.* The *Chronicle,* along with so many similar papers, traces the transformation of Cambridge from small town to borderland to suburb, in part by continuously referring to landscape change. "Cambridge is *out of doors.* Bordered north, west, and south by *the country*—the home of the farmer—the region of rock and hill and running stream, of forest and field,—its streets are scented with the fragrance of orchards, and its air stirred with the sounds of rural industry," enthused its editor on July 19, 1856, a year after Willis published his *Out-Doors at Idlewild.* "Green fields, and salubrious air, and fine gardens, and clustering trees, and the notes of wild birds, and groups of little children carelessly at play,—are attractions which the human heart cannot, or ought not, dispense with and be contented."[33] Such "outdoor" prose is everywhere in mid-century borderland literature, not merely reflecting literary fashion but reminding newspaper readers that the physical environment connotes a wealth of meaning. The virtuous farms are nearby, but not near enough to disturb the newcomers; the air is scented by orchards, not single trees; the children, unlike farm children, play in summer. The scene is romantic, but it is not false. Certainly the journalist picks and omits details in creating it and he uses *country* vaguely, but the commuter, anxious to commute, accepts the deliberate creation, just as he or she sees the surrounding environment in a peculiar way, different from that of the farmer or urban visitor perhaps, but as valid as others.[34] The newspapers deserve reading, for they speak directly of landscape meaning, of the borderland stage set, and of the continuous transformation of rural to borderland to suburb to city—and they speak almost wholly to readers knowing the prose and the landscape.[35]

Newspapers, and especially newspaper advertisements, suggest a hundred subjects deserving sustained analysis, but for which a book of this sort has no room. Insects, for example, irritated and sometimes enraged families newly arrived in the borderlands and unused to mosquitoes and other stinging demons. As early as 1856, one Philadelphia writer had begun analyzing different sorts of window screens intended chiefly for farmhouses but useful also in country residences. As the decades passed, concern over insect-borne disease increased and metal screens replaced fly traps, cheesecloth, and sheer curtains. In the pages of *Country Life, House and Garden,* and even *Vanity Fair,* readers watched technology improve, making possible more pleasant living in borderland areas—even areas near wetlands like those that nearly defeated Olmsted's Riverside development.[36] Bicycling entranced thousands of borderland residents after the 1890s, and local newspapers make clear the peculiar attraction of "wheels" for men and children, and especially for women anxious to exercise and wear risqué bloomers.[37] But the history of window screening and bicycling, like the development of borderland-sited children's literature and the impact of telephone and radio communication, however important in understanding the borderland landscape and however intriguing to readers of borderland newspapers, find little space in the pages that follow, as do many other subjects.

Screens and bicycles comprise only details in the larger picture of borderland structure and space, but they reflect the broader concerns of borderland readers of the borderland press. From the time of the *Rural Magazine* to the mid-nineteenth-century heyday of *The Horticulturist* to the turn-of-the-century period of *Countryside Magazine* and *Suburban Life* and *Country Life in America,* borderland families were never without magazines devoted to their grand experiment in commuter country. To read extensively in that literature is to discover the unchanging nature of so many concerns—urban crime and political corruption, house design that encourages relaxation, the soothing balm of perennial plating, the fruits of commuting—and to realize that borderland landscape from the late eighteenth century until 1940 reflected deep, almost timeless issues.[38] To read beyond it is to see that borderland literature only supplemented the extraordinary attention to borderland landscape evident in so many articles in national magazines like *Harper's Monthly* and *Everybody's,* in specialty periodicals like *House and Garden,* and in women's magazines like *American Cookery* and *Ladies' Home Journal.*[39] The women's journals offer particularly intriguing guidance to anyone seeking the vanished borderland, for that construct of space and structure appears to have been the achievement largely of women concerned with screens and bicycles to be sure, but with far more significant issues too, like the distance from home beyond which it is uneconomical for a housewife to shop for groceries, the best way to wire a house in anticipation of new electric appliances, the rising cost of country vacations, and the usefulness of agrarian values in big-business-era cities.[40]

Women shaped much of the philosophy underlying borderland life in the United States, and they shaped much of the borderland landscape too. Along with a number of powerful male champions of commuter country, female advocates of life in borderland space carried their arguments not only to women, but to men as well. And many, many men heard their arguments and agreed. In writing this book I have encountered for the first time male colleagues and students who dismiss the research subject as a "woman's topic," who see the borderlands as infinitely less important than "the city," who shrug off Susan Cooper as one of the mob of scribbling women Hawthorne disliked, who laugh at the notion that decades ago well-educated people equated proficiency in the flower garden with proficiency at the piano.[41] Over and over I have heard that the borderlands are trivial, that they "are a long way from" the industrial zones and railroad terminals I discuss in *Metropolitan Corridor: Railroads and the American Scene,* that they are, in the end, feminine, frivolous, and undeserving of study. Only rarely, when the conversation strikes past the 1950s framework of a "frontier" of "ticky-tacky houses" and "Peyton-Place morality," have I glimpsed the profound unease with which male champions of skyscrapers and urban avenues view the example of borderland landscape and the arguments made by so many women who looked not *up* to the city, but down upon it.

Even in the late 1980s, New Yorker *cartoons reinforce the half-century-old stereotyping of the outer suburbs as the habitat of cultural traditionalists.*

This 1915 House Beautiful *advertisement emphasizes the closeness of the open-country community; however self-serving, it suggests that farm families enjoyed an immediate closeness often ignored by partisans of city and town life.*

Neighborizing the Farmer

One of the most significant facts of our telephone progress is that one-fourth of the 9,000,000 telephones in the Bell System are rural.

In the days when the telephone was merely a "city convenience," the farms of the country were so many separated units, far removed from the centers of population, and isolated by distance and lack of facilities for communication.

But, as the telephone reached out beyond cities and towns, it completely transformed farm life. It created new rural neighborhoods here, there and everywhere.

Stretching to the farthest corners of the states, it brought the remotest villages and isolated places into direct contact with the larger communities.

Today, the American farmer enjoys the same facilities for instant, direct communication as the city dweller. Though distances between farms are reckoned in miles as the crow flies, the telephone brings every one as close as next door. Though it be half a day's journey to the village, the farmer is but a telephone call away.

Aside from its neighborhood value, the telephone keeps the farmer in touch with the city and abreast of the times.

The Bell System has always recognized rural telephone development as an essential factor of Universal Service. It has co-operated with the farmer to achieve this aim.

The result is that the Bell System reaches more places than there are post offices and includes as many rural telephones as there are telephones of all kinds in Great Britain, France and Germany combined.

AMERICAN TELEPHONE AND TELEGRAPH COMPANY
AND ASSOCIATED COMPANIES

One Policy   One System   Universal Service

Throughout the 1950s, magazine illustrators frequently depicted suburban women as hopelessly witless and wholly unlike the tough-minded suburban pioneers of the prewar era.

I 🌿 Intellectual & Practical Beginnings

An 1870s borderer in her habitat.

R*egard her carefully, the stylish woman on the bluff. Child in hand, she looks below at two others, boys playing in the trees, one turning back to her. Is she mother to the children, the prim girl at her side, the boys at the poplars? Her clothing distinguishes her: the double skirt, bustle, feathered hat, dress not of the farm, but of the borderlands about mid-nineteenth-century Cincinnati. The boys focus her attention. The city, spread out immense before and below her, shimmers as mere backdrop, momentarily forgotten in her particular concern. Secure in her half-wilderness, half-farmland wildflower meadow, secure in her proper day costume, she leans forward toward the children. "The environs of Cincinnati are its distinguishing beauty," argued Sidney D. Maxwell in his 1870* Suburbs of Cincinnati. *"They present as striking a combination of the picturesque and the accessible as can be found in the world; and the topographical features are such as to peculiarly favor, in the development of the landscape, the most artistic plans."*[1] *The stylish woman is a* borderer *then, an inhabitant of Avondale perhaps, or Clifton, Walnut Hills, or some other new community just sprouted above the city.*

1 ❧ WITCH HAZEL

Not surprisingly, when William Cullen Bryant edited his *Picturesque America; or The Land We Live In* in 1874, he chose an engraving of suburban heights to illustrate Cincinnati. Depicting cities from bor-derland heights had been the norm in American "view publishing" at least since 1840, when Nathaniel Parker Willis brought out his massive, two-volume *American Scenery Illustrated* in London.[1] Bryant's even larger three-volume work glorifies not only the wilderness grandeur of the Republic but urban magnificence too. Yet something skews, albeit subtly, the folio renderings of urban prosperity and expan-sion; again and again, Bryant's artists not only depict cities from borderland vantage points, they emphasize the picturesque vantage point as significant foreground. Louisville, Rochester, Boston, Milwaukee—all lie spread out beneath the lush foliage, rocks, and well-dressed men and women of the heights. Urban form, as Maxwell and the creators of *Picturesque America* knew, lacked the half-natural. half-crafted beauty suddenly revalued in the new industrial age. The urban engrav-ings share therefore an almost eerie similiarity, a kinship more among themselves than with those illustrating Willis' book. Consider the frontispiece to the second volume, a crisp "City of New York from Brooklyn Heights." As in the view of Cincinnati, a sylvan foreground frames the harbor and distant skyline, and on a curving gravel walk lingers another stylish woman, reading near a child. Unlike the poplars and other ragged trees of the Cincinnati view, the vegetation is parklike, and wrought iron, not rail fences, grace the bluff. The engraving says more about Brooklyn, dismissed in the accompanying essay as "little more than New York's vast dormitory," than it does about the city across the harbor.[2] Brooklyn Heights, like the suburbs of Cincinnati, is picturesque.

By the 1870s, Americans, and especially American women, understood a new standard of landscape beauty. Older notions of agricultural aesthetics, an aesthetics summed up in the phrase "pretty country," lingered among isolated eastern farm families and governed the thinking of western settlers but no longer shaped edu-cated middle- and upper-class public opinion.[3] Only a handful of wealthy, excep-tionally well-educated easterners found beauty in absolute wilderness, especially in mountain wilderness; paintings of jagged peaks and storm-tossed forests found some favor in a generation prepared by romantic depictions of the Catskills and other half-tamed places, but for most Americans the Adirondacks remained nearly as forbidding as the Rockies, and scarcely more accessible.[4] Sometime between the late 1830s and early 1840s (about the moment when Willis published his sumptuous *American Scenery Illustrated* and established the "view from the heights" format that governed *Picturesque America* and so many other volumes) and the early 1870s, however, educated urban men and women abandoned the once-powerful allegiance to the rural beauty so prized in the early Republic and—still reluctant to honor the aesthetic of wilderness or city—instead embraced the half-wild, half-rural standard its champions called *picturesque*.[5] Opinion-makers like Willis and Susan Fenimore Cooper had swayed the minds of thousands.

Indeed, the finely dressed woman overlooking Cincinnati or some other city depicted in *Picturesque America* might be the daughter of the great novelist. Susan Cooper savored hilltop views, although she devoted most of her energy to viewing and describing picturesque, not urban, vistas. "We were sitting upon the trunk of a fallen pine, near a projecting cliff which overlooked the country for some fifteen miles or more; the lake, the rural town, and the farms in the valley beyond, lying at our feet like a beautiful map," she mused in "A Dissolving View," her contribution to an 1852 anthology entitled *The Home Book of the Picturesque*.[6] Unlike her father, Susan Cooper favored crafted space, not wilderness, and she worried that the rural scenery surrounding her home in Cooperstown, New York, stood a poor second to that of England. Indeed, "A Dissolving View" is a pivotal essay in the intellectual discovery of the American borderland, for it drives deeply into the new nineteenth-century American understanding of the picturesque.

Midway in the essay, Cooper invokes magic to wrench her reader from traditional American spatial aesthetics. After arguing that "it would be comparatively an easy work to remove from the earth all traces of many of the peculiar merits of modern civilization"—everything from "light suspension bridges" to "manufactories moved by steam"—she waves a sprig of witch hazel over the valley beneath, and watches as all built form vanishes in reverse chronological order, until only virgin forest remains. Such retrospective imagining, neither particularly insightful nor particularly uncommon in mid-nineteenth-century writing, gathers force as again the witch hazel branch waves over the valley. Out of the virgin forest emerges a European countryside complete with village, "low, picturesque, thatched cottages," stone church and bridge, and "several country houses" sized according to "various grades of importance" from cottage to former manor house to castle. But nothing follows the detailed description of picturesque landscape. Instead the essay ends abruptly, after a brief, contrived paragraph mentioning a sudden bee sting, the drooping of the branch, and the return of the "every-day aspect" of the countryside.[7] Ahead of her time, perhaps slightly unnerved by the political implications of her understanding in an agrarian nation, Susan Cooper did not draw out her discovery of the flimsy tawdriness of the emergent American rural countryside.

New York rural scenery did please Cooper, but in limited ways indeed. If she liked wilderness half erased by fields and other agricultural spaces, she liked agricultural spaces and activities only at a distance. Her *Rural Hours,* an 1850 book that passed through several printings and proved popular enough to justify a revised edition in 1887, outlines the natural history of Cooperstown, focusing on the habits of birds, the appearance of plants, and the turn of seasons. Mingled with natural history, however, is an nascent dislike of farming, an inability to see beauty in barnyards. "A meadow near at hand would seem to give more pleasure than a cornfield," she argues. "Grain, to appear to full advantage, should be seen at a little distance, where one may note the changes in its coloring with the advancing season, where one may enjoy the play of light when the summer clouds throw their shadows there, or the breezes chase one another over the waving lawn." Distance makes farming picturesque—"rustic," in her terminology—and the more simple and distant the farming, the more attractive. Susan Cooper did not farm. She scorned the farming families who knew the names of only a few wildflowers, jeering that most farmers know almost nothing about uncommon trees, "and as for the smaller native plants, they know less about them than Buck and Brindle, their own oxen."[8] Cooper lived in the country, but she understood it in a way previously unknown in the rural Republic; she understood the country as scenery, as backdrop to her dreams and aesthetic theories, not as an evolving artifact of agriculture.

But neither did she love the city. Along with many other early nineteenth-century Americans, Susan Cooper discerned a virtue in rural life utterly lacking in Boston, New York, Baltimore, and other coastal cities, arguing that "there is, indeed, a peculiar modesty about the wild rose"—a flower not of the wilderness forest but of the edges of meadows and pastures—"which that of the gardens does not always possess."[9] By 1850, however, Cooper knew that rural life had not achieved the standards set by such eighteenth-century optimists as Crevecoeur and Jefferson; even Thoreau knew that. While arguing that he saw "two parties, becoming more and more distinct—the party of the city, and the party of the country," Thoreau admitted that "I know that the country is mean enough, but I am glad to believe that there is a slight difference in her favor."[10] Susan Cooper, Thoreau, and a host of other antebellum observers did not simply juxtapose city and country, religion and nature, wilderness and landscape, nor did they fix their hearts on some rural middle landscape mediating between city and wilderness. They knew the sordidness, the quiet desperation, the meanness of farm life, and they recognized in farmyards and farmhouses, fields and barns a failing dream. For Cooper, and for other contributors to periodicals, drawing-room almanacs, and anthologies of scenery description, only a new sort of space offered a new hope. "The border of an old wood is fine ground for flowers," Cooper decided.[11] Flowers, not crops, did best in the borderland between city and country.

For eighty years following 1790, the borderland welcomed a small but outspoken group of newcomers determined to live better. In the periodical and parlor-table press of the era, in journals like *Rural Gazette* and *The Crayon,* their views shaped public opinion, stirring not only the views of prosperous city dwellers but those of well-to-do farmers too. Willis, Bryant, Cooper, Andrew Jackson Downing,

Donald G. Mitchell, and scores of other discoverers of the borderlands deluged middle- and upper-class readers with essays and books—most illustrated with engravings—championing life in the new space. Novelists picked up on the change, and some based entire plots on it. "It was gradually becoming a favorite summer retreat for some of the metropolitans, who, debilitated or disgusted by the heat and confinement of the city, longed for the charmed air and liberal shade," wrote Caroline Lee Hentz of the new borderland world, the setting for her 1833 novel, *Lovell's Folly*.[12] Soon their efforts not only shaped the content of general interest periodicals like *Putnam's Monthly* and *The Atlantic Monthly* but led to the creation of new journals like Downing's *Horticulturist* and Mitchell's *Hearth and Home*. No one writer addressed every facet of the new theory of borderland life, but perhaps Nathaniel Parker Willis came nearest.

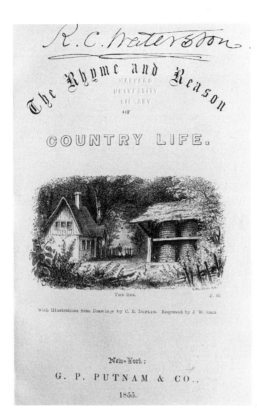

Books like The Rhyme and Reason of Country Life
presented not only textual arguments in favor of
borderland living, but a wealth of illustrations
stressing comfort and peace.

The fertile, prosperous agricultural landscape
surrounded by wilderness that so pleased nineteenth-
century seekers of the picturesque often appeared in
album and magazine illustrations emphasizing not
only the height of the viewer, but the river or lake
offering inviting, easy access into the heart of the
scene, even for a woman.

Rural Letters appeared in 1849, some twelve years after Willis retired to the borderlands. While lacking a cohesive structure—the essays range from Cooper-like natural history records to accounts of daily chores to renderings of rural scenery—the book surveys nearly every important theme in the new literature. Voluntary seclusion, however, underlies the argument Willis advances in favor of his way of life. "There is a charm to me in an in-navigable river, which brought me to the Susquehannah," he writes after describing his fears concerning a proposed new railroad linking his "cottage" to New York. "I like the city sometimes, and I bless Heaven for steamboats; but I love haunts where I neither see a steamboat nor expect the city." Canal boats, steamboats, and railroads all interrupt his rural reveries; he is grateful not only for abutting a shallow river, but for the hills and "a green and wholesome half mile, thickly wooded and mine own to keep so," that lie between his residence and the route of the proposed canal and railroad. Transportation improvements, however, do not spoil his garden or disrupt his quiet life, so long as they remain some distance from his own property. Indeed, the chapter emphasizes the possible delights of living in a rural place linked by the Erie Railroad with Jersey City and New York, by canal with the south, and by other railroads with the north and west. Not only will Willis be able to travel conveniently, the improvements will bring from the city like-minded neighbors. "If I had had the power to people the Susquehanna by the wave of a wand, from those I know capable of appreciating its beauty, what a paradise I could have spread out between my own home and Wyoming!" he remarks in a passage paralleling Cooper's experiment with witch hazel. "It was pleasant to know, that, by changes scarcely less than magical, these lovely banks will soon be amply seen and admired, and probably as rapidly seized upon and inhabited by persons of taste." From the deck of an experimental steamboat chugging along the Susquehanna, Willis catalogues sites for "the distribution of white villas along the shore."[1] Effortlessly balancing his love of seclusion and his love of swift, convenient travel, his love of half-rural, half-wild scenery and his need of neighbors sensitive to it, *Rural Letters* touches the chief constituent elements of the literature of borderland living.

Willis extols the invigorating countryside, but he carefully avoids praising agricultural landscape. Instead, he cherishes a landscape contrived for utility and beauty. His cottage stands near a riverbank, surrounded by land he has tried to make beautiful. A "liberal neighbor" permitted him to cut an "eye-patch" through an adjacent woodlot so that he might see the village church spire about a mile away; on his own land, he "redeemed" a brook from lost strayings to make it water "a fair meadow, laid like an unrolled carpet of emerald" along the shore. The meadow produces hay, of course, as well as "a nodding regiment of lilies." Nothing is regimented, and plants require no money for their beauty: "There is nothing like living in the city, to impress one with the gratuitous liberality of the services rendered one in the country."[2] According to Willis, the country freely offers views and wildflowers, wholesome air and fresh water; implicit in his argument, of course, is not only a love of healthfulness and picturesque beauty but a fierce devotion to a landscape not immediately reflecting industrial capitalism, a landscape of the past, of feudal England.

Along with many other educated Americans of his era, Willis honored the English landscape not merely for its texture or picturesqueness but because it predated the cash economy so intimately tied up in American cities. Precisely as Susan Cooper discerned in "A Dissolving View," the English countryside still reflected its feudal, precapitalist origins, and Cooper, Willis, and others applied to it terms like "quaint" and "rustic" in defining it against American urban space. For nineteenth-century American visitors, rural England represented a sort of "land before," a place before economic and technological change. "In an English lane; with hedges, English hedges, hawthorn hedges, all in blossom; homely old farmhouses, quaint stables, and haystacks: the old church spire over the distant trees; the mild sun beaming through the watery atmosphere, and all so quiet," Frederick Law Olmsted recounted his discovery of rural Eden in his 1859 *Walks and Talks of an American Farmer in England*. "At length we walked on—rapidly—but frequently stopping, one side and the other, like children in a garden."[3] In May, in the English countryside, young Olmsted encountered the original landscape depicted in the hundreds of paintings and engravings so long exported to the new nation across the sea.

Nathaniel Hawthorne experienced a similar sort of amazement in England, writing in *Our Old Home* of the verdant, quaint, decidedly antique beauty of the countryside. In his notebooks, however, Hawthorne confessed that "every point of beauty is so well known, and has been described so much, that one must needs look through other people's eyes, and feels as if he were seeing a picture rather than a reality."[4] *Our Old Home* nevertheless catalogues the hedges, wooded parks, "little hamlets of thatched cottages," ancient farmhouses, "picturesque old mills" and "all those quiet, secret, unexpected, yet strangely familiar features of English scenery that Tennyson shows us in his idyls and eclogues."[5] Hawthorne winced at the

THE FOREST

For mid-nineteenth-century borderers, the second-growth forest offered picturesque locales for botanizing, conversation, and walking, all in one-time agricultural space reverting to nature.

The free woman of the antebellum era, barefoot, loosely arrayed, dancing with flowers, such is the idyll of so many borderland writers convinced that natural surroundings might loosen the bonds of womanhood.

Notions of medieval living entranced many mid-nineteenth-century popular American authors, particularly women increasingly uneasy with urban, industrial circumstances. In the borderland forest, Americans might enjoy the gentle mixing of sexes, if not the costumes, of romanticized feudalism.

rawness of British urban and industrial poverty, the shame of city closes and alleys, but *Our Old Home* emphasizes the relative lack of rural poverty and the picturesqueness of what poverty its author did encounter along footpaths and lanes. James Fenimore Cooper likewise understood that "the prevalent characteristic of the English landscape is its air of snugness and comfort"; in "American and European Scenery," his contribution to *The Home Book of the Picturesque,* he concluded that "poverty and squalid misery" in the English countryside are "kept surprisingly out of the ordinary view."[6] Hawthorne—like Olmsted—encountered remarkably little disconcerting rural poverty, partly because the poor inhabited picturesque cottages, and partly because the extraordinary impact of Wordsworth, Tennyson, and other artists predisposed American travelers to see the rural poor as picturesque, to dwell not on the conditions of present inhabitants but on the rich historical associations of the landscape spaces and structures. "Who that dwells in America has not heard of the bright fields and green hedges of England, and longed to behold them?" asked Melville in 1849.[7] As did other Americans visiting England, Hawthorne, Olmsted, Cooper, and Melville wandered into an almost magical world, the world of poets and other artists, a world in which age, historical association, and lush vegetation combined to create hundreds of miniature set-pieces unlike anything in the Republic, and yet, to anyone familiar with English literature, strangely familiar.

Of chief importance in the English picturesque landscape, the cottage fascinated American observers worried about the rapid transformation of domestic life in the Republic. In his meanderings in Britain, Hawthorne encountered an ancient cottage row, housing for "the poorest order of rustic laborers," which envinced at first view a "stifled, unhealthy atmosphere." But the very age of the structures, the profusion of flowers and well-clipped hedges gracing every dooryard, and the "plump" happy children and mothers therein all combined to quickly change his opinion. "Nevertheless, not to look beyond the outside, I never saw a prettier rural scene than was presented by this row of contiguous huts." The thatched-roof cottages, at first appearance decrepit and mean, soon revealed themselves to be picturesque "nests," beloved by their inhabitants.[8] The power of Wordsworth, Coleridge, and Tennyson overwhelm Hawthorne's American notions of proper rural habitation. In the lush English countryside, exactly as James Fenimore Cooper understood, picturesqueness masked poverty.

In the years just before the Civil War, however, the English cottage began to exemplify virtues missing in American domestic life, and particularly in the domestic life of cities. Since colonization, the American farmhouse had reflected a traditional understanding of family life; the husbandman and housewife, each responsible for a separate sphere of daily chores, labored diligently in simple, austere quarters.[9] "How pleasant things look about a farm-house," mused Susan Cooper in *Rural Hours.* "There is always much that is interesting and respectable connected with every better labor, every useful or harmless occupation of man." *Rural Hours* contains a lengthy, minutely detailed description of a traditional Otsego County farmhouse occupied by a seventy-year-old couple well regarded for their virtuous efficiency. Everything about the farm, from the well-kept fields to the scoured woodwork of the sitting room to the great kitchen exemplifies diligence. The kitchen ceiling, for example, is "a pretty rustic sight," unplastered, carrying from its beams "bundles of dried herbs, strings of red peppers and of dried apples hanging in festoons, tools of various kinds," ears of seed corn, cord, and twine, like the massive brick chimney "garnished all about with flat-irons, brooms, brushes, holders, and cooking utensils, each in its proper place," serving as a kind of scrupulously neat, eminently useful decoration.[10] In popular literature, particularly the literature directed at women, and in popular visual material—perhaps most notably in the lithographs of Currier and Ives—the traditional American farmhouse represents plenty, simplicity, virtue, and beauty, qualities some reformers suddenly found lacking in the homes of urban dwellers.

Author after author lambasted the houses inhabited by the new urban residents, houses reflecting newly acquired wealth, houses inhabited by idle women vexed by idle servants, houses cramped, airless, and fronting ever more noisy city streets. As early as 1838, Emerson argued that a proper home offered its occupants—and particularly the businessman—a haven from the trials of public life, a place of "recreation." For the debilities caused by "studies, handiworks, arts, trade, politics," Emerson proposed the "balsam" of "the garden, the house, and the old and new familiar faces therein contained."[11] Clearly, however, the traditional farmhouse could not serve the needs of the new urban families; after all, as Susan Cooper discerned, the farmhouse required a farm about it, and it derived much of its attractiveness from agricultural pursuits many farmers already considered old-fashioned. Moreover, the utilitarian beauty of the farm devolved all too quickly into barren austerity; not surprisingly, Cooper condemned the virtuously efficient farmer for carefully eliminating all conifers from the woodlot. "The trees were chiefly maple, birch, oak, and chestnut," she concludes. "With us, about the lake, every wood contains hemlock and pine."[12] The modern farmer, who knew the uselessness of softwood as fuel and timber, unconsciously marred the picturesqueness of his woodlot while increasing its efficiency. Mid-nineteenth-century farms and farmhouses, often not even remotely picturesque, made poor models for reformers addressing such pressing concerns as the threatened family. Confronted by the inadequacy of the agricultural present, therefore, American reformers recalled the joys of the traditional farmhouse—but placed them in the English cottage.

Small, decorated by vines, hedges, and other ornamental plantings requiring the work of years, advertising a close-knit family group living simply, the English cottage became the perfect shelter from modern American trial, the perfect nest. In his 1868 *Home Life: What It Is, and What It Needs,* John F. W. Ware summarizes three decades of sustained argument, beginning simply by noting that "a walk though some parts of any large town or city is enough to make the heart ache." He explains the absolute necessity of quality housing, the right of every family to a house suited to its peculiar needs, the importance of seclusion and privacy, children's requirements for a garden and yard, the significance of comfortable furniture. *Home Life* aims at mid-nineteenth-century ills by looking backward at traditional New England village houses, and especially by lovingly describing the "large, cheerful, generous, old kitchen, the place where many a man and woman of silks and fashion was brought up," the kitchen of the "golden days" nearly identical to that described by Cooper. "I do not believe in every thing that is old," Ware continues, "but I do believe we have made no gain in surrendering these homely ways and virtues which clustered about that now dishonored place." Implicit in Ware's arguments is indeed a vision of a vanishing golden age, but there is also something more, a vision of rural simplicity and virtue objectified in a free-standing, simple, unique house surrounded not by fields but by "an enclosure sacred to it," a house enjoying the "blessed sun and air," a cottage.[13]

Cottage designates not necessarily a small house, therefore, but a simple one, a place of rural virtue, the refuge of values assaulted by suddenly complicated modern urban life, a shelter against urban evil. "Let me lay before the reader my favorite idea of a cottage—not a *cottage ornée* but a *cottage insoucieuse,* if I may coin a phrase," offered Willis in *Rural Letters* two decades before Ware.[14] The cottage is simplicity itself, a place lacking "fancy" shrubbery, gravel walks, and exotic plant-ings, a place fit for genuine recreation of the spirit. The cottage blends English picturesqueness with republican simplicity, sheltering the new family from un-precedented challenges.

And around the cottage grows a garden, an Eden defended by white picket fences from the roaming pigs and other creatures of the road, an Eden of climbing roses, honeysuckle, peonies, and tulips, an Eden created by Eve. The cottage garden that so delighted Olmsted, Hawthorne, and other Americans wandering through England boasted no "esculent vegetables," in Hawthorne's words, but only orna-mentals, plants of sensory stimulation. In "On Feminine Taste in Rural Affairs," a *Horticulturist* essay of the late 1840s, Andrew Jackson Downing argued that more American women should actively garden, not only for exercise, fresh air, and health, but to reaffirm their links with nature. "Now we have not the least desire, that American wives and daughters should have any thing to do with the *rough toil* of the farm or the garden, beyond their own household province," he cautioned.[15] Agricultural labor—as Susan Cooper knew too—provided no recreation, and in a nation still predominantly agricultural, no woman of the borderlands suspected otherwise.

Ornamental gardening, however, provided all that Downing promised and much, much more—and soon the borderland "cottages" of leisured women blossomed in flower gardens. Indeed, by the 1850s, ornamental planting, and partic-ularly the growing of annual and perennial flowers, entranced borderland women. On the one hand, a fine flower garden filled with indigenous and exotic plantings advertised the absolute leisure of its creator; after all, no farmwife, not even the efficient farmwife visited by Susan Cooper, could undertake such a task while carrying out traditional responsibilities. More important, the flower garden and ornamental shrubs sharpened the intellect and heightened the emotional sen-sibilities of their creator and her husband and children. Indeed, according to some mid-century authors, it was women's duty to provide their families with floral beauty.

Certainly "the pleasure derived from a fine collection of flowers requires no comment," argued Joseph Breck in his *Flower-Garden,* but "the moral lesson" is equally important, for the beauty of flowers "conveys a pleasing and natural lesson to the most accurate and intelligent observer." In the flower garden, mid-nineteenth-century Americans might encounter natural forms that hinted at the complex structure and beauty of divinity. Breck placed the burden of providing such elevating beauty squarely on the shoulders of the newly leisured family woman. "The cultivation and study of flowers appears more suited to females than to man," he continued enthusiastically. "They resemble them in their fragility, beauty, and perishable nature. The Mimosa may be likened to a pure-minded and delicate woman, who shrinks even from the breath of contamination; and who, if assailed too rudely by the finger of scorn and reproach, will wither and die from the shock." The taste for plants, and especially for flowers, "is a peculiar attribute of woman, exhibiting the gentleness and purity of her sex: and every husband should encourage it; for his wife and daughters will prove wiser, and happier, and better, by its cultivation." Exactly how gardening will make women wiser, happier, and better Breck does not say, but he makes clear the effect of the ornamental garden on the husband. "What can be more grateful to the merchant, or man of any professional business, than to recreate for a short time in a well-selected collection of flowers, neatly arranged and cultivated?"

The Flower-Garden implies that professional men not only respond to ornamental gardens but actually need them. According to Breck, the professional man is "confined," and he needs nature—especially flower gardens—"to tranquillize the agitated passions and exhilarate the man,—nerve the imagination, and render all around him delightful."[16] Farmers and other outdoor laborers either do not need the moral pleasures of the flower garden or else—perhaps like the efficient farmer of *Rural Hours*—cannot appreciate them, simply because they are inured to natural beauty. As professional men grew in number, however, their wives confronted the horror of office illnesses ranging from "nervous prostation" to alcoholism, and the balm of nature often seemed the only certain cure. Moving to the borderlands meant much in the fight against office illness, and flower gardening meant more. Flowers "are the survivors of our lost paradise, the types of what is spontaneous, inspiring, and unprofaned in life and humanity, the harbingers of a blissful futurity," argued H. T. Tuckerman in an 1850 magazine piece that echoed the concerns of Breck.[17] Flowers elevate the minds and recreate the characters of sensitive people—not of the insensitive farm family, but of the professional family resident in a borderland "cottage."

Now and then a harried professional man wrote about the significance of flowers, gardening, and gentleman farming, although few achieved the success of clergyman Henry Ward Beecher, who published *Plain and Pleasant Talk about Fruits, Flowers, and Farming* in 1859. Preaching "began to wear upon the nerves," remarks Beecher in his brief preface, and in a "little one-story cottage, after the day's work was done," he began reading the works of English landscape architects. "There was something exceedingly pleasant . . . in the studying over mere catalogues of flowers, trees, fruits, etc.," he concluded. Gradually his efforts not only "answered the purpose of soothing excited nerves" but increased the pleasure he derived from examining all sorts of vegetation, even roadside weeds.[18] The Brooklyn clergyman became the most influential preacher of his era, and he never lost his love for flowers; for him they existed as "revelations of God's sense of beauty, as addressed to the taste, and to something finer and deeper than taste, that power within us which spiritualizes matter and communes with God through His work." One of his biographers, writing in 1887, remarked Beecher's lifelong love of flowers, noting that "in all his later life he found rest and comfort with flowers and trees."[19] Rest, comfort, and an inkling of spirituality satisfied Beecher, as they did so many other mid-nineteenth-century borderers seeking in flowers some glimpse of a divinity increasingly hidden by urban industrialization.

Understanding flowers and other plants preoccupied some men, and thousands of women, in the 1840s and 1850s. Identifying, classifying, and growing flowers, shrubs, and trees—a range of activities called "botanizing" by practicioners and admirers—entranced educated, leisured women. Botanizing appealed to the intellect mid-nineteenth-century women hoped to develop. "The very logical and systematic arrangement which prevails in Botanical science, has, without doubt, a tendency to induce in the mind the habit and love of order; which, when once established, will operate even in the minutest concerns," asserted Almira H. Lincoln in her 1829 opus, *Familiar Lectures on Botany*. Lincoln's book, a massive, systematic, meticulously illustrated work including not only a careful analysis of the Linnean system of plant classification but an appendix describing practically every plant in the Republic, passed through at least sixteen editions, each aimed, as its title asserts, at "family" audiences. Lincoln wrote for women, telling them that botanizing "seems peculiarly adapted to females," since "the objects of its investigation are beautiful and delicate," but emphasizing the healthfulness of the amateur science too: "its pursuits, leading to exercise in the open air, are conducive to health and cheerfulness." Twisted into her broader discussion of the classification of plants are the strands of many nineteenth-century borderland concerns. Botanizing aids health not only by leading women into the outdoors but by teaching something of herbal medicine; botanizing puts women in touch with divinity; and botanizing leads women into picturesque scenery, "along the banks of the winding brooks, on the borders of precipices, the sides of mountains, and the depths of the forest."[20] Botanizing develops the visual acuity which stimulates accurate thought. Above all, however, *Familiar Lectures* leads women to the precipice of social position. The book argues that women can indeed master a complicated science previously thought accessible only to men, challenging its female readers to develop their intellectual abilities. Lincoln's masterful book and the borderland botanizing movement did not threaten the intellectual supremacy of men, however, for the understanding of flowers, while it trained the mind and exercised the body, produced nothing of political or financial worth—although as Horton Howard's 1832 two-volume opus, *An Improved System of Botanic Medicine,* makes clear, a botanically

Borderland women enjoyed nooks of every kind, and perhaps especially the forest nook that hid them even as they observed events beyond.

Botanizing not only drew borderland women into the open air, into the balm of nature, it stimulated their intellectual capacities.

1st. *Whorl*, (Fig. 87,) an assemblage of flowers surrounding the stem, or its branches, constitutes a whorl, or ring; this is seen in mint and many of the labiate plants. Flowers which grow in this manner, are said to be *verticillate*, from the Latin *verto*, to turn. Leaves surrounding the stem in a similar manner, are said to be *stellate*, or star-like.

Almira Lincoln confronted the intricacies of botany boldly, using technical terms to guide her women readers in the ways of precise description. Her Familiar Lectures are indeed whorl-like, an assembly of lectures surrounding the stem of female intellectual development.

astute housewife might cure any number of ills with plants ranging from skunk cabbage to carolina pink. But no matter how sophisticated, botanical science remained feminine. A borderland woman, trained in botany by a "ladies seminary" teacher or by lengthy self-study, might know every cultivated and wild flower, but her knowledge brought her only a greater intimacy with God, better health, and a calmer spirit, not any sort of career beyond her home.

Playfulness and sentimentality diluted the intellectual rigor of botanizing, and many educated women turned from the science of classification to the gentle sport of floral alphabetizing. Nineteenth-century leisured urban and borderland women created a complicated "language of flowers," a sort of semi-secret code known to themselves and to any man clever enough to inquire into books like *The Floral Keepsake for 1850.* John Keese blended botany and sentiment in his handsomely illustrated album—forty-six flowers appear in full color—but emphasized sentiment. His volume concludes with two alphabets, one describing the "meaning" his contemporaries attached to each flower or tree, the other ordering meanings against specific plants. A woman receiving a bouquet of jonquils, sweet pea, and rosemary understood its message as "Can you return my love? Departure. Remember me." Another bouquet, with everlasting pea in place of sweet pea, signaled "Can you return my love? Wilt thou go with me? Departure." Of course, not every man sending flowers knew the code, but in an era in which leisured women—and some farmwives too—delighted in the language of flowers, intelligent men examined *The Floral Keepsake* and similar volumes until they discovered the encoding alphabets. Under *E,* for example, the perplexed would-be message sender could find a list beginning with "Excess of sensibility—Aspen Tree; Envy—Geranium; Encouragement—Golden Rod" and under *W* he would discover what Susan Cooper knew, that witch hazel meant "a spell."[21]

Serious devotees consulted *Flora's Interpreter and Fortuna Flora,* an incredibly popular opus—it passed through sixteen editions and many enlargements between 1832 and 1852 alone—by Sarah Josepha Hale, editor of *Godey's Ladies' Book,* who struggled mightily to combine precise botanical information with "sentiment." Arranged in encyclopedia format, *Flora's Interpreter* offers not only brief notes concerning the floral code but "sentiments" as well. "The most important aim of the work was to select and incorporate with our love of nature and flowers the choicest and the best specimens of American poetry," Hale explains in the preface, and the avowedly patriotic work reprints excerpts from the poems of Bryant, Willis, Simms, Whittier and other romantics.[22] In anthologizing so much American poetry along with some British writing, Hale recognized the growing importance of flowers and other plants in mid-nineteenth-century poetry and fiction. Hawthorne, Bryant, and their contemporaries delighted in the language of flowers, describing wildflowers, bouquets, and floral arrangements in detail and so adding another layer of meaning to their writing: the bouquet of violets, wood anemones, and scarlet columbines (shaped like a capital *A*) that Pearl brings Hester in Hawthorne's *Scarlet Letter* means, according to Keese, "love, fading hope, desertion."[23] The code spoke most clearly to borderland women, however, and to women determined to leave behind windowboxes, potted plants, and florist shops for the sentimental delights of borderland living.

A borderland cottage gracefully embellished with flowers wild, cultivated, and exotic, screened with evergreen hedges perhaps, or half-covered with climbing vines announced not only the leisure of its mistress, but her developing intellectual and emotional strengths. The garden might originate more in a love of sophisticated botanical study or in notions of floral beauty and messages, or simply in burgeoning love of growing flowers, shrubs, and other nonagricultural plants, but it often reflected a recreation of spirit, a closeness to divinity. Each flower, fragile, delicate, beautiful, thriving in perfect circumstances, wilting in adverse conditions, mirrored the ever more intricate self-image of educated leisured women attempting to rescue their husbands, children, and themselves from the withering blasts of city living, to give them what Willis found in his Susquehanna retreat—peace.

3 SHADOWS

Urban form and life comprise the back-drop against which all borderland form and life acquire definition and vitality. Nathaniel Willis asserts that continually meeting people, acquaintances and strangers alike, creates a "fatigue" that eventually wears down the urban resident forced to live in "a number in a brick block." But the real difficulty of city living originates in a way of life regimented by clocks, wages, employers, and jammed sidewalks and omnibuses. In a long chapter entitled "Open-Air Musings in the City," Willis describes the often happy, satisfied city dwellers and finds much pleasant in restaurant life, shopping, and bustle, in the crowds on Broadway, on wharves, and elsewhere. The chapter twists, however, with the introduction of a "fine, old-fashioned June day," the sort of day that tempts city dwellers not only into the outdoors but away from the city itself, "away to the hills." Urban work, regimented work, demands that the heart be thrust down "like a reptile into its cage," that eye and ear shut out late spring.[1] The attitude of *Rural Letters* is quite clear: urban life is *unnatural,* indeed almost sinful.

Emerson agreed. In "The Eye and the Ear," a lecture of 1837, he argues, "We divorce ourselves from nature; we hide ourselves in cities and lose the affecting spectacle of Day and Night which she cheers and instructs her children withal." Such sentiments derive, of course, from the English romantic poets, particularly from Wordsworth, whose "Recluse" Emerson quotes. But their application is distinctly American. "We pave the earth for miles with stones and forbid the grass. We build street on street all round the horizon and shut out the sky and the wind." Urbanization fosters impaired senses, vulgarity, and "false and costly tastes"; in other words, it destroys the virtues that created the Republic even as it gnaws at the agricultural countryside.[2] Above all, it seduces rural simplicity.

Ancient European tradition fueled the anti-urban bias of so many rural philosophers already convinced that biblical authority condemned city living. American authors needed only the most casual knowledge of Greek, Roman, and eighteenth-century English literature to discover carefully reasoned glorifications of virtuous country life—like Pomfret's paean. They also encountered complete "rural philosophies," tracts like Ely Bates's 1804 *Rural Philosophy: Or Reflections on Knowledge, Virtue, and Happiness Chiefly in Reference to a Life of Retirement in the Country,* reprinted in Philadelphia only three years after its appearance in London. Bates argues bluntly that "there is no magical virtue in fields or groves," concluding that "to exchange the bustle of business, and the gay amusements of society, for fields and woods, silence and solitude, is so far from being alone sufficient to ensure a life of true contentment" that most people would find it "a dreary state of darkness and vacuity." For the unprepared, rural retirement provokes only vice, chiefly idleness, eccentricity, conceit, and incivility; only those determined to live thoughtfully enjoy the true happiness that originates in "the independence of some rural retreat, the peaceful labours of husbandry, the diversions of the field, or the scenery of nature." Bates dismisses the classical poets and scorns the romantics' "sentimental system" that makes "warm and frequent appeals" to "feelings."[3] Instead he struggles to find a purely rational proof that virtue flourishes best in rural retirement. Fragments of his thinking—and that of his fellow modest philosophers—lie everywhere in the emergent nineteenth-century borderland proposal.

Restoration preoccupies Bates. "It is in the silence and calm of retreat that all our powers, natural and moral, are refreshed and invigorated, and made prompt for further service," he asserts in urging all parents and teachers to instill in the young not only "a taste for solitude" but "such knowledge as may enable them to fill up an interval of retreat with advantage to themselves." Even a few days spent wisely in the country restore physical and moral vigor; "the shews and dissipations of a great city," however, may so weary urban dwellers, particularly businessmen, that only a lengthy retreat will prove wholly restorative. Bates examines melancholy and other traditional illnesses, but *Rural Philosophy* grapples also with new and unsettling disturbances of body and mind wrought by urban overexertion. By the close of his book, Bates determines that "from the elevated ground of serene contemplation," the retired moralist "may look down on mankind with an impartial eye, and take large surveys of their different pursuits."[4] Implicit in his argument is a new awareness that late eighteenth-century urban life provides almost no opportunity for sustained independent thought. Over and over, Bates condemns the city for its inability to foster independent contemplation, for its substitution of fashion for truth. City living breeds not so much physical illness as wearied brains and unthinkingly accepted opinions. Only prolonged, intelligent rural residence restores the balance by elevating the "retired man" among the urban throng.

Contemporaries of Bates worried also about physical illness, of course, and about the mental disease that accompanied it. "The city or populous town is rendered less salubrious than the country" lamented physician Thomas Trotter in 1807, by "narrow lanes, high buildings and houses, filthy kennels, small apartments, huge warehouses, manufacturing establishments, cellars underground, consumption of fuel, and a large population." *A View of the Nervous Temperament* examines new and essentially urban illnesses, cataloguing not only symptoms and cures but causes, and holding the "health of the savage" up against the misery of rich and poor urban residents alike. The treatise attacks foul air, rich food, the feminine fashion

From far-off hilltops, large cities struck
mid-nineteenth-century viewers as
manageable, even beautiful, especially if
a foreground harbor or river provided
not only openness and the intriguing
movement of sailing vessels, but a clear
barrier between urbanity and nature.

Nineteenth-century magazine writers
struggled to explain the "New York
flat" to a national readership familiar
with single-family houses. Illustrations
like this of "the new homes of New
York" did little except emphasize the
scale of the apartment houses.

In books like Out-Doors at Idlewild, *Willis and other writers extolled the virtues of the comfortable home nestled in nature, the home in which husband and wife share the joys of spatial creation.*

Early in the borderland experiment, families sought privacy and broad views not only by locating houses on hilltops and behind scenes of trees, but by erecting gates to keep out unwanted peddlers and other visitors.

for pale skin—"a blooming complexion is thought to indicate low life and vulgarity in breeding. What a depraved mode of thinking!"—new and chiefly sedentary forms of work, and a host of other urban enemies of sound health. Trotter lambasts city dwellers' lack of exercise, condemning fashionable women who either find the streets too dirty for walking or who feel faint after walking a block or two, scorning the businessmen who take only "a few strides to the office or counting house," and pitying the restrictions placed upon children. "The whole business of a town-life is transacted within doors: scarcely a house in London has an area attached to it sufficient for the sports of a child, where it may stretch its limbs and ramble about." Lack of exercise produces children resembling hothouse plants, fair-looking perhaps, but susceptible to illness. "Denied the free motion of its limbs," he concludes, the city child becomes a "dwarf," lacking not only "firmness of muscle" but the quality Bates prized too, "energy of nerve." Trotter's popular book—a Troy, New York, publisher brought out an American edition only a year after the English one—lays bare the environmental causes of a new galaxy of diseases, details the uncertain treatments available, and recommends prevention.

Life in the country strikes Trotter as the best prescription. "In what manner then is the city lady to preserve health, or regain it when lost? If she cannot look to a country residence, her situation must be pitiable." Simple relocation, as Bates knew, would work nothing good; the country life must be intelligently lived, with mental exercise accompanying riding and rambling. Only the most nervous require a genuine farm and the stimulation of reading agricultural books and digging in the soil; most middle- and upper-class families—and especially men "employed at a desk"— need only a place to ramble in all weather "to the breaking out of a free sweat." Trotter cares little for the actual location, but he knows it lies beyond the urban edge. "The distance from town, which may be necessary for these excursions, must be measured by the purity of the air, and rusticity of the country: they must be beyond the effluvium of smoke and mud." Of the poor unable to flee, Trotter says little, but his advice to families able to relocate is crisp. Leave or face new and horrible nervous illness.

Trotter shares Bates's faith in the curative powers of "rusticity," but he focuses on the medical virtues of rural places. In particular, he emphasizes the evil effects of impure air on the urban man, woman, or child walking, either on business or for exercise, and he scorns "public walks" not because such parklike places are ugly or lack the trees and flowers that suggest rural thoughts and so invigorate the mind, but because they lie within a realm of polluted air.[5] Fifty years before the creation of Central Park, Bates and Trotter agreed that such urban efforts at rusticity worked little real benefit.

American thinkers understood the import of British reformers like Bates and Trotter and knew that London—the city the English poor called Smoke—foreshadowed American urban growth. And from Hawthorne, Melville, and others, they suspected that Liverpool vice and destitution might accompany such growth. By the early 1850s, as Susan Cooper and Nathaniel Willis rambled in the borderlands and American physicians discovered the mental and physical illnesses so minutely described abroad, reformers began a wholesale denunciation of American cities. More than a national rural tradition, much more than a simplistic anti-urbanism, fueled the condemnation. Indeed, to read any of the diatribes is to discover the fragility of the early and mid-nineteenth-century American urban experience. Urban Americans' lives were so frequently interrupted by rural experience that their European counterparts might have dismissed their urbanity altogether. Had the city dwellers enjoyed fewer such interruptions, anti-urban reformers might have more closely examined the genuine advantages of city life.

Moral Aspects of City Life typifies the nineteenth-century attack on American cities. Published in 1853 by E. H. Chapin, a New York clergyman, the book catalogues the virtues and vices comprising city life, shaping its argument according to Scripture. Chapin recognizes the complex biblical view of urban life and gradually argues that only the scale of the city has changed since biblical times. Many of his similes derive from the biblical, classical, and European traditions that inspired Bates: "Society thus looks like a huge ship, with music, and feasting, and splendor on its deck, and its sail all set and glistening, while down in the hold there are famine, and pestilence, and compressed agony, and silent, choking despair." Chapin transcends such time-honored views, however, as he discovers the extraordinary distance between the "lower depths" and the well-off. He blames the rising power of "fashion" not only for the gulf, but for the distortion of life. "The substitution of night for day, the stifling rooms, the thin garments which are the sacrifice of health to vanity, the compressed lungs, the protracted excitement, the late meal, the indescribable food seasoned with every kind of disease" and a host of other urban evils originate in the triumph of fashion over common sense, which triumph makes the well-to-do as wretched as the poor. The poverty-stricken woman and the society belle wear equally thin winter dresses, the one out of destitution, the other out of fashion; the wretched laborer hunching over his bench and the capitalist crouched over his desk both acquire compressed lungs. Chapin attacks prostitution, alcoholism, gambling, and other evils, but his real enemy is artificiality, an artificiality of unprecedented scale.

Along with Emerson and Ware, Chapin finds his first solution in a reordered home life. Deliberately flouting the criticisms of traditional religionists, Chapin extols healthful home amusements; "amusement itself, relaxation, recreation, call it what you will, finds ground in original faculties or tendencies of our nature." In an age that glorified hard work, Chapin and other reformers directed attention at the need for play, particularly family play within the bounds of the house, to replace public dissipation. On another level, Chapin argues for rural pleasures, for time spent in relaxing work, not play, work resembling that of the farmer working in the "glorious theater of Nature." A proper house, in Chapin's argument, provides not only "pure air, fresh light, and clean water," but a place for relaxing play and work.[6] Only there, away from the public realm, will families recreate themselves, discover simpler ways of life, engage in invigorating exercise, and eradicate the evils of the city.

Throughout the first half of the nineteenth century, American urban dwellers

Urban growth, especially in and around Boston, New York, and Philadelphia, amazed mid-nineteenth-century Americans, especially those old enough to remember that outlying places, like Brooklyn, were once wholly rural, and to wonder if change really meant improvement.

FERRY HOUSE AT BROOKLYN, 1791.

Until after the Spanish–American War, urban Americans recognized in the grassy, long-abandoned ruins of earthworks and other fortifications that coastal cities remained prey to naval assault. However strong the "historical associations" and however delightful the views, the decrepit forts nevertheless reminded pleasure-seekers of the fundamental fragility of urban form.

discovered firsthand the growing strains of city living, and as urban life became more complex, they discovered also a burgeoning literature analyzing, condemning, and seeking to change it.7 But cities grew, drawing immigrants not only from Europe but from rural America, offering a thousand advantages involving work, education, and amusement. While some, disturbed at the evils so frequently catalogued in books, sermons, and periodicals, fled to the borderlands, most did not. The poor could not afford to relocate and for them and many well-off workingmen, country life meant only agricultural drudgery worse than urban work. And the well-to-do, the increasingly prosperous middle and upper classes, did not flee either, for after all, they had the opportunity of temporary visits, and particularly the new custom of the vacation.

No eighteenth- or nineteenth-century farmer vacationed. Keeping dairy cattle alone meant twice-daily milkings, and every other sort of livestock required daily care. Craftsmen in country or city had Sundays free, however, not only for worship but for travel, and the new urban professional groups soon discovered the flexibility inherent in their occupations. By the late 1850s, as reformers like Chapin grew increasingly dismayed with urban life, vast numbers of city residents, and particularly wives and children, customarily deserted residences for summer vacations. "What a thoroughly modern phenomenon it is, this practice of 'emptying' the town!" mused a *Putnam's Monthly* editor in June 1856, as so many of his readers drifted off to the seashore, the New Hampshire hills, the Virginia springs, and even to Canada, fleeing the heat, humidity, and stench of the summer city. Not all New Yorkers thrust down their hearts at the first rare June day as Willis suggested in *Rural Letters*. But the editorial, for all its initial light-heartedness, quickly strikes a different tone, raising the specter of epidemic, of cholera, malignant fever, and other summertime pestilence. New Yorkers fleeing the city ran not so much *to* something, some slow-paced place of rural virtue and exercise, as *from* something atrociously sinister. *Putnam's Monthly* blamed political corruption for the summer pestilence, blasting the "shameful indifference which our authorities have shown to the welfare of the public," deploring the "foulness and filth" heaped in the streets, the unswept tenement houses "teeming with a diseased and neglected population," and championing the good sense of Boccacio fleeing plague-stricken medieval Florence for the "gardens of Fiesole." Most important, the editor implies that the "great public park—which is to serve as the lungs of our metropolis" is too little, too late.8

Year after year, disease haunted Americans, especially those resident in cities. Consider the cholera years, 1832, 1849, and 1866, years of terrifying pandemics, especially in New York. By Independence Day, 1832, almost everyone with means to do so had fled New York City; the crowds reminded one journalist of hordes fleeing Pompeii. After the disease passed, the crowds returned to their filth, only to fall prey to the horror again seventeen years later. After the 1849 outbreak, cholera struck intermittently everywhere in the Republic for five years, but not until 1866 did it come again in fury, destroying whatever hope had blossomed after Appomatox. That year the New York City board of health, terrified into frenzied activity, removed 160,000 tons of manure from vacant lots, disinfected 6,418 priv-

Mid-nineteenth-century magazine illustrations repeatedly depict couples enjoying picturesque borderland scenery. Casualness, not urban formality, characterizes most such images, as in this, where the man sits while the woman stands.

The happy family, the stock feature of so many publications written by women for women readers, struck many readers as one of the few counterbalances to the world of business and busyness seducing husbands and fathers from traditional roles.

Water recreation entranced borderers seeking coolness in summertime, gentle exercise, and broad vistas. Here a small party of pleasure-seekers enjoys the Susquehanna, in a boat designed for pleasure only.

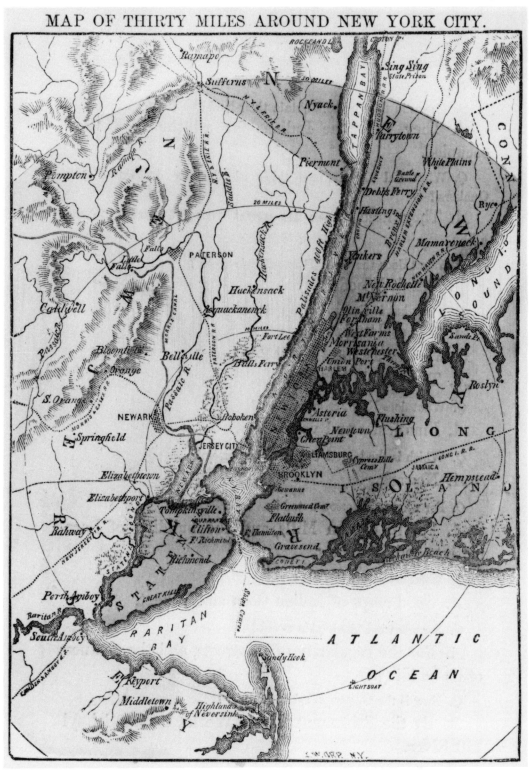

MAP OF THIRTY MILES AROUND NEW YORK CITY.

As early as 1854, James Monteith addressed the significance of the borderlands in his Youth's Manual of Geography, *a textbook aimed at twelve-year-olds.*

ies, and recoiled with horror at the swine and cattle it discovered packed into tenement basements.[9] And as in 1832 and 1849, New Yorkers fled to the country, without a glance at the new park.

Central Park pleased many reformers and delighted its thousands of visitors, but as the *Putnam's* editor argued, it did too little. "Because we have a medicine-chest upstairs, is that any reason why we should acquiesce in a muck-heap under the back window?"[10] Did it not make more sense to improve the domestic environment, to clean the residential streets of manure? In an era of political corruption and inefficiency, however, reformers—and reform-minded families—despaired of such improvement. In summer they ventured forth, into the valley of the Hudson, onto Long Island, south to the Jersey shore; the poor imitated them, trekking to Central Park, walking far out through the farms of Harlem, struggling to get free of urban pollution. But not everyone went. As the *Putnam's* editor concluded somberly, many filled theaters, and perhaps they were better off, for they had become wholly urban people pleased only by wholly urban recreations: they had never heard of Bates, Trotter, or vacation, their amusements aroused the indignation of Chapin; they were unaware of the borderlands and of other sorts of parks.[11]

4 PARKS

In Liverpool and London, the Hawthorne family lived in parks. The novelist, rewarded for his campaign biography of Franklin Pierce with a diplomatic post, commuted to his consular responsibilities. Rock Park, a brief ferry ride from the Liverpool slums, poverty, and social catastrophe he and Melville decried, intrigued Hawthorne for the three years he lived there. From the brow of a hill overlooking Liverpool, he understood it as one of a new type of residential neighborhood. "All round about new and neat residences for city people are springing up, with fine names,—Eldon Terrace, Rose Cottage, Belvoir Villa," he notes in his journal. Surprised to find most houses "a great deal newer than in our new country," he wandered about the villa parks as frequently as he sought out traditional English scenery.[1] But Hawthorne did not just marvel that the "middling classes" might be better housed in borderland Liverpool than in the United States. He lived in villa parks.

Nothing more impressed Hawthorne about Rock Park than the "small Gothic structure of stone" at every entrance, "each inhabited by a policeman and his family." The officers allowed "no ragged or ill-looking person to pass" and charged tolls to nonresident vehicles, precluding "all unnecessary passage of carriages." Occupied solely by "gentlemen" and their families, the strictly private neighborhood of "noiseless streets" and "pretty residences" behind guardposts boasted extensive ornamental planting, not only a wealth of flower gardens, but laburnum and other attractive trees, making altogether a picturesque place to live, a sort of refuge from the noisome streets of Liverpool across the estuary.[2] Hawthorne distills his impressions of park living into a chapter of *Our Old Home,* focusing on Blackheath Park, his borderland London residence, one of the "oases" recently built outside the city. "The scene is semi-rural. Ornamental trees overshadow the sidewalks, and grassy margins border the wheel-tracks," he writes of a place in which the houses appear vaguely American, although fenced off from the street and each other by high walls and hedges. "Glimpses of well-kept lawns, generally ornamented with flowers" ranging from roses to sweet peas to poppies "and a variety of other scarlet, yellow, blue, and purple blossoms, which I did not trouble myself to

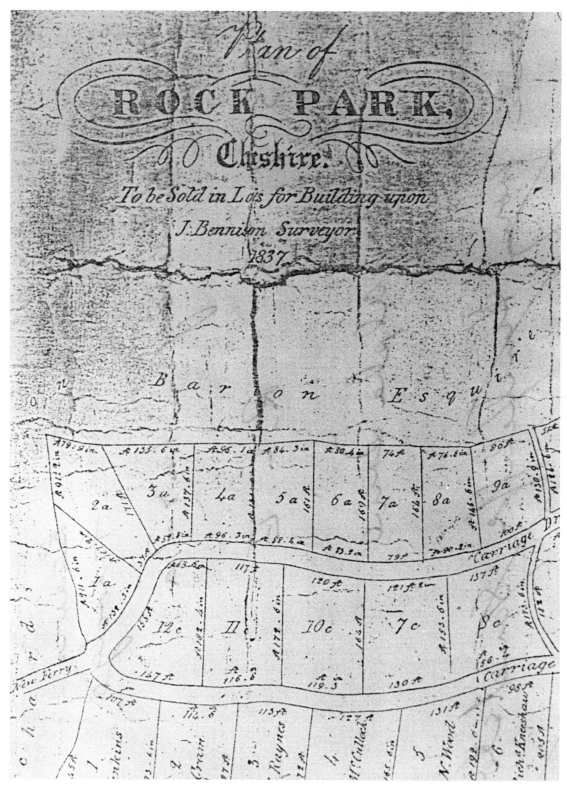

A survey map of Rock Park depicts not only the deep lots that pleased Hawthorne but the curving roads that became the prototype of almost all "exclusive" residential developments in Great Britain and the United States.

*Even in the late 1870s, the gently curving roads of
Rock Park remained quiet retreats offering access only
to very private family grounds.*

*The front porch of the Hawthorne home in Rock Park
offered a nook within the larger nook of the home
grounds, and within the larger nook of the park itself.*

recognize individually, yet had always a vague sense of their beauty about me," delight him in his close-to-home rambles. From rising ground, the serene streets offer views of the "wide waste" of undeveloped Blackheath in one direction, and in the other, of London several miles off, "a glorious and sombre picture, dusky, awful, but irresistibly attractive." The park, a "still eddy" removed from the "turbulence of the vast London whirlpool," surprises Hawthorne by its capacity to soothe. "I was in a manner free of the city, and could approach or keep away from it as I pleased," he muses, sitting in his garden "within a quarter of an hour's rush of the London Bridge Terminus" where the commuter trains regularly roar past a quarter mile away, "screeching to a stop at Blackheath station." Only that "harsh, rough sound" intrudes upon his peace, however; at the edge of Blackheath Park—as at Rock Park—stands the ever-present gateway, "kept by a policeman" insuring "a semi-privacy."[3]

Other Americans in the 1830s and subsequent decades wondered about the villa parks surrounding English cities. As early as 1835, Alexander Slidell Mackenzie described the beauties of Regent's Park, concluding in *The American in England* that "I could not but regret the unfavorable character of the comparison between these charming cottages, and the tasteless masses of brick and mortar in which people of the same class and of greater means are contented to live in my own country." The "pleasing variety of hill and hollow, of rock and glen, and picturesque ravine" naturally beautifying Manhattan Island cry out for similar development, Mackenzie asserts.[4] Frederick Law Olmsted, for all that he disliked the obvious newness of the villas outside Liverpool, nevertheless admired their quality construction, fledgling gardens, and excellent location, and he urges readers of *Walks and Talks* to emulate them in America.[5] Another visitor to the British parks, the New Yorker Howard Daniels, emphasizes in an 1858 *Horticulturist* essay that villa parks focused about a commonly owned picturesque area offered private beauties as well. The villa sites, he advises, should each feature a lawn, flower garden, fruit and vegetable garden, and if possible a pasture large enough for a cow and a horse, providing the owner an opportunity to "spend his leisure hours in cultivating and trimming his favorite trees, shrubs, flowers and vegetables." Such parks provide not only picturesque beauty, "congenial neighbors and good society," but the pleasures of family privacy and private land-shaping too. "A healthy locality, contiguous to a railroad or steamboat route, situated in good neighborhood, having pleasant drives and good building materials are matters of the first importance," Daniels concludes, emphasizing the utter practicality of the English villa park in the New York borderlands.[6] Unlike Mackenzie and Olmsted, Daniels wrote not only from overseas observation. He knew the park idea would work in the Republic: he had seen Llewellyn Park.

In the years just before the creation of Central Park, as the *Putnam's* editor was worrying about vacation habits, foul air, and the prospects of plague, Llewellyn S. Haskell began shaping the first American villa park, about twelve miles from New York, across the Hudson River in New Jersey.[7] Perhaps his Maine boyhood predisposed Haskell to rural, or at least small-town, life; in establishing himself as a prosperous businessman first in Philadelphia and later in New York, he always resided at the edge of the city, where fresh air and trees somehow buoyed his spirit. Perhaps his professional interests directed him to the borderlands too: as owner of a very large pharmaceutical firm that both imported and manufactured drugs, Haskell may have understood the medical problems Trotter and other experts associated with urban living. And, finally, perhaps his European contacts familiarized him with the English villa park, that semi-rural oasis for gentlemen. Inspired first by living in wholesome, picturesque surroundings, he eventually conceived the idea of creating an American oasis.

His vision depended on industrial technology, however, for the railroad alone made practical year-round residence in Orange, the farming community already discovered by New York merchants seeking borderland happiness. Financial panic changed the township from an obscure stop on the Morris & Essex railroad into an incipient commuter Eden. In the 1837 crash, an Orange storekeeper failed, and his New York backer, a wealthy merchant already thinking about a home in the borderlands, took control of his hundred-acre farm. Matthias Ogden Halsted soon erected a magnificent house and began subdividing his acreage, selling the picturesque lots to his city friends. By agreeing to build a depot at his own expense, Halsted convinced the railroad company to stop one morning inbound train and one evening outbound train at the edge of his acreage, making possible not only an hour-long commute each way, but all of Haskell's dreams too.

Alexander Davis, an Orange architect, convinced Haskell that a few miles west into New Jersey lay not only beautiful scenery but also a dry atmosphere that would help his rheumatism. Haskell, only thirty-seven years old and already anxious to maintain his health, found the air around Eagle Rock absolutely invigorating and determined to move, buying 40 acres—and an old farmhouse—in 1853. Davis soon converted the farmhouse into a structure intended to harmonize with the wild scenery about it, and he built a tower, which Haskell equipped with a telescope, on the nearby cliff; almost immediately afterward, the architect acquired 25 acres of land from Haskell and began building his own house. Within four years, the New York merchant had purchased 350 acres, having determined to build a villa park offering "country homes for city people."[8] In succeeding years he acquired another 400 acres, and with Davis and several landscape architects created a strictly private place the size of Central Park.

No site better met picturesque criteria. The Eagle Rock area of Orange Mountain, a six-hundred-foot rocky outcropping covered with spruce, fir, hemlock, and other conifers opened by half-abandoned fields, entranced all visitors. "Threaded by mountain streams, pierced with picturesque ravines, monumented with venerable trees," the place delighted one 1864 writer, who found it "altogether diversified with a beautiful brokenness of scenery."[9] As in so many other places near major cities, no farmer found the slopes attractive or profitable, and rural families laughed as Haskell's designers and workmen began grading roads, creating ponds, and planting shrubs and trees native to the region as well as some imported from Asia, South America, and Europe. Azaleas, dogwood, holly, rhododendron, and other plants, all carefully installed to heighten the wild, tangled, natural beauty of the site, combined in a stunning effect. In seven years, Haskell spent more than a hundred thousand dollars on the landscape work alone, turning land scorned by farmers into sites prized by city families educated in the picturesque tradition.

Above the rocks and trees lay the view, reportedly unsurpassed anywhere south of the Catskills, extending over a hundred miles from Sandy Hook to the Hudson Highlands to the Long Island Hills. In the lowlands covering the twelve miles separating Eagle Rock from New York City lay the bustling little town of Newark, farms, woods, and the salt meadows terminating at Bergen Hill. Beyond the hill stood the steeples of New York and the masts and spars of hundreds of sailing ships, all visible in detail through Haskell's powerful telescope, but all at an obvious distance. From the picturesque heights of Orange Mountain, the inhabitants of Llewellyn Park gazed out over the borderlands, over the great city in the east, and out into the Atlantic, discovering firsthand the thrill of Bates's elevated ground of serene contemplation.

Haskell created a stunning site. Focused about a fifty-acre "ramble," a tree-covered ravine he soon deeded in the British fashion to the association of home-owners, the development opened on the northeast. Visitors entered it by passing a gatehouse and gate, as imposing as those Hawthorne found in England, and moved along narrow, graded roads either directly up the floor of the wooded ramble or along slopes paralleling it. Away from the common ground lay homesites ranging in size from one to twenty acres, all linked by some ten miles of tree- and shrub-bordered carriage roads opening on common areas dignified by "rustic" benches and arbors deliberately sited to emphasize picturesque scenes or spectacular long-distance views. In planting tens of thousands of shrubs of a single species, in offering free rock from the little quarry on the site, and by suggesting houses built in the "romantic" style, Haskell produced what one 1864 visitor called "an enchanted ground or fairy land."[10] Something of Susan Cooper's magic seemed at work, something straight out of Willis' *Rural Letters*.

Llewellyn Park's domestic architecture evolved from the precepts Davis published in his 1838 *Rural Residences*. Gothic, bracketed Swiss, and Italian styles struck Davis as the only ones possible for a wild, picturesque site, for only they emphasized an irregularity of form. In designing the gate lodge, kiosks, and many of the houses in the "romantic" style, Davis helped set the overall architectural appearance of the park.[11] His modest structures—"cottages" in the terminology of era—and his larger, almost castle-like Gothic ones reflected a decidedly avant-garde awareness of the intimacy of natural surroundings and architectural design, a philosophy that did not always suit Llewellyn Park's inhabitants. "The house is rather fanciful for my taste," commented one bride in 1866; "it was built by an artist; it has a funny pitched roof and clustered chimneys and bull's-eye windows, and niches for statuettes, and all sorts of artistic arrangements that don't quite suit my plain taste." But the young housewife determined that she would accustom herself to the modernity, admitting that after all, "the Park is beautiful and the views from our house are lovely."[12] What she thought of her neighbors remains unknown.

Haskell sold land to whomever would buy, making no effort to forbid specific groups or individuals or to inquire into social qualifications. The development quickly acquired a reputation for housing almost scandalous modernists, "long-haired men and short-haired women" in the words of one resident. While many heads of households were simply well-to-do New York businessmen anxious to live in picturesque, healthful borderland surroundings easy accessible by railroad, many Llewellyn Park residents practiced radical Swedenborgianism, atheism, homeopathy, mysticism, spiritualism, and even a sort of nature worship that inspired a May Festival, the only annual gathering in the Park. The park's residents, lively, thoughtful, financially successful, full of originality, wholly modern, shared more than the mix of creeds and practices at first suggests. Not only did they all value borderland life above anything the city offered, they also valued their privacy.

The writer of an *Every Saturday* essay of 1871, focusing on the essence of Llewellyn Park, dwelled not on its picturesque beauty and sympathetic architecture but on its insularity. "Llewellyn Park is a private park, and this is perhaps its most important feature," he wrote. "While in extent it nearly equals Central Park, unlike that, it is strictly private, to be used only by the owners and their friends."[13] Strangers, the essayist concluded, could enter the development by writing their names in a book kept in the gatehouse, but the tone of the article suggests that few visitors ventured past the stone gatehouse and beyond the wooden gates. On Sundays, by order of the residents, the gates stood shut, and the inhabitants of Llewellyn Park—like those of English parks—enjoyed their picturesque fairyland in solitude.

The shutting of the gates may have warped the whole course of American borderland development, for Llewellyn Park became not a prototype, but a half-secret treasure. "We trust and believe that this is but the beginning of many such undertakings," commented one writer in an 1857 issue of *The Crayon*. "There are in the vicinity of our cities many locations now comparatively valueless, which could thus be turned to noblest use, and we know of no way in which combined capital and associated effort could be more worthily employed."[14] Despite such wishes for family salvation through residence in natural beauty, despite the exhortations of Hawthorne, Mackenzie, Daniels, and others, the progress of American borderland development proved otherwise.

5 ❧ HEIGHTS

As early as 1853, when she published her second series of *Clovernook Tales,* Alice Cary discerned the change overtaking the borderlands of Cincinnati, the Queen City of the West. The short stories are among the very first in American literature to address the complexities of borderland life, focusing on the speed with which the borderlands change form. The narrator of the tales, a woman of leisure, surveys the Ohio Valley and Cincinnati from the "hilly country to the west." In the first tale, a mist rising from the river obscures the Kentucky shore, and the narrator tries "in vain to see the young cities of which the sloping suburbs are washed by the Ohio, river of beauty! except here and there the gleam of a white wall, or a dense column of smoke that rises through the silver mist from hot furnaces where swart labor drives the thrifty trades, speeding the march to elegance and wealth."[1] At first reading simply sentimental fiction, the creation of one of the "damned mob of scribbling women" Hawthorne so hated, the tales not only reveal a remarkably forthright understanding of industrial capitalism as the shaper of urban growth and the creator of class-stratified society, they paint a penetrating portrait of the role of women secure in the elevations of quiet contemplation.

Cary's narrator sees both the grand view and the microcosm of happiness. On the one hand, her hilly vantage point enables her to see the distant manufacturing city and even more distant agricultural regions, both spaces distinct from the borderlands. On the other, she sees the happy homes—"cottages"—of other borderland women, and she delights in describing a typical nook, its "cream-white walls, overrun with clematis and jasmine, and the clambering stalks of roses," sited on a lot graced by a smoothly mowed lawn, "various bushes and flowers, and the golden velvet of dandelions." Every detail—the white window curtains, the blue smoke curling upward from the kitchen chimney, the happy housewife singing next to her baby—acquires power as Cary embroiders the picture into a larger whole, a whole as intricate and meaningful as a fine flower garden. "They are plain and common-sense people who dwell here," the narrator concludes, suggesting that in the borderlands traditional virtues flourish. Cary also grappled with the distant city, thrusting her characters into alleys and tenements like the "large dingy build-ing, five stories high and nearly a hundred feet long" that houses some of the poorest of Cincinnati families. Built by a "wealthy proprietor" on "the cheapest possible plan," the immense structure stands not near the central city but in "the meanest suburb of the city," looming like a vast monument to poverty and depravity. Against her image of the hilly borderlands, Cary juxtaposes the suburb slum, detail-ing even the courtyard refuse flung down from windows and balconies. "Dish-water, washing suds, and every thing else, from tea and coffee grounds to all manner of picked bones and other refuse," produce a "filthy and in all ways unendurable spectacle." The characters entering "the vicinity of this money-making device, this miserable house refuge," recoil all the more quickly because they are from the borderlands, "accustomed to the free air of the country."[2] Alice Cary wrote real-istically, avoided romanticizing her characters and settings. Other documentation confirms her courageous description of Cincinnati slum life, just as other sources support her vision of borderland bliss. Now almost wholly forgotten, dismissed as a woman writing trivial fiction for middle-class women readers, Cary recorded the delicate equilibrium of so many women living between city and country and trying desperately to commute the troubles within which their commuting husbands worked.

When Sidney D. Maxwell published his *Suburbs of Cincinnati* some fifteen years after Cary's *Clovernook Tales,* the Queen City borderlands housed thousands of people. A statistician by profession, Maxwell delighted in assembling accurate information on the "environs," and his book confirms Cary's impression of a new world deliberately poised between two others.[3] For all his reliance on statistics, however, Maxwell finally fell back upon the magician's wand that served Susan Cooper so well. When a longtime resident "sees in all directions handsome dwell-ings, numbered by hundreds, surrounded by shrubbery and flowers, and ap-proached by beautiful drives, and witnesses the stream of carriages that, morning and night, carry business men from and to their delightful homes, it seems as if forest and field had been touched by some magic hand."[4] Two decades transformed the Queen City environs from a rural region inhabited by farm families and a few professional families into a wonderfully beautiful, wholly captivating borderland.

Vacationing, Maxwell asserts, stimulated the change, although an 1852 *Gleason's Drawing Room Companion* article suggests that vacationing originated in summertime attendance at rural religious revivals.[5] In the early 1840s a handful of prosperous families, fleeing urban heat and disease, built summer houses on very large lots—some extending over more than forty acres—several miles into the hill country. Adapting themselves to the vagaries of long-distance train schedules or relying upon carriages and poor country roads, the vacationers commuted fitfully into the city. In subsequent years, while experimenting with gentlemen farming—particularly the growing of native and exotic grapes—the summer residents dis-covered improving railroad service and country roads along with growing numbers of seasonal neighbors, and they determined to live in the borderlands year-round. From that moment on, Maxwell relates, the borderlands quickly changed ap-

Over and over again, mid-nineteenth-century illustrators depicted cities from surrounding heights, in this case Brooklyn Heights, and very frequently they included women in the foreground, like this one, who is reading. Who is the thoughtful woman, ignoring the ferry, the Long Island Sound steamer, ocean-going sailing ships, bridge, and city, if not one with her mind on more important things?

pearance. The first summer visitors, having bought farms and portions of farms very cheaply, began selling large lots to newer arrivals, and in the Cincinnati borderlands blossomed a land rush every bit as profitable as those in the Nevada silver country. James Robb, a newcomer from New Orleans, bought land in what became the township of Clifton in 1844: he paid $65 an acre and sold it five years later for $275 an acre. In 1855, as Alice Cary mused about the changing countryside, the land changed hands again, at $1,000 an acre; in 1868 it sold at $3,000 for each acre. "This indicates," Maxwell marvels, "that eligible lands in this locality have increased about forty-six hundred per cent in twenty-four years."[6] It also indicated what Cary knew and said but Maxwell ignored: capitalism moved as certainly in the borderlands as it did in the industrial and business centers of Cincinnati.

Maxwell's book, while based on statistical analysis and street-by-street description, shares the picturesque values of *Rural Hours, Rural Letters,* and so many other books published in the preceding two decades. "These highlands are Clifton, from the slopes of which the beholder looks out upon a valley of great extent and of rare beauty," he writes early in his book. "For many miles to the north are suburban places, beautiful farms, comfortable farm-houses, fields rich in pasturage, interspersed with beautiful groves." The observer sees a new sort of space, not the traditional "pretty country" beloved of American farmers but agricultural space overlaid with borderland structures and spaces. All the scenery necessary for borderland bliss is there, according to Maxwell—at one point he notes that "the landscape is scarcely ever without a railroad train to lend it additional interest"— and anything suggesting urban ills, particularly factories, mechanic's shops, and saloons, is absent. Clifton "is so completely under the control of those who desire to keep it for purposes of country residence, that it must be many years before the general character of the place can change." Clifton and the other borderland communities are in essence pictures, landscapes almost magically created and equally magically maintained in stasis. There, in the "full enjoyment of rural simplicity," the upper- and middle-class families of the Cincinnati metropolitan region enjoy fine churches, schools, and views, and particularly the vista in which Cincinnati figured so prominently.[7] Of the links between borderland and city Maxwell says little, devoting only several pages to the problems of commuting. Cary, the woman novelist writing for women, understood the maze of connections linking the borderlands with factories, slums, and citadels of business; Maxwell, the business analyst, ignored the maze in favor of long journeys into picturesque space.

Within a few years the maze demanded recognition. In *Peculiarities of American Cities,* Willard Glazier addresses the extraordinary dichotomy between the typical "city proper" and its ring of borderland, usually hilly places. A pall of smoke, "caused by the bituminous coal used as fuel in the city," hangs over the valley city, dirtying skin and clothes, permanently soiling clothes hung outdoors to dry, and obscuring the sun. "But beyond the city, on the magnificent amphitheatre of hills which encircle it," Glazier continues, lie the residential places, "as much superior to Fifth Avenue as the country is superior to the city, and as space is preferable to narrowness." In the hills around Cincinnati, Glazier finds "a paradise of grass,

Camp meetings first drew Cincinnati families to the surrounding heights, and many in the vast crowds learned to live year-round in the sylvan environs of the city.

Middle-class families emigrating to the heights around Cincinnati quickly learned that they had moved into a region still dependent on farming, and still offering woodlots and fields where city boys could learn to hunt, and perhaps enjoy views.

In the Cincinnati borderlands, as elsewhere, middle-class families delighted not only in their houses, but in their grounds and stables, setting out all sorts of shrubs and trees, fastening a swing to a convenient limb, and trying to live out of doors, as Willis and other experts counseled.

In the hot summers of southern Ohio, large, tree-shaded porches and lawns offered partial relief from sun and humidity, but they and observation towers also enabled borderers to relax in the enjoyment of fine views.

Industrial Cincinnati sprawled along its riverfront, its manufactories spewing the smoke that overwhelmed the river mists, its giant cranes and foundries roaring day and night. In the far-off heights, such industrial enterprise intrigued the women, who rarely confronted it close up, as did their commuting husbands.

gardens, lawns, and tree-shaded roads," a world of "enchanting scenery" apparently little changed from Maxwell's day.[8] Cary correctly discerned the overwhelming of river mist by the smoke from the factories; no longer was the city healthful or beautiful. Health and beauty, exactly as Trotter argued at the beginning of the century, lay far from the smoke and mud, uphill.

Power, especially aesthetic power, lay uphill too, the power of the observing, discerning, ordering eye far enough removed from urban complexity to arrange complexity into a view, to ignore the shadows of the city. "Lines Written on Prospect Hill," an 1826 *Rural Repository* poem, exemplifies a whole genre of verse announcing the hilltop vision, the prospect:

> The city lies beneath my feet,
> The tallest trees are yet below,
> And yonder smiling country seat,
> It seems a fairy palace now.

City and country seat, merged into one view of nearly magical beauty, float mistily in the poem, touched somehow by the wands of Susan Cooper, Alice Cary, and so many other hilltop scrutinizers.

So what of the innumerable illustrations of the 1840s, 1850s, and subsequent decades, depicting women and children gazing down from the heights covered in wildflowers? Perhaps the illustrations reflect a growing realization of the importance of home and family in a modern industrial society. "Women, in the country, must have some objects of interest beyond their ordinary household cares and joys," argued an 1850 reviewer of Cooper's *Rural Hours*. Without such objects, women fall prey to "a feverish appetite for cities, and the life of crowds." By expanding their interests to include natural history, ornamental gardening, simple, virtuous living, and other "wholesome tastes," women might control the destiny of the nation by rearing children attuned to those forces that will best fit them for life in increasingly difficult times, for life in the cities spread out below the borderlands.[9] In the 1840s and 1850s, Cooper and Cary discerned the changing nature of domestic life and understood the challenge and promise of the borderlands.

And by the 1880s, indeed as early as the 1870s, when Maxwell noted that one residential community, Mount Auburn, was "exceedingly well built up" with an appearance "more of an approximation to the city than any other suburb," every thinking man, woman, and child in Cincinnati—and in almost every other large American city—knew that only in the borderlands lay beauty, fresh air, and a hundred other forces tending toward health and virtue.[10] On the heights, "on the ridge" as Mary Stewart Cutting phrased it in 1907 in her *Suburban Whirl*, lay something attractive indeed—at least after some preliminary improvement.[11]

II "A New Sort of Space":
A Proper Country Home

Westchester displeased many early-nineteenth-century
visitors, especially those interested in agriculture. Too often
the travelers found tottering fences, leaning barns, and the
general decay that advertised pending abandonment and that
mocked any effort aimed at discovering picturesque landscape.

❧ RETIREMENT

"*T*he question has doubtless been often asked, why Mr. Webster retired thirty miles from the metropolis, to the most quiet of all towns, to find a farm, and a country home," asked the editor of The Pictorial National Library in his July 1848 issue. "It may be replied, that the remarkable quiet of the place was one great recommendation of it, to his own mind." Webster had not quit public life. As the editor wrote, Daniel Webster stood among the few from whom the Whigs would select a presidential candidate, he practiced law, and he held a seat in the U.S. Senate. And in Marshfield, in the borderlands south of Boston, he farmed.

In sixteen years Webster transformed the old Thomas farm. He doubled the size of the old house, built new barns and other outbuildings, amassed fifteen hundred acres of land, and introduced the latest agricultural techniques. "Everything is done upon it on the largest scale, looking to future as well as to immediate results," the editor marveled. "He carries on his farm, not merely for the sake of making it profitable to himself, and to gratify his own taste, but to elevate the character of agriculturists, and to introduce an improved mode of pursuing this important calling." By 1848 the place struck visitors as extraordinary. "His farming, like his eloquence, is wholly Websterian in its character."

But Webster did more than farm. He retired. In his garden he located his law library. Along his carriage drive, already lined with elms, he planted an English hedge "interspersed with every variety of tree, of home and foreign production." He dammed his pond with stonework mimicking the horseshoe-shaped falls at Niagara. Everything spoke of leisure even as it announced active agriculture. "The spacious garden and hot houses, with a delightful summer-house, on a little eminence, surrounded with a dense forest of trees, filled with a great variety of birds," combine with "fine cultivated fields" to produce a place of rest, of restoration from the tension of governing under the darkening specter of disunion and war. Webster understood the role of borderland retirement, and the old Thomas farm advertised his understanding.

6 ❧ PROSPERITY

Westchester worried Nathaniel Willis. By 1851, the region struck him as wholly changed, overwhelmed by newcomers seeking rural landscape and borderland living. Away from the railroad, he argued, "you find yourself in a region of 'country seats'—no poor people's abodes, or other humble belongings, anywhere visible." Half in jest, he determined that "this was rather a defect in the general scenery, though any one estate, perhaps, looked better for things exclusively ornamental." In Westchester, some twenty miles from New York City, Willis had blundered into a wholly new sort of environment.

Homogeneity troubled him. "Miles upon miles of unmitigated prosperity weary the eye," he remarked reproachfully. "Lawns and park-gates, groves and verandahs, ornamental woods and neat walls, trim edges and well-placed shrubberies, fine houses and large stables, neat gravel walks and nobody on them—are notes upon one chord, and they certainly seemed to me to make a dull tune of Westchester." At the same time, he found each particular estate, no matter how modest, remarkably handsome, and he marveled at the "charming" grounds from which the larger landscape and Long Island Sound appeared something almost beyond the reach of any painter. Indeed some landscape features seemed beyond the actual reach of any traveler. The Bronx, "a lovely little river," was nearly wholly cut off from public view: "private grounds enclose its banks wherever they look inviting." The river "so aristocratically fenced up" served as the very emblem of the new landscape of rigidly compartmentalized country seats.

Willis longed for traces of vanished traditional rural landscape, asking if "contrast is *always* necessary in out-of-door pictures"—"does no rich man's house show to advantage without a laborer's cottage in the back-ground?" No answers followed his questions, only a hint that some "poor folks" might "humanize" the scene, and a half-quip, half-sneer that "Westchester wants a dash of wretchedness to make it quite the thing."[1] The county, or rather that part he visited following his ride on the "Harlem rail-road," struck him as something carried too far. In lower Westchester, amid the country seats or "residences," Willis discovered a new spatial creation overwhelming—not simply overlaying—an older spatial order, a creation that had driven away the poor folks, the farmers.

7 🌿 SLOVENLINESS

Willis strayed only a short distance from the railroad, however, and his description of Westchester evolved from a hasty tour guided by one of the newly arrived country gentlemen. Elsewhere, if other observers scrutinized the county correctly, Westchester presented a remarkably different appearance, one best designated "slovenly."

Solon Robinson, the mid-nineteenth-century agricultural reformer and editor of *The American Agriculturist,* visited the county in November 1850, only three years before Willis. Robinson thrust deeply into Westchester, ranging into the hilly country and focusing his attention on farming. He too wondered at the Harlem Railroad, although not for its commuting value; instead he marveled at its annual forty-thousand-dollar freight bill for raw milk, remarking the almost unbelievable fact that milk traveled "warm from the cow" to the city fifty miles away "to be used for breakfast the same morning." At first glance, the railroad appeared to have awakened the entire countryside and transformed "the whole course of cultivation."

Only upon closer observation does Robinson discover the shadows in the rosy picture. Certainly "tillable land has increased in value" and "now every article of produce—everything valuable can be sent and daily sold in the city," but farmers prosper little. On the one hand, the hilly, stony terrain is useful as pasture, and so dairymen do well, especially those who choose to fatten some of the cattle driven from the west every spring. But the infertile, uneven ground defeats many potentially profitable crops, making dairying a last resort. On the other hand, the changed Westchester population set up new and seemingly insurmountable difficulties to traditional agriculture. Domestic dogs running amok all but destroyed sheep husbandry when Robinson ventured into the hill sections; even gentlemen farmers desiring choice lamb and mutton for home consumption learned that sheep "are frequently attacked in open day, in some secluded pasture." Working farmers abandoned sloping fields as useless for anything but cattle grazing, for fruit growing had become impossible too. "But now, who will plant an orchard when he knows the fruit will be all stolen?" An apple crop carried off by determined thieves, half a flock of sheep destroyed by roving "curs," such catastrophes turned farmers toward more certain enterprises, toward the level lower fields near their barnyards. Bit by bit, as quality tillable fields increased in value, the farmers of Westchester abandoned sloping terrain.

"Everything has an ancient, and I must say rather behind-the-age appearance," Robinson continues, describing a long ride through the granite hills. "Old-fashioned gambrel-roofed farm houses; old barns and outbuildings, covered with an old mossy coat," wells, buckets, springhouses—everything seems as old as the "old grey granite rocks," existing "through long centuries of old time." Stone walls everywhere, and lines of fallen walls, irritate the reformer, for they bound too-small fields, restricting their owners to outdated tillage practices. The walls and heaps of rocks would do better underground, as drains; if they were removed the arable acreage would be increased by perhaps a tenth. But nowhere does the visitor discern much change for the better. "Close as this county is to the city, the majority of the inhabitants have not yet caught the infecting spirit of improvement," Robinson muses.

The eerieness of Robinson's essay makes his optimistic conclusion—focused on the hope that young farmers will discover agricultural journals and learn new techniques—ring hollow. Westchester farmers seemed caught up in a change as wrenching as any migration to Kansas or Oregon, but a change they scarcely understood, let alone controlled. Robinson noticed the many country estates along the Harlem Railroad and remarks "the singular fact, that these country residences are mainly supplied with marketing from the city, instead of their own vicinity."[1] Apparently the Westchester farmers, despite their proximity to well-to-do families anxious for fresh meat, dairy products, and garden produce, had not shifted to market gardening even as their traditional practices failed. Fifty miles from New York City, and even nearer to the well-off newcomers in the lower part of their county, the farmers of Westchester faltered, growing poorer by the season. And the Westchester countryside turned slovenly.

Between the mid-1820s and the beginning of the Civil War, American agricultural periodicals lambasted the slovenly countryside surrounding eastern cities. Their condemnations detailed the constituents of ugliness. "A barn door, perhaps, for loss of hinges, is propped up by rails or stakes," begins one 1847 *Farmer's Cabinet* piece scrutinizing the farm of a backward man. "Brushwood and trunks of trees lie in fantastic confusion about his doors, whilst the skeletons of departed carts, and wheels, and sleds, and ploughs line the roadside for a considerable distance, as you approach his dwelling." Brush-entangled walls and fences, worn-out tillage land, thistles, johnswort, and mullein holding "title to his mowing fields by right of uninterrupted occupation," all these and more advertise the slovenly resident in the dilapidated house.[2] "Farmer Slack," as one 1851 *American Agriculturist* writer called him, owns a barn unable to "keep the contents from the snows and storms of winter," and "in some places only the traces of a fence are visible"; his cattle wander from field to field.[3] For fifty years, Americans had noticed rural messiness—late in the eighteenth century Dwight condemned it in *Greenfield Hill* as the manifestation of sloth, if not worse—but travelers from abroad aroused domestic concern, and injured national pride, after the early 1810s. William Cobbett called the farmers of Long Island natural "slovens," each content "with a shell of boards, while all around him is as barren as the sea beach; though the natural earth would send melons, the finest in the world, creeping round his door, and though there is no English shrub, or flower, which will not grow and flourish here." He notes that "even in Pennsylvania, and amongst the Quakers too, there is a sort of out-of-door slovenliness, which is never hardly seen in England. You see bits of wood, timber, boards, lying about, here and there and pigs and cattle trampling in a sort of confusion, which would make an English farmer fret himself to death."[4] No American contributor to the agricultural magazines criticized the rough condition of frontier farms, even those settled three or four decades earlier. Readers knew how long pioneers had to struggle simply to make a farm pay, let alone make it efficient. What unnerved the reform-minded editors and letter-writers were long-established, once-prosperous places located near markets—backward, not backwoods places. And as the century advanced, the assault on slovenly farming intensified. "Wherever we see the fields badly tilled, the fences broken, the buildings dilapidated, the dirt in heaps before the door, the garden a wilderness of weeds, and the orchard an untrimmed mass of brush, we turn away in disgust, and say to ourselves, there is no pride," announced Solon Robinson, one of the nation's leading exponents of efficient agriculture, in a barbed 1855 address to some Massachusetts farmers. "That man, like a beggar, has got used to a draggled skirt; his mind is past repair; his children are like the weeds in his garden, growing up to scatter pernicious seed over a fair land."[5] Only vice—drink perhaps, or simple sloth—explained such slovenliness.

While now and then a crusading agricultural editor blamed such conditions not on vice but on pure ignorance of new techniques or on the force of tradition (one 1829 observer claims that "one reason why so many door yards are neglected, is that it is a spot of doubtful jurisdiction, neither falling exactly under the scope of the word 'farm' which it is the man's to oversee, nor being properly in the house, where woman reigns") most ignored the debilitating effects of the Revolutionary War— during which British and patriot armies swept repeatedly over farmland adjacent to eastern cities, devastating structures, fences, and optimism—and of the floods of produce from Ohio, Indiana, and other states connected by canals to eastern markets.[6] Most of the time agricultural writers blamed immorality, and particularly thriftlessness and laziness, for the condition of eastern farms. One 1842 *American Agriculturist* author, who signed himself "Octogenaria," argues that "this moral deliquency can be traced" from the time when parents stopped raising sons and daughters "in habits of *industry*, morality and religion." A *New England Farmer* writer of the same year echoed the sentiments, arguing that the daughters of well-off farmers received ornamental educations making them too delicate for the dairy barn and anxious for store-bought, not homemade goods. Five years later, a *Farmer's Cabinet* columnist directed attention at the farmers in the vicinity of Philadelphia, beginning his lengthy diatribe with a detailed catalogue of the wonderful produce available at the city marketplace only ten years before. "In truth, it was a goodly

Vacationers in the borderlands around Boston stumbled upon ramshackle farm structures like these depicted in an 1848 issue of Pictorial National Library. No matter how evocative of older times, the tottering buildings announced the gross slovenliness of their owners.

Farmer Slack, learned readers of mid-nineteenth-century agricultural journals, lived on a farm that reflected his moral and mental weakness.

In the capable hands of Farmer Thrifty, however, the slovenly farm abandoned by Farmer Slack becomes prosperous and attractive. Reform-minded editors of agricultural journals often failed to realize that Farmer Thrifty might well be a gentleman farmer newly arrived in the borderlands.

sight to see the farmer part with his treasures, to adorn the domestic feast and gladden the hearts of civic partakers—whilst he, in exchange therefore, was gladdened with shining stores of gold and silver." Whatever the truth of the writer's memories, present conditions, he reports, are disastrous. So many farmers have concentrated on dairying that many must produce and sell ice cream to prosper, and urban "housekeepers groan at the scarcity and dearness of produce." As the city marketplace grows bare, so the countryside grows slovenly, as farmers abandon all but land suited to dairying. "It is undoubtedly true that the present high price of provisions is partly owing to the fact that so many farmers in the neighbourhood of our Atlantic cities have turned their attention wholly to the manufacture of luxuries to tickle the palates of our dainty loving citizens."[7] The farmer, anxious to increase his immediate profit, thus abandons the mixed agriculture of his father, the agriculture of simple virtue, the agriculture that created a beautiful landscape.

Other critics, more intimately familiar with the awesome difficulties confronting farmers near eastern cities, discerned a fundamental economic equation reshaping the landscape. "Instead of asking how he can make every acre of his land productive, the farmer inquires how he can subsist with the least possible expenditure of labor in its cultivation, or of capital in its improvement," asserted one critic in an 1842 issue of *The New England Farmer*.[8] Certainly laziness played a role in such cases, but other forces proved more powerful. A farmer owning a hundred acres outside an eastern city quickly learned that grain made a poor crop: the Erie Canal and other transportation arteries buried the east under cheap grain from the Ohio and Mississippi Valleys. Cereals and other field crops depended by 1840 on complicated horse-drawn equipment wonderfully efficient in western flatlands but nearly useless on hilly terrain; sloping land turned a profit—and a scanty one at that—only as pasture. Eastern farmers knew too that nearly two centuries of tillage had often eroded their land and exhausted their soils, that borrowing money to buy new inventions might bankrupt them, that industrious sons departed for the west rather than working to improve old acreage. Given such challenges, many farmers wished their sons well as they left for city jobs or frontier farms.[9] Only a handful understood the equation and abandoned most of their land to concentrate on a few acres dedicated to high-profit crops that tickled urban palates.

Manufacturing added to the woes of agriculturists. Air pollution alone tormented many farmers, especially those in the vicinity of New York City. By the 1840s, Westchester County farmers knew that smoke and noxious gases from the dozens of brickyards producing bricks for city building drifted over vineyards and orchards with ghastly results. The New York Farmer's Club devoted much attention to the new peril, which worsened as brickmakers shifted from wood-fired to coal-fired kilns. One superb orchard in the Westchester town of Cortlandt, "containing from 1000 to 1500 trees, was entirely ruined, principally by the gases from numbers of brick-yards in the immediate vicinity," remarked one *Farmer's Cabinet* writer.[10] The problem, first reported on a large scale in the late 1830s, spread through the entire Hudson valley; dew, rain, or fog caused the airborne poisons to settle over orchards and vineyards, causing leaves to wilt, unripe fruit to fall, and whole trees to die. "If the fruit trees should happen to be in blossom when these gases were in the air, the destruction of fruit would occur fifteen miles in the direction of the wind," asserted one physician familiar with the issue. "Orchards have been killed ten miles off by it." Grain crops, vegetables like carrots and sugar beets, and forest trees too suffered, and at times farmers came in from their fields half-sickened by the stench. New York farmers knew by the late 1840s of British experiments and litigation involving manufacturing plant pollution and timber damage near Liverpool, and they followed overseas news with interest.[11] Determining cause and effect proved difficult, however, not only because aphids and other blights newly arrived in North America also caused much damage, but also because even the chemists addressing the Farmer's Club knew little of the reactions involved and could suggest no material that might be mixed with the coal or clay to eliminate the noxious gases. Amidst all their other difficulties, farmers near large cities, and especially those farming near deposits of clay and rivers deep enough to float bargeloads of bricks, learned that the brickyards every city dweller considered an exportable nuisance meant the impossibility of growing the fruit—and possibly the vegetables—that would sell so profitably in those cities.

Some farmers tried to adapt to changing circumstances. Many embarked on frantic weed-control programs, discovering that uprooting weeds along roadsides, fences, and walls not only mitigated weed infestations in fields but provided nutritious fodder for hogs and other livestock and destroyed the habitats of harmful insects.[12] Others began hauling city manure to their farms. "Street dirt and stable manure," sometimes free for the taking, provided valuable fertilizer, although some experts pointed out that rainfall leaches most nutrients from street manure before the farmer scavenges it. Offal from fish markets struck some reformers as a marvelous free fertilizer, and one 1842 *American Agriculturist* commentator learned that fishmongers would be glad for farmers to cart away the scraps, "if it could be done daily." Charcoal dealers offered to sell barrels of dust at nominal prices to any farmers willing to supply barrels, and "the broken brick, and lime rubbish, of buildings pulled down in New-York and Brooklyn," usually carted off to fill low-lying ground, also struck agricultural reformers as a perfect soil sweetener. One farmer outside Boston, having taken possession of an abandoned brickyard, discovered that the ground produced 2.5 tons of hay per acre each year; whatever the evils of brick-kiln air pollution, brick powder enriched worn-out soil.[13]

Destroying weeds and applying traditional and novel fertilizers helped, of course, but the most industrious farmers chose to focus their energies on spectacularly profitable crops grown on intensively worked acreage. Along with the shiftless, these serious farmers abandoned second-rate terrain: "Think very seriously on the advantages to be derived from the system of cultivating no more land than can be well manured," argued "An Old Farmer" in an 1840 letter to *The Farmer's Cabinet*. If ten intensively managed acres can yield the crop of a hundred worked in the old way, the farmer will have saved, if not nine-tenths of his effort and expense, at least half, leaving him time, energy, and funds to work another ten acres, and so double his income.[14] "Instead of planting five acres, plant two, or one even; and cultivate this small field to the neglect, if need be, of other acres."[15] So urged one 1855 issue of *The Plough, the Loom, and the Anvil.*—and so urged every eastern agricultural periodical in the years just before the Civil War. And here and there, farmers appeared to listen.

If Westchester seemed somewhat backward to agricultural experts, Long Is-land struck many mid-nineteenth-century observers as slightly forward in adjusting to the changed conditions of agriculture near large cities. Long Island farmers suffered from poor-quality soils, but they soon realized the advantages of importing stable and other manures from Brooklyn and New York, and when manure dealers in New York began adulterating manure with sawdust and tan-bark—"giving the whole a rich dark color by a liberal use of the leaves of the sumac" in the words of one New York State Agricultural Society member in 1843—they imported a purer variety from Albany.[16] Many Long Island farmers abandoned extensive agriculture in the 1820s, concentrating their efforts on reduced acreage. While as late as the 1840s some raised corn, oats, and wheat, most had shifted to growing hay for the immense New York market; indeed by 1843 hay had become the dominant crop.[17] Others concentrated on large-scale gardening; parts of the island specialized in cabbages raised from seedlings started in hothouses in early spring, then trans-planted into manured fields. One farmer explained to the editor of *American Agri-culturist* how he had averaged a twelve-hundred-dollar profit per acre for ten years by growing cabbages; one year he had netted twenty-six hundred. "We know of many a farmer occupying from 300 to 500 acres of land who does not on an average clear half this amount," the editor concludes soberly, "so that it is not the number of acres after all, so much as the crop and method of cultivation, which gives the largest profits."[18] Within a radius of thirty miles from the center of New York, the editor estimates, farmers must be growing several million head of cabbage, along with spinach, broccoli, lettuce, and cauliflower. Certainly the harvest of fruit and vegeta-bles staggered European observers; in 1830, one Englishman determined that "much of the land in the neighbourhood of Brooklyn appears to be devoted to the raising of fruits and vegetables for its own and the New York markets." Awed by the "prodigious quantities" ferried to New York, John Fowler "counted eleven waggons driven off one steam-boat at a time."[19] On Long Island especially, farmers by the late 1820s appeared to be prospering by concentrating their energies on less land and new crops.

Hidden in the glowing descriptions lie hints of serious difficulties, however, troubles not always apparent to mid-nineteenth-century observers. In the Brooklyn distillery district near Furman Street, for example, one observer discovered an indoor dairy. Formerly enclosing one thousand cows, in the autumn of 1843 the immense structures housed only half that number, although the reformer found that "just 500 too many." Cows feeding upon the slops of the distillery produced milk retailed in Brooklyn "under the false names of 'pure milk,' 'Orange county milk,' 'grass-fed milk,' 'Connecticut milk,'" and other bucolic designations. Even with the low rates offered by railroads and steamboat lines, such a "foul, loathesome place" challenged farmers by producing milk extremely inexpensively, and perhaps it ex-plains the relatively slight attention given traditional dairying further east on Long Island.[20] At the same moment, descriptions of model Long Island farms suggest how much prime agricultural land belonged to city residents astute enough to employ salaried managers. Over and over, agricultural periodicals extolling the wonders of innovative farms mention absentee owners willing to provide capital for large-scale improvements overseen by well-educated farm managers. Perhaps the periodical editors and columnists sensed the scale of the change in ownership; by the late 1840s many articles describe farms "cultivated" by industrious men, using a term less specific than words like *owned* or *managed*. But Fowler, the sharp-eyed English observer of orchards and steam-ferries, realized in 1830 that "Long Island is rather a situation for an opulent farmer than for one of limited means," because acreage "is much dearer than in other parts of the state" and because the necessity to manure increases cultivation costs.[21] "Retired, or half-retired merchants are therefore commonly to be found amongst the proprietors, a class of persons farming about as much for amusement as profit," and "whenever they feel a taste for business, or the city," quick to temporarily desert their farms.[22] Moreover, the periodicals suggest that many farmers, including the successful grower of cabbages, rented their acreage and concentrated on improving it only enough to make a profitable next crop. Even on Long Island, mostly free from the air pollution vexing Westchester County farmers, the landscape reflected agriculture in transition. Farming slid slowly into truck gardening, forest retook sloping land, barns and other structures from the bygone days of mixed farming fell into disrepair, and villages blossomed as the newcomers moved into the "country" around them.

"Casting the eye to the southward, over Centre Island, we see the pleasant village of Syosset (formerly Oyster Bay), with its white houses, peering out amidst green trees and verdant fields, contrasting beautifully with the high and densely wooded hills, which rise directly behind it," wrote one 1847 *American Agriculturist* columnist describing Long Island farming. "Turning the eye still more to the south we see Cold Spring Bay, a beautiful sheet of water, and catch a glimpse of a little village, bearing the same name, lying snugly ensconced among the green hills by which it is surrounded."[23] By the late 1840s, even agricultural reformers no longer worried about reforested hillsides; together with villages, they reflected the changed circumstances of borderland life about which Willis and others could only wonder. "No better field can be found for the display of a refined and cultivated taste than is opened to us here," mused a *Horticultural Review* columnist in 1854, "for it is the surroundings of home that clothe it in a comely garb, and commend it to our admiration." Samuel Gookins knew the slovenly farmstead, knew clearly the garden of "Rag-weed and Crab-grass," the approach through "a rank smell, compounded of various odors, in which worm-seed, and stale bacon rinds predominate," and he knew only that the newcomers could correct it. His "Culture of Rural Taste" argues that the newcomers, and particularly the new woman concerned about the moral condition of her family and her nation, the new woman alone most of the day, married to the new husband "entertaining pretty liberal views on the subject of women's rights" and wholly willing to buy nursery stock and arrange grounds, could eradicate the farmers' slovenliness purely by example. "Here, then, is a field for the exercise of women's rights, the possession of which no one will contest and the power of which no one can deny."[24] With effort, the borderers could clean up the countryside and restore the moral order of the Republic.

As late as the 1870s and 1880s, agricultural reformers kept alive the relation of slovenly farms and moral decay. Here is the habitat of a good-for-nothing farmer, one so cruel as to whip scrawny, overloaded horses.

In the hands of a "thrifty" family, however, the run-down farm can be made orderly, beautiful, and profitable, a proper home for moral people.

Joking, patronizing, slightly sneering, urban Americans turned on village life in the waning years of the eighteenth century. In the pages of urban periodicals and Christmas gift books published after 1790, farming remained noble, if ever more vaguely described, and pioneering became more arduous, and ever further away. Authors depicted polite city society as ever more sophisticated and introduced the romantic love of wilderness to urban readers. Subtly at first, then explicitly, urban writers sliced village life from respectable existence. Villages sheltered old-fashioned ways and irritating modern problems. They offered nothing to guide the nation into the new century. Villages represented smallness—smallness of thinking, of imagination, of social life, of everything.

At first glance, the shift in attitude appears almost evanescent. The expression *village life* certainly designates the ostensible subject of resoundingly affirmative works of the period. Perhaps the best known in its day, Timothy Dwight's book-length poem entitled *Greenfield Hill* appeared in 1794; a nationalistic demonstration of post-Independence life, the poem juxtaposes, against the poverty-stricken English community described by Oliver Goldsmith in "The Deserted Village" (1770), a prosperous, attractive, near Edenic place:

> *Sweet smiling village! loveliest of the hills!*
> *How green thy groves! How pure thy glassy rills!*
> *With what new joy, I walk thy verdant streets!*
> *How often pause, to breathe thy gale of sweets;*
> *To mark thy well-built walls! thy budding fields!*[1]

An exclamatory style befits Dwight's glorification of the "flourishing village" and masks the essential character of the place. Greenfield Hill is an entire rural landscape, something like the "fair field full of folk" described by William Langland in *Piers Plowman* in 1550.[2] Its inhabitants farm, and only a few live in closely clustered houses. *Greenfield Hill* is a hymn of praise indeed, not to a specific village or to village life, but to traditional rural New England space and calling.[3]

Many authors used *village* as Dwight did, to signify some collection of rural smallholdings. In 1772, for example, Philip Freneau published his "American Village," a long, incredibly detailed paean to the virtuous rural landscape where "each year tall harvests crown the happy field."[4] About an actual group of structures, however, Freneau is silent, clearly favoring the fields and forests over the inn, blacksmith shop, meetinghouse, and other buildings implicit in his title. Within fifty years *village* clearly designated a group of closely ranged structures, not fields, but many American writers no longer unthinkingly accepted the innate perfection of the place. An anonymous biographer of the poet William Martin Johnson, writing at length in an 1838 issue of *United States Magazine and Democratic Review* about his subject's boyhood in the Long Island town of East Hampton, unconsciously splits the meaning of the term. On the one hand, East Hampton "is a beautiful oasis, so surrounded by sands and barrenness, that the inhabitants are confined to farms barely sufficient" to sustain them; on the other it is the place "built on the two sides of a very wide grass-grown street; the most of its houses low, with one end to the street, and the roof of that old-fashioned and unintellectual form, which may be compared to a face without a forehead, shooting abruptly backward from the eyebrows, to the high phrenological bump of veneration, on the apex of the skull." East Hampton is beyond doubt a good place for a boy to grow up; its people cherish rural virtues like frugality, hospitality, and family unity. As a place for a budding artist, however, it is something of a joke: time-bound, "quaint," deeply distrustful of innovation. "Some alarming cases of genius had actually broken out among" the residents, the author remarks in discussing a man who invented a combined flour mill and threshing machine and another who crafted an orrery, only to endure the laughter of neighbors. On most days the main street—the only street—hosts only gaggles of geese. The township (*town* in New England usage) exemplifies rural industry and agricultural beauty; the village is a collection of outdated religious services and political discussions, small-minded people, and houses best understood through the prism of the new—and urban—science of phrenology.[5]

Between 1794 and 1838, a number of urban writers felt village bumps, snickered, and pronounced village life impossibly dull. In 1832, for example, another anonymous writer, this time in *New England Magazine,* recalled the village boredom he abandoned for urban living. "There is in a village no common place of meeting, but at the public fire-side of the inn," he remarks in "Some Recollections of a Village." "The high discourse held there includes all that is difficult in morals, religion, law and government. Much talking creates thirst, and thirst at an inn perpetuates itself." But the author's whole article mocks the notion of high discourse; it satirizes the "small statesmen" thriving on gossip, the aristocracy of doctor, lawyer, and "merchant" secure in its pretty pretensions, and the schoolmaster smug with birch cane and grammar book.[6] "Recollections of a Village" unwittingly defines the semantic issue implicit in *Greenfield Hill* and other turn-of-the-century works. Just as *village* once designated in English law a community too poor to support a church building, so by the 1820s it designated a community undeserving of the title *town.* A village *might* possess a schoolhouse and even a church building, but it lacked the stores and other businesses that facilitated buying and selling—and the social interaction accompanying the transfer of money, goods, and services. Villagers lived in limbo, neither farming nor engaging in townlike enterprise. Many eked out livings from blacksmithing and other semi-rural handicrafts; the elderly lived modestly on incomes from wise investments or the sale of slovenly farms. And by the 1800s, many worked machines.

Mechanics, the inventors, builders, operators, and repairers of machines, grew in number everywhere in the eastern states after Independence, and especially during the embargo years of the 1800s, when merchants unable to trade with Europe invested their money in clothing mills, iron furnaces, and other workshops or "manufactories" located near the waterfalls that powered novel machinery. Everywhere in the eastern states north of slavery and the plantation system, small manufactories blossomed near falling water, and the fledgling industries sparked others less dependent on hydropower. Throughout New England, New York, New Jersey, and Pennsylvania, farmers shifted away from full-time agriculture, at first making shoes or nails or clocks during the slow winter months, then abandoning farming altogether for work in a "shop" or small mill. In an 1851 discourse entitled "The Age of Homespun," the nationally known clergyman Horace Bushnell remarked the migration from eastern hill farms to "the close villages and populous towns, that crowd the waterfalls and the rail roads."[7] The migrants moved as dramatically as families pioneering west of the Appalachians, but they moved only a short distance, sometimes to a thriving town but more often to a village, buying, renting, or building a small house on a small lot and looking forward, however imprecisely, to industrial life.

Nowhere is this transformation of the American landscape more clearly noticeable than in the gazetteers published after 1800. *A Gazetteer of the State of New-York*, published by Horatio Gates Spafford in 1824, for example, details the transformation of the agricultural township of Florida. Some 569 farmers and their families worked 20,436 acres of improved land, managing some ten thousand head of livestock. "In the centre of this town is a handsome hamlet, or small village, called *Yankee Street*, where is kept the Florida Post-Office, 4 miles S. of the Erie Canal," Spafford notes. Clearly Yankee Street is prosperous. Home to 108 people working five grist mills, five saw mills, two fulling mills, two carding machines, and one ashery, the township focuses on its manufacturing village and the stimulation of canal traffic and markets. Cloth-making appears to have shaped the life of Yankee Street and of the farm families; in 1821 the whole population produced 24,168 "yards of cloth made in families."[8] But Spafford implies that Yankee Street is not mature; not only does it remain politically indistinct from the larger township, it and the farm population can support only eight "traders." Beyond doubt, Yankee Street is a handsome *hamlet*, but only a small *village*. In the eyes of men like Spafford, it deserved attention only for what it might become.

Twelve years later, Thomas F. Gordon published his gazetteer of New York, and his meticulous attention to detail reveals that the transformation Spafford noted not only continued, but intensified. Gordon favored spartan entries, but he frequently cited the number of houses in a village; his *Gazetteer* suggests something of the meanness of the many mechanics' villages throughout the state. Hatsville, for example, "has a small woollen factory, 1 tavern, 2 stores, and 16 dwellings," and "Nyack, on the river, 28 miles from New York, is a thriving village, containing 3 taverns, 3 stores, 1 Presbyterian, 1 Methodist, churches, and about 50 dwellings." Gordon distinguished between simple villages and "thriving" or "flourishing" ones, deciding that a church building indicated flourishing circumstances, but he understood that *village* designated something definitely more sophisticated than a harbor hamlet and much less grand than a town. "Easthampton, village, extends along the road about 1½ miles," Gordon noted two years before the *United States Magazine* writer snickered at its unintellectual houses, "having about 100 plain dwellings, a Presbyterian church, the Clinton academy, 2 school houses, etc."9 The residents of the township of Easthampton, "agriculturists and mechanics," appear to have been unable to support a store or a tavern.

Gazetteers display the extraordinary transformation of the borderlands in the antebellum decades, a change almost as magical as any wrought by Susan Cooper's magic witch hazel. Villages produced hoes, twine, chemicals, India rubber, carpets, rifle cartridges, flint glass, varnish, needles, lime, and files—and innumerable other items—almost always in small wooden buildings that gazetteer-compilers called *manufactories* or *shops,* sometimes inside houses, in back rooms or lean-to sheds. Only rarely, however, do gazetteers describe the appearance of villages or of any other part of the rural landscape; for descriptions of slovenly farms or neat villages, only "historical collections" suffice.

John Warner Barber specialized in compiling historical collections, each a thick, illustrated volume containing not only "history and antiquities" of every town and village in a state but also "geographical descriptions." Barber understood the economic and cultural significance of early nineteenth-century villages, and he distinguished among several types. In Connecticut, he discovered Colinsville, established in 1826 as a "company village" within the town of Canton. The houses of the workmen, he observes, "which are built precisely of the same form, are compactly set together on the side of a hill" and "are painted white, and when contrasted with the deep green foliage in the immediate vicinity, present a novel and beautiful appearance."10 The five hundred inhabitants of Colinsville, who make axes, reside in a new sort of community space—the village of identical houses. In Clinton, New Jersey, Barber found another sort of village, the fast-growing type focused on several unrelated industries. From 1820 to 1838, when the Federal government established a post office there, Clinton existed as a hamlet of three houses and a mill; by 1844 it contained "3 mercantile stores, 2 large merchant-mills, with one of which an oil-mill is connected; 3 public houses, about 15 mechanic shops of various kinds, a brick-yard, a valuable limestone quarry, 3 churches, 62 dwellings, and 520 inhabitants," along with two schools.11 Conway, Massachusetts, exemplifies the third type—the stagnating village. While Conway township struck Barber as reasonably prosperous, it boasted a village consisting only of "about thirty dwelling-houses and other buildings." Two of the other buildings were churches, but since Barber took

The Connecticut village of Colinsville intrigued
Barber, who rather admired the regularity and
efficiency single ownership brought to the landscape
and to work.

Conway, a typical hill village, straggled down a long
and quiet road barely deserving to be called a street.

A "factory village" within the larger town of Medway, Massachusetts, slightly perplexed Barber, who glimpsed the social and economic importance of such communities of mechanics and manufactories.

"Village of Four Corners," Barber called the nearly treeless place he described in Historical Collections of Massachusetts.

pains to note that the Baptist edifice lacked a spire, it seems likely that the peripatet-ic historian-geographer found the straggling village less than impressive.[12] Barber's hundreds upon hundreds of descriptions and engravings confirm what gazetteers and maps suggest; by the 1840s, a thick sprinkling of villages lay everywhere in the borderlands of Pennsylvania and other northeastern states.

A typical village straddled a main road or huddled about a crossroads, usually extending little more than a half mile.[13] Comprised of small houses set closely together on narrow but deep lots, the village provided affordable housing for ar-tisans and mechanics working long hours at low pay. Living near the workplace shortened the twice-daily journey to and from shop or manufactory and provided neighbors for wives freed of farm chores and suddenly blessed with time for visiting, unless they too were employed in the shop or mill. Clustered houses conserved fuel, too, for the mass of structure broke winter winds while providing other advantages, like shared wells and stables. Land prices encouraged compact villages, simply because farmers reluctant to sell profitable arable acreage caused village landowners to subdivide their lots, snuggling more houses into the place and encouraging some to build two-family "double houses." As Barber so crisply relates in prose and engravings, early nineteenth-century travelers entered villages abruptly, leaving behind farmland and stepping into a different sort of space. Just as abruptly, they left village compactness, moving into fields or woodlots that stretched on past farm-houses and hamlets, leading, eventually, to another village.

Despite some advantages, villages presented real difficulties to their inhabi-tants. Their smallness meant the frequent lack of a church building or general store; almost always it spelled a lack of hardware, dry goods, and other specialty stores. In most instances, villagers numbered too few for incorporation as a self-governing municipality; beyond its name and perhaps its post office, the village lacked legal identity. Of all disadvantages, however, the lack of effective fire protection proved most worrisome, especially on frigid, windy winter nights.

Wildfire terrified farmers and city residents alike; the farmer lived far from help—including the horse- or hand-drawn, hand-powered pumping engines capable of squirting thin jets of water into second-story windows and barn-loft doors—and the urbanite inhabited a house or flat jammed against others equally flammable. Nevertheless, both farmer and city dweller enjoyed some safeguards. The farmer could employ a hundred prudent practices, many reiterated regularly in the agri-cultural press. "A cat should not be left in the house at night," counseled an 1824 *New England Farmer* piece. "They have often, by getting in the ashes, and having coals stick to them, communicated fire to the house." Much of the advice contra-dicts urban guidelines: "Never give an alarm of fire, unless you be pretty sure you cannot put it out without further assistance; for a small fire may be easier ex-tinguished by one, than by twenty men."[14] By carefully repairing and sweeping chimneys and keeping a ladder propped against the roof beneath the chimney top, by installing lightning rods atop barns, by digging "fire wells" next to both barn and house, by putting out the cat at night, wise farmers greatly reduced the likelihood of fire; secure in their isolated locations and equipped with simple fire-fighting equipment, farmers slept almost soundly. Far off, in cities like New York, Philadelphia, and Cincinnati, where wildfire exploded easily into conflagration, residents aware that not everyone practiced good habits around stoves, fireplaces, candles, and whale-oil lamps voted funds for fire-fighting equipment—especially pumping engines they optimistically named Extinguisher or Niagara—invested in fire insurance, policed the manufacture of hazardous products, and thought about building in brick. "Experience has proved that a wooden city is a vast tinder-box, kindling at every transient spark; an immense mass of phial'd phosphorous, blazing out by mere communication with the air," argued John Quincy Adams in an 1802 address to the Massachuetts Charitable Fire Society. As late as the 1760s, clergymen told parishioners that a wrathful Providence sent wildfire; by the early years of the nineteenth century, Adams and other reformers blamed human causes. "But clapboards and shingles! What mysterious fascinations can they possess?" Street trees, thought by many to spread urban fire, especially in autumn, worried fledgling insurance companies so much that several forbade policy owners from planting ornamental trees near "assured" property.[15] Villagers, however, knew neither the security of isolation nor that of fire apparatus, and only rarely did they have funds enough for brick construction. Wildfire continually threatened their closely built, sometimes multiple-family houses and workshops, and their small numbers precluded the purchase of hand- or horse-drawn fire equipment acquired by cities and towns.

In December 1825, a *New England Farmer* column warned villagers about their danger. "Causes of Fire" addressed the dangers threatening isolated farmsteads but introduced novel issues too, such as "smoking cigars in the street and about the stables of publick houses" and "workmen leaving fires in merchant's shops." Implicit in the editorial is the awareness that villagers do endanger themselves; the mechanic returning home on a dark December evening *might* carry an exposed candle or lamp into his barn or stable simply because even village-scale agriculture demands daily attention, even after dark. The editor ominously concludes, "There is not less danger from fire in country villages than in large towns; frequently the former are more combustible than the latter."[16] Many villages, with their convivial taverns, bustling little manufacturing shops and mills, and closely built frame houses, connoted *fire-trap* to citizens increasingly aware of urban conflagration caused, for example, by carelessly discarded cigars.

But more than fire hazard caused the condescension that characterizes early nineteenth-century city writing about villages. Over and over again, travelers wondered at the ugliness of villages, an ugliness sometimes the result of cheaply built houses but more often of siting and maintenance. The Connecticut village of Litchfield disturbed one observer, who found "fragments of old fences, boards, woodpiles, heaps of chips, old sleds bottom upward, carts, casks, weeds, and loose stones lying along in wild confusion," the whole mess fitfully grazed by wandering sheep and hogs.[17] What explains such conditions? An *American Agriculturist* writer concluded somberly in 1857 that villagers shared the ignorance and slothfulness that contributed to slovenly farming. The anonymous letter to the editor asks, "how many of our villagers neglect the little plots where a bed of salad or radishes might be cultivated," losing the "double satisfaction" of eating fresh food and acquiring gentle exercise? Its author offers an example of a "village 'tenement' in a block of buildings that had attached a back yard" filled with "old shoes, stovepipes, etc., until it was not far removed from a nuisance." After burying the rubbish from the shops of a tailor, shoemaker, and butcher, the letter writer prepared the soil and raised—to the surprise of his neighbors—a fine vegetable crop.[18] But the gardening writer suggests something of the difficulty involved in beautifying the typical village, and the most casual reading of nineteenth-century "improvement" literature confirms his or her implications.

In 1849 and 1850, Andrew Jackson Downing lambasted the condition of villages, and while he admitted the beauty of some long-settled New England ones, he found on the whole a national ugliness. His *Horticulturist* essays endeavored to turn "neglected, bare, and lanky streets into avenues of fine foliage, and streets of neat and tasteful houses," chiefly by recommending the planting of shade trees along village streets. "A village whose streets are bare of trees, ought to be looked upon as in a condition not less pitiable than a community without a schoolmaster, or a teacher of religion," he asserted in some of the strongest language he ever used, "for certain it is, when the affections are so dull, and the domestic virtues so blunt that men do not care how their own homes and villages look, they care very little for fulfilling any moral obligations not made compulsory by the strong arm of the law." How many villagers read *The Horticulturist*'s advice? Probably not many, for Downing simultaneously insults the typical villager and explicitly suggests that "apostles of good taste" resident in the borderlands will have to plant trees for the villagers to enjoy, or else pay a bounty to any villager willing to plant one himself.[19] Only by imitation, not by recommendation, will American villagers plant street trees, build appropriate, simple, genuinely beautiful houses, and otherwise improve their compact communities. Middle- and upper-class readers, not village mechanics, comprised most of Downing's audience, and it is not surprising that Downing felt free to criticize the underlying causes of village ugliness.

Irish immigrants struck Downing as one cause of village ugliness; he saw them as chief impediments to street-tree planning. Pigs and other livestock wandering village streets angered Downing, who knew that the rapacious creatures soiled the ground and devoured vegetation, including newly planted saplings. "We believe we must lay this latter sin at the doors of our hard-working emigrants from the Emerald Isle," remarked Downing in a footnote on the ranging of swine. "Wherever they settle, they cling to their ancient fraternity of porkers, and think it 'no free country where pigs can't have their liberty.'"[20] Newly arrived immigrants, especially Irish fleeing the potato famines, landed in the Republic too poor to acquire farms, even in the frontier country; many became village mechanics and stretched their wages by keeping livestock, particularly pigs and geese whose foraging ability decreased feed costs. Too poor to own quality village housing, they frequently either rented or lived in shacks such as those Thoreau found in Concord. Working long hours in small manufactories, managing vegetable gardens and a few animals before and after work, all the while hoping to escape rented housing and move on to a western farm or more profitable employment, these immigrants were not interested in planting trees and making other improvements that—as Downing admitted—show results only after years, and sometimes decades. Downing's anti-Irish comments, brief as they are, give force to his remarks about the baseness of character that undoubtedly stands reflected in the lanky "graceless village." Indeed, his constant use of the phrase suggests that he somehow associated village ugliness with the sinfulness so much discussed by clergymen caught up in a national religious revival woven not only out of spiritual concerns but from a fervent nationalism and dread of civil war. An ugly borderland village—especially if churchless—announced all kinds of disconcerting issues ranging from sloth to fire hazard to un-American immigrants to godlessness.

Of course, not every village struck sensitive observers as ugly. Timothy Dwight, in fact, smiled upon any village, no matter how small, blessed with a church building, and he beamed upon any ornamented with two; three decades later, Thomas Gordon continued the standard in his New York gazetteer. Andrew Jackson Downing delighted in describing many "flourishing" Massachusetts villages "with broad streets lined with maples and elms, behind which are goodly rows of neat and substantial dwellings, full of evidences of order, comfort, and taste." But while he understood the advantages of Massachusetts outlawing roaming livestock, Downing missed the significance of Massachusetts town order. Many of the villages that pleased him were township "centers," the legal hubs of prosperous agricultural communities settled nearly two centuries earlier, long possessed of tax-supported church buildings and growing only slowly—if at all—in population or manufacturing. Most villages deemed attractive by travelers in New England—and elsewhere too, it seems—were large, almost towns, long settled, and graced with church buildings. South Norwalk in Connecticut offers a useful example.

Barber found South Norwalk "flourishing" and enumerated its "upwards of 100 houses, 26 mercantile stores, 2 churches" and other advantages, including a bank, two newspapers, and an "extensive pottery." The harbor village bustled with transshipping activity; farm produce from an extensive area flowed into the community for shipment to New York City.[21] In South Norwalk, according to an 1857 *American Agriculturist* article entitled "Half an Acre," Mr. H. Smith, "a hardworking mechanic, who labors ten hours a day in his shop," created a handsome home lot, from which he realized "a great amount of real enjoyment, as well as profit." Illustrated with an amazingly complicated plan of the lot showing the wealth of fruits, vegetables, and ornamental plants on the 19,680 square feet—less than half an acre, the editor admits—the article shows what can be done with a "village plot" roughly three times as deep as wide.[22] Undoubtedly, Mr. H. Smith had created over some years a remarkably productive and somewhat ornamental place—he took pains to include a small lawn decorated with Norway spruce and balsam firs—but certainly he intended to live long on the site. He had planted some fruit trees with the intention of thinning them in years to come and had even planted an asparagus bed, one of the slowest of vegetable-growing endeavors. "Half an Acre" demonstrates the very forces keeping small villages small, and often ugly.

In Connecticut Historical Collections, Barber assured readers of the prosperity of many towns, especially seaport ones. His "Southern View of the Borough of Norwalk" illustrates the commercial and manufacturing liveliness of the place.

On half an acre, according to an American Agriculturist article, one Connecticut mechanic created a superb village houselot, demonstrating the adaptability of traditional gardening practice to a new sort of settlement arrangement.

Large villages and small towns offered permanent employment and the prospect of sustained economic growth, the advantages that encouraged mechanics to improve their grounds and houses and savor the "double pleasure" of fresh food and gentle exercise.

Villages near very large towns, and adjacent to cities like Boston and New York, changed form in the early nineteenth century just as farms did. Road traffic caused the transformation. As Dwight, Barber, Downing, and so many other early nineteenth-century observers knew, most villages stretched along a short section of road; indeed, having only a single street, not three or four intersecting and parallel ones, appears to have helped observers distinguish villages from small towns. Wagon, stage-coach, and horseback travel increased in the vicinity of cities as roads converged, and the condition of such well-traveled roads struck many travelers as infinitely better than that of back-country rural highways. A few miles outside Boston, for example, Dwight found most of the highways good, "and some of them excellent." Several of the roads, he determined, "are lined throughout their whole extent with almost a continued village, formed of houses, neat, well built, and strongly indicative of prosperity."[23] In the very last years of the eighteenth century, Dwight rode through a novel sort of space: "from Weymouth," he remarked of the landscape as he rode toward Boston, "the country may with little extravagance be considered as one continued village, raised up by the commerce of Boston, and forming a kind of suburb to that capital."[24] Dwight had discovered the first of the ribbon villages, stretching along very well traveled roads and inhabited by families dependent on occupations other than farming.

Most men in the ribbon villages worked close to home; only a few commuted from the borderlands to city workplaces. Indeed, most appear to have worked in the multitude of small manufactories springing up everywhere in the regions around major coastal cities. Often the mills and shops stood near waterfalls that marked the limit of estuary navigation; the inlets provided convenient transportation for raw materials and manufactured goods. Further inland, material moved by wagon over the roads Dwight found so congenial; within a half-day's journey of major cities— the zone in which a teamster could deliver a load and return home before bedtime— tiny manufacturing enterprises enjoyed many advantages. Land prices, far cheaper than in city locations, encouraged small entrepreneurs, as did a plentiful part-time workforce comprised of farmers idle in winter months. As metropolitan farmers shifted away from traditional mixed agriculture, often abandoning livestock raising completely, many discovered months of wintertime idleness, during which they became clockmakers, shoemakers, and seasonal employees of small manufacturing concerns. As mixed agriculture declined in profitability, as thousands of young men migrated to the West or to cities, the ribbon villages, especially around New York and Boston, increased in density, and—for the traveler—in importance. After all, they frequently defined the view of the traveler and shaped his estimation of the entire region.[25]

Dwight and many other sojourners focused on the ribbon villages out of necessity; as they neared cities the main roads indeed resembled lengthy village streets.

Jamaica, an increasingly important town on Long Island, struck Barber as the sort of place that might amount to something someday.

In 1856 the editors of Illustrated Annual Register of Rural Affairs *told readers that the stable sheltering a single horse and buggy "is all the accommodation that many village and suburban residents need," implying long before the garage era a vague understanding that village and suburban transportation needs might be similar.*

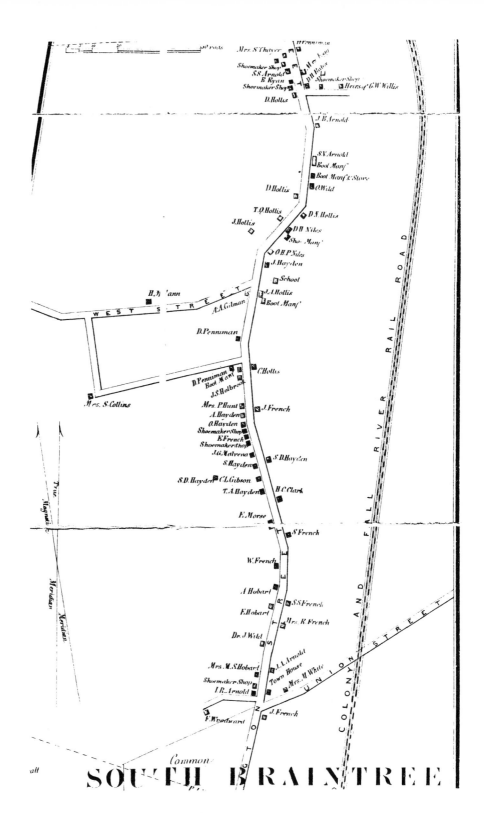

Often the village houses and small industries presented a picture of prosperity that masked the failing traditional farms lying farther back from the roadside. Only rarely did commentators notice another equally important borderland landscape feature, one lying off or back from the main roads. "Villas, pleasantly situated, commanding handsome views, exhibiting more lightness and elegance of architecture, and ornamented with more suitable appendages than I have elsewhere seen, adorn at little distances a considerable part of this region," remarked Dwight of the countryside away from the ribbon villages outside Boston. But Dwight found similar beauty on the coast just east of New York City, too, commenting in 1804 that "the villas rise in perpetual succession on the shores and eminences, embellishing the landscape and exhibiting decisive proofs of opulence in their proprietors."[26] Clearly, while the houses in the ribbon villages, and in the abbreviated villages also near cities, sheltered the new mechanic class along with retired farmers, clergymen, storekeepers, and a host of other Americans defying classification as a group, the villas beyond, and often uphill from the villages housed a different sort of inhabitant altogether—the country gentry secure in "seats," "situations," or "residences." Away from slovenly farms and pretty villages lived—if not always year-round—a new sort of American anxious to avoid the opprobrium urban intellectuals heaped upon backward farmers and narrow-minded villagers alike.

"One does not need to be much of a philosopher to remark that one of the most striking of our national traits, is the *spirit of unrest*," mused Downing in an 1847 *Horticulturist* editorial. By and large, he admitted, the spirit worked only good; it propelled families into virgin forest, "across vast sandy deserts to California," over mountains, even into the empire of Mexico. On the other hand, he noted, Americans seemed "fonder of no one Anglo-Saxon word than the term *settle*," using it constantly in phrases referring to making a new home in the frontier, paying off debts, laying to rest every sort of matter. However powerful the spirit of unrest, Downing determined, the spirit of settling down appeared stronger by the day: "in all the older portions of the country," he discovered "growing evidence that the Anglo-Saxon love of home is gradually developing itself out of the Anglo-American love of change." In the East, especially around Philadelphia and Boston, and to a lesser extent around New York, he found ever more families engaged in ornamental horticulture, the sort of gentleman farming that inspired love of locality. Horticulture, he announced triumphantly, "transforms what is only a tame meadow and a bleak aspect, into an Eden of interest and delights." It buries any vestige of the spirit of unrest.[1] But Downing misinterpreted the causal relationship. Only after the spirit of unrest loosened its grasp on some eastern families did horticulture further cement the marriage of interests to topography. Not in farms, not in villages, but in a new sort of space, the *country seat*, did a new sort of American flaunt a dislike of change and unrest.

Nothing restful characterized the decades immediately following the Peace of Paris. Independence brought social and economic disruption; high taxes, currency shortages, credit difficulties, and above all the blatant weakness of state and national government tormented farmers, shopkeepers, craftsmen, merchants, and housewives. After the revolution, the new upper-class elite—the "aristocracy of wealth and talent," in Jefferson's phrase—found itself governing a restive public well aware of revolutionary change. Federalists especially worried about the perils of too much democracy—even the adoption of the new Federal Constitution emphasizing an elaborate system of checks and balances intended to stymie power-hungry demagogues and factions did little to allay their fears. Economic instability further weakened the grasp of the new governing elite; financial disasters caused by the Embargo Acts, by ill-advised land speculation in the western territories, and by early manufacturing failures shook many wealthy families and unnerved voters expecting competent business sense in its elected officials.[2] Moreover, the new elite discovered the longevity of an old English and colonial ideology, a way of thinking that soon threatened the very fabric of post-revolutionary society.

No one name adequately designates the ideology, let alone connotes its complexity. Old Whig, Commonwealth, or Country identifies a political philosophy born in the reign of Charles II and focused on opposition to a standing professional army, systematic public credit, national debt, and royal patronage. Essentially, the Country ideology opposed the creation of a new group of powerful political functionaries owing its existence to an ever bigger government. Its adherents further decried the weakened Parliament and judiciary that would result from a crown's unwisely expanding the national debt while creating vast ranks of individuals loyal only to ever bigger government. Against the bloated, unbalanced government it called Court, the Country ideology juxtaposed the true guardians of virtue—the landed gentry supported by agriculture and honored in "georgic" poetry and, to a lesser extent, the independent merchant.[3] The gentry and the merchant, so proponents argued, honor virtue, and particularly moderation and stability, because they must; their daily affairs require diligence, forbearance, and self-discipline. In honoring virtue they defend the traditional rural lifestyle and the sanctity of private property, the true creators of national greatness, against a selfish, rapacious, often erroneous Court enslaved by fashion and addicted to levies.

In the two decades before the gunfire at Lexington and Concord, the American adherents of the Country ideology adapted it to colonial issues; in the war years, the ideology prospered, becoming the force behind political theory; and in the postwar decades, it shaped the Federal Constitution. The prohibition of a standing army, the restrictions on multiple office-holding, and especially the separation of powers among the three branches of government derive from Country thinking. But after the loyalists sailed off to Nova Scotia or Jamaica or England, the Federalists discovered the deeply rooted power of Country ideology shifting against themselves. Now it was the Federalists who held office and braved charges of patronage, government indebtedness, overripe complexity, and instability.[4] Indeed the very fact that many Federalists purchased houses and farms seized from Loyalists furthered the popular equation of the new elite with the hated old. Not surprisingly, the new elite struggled to defuse the opposition. It worked hard to limit the immediate political power of the voters—by enforcing poll tax laws and empowering state legislatures to elect United States Senators, for example. And to better demonstrate its love of virtuous simplicity and stability, it favored a new architecture.

Federal domestic architecture objectified the virtuous simplicity genuinely cherished by the governing elite. The solid, forthright facade exemplified balance and order; the symmetrical arrangement of windows around a central front door, the paired chimneys, and the emphasis on rectilinear forms announced a distinct if not total departure from the late-colonial Georgian style. Change in details, particularly the shift from fan-shaped windows to rectangular ones, derived from more than faddishness. Post-revolutionary building by the new elite evolved from a deep-seated concern with political stability in a turbulent era. In the Federalist mind, the big new house ornamenting a growing seaport city or inland market town must not insult the sensibility of farmers and mechanics. Instead it must reinforce the popular understanding of shared beliefs linking the farmer or workingman with the well-to-do merchant or lawyer. By the first years of the nineteenth century, however, the new architecture proved insufficient, and the elite adopted a new, even purer style reflecting the virtues of classical antiquity. Classical Revival houses, dignified by pilasters or pillars, displaying chaste gables to rural roads and town streets, announced their owners' continuing allegiance to a virtuous simplicity alien to Old World courts and cities.[5] But as growing numbers of Democratic Republicans railed against the supposed artificiality, ostentation, and self-interest of Federalist leadership, the governing elite sought a new image—and personal refuge—in country living.

In acquiring country residences, the wealthy governing elite advertised its adherence to "rural" qualities, to moderation, simplicity, and stability, to the "virtue" increasingly designated *republican* or *republican simplicity* by growing numbers of writers and voters.[6] The Federalists' move to the country—if only for the summer months, at least in the beginning—and fervent devotion to agricultural improvement deflected much criticism, for it confused the embryonic forces remaking the old Country ideology into something new.

Almost imperceptibly, anti-Federalists substituted *city* for *court* and attacked the urban governing elite as the colonial elite had once attacked the court of King George III. "To the strong influence that cities,—where wealth accumulates, where luxury gradually unfolds its corrupting tendencies, where aristocratic habits and social classifications form and strengthen themselves, where the congregation of men stimulates and exaggerates all ideas—to the influence that cities exert upon the country, no inconsiderable effect is to be ascribed," argued the editor of *The United States Magazine and Democratic Review* in 1837, in an essay that might have heartened Ely Bates. He blasts the "influence of the mercantile classes, too, (extensively anti-democratic) on the young men of the professions" and the susceptibility of the clergy to urban, anti-democratic notions.[7] By 1837 such arguments had triumphed despite the Federalist effort to demonstrate a loyalty to republican virtue, and in a maelstrom of political unrest, Federalists and a handful of well-to-do Democratic Republicans turned away from politics, inward to the family, and often outward to the borderlands.

In the Federalist mind, only an elaborate system of political checks and balances produces genuine human progress; wise restraints channel the self-interest and passionate factionalism of "the people" into fruitful paths. As Democratic Republicans gained political power, Federalists shifted ground, attempting to demonstrate the intimate relation of correct politics and sound religion. Federalist

By the late 1850s, periodicals aimed at prosperous farmers and at gentlemen farmers regularly emphasized the ornamented farmstead laid out as much for efficiency as for beauty.

This 1858 Rural Affairs illustration depicts the ideal borderland home as a house in a nook of trees, protected from storm and public view, and offering lesser nooks perfect for sitting and enjoying views.

clergymen struggled to prove the divinely ordained nature of a hierarchical, deferential society, and between 1815 and 1830, as Federalist power slipped, organized more than a dozen moral reform societies intended to save the nation from egalitarian democrats owing no allegiance to established religious denominations— or to any religion at all.[8] But the conservative clergy—the very divines the editor of *The United States Magazine and Democratic Review* suspected of serving the elite— discovered the burgeoning force of the theological change. In the first quarter of the nineteenth century, east coast Americans wholeheartedly rejected the old Puritan doctrine of determinism and substituted for it the theology of perfectionism. Once free of the doctrine that God had determined that some or most people would live sinfully and eventually arrive in Hell, Americans suddenly understood evil as voluntary sin that industrious effort might correct.[9] The very moral reform societies organized by conservative Protestant clergymen thus led their members directly into the anti-establishment way of thinking, deflecting them from traditional Congregational and Presbyterian theology—and Federalist orthodoxy—into Unitarianism and other new creeds. Instead of reinforcing the need for checks and balances, they strengthened a perfectionist spirit that built upon the "more perfect Union" thinking of the Federalist Constitution and in time produced Downing's insistence that tree-planting would help perfect village life and village character.[10]

Out of perfectionism evolved such massive reform efforts as the abolitionist movement and such relatively minor ones as the improvement societies struggling to reform slovenly farmers and narrow-minded villagers. Out of it too evolved a new appreciation of the natural world, and particularly of natural scenery. Perfectionist reformers argued that the curative powers of nature could restore individual spirit and in time improve the Republic. Coupled with the powerful intellectual impact of English romanticism, the perfectionist impulse reoriented the thinking of most well-informed borderland residents, whatever their political affiliation. By the 1840s, an intelligent appreciation of wilderness scenery marked a genuinely educated man or woman, exactly as Susan Cooper explained in *Rural Hours*.[11] But perfectionism never wholly replaced the old Country ideology, and the Federalists who moved to the borderlands four or five miles from seaport cities, the Federalists who favored Federal, then Classical Revival architecture, understood the lingering anti-urban echoes in the new language of perfectionism. Democratic Republicans understood them even better.

Family perfectionism preoccupied educated Americans in the first years of the nineteenth century, and many reformers argued strongly that children ought not be raised in cities. Henry David Thoreau, for example, worried about the long-term effects of urban childhood and, in the tradition of Bates and Trotter, scrutinized city children. "What right have parents to beget, to bring up, and attempt to *educate* children in a city?" he asked in 1851 after finding some "ill-dressed and ill-mannered" twelve-year-olds smoking cigars. "A true culture is more possible to the savage than to the boy of average intellect, born of average parents, in a great city." His journal entry illuminates the decades-old impact of perfectionist thinking. "How can they be kept clean, physically or morally? It is folly to attempt to educate children within a city; the first step must be to remove them out of it."[12] Only individual attention—and especially transportation to a country home—will reform the ill-mannered boys. But how life on slovenly farms will actually help is something Thoreau ignores, perhaps because *country* to Thoreau meant a borderland place, a place—like Concord—in the borderlands, not an agricultural region isolated from the ferment of novel ideas.[13]

Other reformers shared Thoreau's thinking about urban childhood. In *Modern House Builder from the Log Cabin and Cottage to the Mansion*, Zebulon Baker argued that children raised with a love of trees and flowers "are more likely to retain the integrity and virtue of childhood in mature years; their aims in life will be truer and higher, and patriotism almost alone here fostered and encouraged. Hence so little of this feeling in large towns by those reared therein."[14] Baker's equation of love of nature and love of nation derives from two decades of childrearing reform, and his insistence on borderland living as the only proper way to raise a child gathers strength from the equally powerful literature of family order.

Early nineteenth-century books and periodicals, especially the Christmas "annuals" aimed at women, emphasize the changing character of housewifery and the new challenges confronted by wives and mothers free of farm work. Reformers repeatedly characterized the home as a refuge from urban disorder and the tumult of commerce and manufacturing, stressing the role of women in perfecting the characters of husbands and children. In "How to Make a Happy Home," an 1848 *Ladies' Wreath* essay that typifies the Christmas annual genre, Mrs. S. T. Martyn warned that the effects of domestic happiness "on the character and habits of the children of a household, cannot easily be estimated."[15] Implicit in this and other essays pulses the conviction that the home must be a refuge of correct living for the husband ensnared in urban business—and an ideal microcosm for children—only a perfected domestic architecture will surmount the challenges posed by social and economic change. Romantic perfectionism transformed the borderland houses of the educated elite, replacing the Federal or Classical Revival style with villas or cottages of no precise style whatsoever.

Reaction against Federal and especially Classical Revival style houses gathered force in the 1820s and 1830s, even as well-off farmers constructed houses aping those of businessmen "retiring" to borderland seats. "Neatness, comfort, and economy are sacrificed to fashion and false pride," railed an anonymous observer in a long *New-England Magazine* article in 1832. "In the first place, our houses are too large for comfort, convenience, or beauty," often costing so much to build that no funds remain for proper maintenance, and "the wife and children" are "too strongly marked with the seal which ruin has set upon them, to make such a spectacle anything but painful and melancholy." Arguing that such houses can be found in every town in New England, the author traces the propensity for overbuilding to gross misunderstanding of political equality. "In the consciousness of acknowledged equality, he cannot bear with patience to be surpassed in the *externals* of style or independence," the author writes of men anxious to demonstrate their social position. Given the ubiquity of such misunderstanding, the person building a grand house in a village does the place genuine injury, for he sets off a house-building or house-improving competition resulting not only in "comfort, and fitness, and neatness" being sacrificed to a "false and ill-grounded jealousy or pride," but in the withdrawl from village use of the "active capital, that gives life to business." Often, the author claims, has he or she found the "marks of dilapidation and decay in a village" impoverished by such a competition.

Moreover, the new sort of house—"towering up into its two stories in height, with its large and numerous windows, its white glaring walls, and its white fence in front, enclosing a green plat of untrodden grass, but without a tree near it to shade or shelter it from the sun and storm"—is so massive that only half of its rooms are regularly used. So senselessly is it designed that the winter wind enters its many openings with "a sound that is truly appalling," and the summer sun scorches its occupants. "Nature is, indeed, shut out entirely. She is not permitted to lend the cooling shade of her forest trees, nor the bright and beautiful flowers of her exhaustless store of shrubs, to deck what man, not art, has tortured into the abode of a rational being." Only "slavery to fashion and custom"—in other words, submission to urban extravagance—explains the building of such expensive, wretched houses so ill suited to the urgent home-life needs of nineteenth-century families.[16] In honoring the traditional rural virtue of simplicity, the essayist of course strengthens the argument with all the power of Country ideology, but in emphasizing the curative powers of natural surroundings he or she directs the full force of romantic perfectionism against the ornate structures fashion adored.

Midway in the article, the essayist pauses to compare the traditional rural cottage with the newfangled symbols of status, finding the simple, small house carefully sited with regard to climate and natural beauty a far better home. The writer's contemporaries shared this enthusiasm. An anonymous New Jersey author, in an 1836 issue of *American Gardener's Magazine,* remarked that the cottage "by the side of a wood, which serves to protect it from the cold winter blast, and has the effect of a shady retreat for summer" is most likely to impart "pleasing ideas of the fertility and domestic comforts, blended with rural economy," of the countryside in which it sits. Snugness, the chief virtue of the cottage, is augmented by hospitality advertised by a flower-bedecked arbor and ornamental garden tended by wives and children. The proximity of woods for botanizing, the healthfulness of flower and vegetable gardening, the relaxation of bird-watching, and a library of good books combine to create a home strong enough to counter "a life of bustle and business."[17] By the late 1840s such articles had borne fruit.

"Within the past twelve years, the number of country houses for gentlemen, on the banks of the Hudson River have greatly increased, and the style of them has undergone an entire change," remarked the editor of *American Agriculturist* in 1851. "Formerly, there were very few, and most of them were in the Grecian portico style, with tall, two-story pillars in front, than which nothing is more ugly and absurd, in our estimation." Of chief importance in the editor's mind, the piazza signaled a radical change in the understanding of nature, but a surface plainness, an airiness, and an openness on a beautified landscape also marked the transformation.

In the years before the Civil War, American Agriculturist illustrators now and then depicted the perfect borderland residence, simple, small, inexpensive, and always graced with trees.

Alexander Jackson Davis glimpsed something of the immense potential implicit in the borderlands: here a Rural Residences drawing reveals a proud father leaving for a walk, and a proud mother enjoying her new front porch.

The vine-embowered cottage-with-a-view
proved appealing everywhere in the
borderlands, even in the newer states, as
this Western Horticultural Review
illustration of 1850 attests.

Even American Agriculturist writers
advocated "tasteful" modern houses, not
only for well-to-do farmers but, as in this
case, for gentlemen farmers assiduously
erasing slovenliness.

Terms like "chaste Italian" and "castellated Gothic" inform his essay, but the significant term is "cottage *orne.*" The ornamented cottage, "of great variety of style, picturesque chimneys, bracketed roof, bow windows, *port cochere,* verandas and piazzas, all surrounded with ornamented grounds," reflects a reorientation in the attitudes of borderland Americans.[18]

Andrew Jackson Downing, the architect Andrew Jackson Davis, and other mid-nineteenth-century reformer-designers in time devised two designations for country houses, *villa* and *cottage.* Essentially, *villa* designated a large, frequently asymmetrical, ornate house, often Gothic or Italian Revival in decoration, intended as the residence of a wealthy family employing three or more servants. By *cottage,* Downing and Davis understood a much smaller house, symmetrical in plan, and ornamented chiefly around the entrance, chimneys, and gable. In *The Architecture of Country Houses,* Downing emphasizes that "industrious and intelligent mechanics and workingmen, the bone and sinew of the land" are the proper owners of cottages, and clearly Downing intended his designs for such owners.[19] But the agricultural press scorned the designs, dismissing their floor plans as inefficient for farmwives and their cost as absurd.[20] Nevertheless, Downing and Davis redirected American architecture after the late 1830s, introducing, almost by accident, the cottage as the perfect borderland house. They and other reformers and builders familiarized themselves with the needs of people too poor to afford villas, and they gradually addressed several overarching needs of borderland residents anxious to demonstrate their allegiance to Country virtue, to perfect their family lives, and to provide examples to fellow citizens not yet on the path to perfection.

A greater appreciation of natural light, and consequently of window design and placement, for example, evolved from early nineteenth-century health concerns. "It has been found that light gives color to the blood, and the color is the life," argued Zebulon Baker. Bedrooms in particular required full sunlight all day in his estimation; basing his arguments on the evident need of plants for sunlight, he concluded that every freestanding house ought to have windows carefully placed to admit as much sunlight as possible, and that the windows should nearly reach the ceiling, in order that light might come in from above the eye. Moreover, large windows correctly sited would admit the life-giving fresh air absolutely necessary to sound health, particularly the health of children.[21] No wonder that the borderland house blossomed with so many windows of so many sorts—particularly bow and dormer—and that the symmetrical floor plan and facade favored by Downing and Davis frequently became asymmetrical and open to light and air.

Of equal if not more importance was the porch, which opened the house into its surroundings. In an 1856 sketch entitled "The Piazza," Herman Melville detailed his love of porches, "as somehow combining the coziness of in-doors with the freedom of out-doors." He describes acquiring a seventy-year-old farmhouse with no porches at all, determining that poverty prevented his building "a panoramic piazza, one round and round," and finally choosing, despite the ridicule of neighboring farmers and carpenters, to have carpenters build one on the north side of the house since to the north lay the finest view. Just as adjacent farmers laughed when

Haskell's crew began work on Llewellyn Park, the neighbors joked about the "cit," the citizen, the city man smitten with new ideas.[22] Even as late as the 1840s, the isolated Massachusetts hill town of Pittsfield apparently knew little of piazzas, but elsewhere, closer to cities, these outdoor livingrooms formed an essential part of seat architecture. As liminal zones between indoors and out, the piazzas provided observation decks where families might imbibe fresh air and good views, simultaneously improving lungs and spirit.

A third important characteristic of the borderland seat, whether large, middling, or small, involved paint, or rather coloration. Downing and most other champions of rural retirement mercilessly attacked the love of farmer and villager for white paint, not only remarking the pain of approaching a glaring white house on a bright day but also emphasizing that white structures fail to harmonize with the rural landscape and indeed mar the overall beauty of scenery. Wordsworth disliked white structures in the English lake district, and other British authors seconded his antipathy.[23] In arguing that landscape painters know best the palette of beautiful scenery, Downing accepted the British argument and eventually arrived at a painterly solution: "the color of all buildings in the country should be of those *soft and quiet shades,* called neutral tints, such as fawn, drab, gray, brown, etc., and that all positive colors, such as white, yellow, red, blue, black, etc., should always be avoided." In advocating colors taken from nature, Downing contradicted the post-Independence love of classical white as well as the intense desire of farmers—especially frontier farmers—to emphasize the separation of house and fields from wilderness. Beyond that, however, in asserting that a large mansion ought properly to have a sober hue implying dignity and that a cottage deserved always "a cheerful and lively tint," he found himself confronting the "country house, of moderate size," which "demands a lighter and more pleasant, but still quiet tone" advertising its occupants' love of moderation and stability.[24]

In worrying about the coloration of "moderate" houses, Downing implicitly recognized not only the proliferation in the borderlands of smaller houses defying stylistic designation, but also the new reality of urban filth. By the early 1850s, when the *Western Horticultural Review* published spirited defenses of both white-painted country residences and bright red city houses enlivened with chrome-green venetian blinds, Ohio Valley aesthetes knew the impact of coal fires. "Since the introduction of coal has hung its funeral pall over us blackening everything it touches," one *Review* writer lamented, Cincinnati homeowners no longer experimented with the fanciful colors that once delighted visitors and elevated urban psyches. City dwellers learned quickly to live with drab-colored buildings simply because the dense coal smoke smudged every outdoor surface.[25] For the far-off borderland narrator in Alice Cary's *Clovernook Tales,* the smoke meant only intriguing atmospheric effects; for Cincinnati residents, it announced the griming over of color. Borderland residents embraced white and other light colors, especially a yellowish cream, out of the ecstasy that followed successful escape from airborne soot, and even Downing and his fellow opinion-shapers learned the force of cleanliness within the larger argument of perfectionism. Borderland paint might suggest

In the years immediately following construction, many borderland houses offered only hints of the carefully chosen plantings with which their owners surrounded them. Only as the trees and shrubs matured did houses acquire the aura of age first evident in revival styles.

The wholesale arrival of gentlemen farmers reshaped the slovenly farms of Westchester into handsome seats.

For many mid-nineteenth-century
Westchester borderers, a handsome house
was only half the home; the other half, a
model hobby farm, lay elsewhere on the
grounds, but equally near the heart.

For some middle-class borderers, fondness
for botanizing and hobby farming
combined in a love of greenhouses and
extravagant flower beds, the delight of both
wives and husbands.

moderation and appreciation of natural scenery, but it *must* extol a fresh cleanliness announcing purity.

Antebellum architectural reformers, caught up in the force of romantic perfectionism, undeniably considered the improvement of domestic architecture immensely significant to the long-term improvement of the Republic. By 1840, perhaps even a decade earlier, well-designed "country houses" reflected not only the gradual transformation of Country ideology and the irresistible force of romantic perfectionism but the establishment of an enduring standard of domestic architecture. No city house, no matter how opulent, few houses in large towns (except those on their edges), and certainly none in villages and rural places compared favorably with those erected "in the country" by reform-minded families.[26] Parents anxious about the health of children, women striving to make orderly, pious homes for husbands ground down by business cares and for sons and daughters facing uncertain challenges, couples caught up in the intellectual excitement of romanticism, transcendentalism, and reform all learned of the advantages of the new sorts of houses, the light, airy, carefully colored houses symbolizing stability, whispering of the old Country ideology, and announcing the promise of romantic perfectionism. And beneath all the exuberant reform, underlying the tracts, conventions, lyceum lectures, political oratory, and architectural guidebooks, murmured the old come-outer tradition. Perfectionist families abandoned city shadows and built their new houses away in the borderlands, on lots large enough for every sort of family experiment in outdoor stability. As Downing knew, they had met the spirit of unrest, and had settled.

Before the Civil War, essayists emphasized that old, boxlike houses might be renovated into stylish borderland residences fit for leisured women awaiting commuting husbands.

10 ❦ GROUNDS

Around the proper country house blossomed its grounds, the acreage devoted to kitchen garden and ornamental trees, greensward and flower beds. As did the structure at its center, the houselot objectified the concerns of early nineteenth-century borderland settlers. A wisely planted tree, a carefully curving walk, a judiciously shaped plantation of shrubs reflected not only the educated homeowner's desire to distance himself from slovenly farmers and narrow-minded villagers but also his love of American, agrarian ideals. It is not surprising, then, that the early nineteenth-century borderland seat, cottage or mansion, stood surrounded by very remarkable plantings indeed.

"The art of embellishing the grounds of a country residence, holds a very high rank," opined George Jaques in an 1852 *Horticulturist* essay. "Compared, indeed, with its productions, there is no work approaching so nearly . . . the creative power of his Maker. Of all earthly pleasures, this claims to be the most fascinating, while it acknowledges itself capable of becoming the most ruinously expensive."[1] Jaques precisely if implicitly identified the coexistence of religious doctrine and financial display working to produce the handsome grounds that delighted turn-of-the-century borderland settlers. While a range of authors and reformers argued that avocational gardening, or *horticulture* as they called it most frequently, evolved from and encouraged moral energy, another group of observers perceived its extraordinary financial underpinnings.

Horticulture rescued the merchant from the snares of hard work and materialism, at least in the mind of many reformers. In choosing to plant and tend fruit trees, ornamental plants, and even vegetables, the urban businessman embraced a sphere distinctly different from that of his countinghouse. "In the present age," mused a writer in the 1840 *Godey's Lady's Book,* horticulture works as a sort of tonic. "The restlessness and din of the rail-road principle, which pervades its operations, and the spirit of accumulation which threatens to corrode every generous sensibility, are modified by the sweet friendship of the quiet plants."[2] Many, many businessmen agreed with Lydia Sigourney, as diaries, letters, and public testimonials demonstrate.[3] The double life of Marshall P. Wilder, Boston merchant and

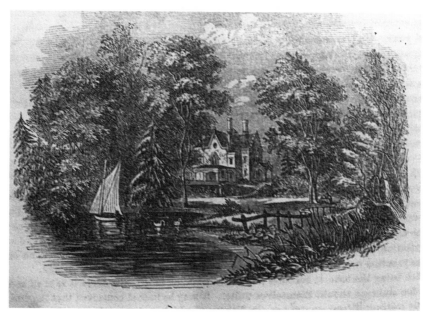

*Placing the proper borderland house in a
proper borderland setting preoccupied not
only borderland families but the many
Horticulturist essayists and illustrators
working out month after month an
American notion of picturesque beauty.*

*Many nineteenth-century illustrations
suggest that the borderland house often
functioned as a sort of home base from
which inhabitants made long and frequent
forays into the grounds or the larger
landscape beyond.*

amateur horticulturist, typifies the absolute integrity so many Americans associated with ornamental gardening.

According to an 1848 *Horticulturist* essay, Wilder moved easily from his immense Pearl Street textiles warehouse to his seat in Dorchester four miles south of the city. "In his countenance you see only the engrossing cares of commerce, and his ample brow, and clear penetrating eye are full of plans for the increase of cotton mills and American manufactured goods," remarked his visitor. But in Dorchester, "one of those agreeable rural suburbs of Boston, which the sturdy city . . . is fast overtaking and swallowing up with its vast commercial appetite," the merchant inhabits Hawthorn Grove, "grounds which are a complete museum of horticulture, full of every known variety of fruit tree; orchards well planted; and long, fruitful alleys." Every sunrise and sunset found Wilder enjoying his gardens; by 1848 he had enjoyed them for sixteen years, employing "every moment of *forced* leisure— leisure borrowed, not from business, but from the ordinary relaxations of the business man, in carrying out his favorite study of horticulture." Wilder did more than garden; for eight consecutive years he served as president of the Massachusetts Horticultural Society, and he conducted experiments on hybridization. His horticultural pursuits not only provided a perfect counterforce to the ever-present danger of materialism that loomed over all capitalists, they also enriched the lives of his countryman. In collecting and improving fruit trees, particularly pears, he actively assisted the farmers of his young nation, and in directing the Horticultural Society, he benefited not only farmers but amateur gardeners too. "It is only indeed by making horticulture the *great working pastime* of his life, that he has been able to accomplish so much," the essayist concluded.[4] Trivial urban recreations, the frenzied entertainments reformers scorned, compared not at all with the uplifting quality of horticulture.

Fifteen years before the *Horticulturist* appreciation of Wilder, another member of the Massachusetts Horticultural Society spoke out explicitly in favor of moral uplift. In his address, Henry Alexander Scammell Dearborn argued that voluntary societies are "one of the most efficient means of accelerating the progress, and enlarging the bounds of knowledge," and that horticultural societies are no exception.[5] By 1833, however, Federalist power had nearly died, and Dearborn and his fellow Society members knew that the only hope for the infant Republic lay outside the confused, egalitarian government of Democratic Republicans. Dearborn emphasized that the pleasures of gardening and the instruction and moral wealth it provides are "not too humble for the most exalted, or beyond the reach of honest and retiring industry." His message endured for years, as Society members insisted that horticulture elevates even the mind of the workingman. "What truly, may we not hope from its effect," wrote one essayist, "when such men as Abbot Lawrence are heard publicly to declare that even in the act of choosing a mechanic, he would go out of his way to find one who 'had been seen on Saturday night taking home *a flower-pot under his arm.*'"[6] By setting a strong example, the upper-class horticulturists hoped to inspire all Americans, even the working classes.

From the 1820s on, periodical writers argued that horticulture would not only rescue the merchant from materialism, but might actually financially enrich its upper-class practicioners. "A pursuit, which is absolutely exclusive and unremitted, is very apt to become a feverish one; and he who pauses occasionally from his labors may gain more in cool reflection that he loses in actual effort," asserted an 1838 *North American Review* contributor. Time spent among fruit trees and flowers, however much it elevated the spirit, might spark excellent ideas for future business ventures too. The essayist offers the example of Philadelphia banker Stephen Girard, who cultivated a seat a few miles outside the city "with the same zeal and exactness, which rendered him so conspicuous in the commercial world."[7] Girard, Dearborn, Wilder, and thousands of other businessmen found in their tiny private Edens both a refuge from temptations and perhaps a place for worldly reflection.

Temperance reformers, members of another of the voluntary associations Dearborn and other upper-class citizens so cherished, argued that horticultural pursuits furthered their cause too. Few aids to the temperance cause are more powerful than fine fruits, continued the *North American Review* essayist. "A fondness for these and for the fiery products of distillation cannot long exist together in the same individual; and, with a fair opportunity, the contest between them cannot well be a doubtful one."[8] The confused link between horticulturists and temperance crusaders proved strong, amazingly enduring, and productive of bizarre effects. In 1850, Downing noted that temperance reform seemed to parallel horticultural developments, to the effect that "a large amount of vice and crime have disappeared from among the laboring classes;" and in subsequent years other authors noted—or imagined—the link, almost always from the awakened, elitist point of view articulated in horticultural periodicals and other borderland-oriented journals.[9]

Well-to-do merchants and professional men discovered the political safety of horticultural pursuits and capitalized upon it. Large houses and magnificently ornamented grounds might have excited comment from Democratic Republicans, especially if the estates had once belonged to hated Loyalists, had not the trees borne fruit. Fruit trees, fruit-bearing shrubs, and vegetables demonstrated not the immense wealth of their owners but also their public-spiritedness. By importing rare fruit trees, the borderland resident indirectly or directly furthered traditional agriculture while enriching the diet of all citizens. The preponderance of fruit trees masked the practical uselessness of strictly ornamental specimens and cast about Hawthorn Grove and other estates an aura of patriotism. Moreover, the vast, intricate plantings demonstrated the stability of their owners. A merchant planting and tending expensive trees and shrubs advertised not only his wealth, but his intention to prosper in the future. Such farsightedness combined with the traditional, almost mythological strength of the American respect for efficient, "thrifty" agriculture to make borderland estates monuments to the staying power of the post-revolutionary elite.

Political figures also embraced the practice of model farming and model horticulture, working diligently to improve their grounds for the good of the Republic.

While some politicians, most notably Washington and Jefferson, farmed as a matter of course, others, particularly northerners, took up farming either as summer recreation or a retirement obsession. In Massachusetts, for example, John Quincy Adams lavished attention and funds on his Braintree residence, struggling to create an up-to-date, handsome, and profitable farm around a house that had once belonged to a Loyalist family. A few miles south, Daniel Webster worked industriously on his Marshfield farm, planting thousands of trees from everywhere in the new nation, experimenting with Swedish turnips, even importing a handful of llamas. Adams and Webster not only directed work done in their absence but labored with their own hands in hotbeds and fields. Adams in his manure piles, Webster in his cattle barn, and dozens of lesser politicians working on the grounds surrounding their seats drew strength, perhaps especially at election time, from the national love of agricultural effort.[10] At the same time, they displayed—as did their merchant neighbors—the solidity of their offices. Clearly men so entranced with planting trees understood the permanence of the Constitution and the Republic.

Country seats and their magnificent grounds attracted much public attention, not only from travelers along roads and the new railroads but from editors of periodicals. In the three decades before the Civil War, American readers visited borderland estates secondhand in the pages of general and special-interest magazines. Rarely embellished with a woodcut or engraving, the articles nevertheless deftly describe not only the handsome houses and grounds but the upright character and continuous, self-disciplined effort that create and maintain them. Size of house or grounds remains strictly secondary in the essays. Other characteristics matter more.

In Flushing, a Long Island town only a few miles from New York City, an 1843 essayist discovered the farm of G. G. Howland, a retired shipping merchant. In a lengthy *American Agriculturist* piece, the observer describes the three hundred acres, the structures, and the crops, making it clear that the farm is anything but slovenly. Howland employs only the latest techniques of field husbandry, producing amazingly rich crops of hay for the city market. "The farm is handsomely laid out, and conveniently arranged," the essayist continues, "the fences principally stone wall, and made in the most durable manner—the foundation being laid one foot below the surface of the earth, so as not to be endangered by the heaving of the frost." Such magnificent husbandry and building characterized the entire farm. Howland used several types of manure, including imported guano, owned a breeding cow brought directly from the Netherlands and hens from China, employed two treadwheel dogs for churning, and delighted in a forty-two-thousand-gallon cistern for rainwater storage. "From an eminent and successful shipping merchant, Mr. Howland has transferred himself to an equally eminent farmer, and judging from appearances, we presume that he takes more pride and pleasure in the latter occupation, than he ever did in the former," concludes the awe-struck writer.[11] Of course, only Howland's mercantile career enabled him to farm so well; everything about his operation, from the massive stone walls to the Chinese hens, cost vastly more than the typical Long Island farmer could begin to afford. Like his collection of dahlias, his plantings of shrubs, and his fine ornamental trees, his hay crop and potato harvest reflected the fertilizing power of money.

Model farming may have irritated some farmers unable to make the massive capital investment necessary to farm profitably in borderland areas, but others appreciated the experiments of wealthy neighbors. "The bold and liberal spirit of improvement, which persons bred to trade or manufactures have often exerted on the improvement and embellishment of their land estates," remarked one traditional borderland agriculturist in an 1822 letter to *The New England Farmer,* helps working farmers, who lack the money for experiments but see the advantages of new methods of cultivation.[12] Such thinking had precedent; four years earlier, William Cobbett claimed that Long Island farmers remained slovens because "the *example* of neatness was wanting," there being "no gentlemen's gardens, kept as clean as drawing-rooms, with grass as even as a carpet" to serve as encouraging models.[13] How much real help hard-pressed farmers—particularly those fruit growers battling blight, thieves, and air pollution—derived from gentleman horticulturalists, however, agricultural editors never asked.

Most newcomers to borderland life favored horticulture over model farming. Two years after its essay on the Howland estate, *American Agriculturist* published one in its lengthy "villa" series, an article entitled "villa of Mr. Halsey." In Astoria, "so easy of access that one can reach it in a single hour from the City Hall . . . making one of the most delightful rides or steamboat excursions around New York," stood Halsey's "commodious" seat, a "mansion" of "dark freestone, roomy, and of a pleasing style of architecture," surrounded by ten acres of lawn, garden, and orchards running downward from the house. "And pray what can be more ornamental, we would ask, than many varieties of fruit trees?" asks the essayist before detailing Mr. Halsey's "experiments" with peach and plum trees and with several massive hothouses devoted to grapes and figs. Although Halsey experiments with poultry—the essayist wonders at his Mexican pheasants—and a few cows, his real love is fruit growing. Halsey deals chiefly with elevated crops, not field varieties. And he at least tries to cover his operating costs, selling his grapes, nectarines, and other scrumptious produce in the city market, as might be expected of any wise businessman. The article makes plain the differences separating the gentleman farmer from the gentleman horticulturist: Halsey owns far less acreage than Howland, focuses his energies on fruit and other delicacies, and lives in close proximity to the city, so close, indeed, that the essayist worries "that as the city spreads, Astoria will be too soon incorporated within its limits, and thus lose the rural beauty for which it is now so greatly admired."[14]

In the 1830s and 1840s countless wealthy borderland families shifted their attentions from farming to horticulture, and periodical articles reflect the change. In an *American Agriculturist* article of 1851, "Villa of Mr. Sargent," an anonymous essayist details the grounds of a seat about one mile south of Fishkill Landing on the Hudson River, again within easy commuting range of New York. After ten years of work, Henry Winthrop Sargent had not only erected a handsome house and out-

Borderland women crossing Brooklyn Ferry to
Manhattan for a day of visiting and shopping
crossed at mid-morning not with the carriages of
commuting men, but with wagonloads of hay, often
the product of the grounds of gentlemen farmers.

The love of ornamental gardening prompted many
borderland families to join houses to greenhouses,
making gardening a year-round activity and
bringing grounds indoors.

buildings but had even produced a fine lawn, chiefly by folding sheep within "a handsome iron hurdle fence" and so profiting from the manure. Extensive gardens and orchards delighted the visitor most, however; the writer recorded finding 180 varieties of pear trees, 60 each of apple and peach, 46 of plums, 12 of nectarine, and 9 of apricot. Moreover, Sargent had built a great glass-enclosed greenhouse for grapes; within the grapery flourished a wide range of exotic vines. Outdoors prospered "rare ornamental shrubs and trees;" the writer notes that "Mr. Sargent has devoted no inconsiderable amount of money, together with years of unremitting attention, to their introduction from every part of the world."[15] As did Halsey's ten-acre estate, Sargent's Wodenethe represented the subtle but significant change in attitude, the origins of which can be traced to the 1820s. Horticulture, along with landscape aesthetics, preoccupied Sargent; field crop improvement held little interest for him. His grounds represented a devotion to delectable but useful fruits and an evolving love of exotic plants kept only to delight the senses.

In the 1830s the split produced new periodicals aimed at borderers who chose horticulture over farming. In the pages of *The Horticulturist* and *The Magazine of Horticulture,* and in general circulation magazines too, flamed a rich new literature focused not on model farming, but on grafting, fertilizing, and hybridizing fruits and ornamentals.[16] Moreover, the new periodicals championed an organic arrangement of trees, shrubs, and flower beds, an arrangement born not only of European romanticism and the quickening educated American love of wilderness scenery, but of a continuing distaste for slovenly farming, stark villages, and cities. Handsome, almost sumptuous color plates of peaches, pears, grapes, and flowers announced the publishers' willingness to splurge mightily in the attempt to gain favor with borderland horticulturists.

In 1866, after more than four decades of argument, Wilson Flagg summed up the debate in a *Magazine of Horticulture* article entitled "The Old and the New." Years of championing one position had somehow mellowed Flagg, who finally admitted that many Americans dearly loved rectilinear form, white houses, and land stripped bare of trees. "Our people encounter vast woods, which must be cut down, before they can attain any material prosperity," he determined. "In a new settlement, a row of clean white-painted houses is conspicuous evidence that nature has been partially subdued; and these sights justly affect the pioneer with a great deal of pleasure." At nightfall, he continued, when traveling in the wilderness, even the educated wayfarer feels pleasure in finding a village.[17] The vast majority of Americans indeed dearly loved straight lot lines and white-painted houses, especially west of the Appalachians, where the Federal land surveyors had spread an immense grid across the wilderness and pioneers lived in square houses on square farms beautified by few trees and many straight furrows.[18] Agricultural experts sang the praises of square fields on all but the most irregular of sites; the editor of *The Annual Register of Rural Affairs* warned in 1853 that "fields should be made nearly square, for economy of fencing material and to save occupancy of land by boundaries."[19] In a similiar way, the builders of cities and towns—and maybe villages too—delighted in straightness for its suggestion of anti-wilderness artificialty.

"Curved lines, you know, symbolize the country," remarked one early nineteenth-century Cincinnati resident; "straight lines the city."[20] In the end, however, Flagg and others argued that truly educated, genuinely sensitive people favored the natural style, not the gridiron arrangement.

The gridiron or geometric arrangement symbolized order, and in a nation not far removed from wilderness chaos, order mattered. But as the educated elite increasingly valued natural scenery and romantic spontaneity over agricultural and urban regimentation, it increasingly scorned any place ordered—and especially ornamentally ordered—according to the geometrical style. As early as 1820, one *Rural Magazine and Literary Evening Fireside* author, well aware that his essay risked the ire of farmer readers, argued that grounds ought to follow "what the painters, perhaps a little fantastically, call the line of beauty, so as to have but few sharp corners or square beds."[21] After three decades, however, only the cognescenti favored the curving line. "The great mass of the people prefer symmetry, stiff formality, straight lines, and the geometrical forms of the ancient or artificial style of laying out grounds," asserted George Jaques. His 1852 *Horticulturist* essay particularly bemoaned the fascination for symmetry. "Some of these places afford a ridiculous exhibition of the proprietor's insane passion for symmetry," he wrote of grounds laid out by newly wealthy residents of villages and open country. "Every angle is a stiff right angle; every row is formal and straight; every plant of a row equidistant, of equal form and equal size. . . . Everything is so prim, so square, so sharp, we almost expect to see the house leap from its foundations and fly away."[22] Horticulturalists, periodical essayists, and borderers as well educated as Susan Cooper and Nathaniel Willis could and did enjoy the beauties of uniformity—the essayist describing Howland's Long Island model farm praised a hay field "80 acres so alike, that one square rod would hardly differ from another over the surface"— but only in strictly agricultural and urban space.[23] In places intended to be beautiful, symmetry, rectilinearity, and other sorts of uniformity advertised only warped sensibility, weak education, and—worst of all—"quick-made wealth" anxious to show off.[24] Only the "natural" or "modern" style of ornamental space reflected true accomplishment.

Two great forces combined in the natural style. One originated in a sophisticated, European-inspired love of picturesque scenery, but it gathered energy from patriotism too. Arranging new plantings in ways evocative of natural patterns did not suffice in early nineteenth-century America. The plants themselves had to come chiefly from American locales; just as the educated elite searched for a distinctly American poetry, a clearly American painting, so it tried to eschew imported ornamental plants. Of course, borders enjoyed importing any useful animal or plant, and they frequently acquired European and Asian ornamentals, but the well-to-do shied away from planting only exotics. Throughout the late 1850s, Wilson Flagg argued in a long series of essays in *The Magazine of Horticulture* that "embellished landscapes indicate luxurious habits, and consequent effeminacy."[25] He emphasized over and over again that native American trees—birch, elm, cherry, poplar, maple, and others—ought to be used by any right-minded borderer, not only for

In the heights around Cincinnati blossomed a landscape of carefully ordered, impeccably maintained grounds, graced everywhere by houses equipped with observation cupolas.

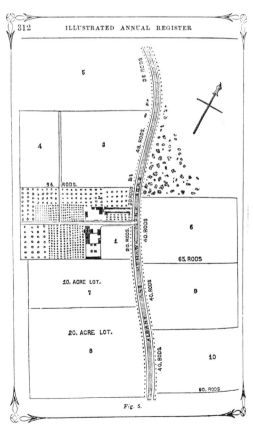

5

36 RODS

48. RODS

4   3

96. RODS.

51. RODS

1   20. RODS   6

40. RODS

65. RODS

10. ACRE LOT.
7   9

40. RODS

20. ACRE LOT.
8   10

ALBANY LANE

40. RODS

90. RODS

Fig. 5.

Farm-journal illustrations depict the subtle shift away from mere efficiency in laying out and dividing farms. In this illustration of 1857, only practicality governs the arrangement of farmstead and fields.

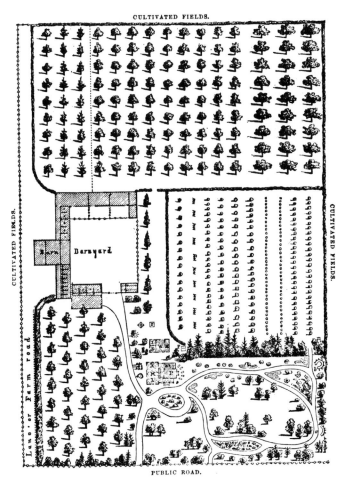

CULTIVATED FIELDS.

CULTIVATED FIELDS.

CULTIVATED FIELDS.

Barnyard

Barn

Lane or Farm road

PUBLIC ROAD.

This 1858 Illustrated Annual Register of Rural Affairs *plan of a "Complete Country Residence" reveals not only a continuing commitment to efficiency but a growing attachment to ornamental grounds as the setting from which passersby view the comfortable farmhouse and well-ordered orchards.*

Agricultural periodicals advised both farm families and newly arrived borderers to ornament their entrance drives, especially by designing curving lanes and footpaths graced with purely beautiful plants.

their genuine beauty but for their patriotic associations. "The American elm, indeed, is a fair symbol of a well-bred New England country-gentleman, who has strength without rudeness, politeness without effeminacy, and courage united with a mild and gentle deportment."[26] His series and sentiments culminated a long argument by many authors, some of whom advertised the ornamental virtues of such little-known species as the Virginia fringe tree.[27] Other experts argued in favor of native plants by attacking exotics, especially the ailanthus tree imported in the early part of the century as a plant useful in tanning leather; when the native sumac proved equally valuable, a canny nurseryman advertised the foreign trees—which spread so fast that they overrun all other plants—as "the tree of heaven."[28] Within two decades Americans learned to loathe the hardy, spreading immigrant and to beware other exotics as well.

On the other hand, a developing love of time past deflected well-educated borderers away from ornamental plants. In 1847, Downing warned his *Horticulturist* readers searching for borderland building locations to "choose a site where there is *natural wood*." Finding such a location ensures finding the means to the illusion of a time-honored structure. "The masses of trees are easily broken into groups that have immediately the effect of old plantations, and all the minor details of shrubbery, walks, and flower and fruit gardens, fall gracefully and becomingly into their proper positions." Mature trees provide privacy from road traffic and pleasing effects of light and shadow in Downing's estimation, but chiefly they "dignify" the newly built house, making it seem old.[29] Many other savants agreed with him. "Where a fine cluster of half a dozen elms, oaks, chestnuts, or other beautiful indigenous trees, grow near the site of the house, the buildings may be located as it were, beneath the protection of these forest guardians, so that the whole place shall at once produce an effect which would otherwise cost the labor of years," cautioned another writer five years later.[30] Architects too extolled the innumerable value of mature trees. "Do not allow picturesque rocks, or wild forest trees to influence your decision against any site," explained Henry Hudson Holly in his immensely popular *Country Seats* in 1863. "Your landscape gardener can always reconcile them, domesticate them, as it were; in short make them beautiful and appropriate; and your architect, if a man of taste and education, can arrange your house to combine gracefulness with any peculiarities of country, and give it such character as will be congruous with surrounding scenery."[31] In the post-Revolutionary decades, and especially when economic instability worried all Americans, the wealthy elite prized the image of time-honored stability that mature trees have to a new house. Money might build a mansion nearly overnight, but only time seemed able to produce a magnificent stand of trees. Native trees only added to the evidences of public-spirited patriotism announced by orchards.

Flagg and others suggested further, however, that the natural style of grounds and the congruous sort of architecture originated in such a heightened sensibility that only well-read women, and a few businessmen so prosperous that they had time for intellectual improvement, could appreciate them. Most boys and men "on their way up" admired only the new, according to Flagg, and city life further warped their notions of value: "Their minds are crowded with a multitude of ideas, which are but *photographs* of painted houses, dusty streets, fast horses and showy vehicles," he exclaimed. Educated women, on the other hand, valued less transient things, while following "moral and benevolent enterprises" and cultivating "moral and intellectual" topics.[32] Thus a businessman carefully choosing a wooded site in the borderlands, erecting on it a tasteful house, painstakingly improving the existing natural planting, and then engaging in horticultural and other recreational but potentially useful pursuits, displayed not only his "gentle" character and fine education—the traits Flagg found reflected in the mature elm—but his absolute success in business. A merchant, investor, or professional man who no longer needed to think constantly of business, who needed no cheap "gewgaws" like tiny exotic trees symmetrically grouped before his ostetatious new country house, was a businessman not only rich, but *securely* rich.

The upper- and middle-class values spread throughout society as nineteenth-century America progressed toward disunion and the Civil War, the very nadir of instability. The Brooklyn author of "Suburban Gardening," an 1852 *Horticulturist* essay, forcefully announced that "if there were a necessity for confining gardens to one class alone, then I would say, let that class be the poor. Let them have at least one little spot where they can pass the evening of their days in quiet repose under their own vine and peach tree. How much brighter and better this world would be, if each man had a spot that he could call his own!" Some writers despaired of teaching the working class much about the natural style—Flagg argued that "it matters nothing at all, if the owner of such a piece of ground be satisfied, whether it be round or square, geometrical or hieroglyphical; whether the beds and paths resemble checkerboards or goose-tracks; whether the plan be that of a kidderminster carpet or a map of the moon," simply because the tiny yards scarcely affected the larger landscape in the way one or more county estates did—but most agreed on the moral effects resulting from land-owning and gardening.[33] Even villagers might improve themselves, as one *Annual Register of Rural Affairs* expert argued in 1855. "The simplest grounds for the exercise of taste in planting, are those of the village residence where a space of only a few yards intervene between the dwelling and the boundaries. But here one great advantage exists—the narrow dimensions enable the occupant to preserve the most finished appearance, as he has but little space over which to extend his labors."[34] Of course, the writer continued, villagers and other owners of small lots might easily blunder into "stiffness," but at least they had space enough in which to experiment.

Villagers and other poorer adherents of elite aesthetics turned not to horticulture—for after all, most lacked room for more than a fruit tree or two—but to floriculture. Space not devoted to kitchen gardening blossomed in flowers, and as early as 1838 *The Magazine of Horticulture* devoted a lead article to "The Picturesque in Floriculture." Despite the periodicals' emphasis on native, perennial flowering plants, mechanics—or perhaps their wives—lavished their attentions on geraniums. Between 1834 and 1836, a geranium-collecting fad struck New York City, and one florist, Thomas Hogg of Bloomingdale Road, did amazingly well importing English varieties. But despite articles like "Influence of Poetry on the Cultivation and Appreciation of Flowers," an 1856 *Yearbook of Agriculture* piece, floriculture remained distinctly secondary.[35] By the 1830s, only grounds embellished with fruit trees, native ornamentals, and perhaps a few exotics announced stable wealth and exquisite taste.

Providing such plants preoccupied the growing ranks of nurserymen inhabiting the borderlands. Beginning in the 1830s, horticultural magazines devoted much space to describing the nurseries near Boston, Newark, New York, and Philadelphia; the articles suggest the burgeoning power of taste-makers like Downing, who himself ran a nursery in Newburgh, on the Hudson River. But the articles also suggest something of the pace of urban expansion. As cities expanded, urban nurserymen learned that rising land values meant the end of renting acreage for nurseries—New York City ran a street through Hogg's garden in 1836—and immense profits from selling owned land.[36] Another New York nurseryman "sold his estate for building lots" in the middle 1830s and moved his nursery to Harlem, far from the speculators and nearer to horticulturalists and other devotees of borderland moral recreation.[37] In the 1830s, few realized that the fate of city nurseries foreshadowed the fate of borderland estates, both large and tiny.

In 1836 appeared *The Philadelphia Book:
or, Specimens of Metropolitan Literature*, one of many anthologies pesenting American writing to an American audience concerned about the development of a genuinely home-grown literature. The word *metropolitan* implies a growing awareness
of the spread of Philadelphia, however, and an acute realization that in the borderlands lived an ever larger portion of educated readers. Toward the end of the
volume, a brief essay by Sarah Hall confirms such speculation.

"Reminiscences of Philadelphia" begins by emphasizing that a few aged people
"well remember when this wide-spread metropolis was comparatively a village, and
had the simple manners of a village." Speed almost beyond comprehension characterized the spread of the city, and Hall details the block-by-block takeover of rural
space by urban form. Fifty years ago, she wonders, a large house "between Fifth and
Sixth, stood alone, and was considered *out of town*." Men "not much beyond the
middle age" recall skating on ponds "as far east as Seventh, and even Fifth, streets;"
and others "remember lots, inclosed by post and rail fences, in the now most
populous and busy streets." Uniformity characterized the reach of urban fabric;
"springs, creeks, groves and copses, which once broke and diversified the ground,"
Hall marvels, are "now levelled and drawn out into streets." No wonder, she notes,
that urban expansion orders so many casual conversations. The rapid changes
erased childhood landscapes, and disoriented many citizens returning from brief
absences.

Hall implies that genteel people, her term for the wealthy, desert their old
urban houses for residences either in more fashionable parts of the city or in the
borderlands. "Many houses in these days, which are not now thought sufficiently
genteel or convenient for a second-rate tradesman," she remarks, "were then inhabited by the rich and honourable of the land." Genteel people living away from
"town" retained their business interests in the city, however, and in Hall's time
Philadelphia guidebook writers realized that *Philadelphia* no longer designated a
place bounded by city limits but connoted a place of shared interests, business and
otherwise. Rapidly expanding to include "places of genteel and frequent resort"

easily reached by "the Daily Lines of Steam-Boats and Rail-Roads," Philadelphia had become metropolitan.[1]

In the 1840s two inventions opened the borderlands to families other than those wealthy enough to afford horseback or carriage commuting. Steamboat service, particularly in New York along the Hudson River but also around the western end of Long Island, enabled many families to live in small seats; Brooklyn, only a short ferry ride from Manhattan, began to prosper as the home of middle-class commuter families. Railroad travel, however, precipitated a revolution, exactly as Nathaniel Willis knew it would; it made possible not only the success of jewels like Llewellyn Park but also square miles of borderland country cut into one- to three-acre lots. "Now every railroad which can convey the pent up denizen of closely packed squares, carries *to the country* the sensible father or the youthful husband, in numbers which statistics render perfectly wonderful," marveled a *Horticulturist* columnist in the summer of 1858.[2] In running through the list of borderland enjoyments, which smack not of the farm or the village but of the seat, the essayist repeats the message driven home monthly in this and a dozen other magazines aimed at a growing population of educated city people prospering in an industrializing economy and anxious for the rewards of hard work.

Obtaining the rewards—right education, moral home life, aesthetic understanding, stability—proved tricky as railroads threaded their way through the borderlands. Newcomers unable to afford the ten-acre lots of the carriage commuters found their options limited, and they learned the absolute necessity of following the advice of Downing and other experts, lest they buy into a village existence. "The improved taste which is consecrating the shores of the Hudson, of the East River, and of Staten Island" and "the increased demand for flowers and trees, the growing interest in landscape study, and in the multiplication of the out-of-town houses for working men which are springing up in every direction" heartened the editor of *Harper's New Monthly Magazine,* but the village-like appearance of many new borderland places worried him. "We wish to suggest a more pleasing outlay of streets, and villages, than at present characterizes the bulk of new suburban towns." A rectilinearity completely at odds with natural topography and scenery coarsely cheapened beautiful sites. After asking what sort of taste would "carve up" magnificent sites "into rectangular squares, with streets gullied by every rain, and basement houses tottering upon the meagre patches of grass," the editor asks why speculators and "engineers with their theodolites" never ask if "the pattern for a flat, commercial town, may not be altogether the most judicious for a picturesque river bank?" His satire implies that a borderland place ought to be free of commerce-inspired form and should reflect the lines of art, not brute engineering. The remainder of his editorial explains why.

A "suburban town" is a place where "people go for quiet, and for a small measure of rural enjoyment." Consequently it ought not have straight streets, for those encourage the quick transportation and noisy traffic that contribute to urban nervousness. Moreover, "country roads, and roads in country villages *ought to wind,*" not only because winding roads make for easier grades and expose better hillside views but because winding roads increase the number of odd-shaped house lots. "Irregular-shaped lots increase the devices of ingenuity," he continues. "Queer, jutting, lozenge-shaped lots tempt all the prettiness of gardening; odd nooks and corners of a town, charm the rural architect."[3] Woven into his editorial are two strands of argument, one stressing the importance of picturesque scenery, romantic landscape arrangement, and peaceful, curvilinear form; the other displaying a real confusion of language.

In the editorial, terms like *village* and *town* float detached from their early nineteenth-century connotations. A *country village* differs from the prosaic places described by Barber and other gazetteers, just as a *suburban town* connotes something unlike the main street towns Americans knew. No longer did the mix of slovenly and model farms, mechanics' villages and country seats bring to mind easily defined words, and the lightning-like sprint of cross-hatch residential streets across the countryside perplexed even masters of language.[4] In 1870, when he published *What I Know of Farming,* Horace Greeley struggled to describe the Manhattan region where he first farmed for fun. "None of the avenues east of Third was then opened about Thirtieth Street, and the neighborhood, though now perforated by streets and covered with houses, was as rural and secluded as heart could wish." The gentleman farmer, who then managed his fields in Westchester County some thirty-five miles from City Hall, settled on the term *open country* to designate the landscape lost to Fiftieth Street.[5] Thirty-three years later, when James Buckham published a series of essays describing the wildlife and landscape of the borderlands some ten miles beyond the city limits of Boston, he chose *Where Town and Country Meet* as a title, suggesting what his essays reveal, a continuing difficulty concerning landscape terminology. As so many nineteenth-century observers knew, Sarah Hall perhaps best of all, the borderlands forever retreated before the creep or sprint of urban form, but whatever their location, their peculiar landscape defied designation.

No wonder Westchester worried Willis. No wonder urban authors moved so deliberately in borderland space. Only a few miles from city centers, only a few miles from editorial offices, accomplished writers discovered the poverty of language and the richness of landscape change.

III 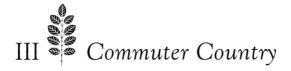 Commuter Country

*In the 1830s Philadelphians began exploring not only the
Fairmount Waterworks but the handsome regions west and
north, regions that fitted the emerging American notion of the
picturesque.*

PHINNEY

Elias Phinney commuted. In the 1830s and 1840s the clerk of court drove daily between his little farm in Lexington and the county courthouse in East Cambridge; except on Thursdays, when court adjourned, he and his buggy were a familiar and respected site in the borderlands of Boston. His long ride over rough, unpaved roads consumed immensities of time; by his own admission, he spent sixteen hours a day—except on his beloved Thursdays—at the courthouse or on the road.[1] Yet he gloried in spending every morning and evening at home with his family.

What made him drive so far, in fair weather and bad? He farmed, not really for income, but for love. His little farm, a jewel-like demonstration of scientific agriculture, consumed his residual hours. As elected secretary of the New England Society for the Promotion of Agriculture, he wrote extensively on agricultural improvement, specializing in the propagation of Ayrshire cattle and the most efficient means of draining wetlands. Granted, he relied on foremen, but the foremen through the years made daily, meticulous notes of their activities for the attorney-farmer they saw only at twilight. "The principal part of the time I have devoted to farming is while others have been in bed," Phinney confided in a letter.[2] For fourteen years, he averaged five hours of sleep a night, consumed not only with a passion for his legal duties but with a passion for borderland estate-making, for the virtuous life of moderation, self-discipline, and simplicity he grounded in the country.

Phinney's twenty-four-mile daily trip was uncommon, especially on a daily basis in pre-railroad times, but it carried him through interesting regions. In 1841, Henry Colman, describing Middlesex County in an agricultural report, noted that it "presents nothing interesting or picturesque," although its well-kept truck farms delight the eye of agriculturists. "Trade and manufactures greatly predominate over the agricultural interests," Colman concluded, but many of the newcomers—like Phinney—farmed for pleasure and small profit. "Though in general their occupations are on a small scale, yet their means give them the power of free expenditure and their establishments do much to improve and adorn the country."[3] Despite the success of truck and dairy farming and the aesthetic improvements wrought by gentlemen farmers, the eastern edge of the county—the site of Phinney's courthouse—had become urban, a place of manufactories, shops, wharves, foundries, and closely spaced houses. Colman understood the inexorable creep of brickyards and other enterprises at odds with farming, picturesque or practical.[4]

Phinney passed each morning from borderland across places still undesignated, even by Sarah Hall, which linked, somehow, borderland with city. His wife, left behind on what passed in Middlesex County for heights, remained in borderland space. Something noticeable—and noteworthy—but nearly indecipherable separated her from the urban form in which her husband stabled his horse and kept his records. Far off to the south, in the environs of Philadelphia, the something took shape faster and more boldly, and there it underwent first-class observation.

12 ❧ PHILADELPHIA

"Hundreds of omnibuses are con-
stantly in motion in every direction," marveled A. M. Maxwell, a British military
officer touring Philadelphia in 1840. "We put ourselves into one, and went to the
Fairmount Waterworks," a borderland engineering wonder serving the fast-growing city to the east. "The grounds are tastefully and beautifully arranged," Maxwell
continued, and popular enough as a park to justify frequent omnibus service.[1]

Omnibuses appeared in Philadelphia near the end of 1829. For years, stage-
coaches had operated regularly to Germantown, Hamiltonville, and other locations
near the city as well as to New York and Baltimore, but an announcement that "the
Chestnut street accommodation stage would run regularly from the Coffee House
along Chestnut street to the Schuylkill and return" signaled the advent of a new
form of transportation. Operating between nine in the morning and five in the
afternoon, the first omnibus soon proved its worth; the ten-cent fare made its service
accessible to many Philadelphians, and soon tickets could be had more cheaply,
twelve for a dollar. Within a few years additional omnibus lines crisscrossed the
city, and competition drove down the price of single-ride tickets to five, four, and
eventually three cents; holders of season tickets enjoyed fares of one cent per ride,
and as Maxwell discovered, the large, boxlike conveyances jammed with riders
thronged Philadelphia streets, rattling over cobblestones and lumbering along the
dirt roads at the city's edge.[2]

Omnibuses made possible the dramatic extension of urban form that so dazzled
Sarah Hall and made difficult the composing of guidebooks. R. A. Smith, for example, worried in 1852 that existing guidebooks to Philadelphia "necessarily fail to
arrest the attention, or impart that information and instruction, which books of this
character are expected to afford," largely because they focus on individual structures, not the overall urban fabric. His *Philadelphia as It Is in 1852* emphasizes in
text and handsome, colored maps the extraordinary growth of the city and its
"vicinity." "The city is extending with wondrous strides; year by year streets are
being laid out, and houses extending away for squares, arise, as by the hand of magic,
on ground that lately 'waved in golden harvest,'" he exclaims, using the simile

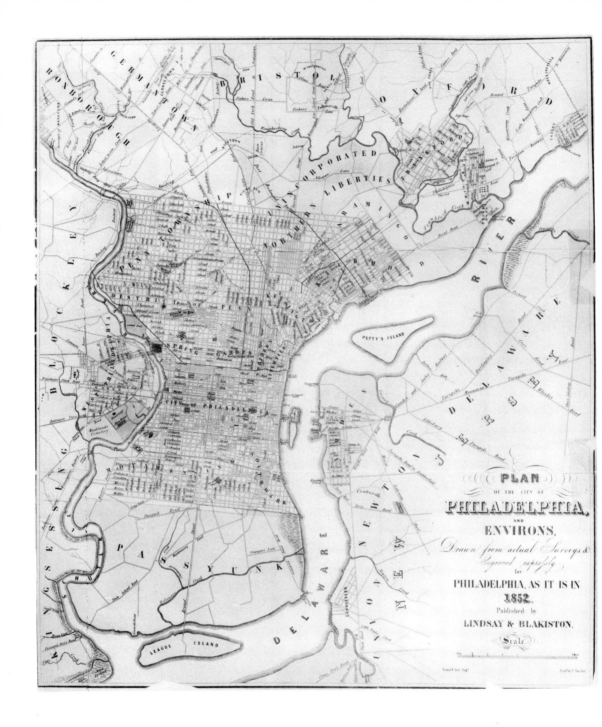

Throughout the nineteenth century, Philadelphia mapmakers
detailed the extraordinary growth not only of the city proper,
but of the borderlands north of it and those across the
Delaware.

favored by Susan Cooper, Nathaniel Willis, and other borderland scrutinizers of rapid, seemingly instantaneous spatial change. "Spring Garden and Penn, twelve years ago, were rural districts. Now look at them! We remember rambling, five years since, through fields immediately north of Poplar Street, where are now beautiful streets, adorned with tasty, and, in many instances, magnificent houses." Unlike previous guidebook authors, Smith not only emphasizes the environs or borderland surrounding the built-up city proper; he also explicitly stresses the typical Philadelphian's ignorance of borderland change, quoting one citizen's amazement at the unparalleled growth. "The Schuylkill no longer bounds us. Improvement is now in rapid march through the beautiful District of West Philadelphia. And no less marvelous are the changes taking place in Southwark, Moyamensing, etc., etc." Perhaps most marvelous of all changes was the improving "accommodation" in housing: "Not only the merchant, wealthy manufacturer, and persons well to do in the world, occupy each an entire dwelling, but tradesmen of the most humble class can have a house to themselves." Surely the rattling, bumping omnibus had wrought magic, for it made possible cheap daily commuting from the further reaches of the city, and from the inner borderlands as well. And it caused Smith to broaden his guidebook horizons, to use the word *metropolis* with sureness, to emphasize that neighboring communities closely tied by omnibuses to "the city" must "always be considered as forming a portion of the city, in a general and descriptive view."[3] Only the slightest uncertainty, the slightest faltering in his prose suggests that Smith wondered a little if improvement marched through West Philadelphia, or something else, something masquerading as progress.

If omnibuses smacked of magic, horsecars spoke boldly of wizardry. From the day the first horse-drawn streetcar glided along the rails newly laid on Fifth and Sixth Streets in January 1858, Philadelphians grasped not only the transit significance of the invention but its real estate implications as well. The cars, each seven feet wide and fourteen feet long, operated behind two-horse teams; low to the ground, smooth-riding—at least on smooth city streets—and traveling at about six miles an hour, the horsecar or "passenger car" immediately shamed omnibus proprietors. Within two years, Philadelphia boasted a dozen horsecar lines; investors literally mobbed offices at stock sales, for the lines—even with the six-cent fare— proved tremendously profitable to their owners.[4] But borderland real estate speculation and development soon proved even more profitable, for the swift-moving cars opened vast regions to families unable to afford their own horses and carriages or to commute by the new steam-driven railroads.

Of all Philadelphia observers, Sidney Fisher best grasped the staggering importance of the horse-car revolution. A city attorney deeply attached to rural pursuits—he devoted much energy to improving his plantations in Cecil and Kent counties in Maryland and to addressing assemblies of farmers on the necessity of crop rotation—he recorded his borderland business and social travel in a minutely detailed diary.[5] His long entries reveal his conviction that borderland life best combines the virtues of city and rural living, displaying his sharp awareness of the financial underpinnings of borderland spatial change. Fisher understood the horsecar line as a sort of magic wand transforming not only the borderland landscape but the very form and concept of the city.

"They offer great facilities in traversing the city, now grown so large that the distances are very considerable from place to place," he wrote in February 1859 of the vehicles banishing the "jolting, slow, and uncomfortable omnibus." Fisher rode the horsecars frequently, recording his paths in an attempt to understand how the lines functioned as a system. "Their remarkable success proves how much they were needed. They are all crowded, too much so, indeed, often for comfort." Their real importance, however, lay perhaps a half decade into the future. "They will also soon stretch out to the neighboring villages, thus merging them in the town. Then, in a remarkably prescient passage, he detailed his vision of the horsecar future.

"A beneficial effect of this will be to enable everyone to have a suburban or villa or country home, to spread the city over a vast space, with all the advantages of compactness and the advantages, moreover, of pure air, gardens and rural pleasures," he mused. "Before long, town life, life in close streets and alleys, will be confined to a few occupations, and cities will be mere collections of shops, warehouses, factories, and places of business." Along with his contemporaries in Pennsylvania and elsewhere, Fisher had difficulties with terminology. Was *suburban* the right name for the changed borderland space? Did *country home* better designate the house along the horsecar route?

Within a few months Fisher knew more about the horsecar transformation. Early on he realized that the city streets crowded with horsecars made carriage driving difficult if not impossible, and that the rails laid in the cobblestone pavement made riding in carriages unpleasant. Five months later he wrote with certainty about the effect of horsecar lines on carriage travel and borderland real estate development. "They operate in two ways to disperse the population over the country, by making the streets inconvenient for all other vehicles and by offering cheap means of reaching the country. It is very unpleasant to drive the streets now because of the rails, so that private carriages have become useless whilst the cars, comfortable & easy, offer to those who live in the country a pleasant way of going to town at all hours & in any weather at trifling expense." Fisher knew that the new line to Germantown "spoils the road for driving," but cars operating every ten minutes and ten-cent fares would delight the residents of that fast-growing village north of the city.

"One consequence of this is the immense improvement of the country and rise in the value of property," he continued, speaking of the borderland extension of horsecar lines. Of course, wealthy urbanites had discerned the enticements of borderland places before the horsecar era; one 1839 commentator noted that Germantown and Frankford were "accessible in less than half an hour, by rail-roads," and that "these villages have become greatly improved, within a short time, having become the resorts of many citizens, as summer residences." Only four years later, a gazetteer remarked that Germantown remained a place without "lateral streets," "composed of dwellings, stores, taverns, and occasionally splendid mansions extending for four or five miles on each side of the turnpike." The citizenry of the *lengthy* place"—a sort of ribbon village in the making—included many who were wealthy, "retired from business in the city," savoring "that happy competence that results from quiet industry, uninterrupted by the excitement and expensive luxuries of a large city, but still enjoying all the advantage of its market." By 1859, however, Germantown boasted water and illuminating gas piped into every house; there had been an astonishing rise in land values and other evidence of the horsecar metamorphosis on which Fisher devoted increasing attention. "Shops & mechanics follow the rich population of the villas, and soon every luxury of a city can be had in the neighborhood. All the families who own much land here have been enriched." He talked with his borderland friends who owned country places—often farms—in Germantown, and learned that one family had nearly a thousand acres "worth now millions"; another had sixty acres, worth "$5000 per acre & increasing in value." As the horsecar lines snaked into the borderlands only recently crossed by steam railroads, the landscape changed almost before his eyes.

On his way to the farm of a friend, a Chestnut Hill country gentleman, Fisher explored one or two streets near Germantown that he had not seen for many years. "Now lined with cottages & villas, surrounded by neat grounds, trees, shrubbery & flowers, many of them costly and handsome, all comfortable and pretty," the streets represented the recent transformation "everywhere, in short, within ten miles of the city where a railroad runs," in territory just reached, or about to be reached, by horsecar lines too. Fisher learned that "shopkeepers, manufacturers, and merchants" owned the new places, and he determined that "their beauty and general good taste and the care and attention lavished on them show what sources of enjoyment they are and how superior is the life they promote to that of the streets."[6] What he saw had already appeared in the pages of national magazines, of course, depicted in sketches, floor plans, and essays.[7]

"A Suburban or Country Residence" typifies the articles concerning Germantown houses.[8] Written by R. Morris Smith, a Philadelphia architect, the piece reflects the confusion characterizing Fisher's diary entries. The two-story "cottage," designed "as a suburban residence," would be "suitable as a country residence, or, with some small additions, as a farm-house," begins Smith, clearly at a loss how to precisely designate the structure. Yet the form and purpose of the house are clear: with "some degree of luxury in the interior, and picturesque ensemble, with a neat, yet roomy compactness," the two-and-half-story building opens on the outdoors. The large drawing room, "with a bay window, 6 feet by 4 feet, which commands a very fine view, fifteen or twenty miles in every direction," opens through glass doors onto a "wide veranda; a small, second-story porch overlooks another view. But surmounting the house, above the roof, is the crowning glory, a cupola nearly eight feet square from which "a most magnificent prospect is commanded." All conveniences, the hot and cold running water, upstairs bathroom, central heating, finished attics, pale beside the perfect openness of house to site, and particularly to vista. Surrounded by gravel walks, lawn, flowers, shrubs, and a view

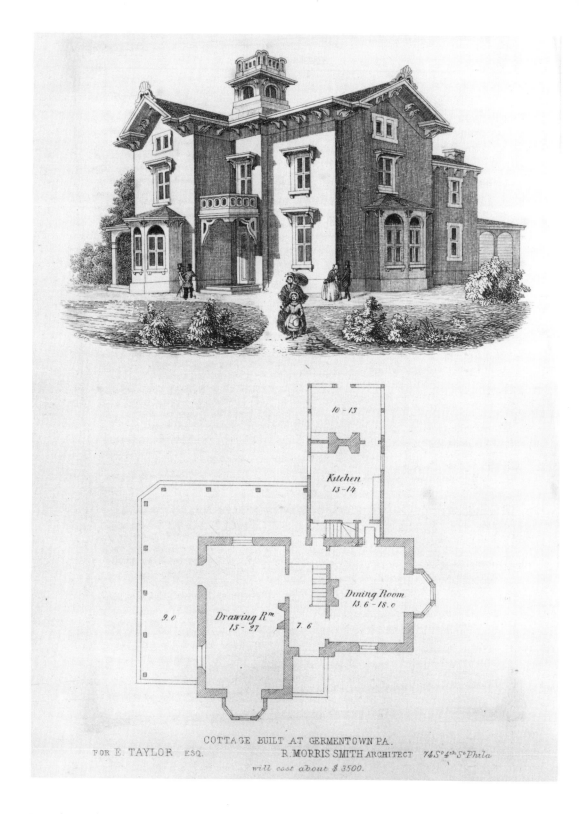

COTTAGE BUILT AT GERMANTOWN PA.

FOR E. TAYLOR ESQ.   R. MORRIS SMITH ARCHITECT 74 S° 4th St Phila

will cost about $ 3500.

Everywhere in the borderlands north of Philadelphia, railroad and horsecar commuters left the houses of the heights to travel to the city visible from observation towers.

of several hundred square miles, the thirty-five-hundred-dollar house objectifies the love of picturesque scenery and outdoor living, the love of openness, that prompted the Germantown boom.

In the end, Fisher concludes that "fresh air, space, trees, flowers, privacy, a convenient & tasteful house, can now be had for the same expense as a narrow & confined dwelling on a pavement, surrounded by brick walls & all the unpleasant sights & sounds of a crowded town." Again, his language reveals the confused complexity of his thinking; his diary entry mixes specifics like flowers with generalities like privacy, while nevertheless capturing the peculiar character of the locale. Then, within the aesthetic, moral, and political framework developed by the Coopers, by Willis, Chapin, Ware, by Bates and by Trotter, Fisher evaluates the transformation wrought by railroads and horsecar lines. "The advantages are so obvious that this villa & cottage life has become quite a passion and is producing a complete revolution in our habits. It is dispersing the people of the city over the surrounding country, introducing thus among them, ventilation, cleanliness, space, healthful pursuits, and the influences of natural beauty, the want of which are the sources of so much evil, moral & physical, in large towns."[9] What Fisher saw that hot July day in 1859 (riding with a friend to view some cattle in which they both had an interest as gentleman farmers) struck him as good, as *obviously* good, as the only intelligent future in a nation perilously close to disunion.

Who, a quarter century earlier, foresaw such change in the Philadelphia borderland? Certainly civic boosters thought that the city would grow, but their projections suggest a slow, purely urban growth, one like that depicted in the guidebook *Philadelphia in 1824,* especially in its map. The publishers clearly understood the real estate significance of the new "permanent bridge"—so called because it replaced a pontoon bridge—over the Schuylkill River. Their map shows a cross-river neighborhood, "Part of West Philadelphia," sliced by proposed straight streets matching the grid pattern of the city to the east. And just as clearly, the map displays proposed or unfinished straight streets within the established grid nearer the city. Almost nowhere does it record the curved lines thought to emblematize the country. But in the final analysis, Carey & Lea (the publisher of the guidebook) proved more farsighted than Fisher.

In the middle eighteenth century, a handful of wealthy Philadelphia families rediscovered the Schuylkill, the marsh-lined watercourse named Hidden River by Dutch explorers. Building on high ground west of the river, they enjoyed picturesque views of the water and of the growing town east of it, a town reasonably accessible by ferry, and later by floating bridge.

The Woodlands, the family home of the Hamiltons, epitomized West Philadelphia country living in the late eighteenth and early nineteenth centuries. Eventually extending over more than five hundred acres, the estate reached its zenith under the ownership of William Hamilton, who improved not only the immense Adamesque Federal style house but the grounds as well. Based partly on his reading of British romantic writers, especially experts on the picturesque, and on a careful tour of English estates, Hamilton set about making The Woodlands the equivalent of any European country seat. He erected a 140-foot-long greenhouse for his collection of some ten thousand exotic plants—a collection that entranced Thomas Jefferson and other contemporaries—and altered the form of his stable and coach-house to complement his renovated house. Every outdoor plant he carefully selected and sited, considering its appearance, fragrance, and usefulness in framing views of the Schuylkill and Philadelphia. Hamilton brought into North America the ginkgo tree and the Lombardy poplar, spice plants and tea bushes, along with many other plants that eventually spread over much of the continent. Hamilton succeeded in his efforts, at least in the opinion of Jefferson, who remarked in 1806 that The Woodlands was "the only rival which I have known in America to what may be seen in England."[10]

Hamilton died in 1813, eight years after the opening of the permanent bridge and the beginning of a new era in West Philadelphia, an era Hamilton anticipated and indeed helped inaugurate. In 1804, he subdivided the northeastern part of his estate into a new settlement he called Hamiltonville. Envisioned as a replication of the grid pattern of Philadelphia streets, the place, at least as it appears on Hamilton's development map of 1804, was to be a community of quarter-acre houselots, most fronting on major east–west streets, and lots for a school and a church. Hamilton, whom many contemporaries knew as a wealthy miser, early grasped the opportunities for profit implicit in borderland growth, and his love of picturesque landscape gardening did not deter his speculative efforts. Within three decades of his death, his heirs had sold almost all of his acreage, and most of his trees had fallen to house builders; his own residence and some acreage remained as the administrative center of Woodlands Cemetery.

Hamilton's efforts in real estate development served as prototypes for other wealthy landowners, who learned that the new bridge not only opened into countryside perfect for summer and year-round residences, but made possible the subdivision of land for omnibus and, later, horsecar commuters. At first, however, well-to-do newcomers bought lots of one acre or more facing the wide new streets aligned with fashionable city streets across the river. The newcomers with their Italianate style houses combined with long-time residents of older estates to give an aura of comfort and wealth to the region; one family entertained Andrew Jackson during his visit to Philadelphia, and all tried to achieve, albeit on a smaller scale, something of the gracefulness that characterized life at The Woodlands and other estates. But within a few years, speculator-developers capitalized on both location and aura, reshaping the fabric of West Philadelphia into something married more closely to horsecar urbanity than to the picturesque gardens of The Woodlands.

As the nineteenth century progressed, well-to-do West Philadelphia families learned firsthand of village growth. Working farmers, mechanics, and their wives and children had long lived in the West Philadelphia region, the mechanics and laborers attracted in part by the traffic generated at the junction of the Lancaster Turnpike and several lesser long-distance roads converging at the Schuylkill ferry, and later, at the bridges which replaced it. River traffic caused boat builders, chandlers, and other craftsmen to locate in the village too, and the combined road and river trade supported several inns. As wealthy families settled the West Philadelphia uplands, the villagers found new occupations, especially the unskilled laborers who learned that house builders and newly arrived families needed strong backs. Canal- and railroad-building enterprises fueled the growth of the village, chiefly by making possible small-scale riverfront manufacturing and transshipment businesses, especially coal docks.[11] In 1844, Fisher cannily fathomed the meaning of village growth. In describing Powelton, the magnificent country seat of John Hare Powel "in a fine park timbered with noble old woods," the diarist concluded that the estate stood in the wrong place. "If it were 10 miles from town it would be a delightful residence, but it looks on the coal wharves and mass of brick buildings on the other side of the river & is so near the city that it is constantly liable to trespass & intrusion."[12] Thirty years after Hamilton's death, less than a year after what was left of The Woodlands became a cemetery, West Philadelphia displayed all the bright and shattered dreams of antebellum borderland effort.

Essentially, wealthy West Philadelphia landowners early established a development pattern that eventually transformed the innermost borderland landscape everywhere in the pre-Civil War eastern United States. Holders of large estates subdivided their property two ways, laying out large lots for prestigious houses facing main streets, and creating on side streets and along service alleys, especially near existing villages, semi-detached and row houses for far less wealthy buyers anxious to savor something of upper-class aura. Consider the activities of two partners, a tile manufacturer named Samuel A. Harrison and an attorney and West Philadelphia landowner, Nathaniel B. Browne. In 1851 the men hired the noted architect Samuel Sloan, designer of the West Philadelphia mansions for industrialists and financiers, to build a row of modest single and twin houses on a dirt road passing only a few farms and several large new country seats. From 1851 to 1856, Sloan built more than twenty houses for the partners, all aimed at omnibus commuters affluent enough to afford sites nearby the estates of the rich. The partners provided quality housing and took up residence in one of their developments, each occupying with his family a single-family house surrounded by single and double houses designed by Sloan. Harrison and Browne simply followed the example of many upper-class West Philadelphia estate-owners-turned-developers, living amongst the middle-class occupants of their speculative enterprises.

Subsequent developers, however, embroidered the pattern Hamilton originated. In the years just following 1868, Annesley R. Govett, a lumber dealer and resident of West Philadelphia, embarked on three projects. On prominent, stylish streets he built brownstone twin-family and row houses; on cross streets he built only row houses, each smaller than those erected on broad thoroughfares. And in mid-block alleys he built tiny row houses, each twelve feet wide by twenty feet deep and opening onto a tiny back yard, intended for laborers and other service workers employed in West Philadelphia. On land he purchased from one of the original buyers of the fragmented Woodlands estate, Govett built decidedly urban housing.

Despite rear-facing bay windows, arched doorways, iron railings, and third-story mansard roofs, the middle-class housing provided almost nothing of the rural bliss Fisher encountered a few years earlier a few miles beyond.[13]

In 1880 West Philadelphia struck visitors as distinctly urban, although graced by many fine, detached houses sitting on large lots. Attorneys and real estate agents, butchers and plumbers, dry goods retailers and carpenters had established offices and shops along one horsecar route, and black and immigrant families lived close by, in cramped row housing. Many parts of West Philadelphia remained wholly upper or middle class, but others displayed a marked integration, or rather confusion, of housing types and social classes, the end result of fast-paced real estate development, the financial panics of 1857 and 1873, and, above all, the horsecars that brought urban form across the hidden river. No longer borderland, yet not wholly part of the urban fabric of Philadelphia east of the river, the district advertised the perils of disorganized real estate subdivision. Only the environs of Chicago surpassed it in confusion.

13 ❧ CHICAGO

"Railroads have been the making of Illinois," marveled Caroline Kirkland, who anonymously published "Illinois in Spring Time," an 1858 *Atlantic Monthly* essay aimed at eastern readers still convinced that log cabins decorated the prairies bordering Lake Michigan. Away from the forests and mountains of the eastern states, railroad travel changed into a magical experience, as the comfortable "steam cars" seemed to glide above the rolling, open grassland, prompting the essayist to ruminate about Arabian flying carpets. In the expanse of prairie, even light and "atmosphere" changed character, delighting the traveler with mirage-like visions. "No Loudon or Downing is invoked for the contriving or beautifying of these villa-residences and this landscape-gardening," Kirkland continued of the "loomings" of structures and spaces in yet unsettled territory. But actual pioneer farms proved almost as attractive as those of light and mist.

"One of the marvels of this marvelous prairiedom . . . is the taste and skill displayed in houses and gardens," Kirkland explained. Despite her expectations, the new farmhouses and vegetable gardens reflected a genuine aesthetic sensibility. She decided that freedom from the onerous task of tree-felling and stump-pulling gave farm families "leisure for reflection and choice as to form." Almost nowhere did she discern the slovenliness characteristic of so much of the eastern rural landscape.

Nearer "the Garden City," the *Atlantic* essayist discovered that "the vicinity of Chicago is all dotted with beautiful villa-residences." In the outer environs of the booming, rapidly changing city, she found another mentality, one dramatically different from the downtown drive for growth. The "substantial excellence" of the stone houses "inspires a feeling that all this prosperity is of no ephemeral character. People do not build such country-houses until they feel settled and secure." Moreover, the environs, the fresh borderlands of the new city, demonstrated a delicate aesthetic sensibility wholly absent from the unpaved city streets and gross business structures. "To drive among them is like turning over a book of architectural drawings,—so great is their variety, and so marked the taste which prevails."

But in the environs of Chicago Kirkland glimpsed—but failed to recognize—

the changing relationship of borderland and city. She failed to connect the beautiful villa-residences with an oddity of Chicago street life. "There is, to the stranger, an appearance of extreme hurry in Chicago, and the streets are very peculiar in not having a lady walking in them," despite the vast crowds there of all sorts of men from immigrants to the "greenist rustic" to gentlemen.[1] In antebellum Chicago, the easterner encountered a new sort of urban existence, one still alien to New York, Boston, Philadelphia, and other older cities. Middle- and upper-class women tended to remain at home in the borderlands; entering the city, on shopping missions for example, meant difficult road travel by carriage or schedule-structured travel by long-distance trains. Mere distance precluded casual walks from home to shop.

Unlike Boston, Philadelphia, and even Cincinnati, Chicago developed almost wholly within the railroad era; eleven separate railroad lines entered the city between 1847 and 1861, running across essentially rural or half-settled territory. Railroad building there prompted an extraordinary, and very long-lived, fascination with subdivision and subdivision speculation. Chicagoans of nearly every income level hoped to prosper by investing in real estate, and many directed their attention—and money—at outlying areas. "Land is the grand topic of conversation in the streets, hotels, and liquor saloons of Chicago," asserted William Hancock in an 1860 book detailing five years of observations. "The columns of the newspapers are crowded with advertisements of 'eligible lots,' and the land agents suspend huge maps in their windows to attract the speculator."[2] The speculators at first concentrated on land crossed by the plank roads constructed between 1848 and 1855 by toll-road companies; about a third of all such land underwent subdivision between 1845 and 1858. Plank roads assured travelers of safe, convenient, and reliable routes from borderland places to downtown; they assured real estate speculators of accessibility to land previously valuable only for agriculture.

Railroad building likewise encouraged acquisition and subdivision of outlying land, but not every railroad line attracted speculators in equal degree. South of Chicago, in the region enjoying the first railroads, speculators moved more slowly than they did a few years later in the west. In many instances, of course, railroads paralleled plank-road routes through land already subdivided. Nevertheless, within five years after the completion of routes west of the city, a fifth of the land crossed by the magical trains that so delighted Caroline Kirkland had been either resold or subdivided or both. Subdivision did not, however, alter the landscape much.

Neither plank roads nor railroads caused individual families to purchase lots in the newly subdivided areas, at least not within the first five to ten years following subdivision. Most of this land lay too far removed from Chicago proper, and speculators intended either to sell their subdivisions whole to other speculators or to wait patiently for residential expansion. As in the borderlands of Philadelphia, only the horsecar sparked large-scale sales of individual lots, and then only near the edges of built-up land. The horsecar lines reaching north, south, and west made daily commuting practical and inexpensive. Between 1864 and 1888, the horse railways of Chicago combined with steam lines to fuel a transformation of the borderlands even more dramatic than that so painstakingly chronicled by Fisher.[3]

North of Chicago developed a borderland of modest houses, not immediately graced by mature trees perhaps, but offering in their shrubs and flowering vines some indication that eastern borderland values had taken deep root in the prairie.

At the beginning of the Civil War perhaps three thousand people lived in the immediate borderland area north of the city; another two thousand lived in the southern environs. As around Boston and other eastern places, some of the borderland residents had little daily contact with the city; some farmed, and some, in the area that became Hyde Park, fished in Lake Michigan. While the Panic of 1857 temporarily slowed the craze for buying and selling borderland acreage, a clear pattern of development had caused journalists to foresee massive changes in the immediate future. In 1854, for example, families involved with the founding of Northwestern University established the town of Evanston north of the city along the Chicago & Milwaukee Railroad, and two years later, a real estate developer who had acquired land south of the city convinced the directors of the Illinois Central to add two stops at his new Hyde Park. "The former verdure-clad prairie now in thousands of little spots teems with humanity," remarked one 1865 newspaperman. A vast, vast settling had begun.[4]

In 1875, only several years after the Great Fire and the national Panic of 1873, J. W. Sheahan grasped the enormous financial and social energy of Chicago and its suburbs. "There is a large portion of the people who do business in Chicago who reside in the suburban towns and villages," who "reach the city and return by railway." For thirty miles north along the lake shore he traced a succession of towns—Evanston, Winnetka, Highland Park, Lake Forest, Waukegan; to the south he noted Hyde Park, a town of some four thousand people, and "in all directions," he concluded, "are rural towns where our people have built residences." In Sheahan's view, the railroad system—and particularly the marketing techniques of reducing or "commuting" ticket prices for regular riders and operating special trains to the outlying communities—made possible the burgeoning growth of borderland living. Between 1869 and 1874, the number of building lots increased by a hundred thousand; Sheahan anticipated a further—and equally astounding—increase in 1875. Almost everyone shared his vision of a prosperous, largely borderland future; one promoter argued that borderland lots are "the natural Savings Bank of a Chicago Man that tries to get ahead." Exactly as Hancock perceived, speculation in lots—from the scale of a 640-acre "section" to that of the 25-by-125-foot lots Sheahan counted so optimistically—entranced people of almost every economic level.[5]

Certainly the Great Fire convinced many Chicagoans to imitate the well-to-do and live away from the commercial-industrial heart of the city. With an unparalleled rapacity, fire consumed the downtown in 1871, destroying not only businesses but houses as well, proving the accuracy of Adams' long past predictions concerning wooden Boston. Chicago rebounded quickly from the fire, but the inferno accelerated borderland growth. First, many industries remained in the temporary borderland locations their owners found immediately after the fire. Cheaper land, convenient rail access, and room for future expansion made away-from-center situations attractive to many manufacturers. Second, a strict new fire prevention ordinance forbidding frame houses forced many poorer Chicagoans to buy lots outside city limits. One anonymous *Lakeside Monthly* commentator, in an

1872 article entitled "The Effect of the Fire upon Real Estate," clearly perceived the rearrangement of property types. "Chicago property now stands better classified, and its future more distinctly marked, than could have been possible before the fire." In particular, the shift of manufacturing enterprises to a fringe industrial zone heralded extensive building of houses for workingmen and their families. The vast, subdivided but unbuilt borderland region included "an amplitude of area that postpones the future, when the thrifty mechanic will be unable to purchase a cheap lot." Manufacturing relocation would not only free downtown land for commercial building, it would terminate the tenement problem. "There is an aversion among our industrial classes to herd in tenement premises," the essayist concluded hopefully, "and this will secure to the great main quarters of the city an aspect peculiar to themselves—distinct households in place of closely ranged and packed factory tenements." In the eyes of many, especially the moneyed holders of prime downtown real estate, the fire brought only good.

Jefferson Township, for instance, changed rapidly in the years following the Great Fire. The thirty-six-square-mile township, just northwest of the city, remained chiefly agricultural from its settlement in the 1830s until the late 1860s. Its farmers brought garden and dairy produce, potatoes, corn, oats, and hay into city markets, and as late as 1850, 110 of its 115 families farmed. Once the Chicago and North Western Railway crossed Jefferson Township, however, land values, at least near the right-of-way, soared, and by 1870, when its population had increased from 744 (in 1850) to 1,813, only half its residents farmed. Some worked in a pickle and sauce works and others manufactured fireworks; no longer was Jefferson Township the agrarian community that would have so pleased its namesake.

But the real change emerges only from land-holding records. In 1870, 87 percent of the township's landowners lived outside its borders; subdividers and speculators had acquired control of much of the land. Many nonresident owners held title to very small pieces, probably building lots that they intended to live on at some future time. The coming of the Chicago, Milwaukee, and St. Paul Railroad sparked a shift from potential growth to actual growth, however, and when coupled to the effects of the fire rapidly and irrevocably changed the appearance of the place. Between 1870 and 1880, Jefferson Township underwent a striking metamorphosis. Much of it changed from rural to borderland—and in some areas to urban—and it did so at least five times faster than West Philadelphia.

Horsecar service precipitated change too. After 1874, when the first horsecar line reached the edge of the township, land values skyrocketed. Some real estate that in 1865 sold for under a hundred dollars an acre sold for one to three thousand an acre in the early 1870s, and typical lots in the part of the township closest to Chicago sold for a minimum of four hundred dollars an acre. As in West Philadelphia and Germantown, long-time residents, usually farmers, subdivided and sold their acreage at stupendous profit, and newly arrived gentlemen farmers, discovering the advantages of selling out, prospered mightily too. One gentleman farmer divided his acreage, built a railroad station at his own expense, and soon advertised reasonably priced houses in Irving Park, a brand-new place graced with commuter trains every thirty minutes, seven-cent fares, and situated only twenty minutes from downtown depots. Just southwest, a banker subdivided a small area, erected "twenty-one exactly similar houses," and called their location Avondale. An eighty-acre parcel that remained a cornfield until 1870 sold for two hundred thousand dollars that year; its new owners divided it into sixteen blocks and prospered.

Much of the 1870s profit occurred in a time of financial panic and depression; indeed, economic crisis spurred many Chicago families to consider buying a tiny frame house in some part of Jefferson Township. In 1877, for example, several Chicago savings banks failed; real estate salesmen emphasized the security of land-owning against the fragility of banks. "People of moderate means, who disregarded the real value of money until the late financial strigency came on," opined one contributor to the December 13, 1873, issue of the Chicago *Real Estate and Building Journal,* "are beginning to see the necessity of owning their homes, and are making every possible effort to secure that end." Chicago families suffered two awakenings in the early 1870s, one by fire and one by financial catastrophe. Not surprisingly, a snug house on a tiny lot in Jefferson Township appeared to many as a relatively safe refuge.

By 1880, however, Jefferson Township no longer remotely resembled a homogenous agrarian community. It had splintered into half a dozen distinct places, all defying precise description. At the far edge of the township lived some farmers, still in rural surroundings, still outside the jurisdiction of the five communities incorporated as self-governing villages. Jefferson and Bowmanville, the municipalities farthest from Chicago, included some working farms, but although some residents worked in a wagon-making firm and a pickling factory, most men commuted to Chicago. Nearer Chicago, in fact only four miles from the city center, Humboldt and Maplewood revealed much less of their agrarian past; workingmen and their families comprised most of the Humboldt population. Humboldt, much of which a German-American building society developed for its members, offered lots only one-ninth of an acre in area. Irving Park, the fifth village, retained some traces of its gentleman-farmer origins and remained a haven of upper-middle-class families; more than half of its heads of household did nonmanual work, and many commuted daily to Chicago. Humboldt houses, simple frame structures, sold for about three thousand dollars; houses in Irving Park, where the gentleman-farmer-turned-developer still lived, went for between three and twenty thousand, but most of them, with seven to ten rooms, brought from three to six thousand dollars. Marble fireplaces, artesian wells, and other amenities combined with the security of a good address to keep prices stable. As in the environs of Philadelphia, a mix of house types and land uses characterized the once uniform township.

Unlike West Philadelphia, however, Jefferson Township residents remained deeply committed to single-family houses; and industry, not multifamily housing, accomplished the transformation of the region from borderland to urban. While many large pieces of land lay vacant for years after 1880, property adjoining railroads shifted to manufacturing uses. Factories producing brick, steel wheels, furnaces, and a wealth of other products spawned around them clusters of single-family "workingmen's cottages." Such houses, often only eighteen by twenty-eight feet and containing kitchen, parlor, and two bedrooms, cost about six hundred dollars. Jammed side-by-side on tiny lots, they mocked the borderland ideal of gardens and picturesque virtue, let alone the wishes of fire insurance companies. In time, as manufacturing enterprises expanded and land values rose ever higher, apartment housing replaced the cottages. But until the turn of the century, the ideal of detached houses—buttressed by fervent hopes for physical and financial security—shaped the built form of much of the township.[6]

In 1873 *The Chicago Times* published a lengthy supplement entitled "Our Suburbs: A Resume of Their Origins." Reprinted as a pamphlet later that year, the document presages Everett Chamberlin's 1874 tome, *Chicago and Its Suburbs.* Together the pamphlet and the lavishly illustrated book demonstrate a boundless optimism, offering a vision of metropolitan Chicago stretching even into the provinces of British North America and knit together by a "pneumatic tubular railroad." *Our Suburbs* piles detail upon detail, becoming by its conclusion a subtle advertising brochure for the real estate agents "kept busy from morning till night explaining subdivisions, answering questions regarding railroad facilities, the water supply, educational advantages, and such other points as the prospective ruralist would naturally take into consideration." Its descriptions of one community after another eventually grow formulaic; the mention of Lake View, for example, might describe any number of railroad-reached places: "church, academy, and large brick schoolhouse—an energetic and thriving neighborhood—just the place for parents looking for a healthy and accessible suburban locality wherein to rear and educate their children." But in briefly emphasizing the importance of the railroad links between Chicago and the places "considered more salubrious locations," the vitality of new religious congregations engaged in erecting houses of worship, the funds lavished on schoolhouses, and the wonders of well-drained land and brick foundations in promoting family hygiene, the pamphlet published by a city newspaper indirectly condemns the immense place deserted every evening by businessmen whose "stores, warehouses, elevators, and offices are here."[7]

A year later, Chamberlin attempted to demonstrate the essential wholeness of the Chicago region, arguing that the city and its surrounding communities formed a single entity best understood by businessmen. One of the very first studies of a metropolitan region employing statistics, *Chicago and Its Suburbs* is more than post-conflagration boosterism, for its author admits an unnerving development in land sales. Midway in the volume, he concludes that the new building code mandated by the fire prevention ordinance has produced a "chronic dullness in the market for moderately choice lots" inside city limits. "It has made the market for much semi-genteel property very slow ever since its passage," he determines, and "has acted decidedly in favor of suburban localities." Chamberlin's analysis becomes remarkably acute at this point, shifting away from mere numbers to a discussion of populations and tastes difficult to quantify. "Professional men, clerks, and others of moderate income but whose tastes rise above rows of cheap cottages, have been attracted in great numbers," he argues in a sentence worthy of scrutiny.[8] By *profes-*

sional men, Chamberlin evidently means salaried employees of large firms as well as middle-class, self-employed experts like attorneys; *clerks* apparently designates white-collar, upper-working-class heads of families able to pay railroad commuting rates. Rows of cheap cottages repel both types of man, but neither group is financially able to build brick houses—semi-genteel property—on lots within the area covered by the new building code. What Chamberlin implies is of enormous importance in any interpretation of urban and suburban built form, and especially in understanding not only the late-nineteenth-century appearance of borderland Chicago, but the very structure of his book.

Many Chicago families might have remained city residents had they been able to afford first-class—or even second-class—urban houses in neighborhoods likely to remain pleasantly residential. Deprived of such opportunity by the tremendous demand for housing caused by the growth of the city and accelerated by the fire and by speculator manipulation, they looked to borderland areas for relief. But not all borderland locations satisfied their desires. Once they determined to leave the city, they wanted what Downing and so many other authors had for so long described. However vague that description, places—like Humboldt—just beyond the city limits, places of tiny wood houses jammed together, simply missed the mark. By the mid-1870s, such places existed in the minds of many Chicagoans as urban fragments not yet attached to the city proper, as working-class neighborhoods offering neither mid-quality—what Chamberlin calls *semi-genteel*—urban houses nor mid-quality borderland pleasures like lawns, pear trees, and vegetable gardens. In the last quarter of the nineteenth century, thousands of Chicago families readjusted their dreams, skipping over the innermost ring of largely residential places and fixing their sights on outer areas. Chamberlin understood the reorientation. His book devotes almost no space to working-class communities like Humboldt—which he says ought to be incorporated into the city because its "inhabitants are anxious to have the gas and water improvements"—and instead deals at length with distant borderland Edens in which Country ideology and romantic perfectionism take physical form.[9]

In such Edens businessmen found peace, or at least temporary diversion from urban money-making, as well as safety from the upheavals of urban growth. Within city limits only the very rich could afford the ostentatious mansions of North Dearborn or Clark streets, and even those citadels of domestic accomplishment seemed likely to fall before the continuous encroachment of downtown, perhaps in summer, when their owners had left for rural estates. What Chamberlin discerns as "the *centrifugal force* of business in Chicago" overwhelmed many residential avenues. "The former residences of the aristocracy still remain," he notes of Wabash Avenue, "some of them still occupied as shops, but the most of them given over to that close follower-up of retreating aristocracy, the genteel boarding house keeper." And even as the central business district swallowed the wealthiest residential neighborhoods, the burgeoning industrial zones athwart the railroads entering the city limits swallowed the inner municipalities, converting many into barracks for thousands of industrial workers. Consider the "Iron-workers' Addition to South

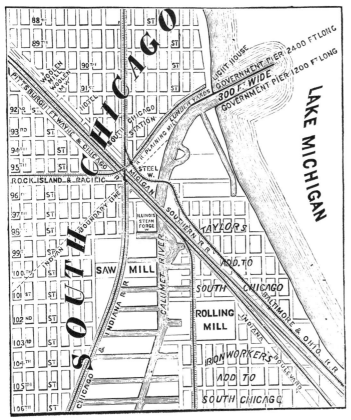

Along the shore north of the city evolved a carefully wrought borderland landscape in which businessmen found solace and gentle exercise and women found relief from urban frenzy.

South of the city, especially near the shore of Lake Michigan, heavy manufacturing and industrial housing sprawled around the fledgling borderland settlements and changed the entire character of a region.

Chicago," a place of a thousand houses intended by the Silicon Steel Company as the home of its workers. The very scale of such nearly instant neighborhoods at the corporate limits of the city combined with the complexity of their industrial hearts to defy description, but nothing about them struck Chamberlin and other observers as rural or traditionally picturesque. Unwittingly, therefore, Chamberlin discovered the reason behind the scarcity of quality urban housing. Even as the downtown swallowed the houses of the rich and the middle class, the fringe industrial zones stretched into and around the innermost residential neighborhoods and the oldest residential municipalities, walling them off from the more distant borderland places *Chicago and Its Suburbs* so lavishly praises.

Chamberlin's lengthy descriptions of Evanston, Lake View, Wilmette, Winnetka, Riverside, and other "picturesque" places, most illustrated with engravings of houses and lush lawns seemingly lifted straight from *The Horticulturist* or other borderland publications, eventually wear thin.[10] Essentially as formulaic as any in *Our Suburbs,* they emphasize the ecclesiastical and educational "advantages," the fine houses, grounds, and graded roads, and above all, the startling advances in real estate prices stemming from careful, suitable improvements like sewers and convenient commuter train schedules, and from natural advantages like fine vistas and attractive forest cover. Chamberlin undoubtedly knew that the northern borderlands had already received careful attention a year earlier in *North Chicago: Its Advantages, Resources, and Probable Future,* a document that not only made explicit the wonderful attractions of the northern borderlands but implicitly suggested the perils of rusticating south of the city.

"It would be a new revelation to many of the citizens of Chicago to visit these spots and see the surprising variety of scenery so near by, and a still greater surprise, no doubt, to observe how quietly this region has become occupied by the country seats of the wealthy and cultivated," muses the author of *North Chicago* early in his booklet. North of the city the land rises, becoming a "romantic wildness" in the suburbs of Lake Forest and Highland Park, and everywhere exhibiting a perfectly picturesque roughness of forest trees, small hills and ravines, and eminences offering views of Lake Michigan. "Over the ground a cultivated taste has spread all the rich variety of horticulture and floriculture that may be conceived of," Henry C. Johnson continues, extolling the delights of "grounds varying in extent from one to five or ten acres."[11] The rising ground provides a suitable nickname for the group of towns—"The Highlands of Chicago"—and becomes a metaphor for the elevated classes responsible for the improvement of fine natural topography and vegetation. In the highlands, the women and children of the heights gazed about at healthful ordered nature and, when they chose, at the far-off city smoking beyond less fortunate residential districts.

Implicit in the lavish descriptions of the northern borderland lies a warning about the "south side," the vast area of flatness, marshes, and booming industrial plants. With only a few exceptions, southern borderland districts rapidly evolved into quasicompany towns or semi-industrial neighborhoods. The level topography and lakeshore access attracted industrialists, and land speculators quickly learned the profits involved in developing single-family residential neighborhoods for workers in nearby factories. Astute visitors immediately realized the predestined future. "South Chicago is a place of great expectations," noted J. W. Sheahan, writing in *Scribner's Monthly* in 1875. "It has a harbor, and the owners look forward to the time when it will be a great manufacturing center, and the grain warehouses will all be transferred thither."[12] Sheahan grasped the implications of south side development: the city proper kept expanding by annexing adjacent territory, and clearly the southern borderlands lay in the path of annexation. Maximization of profit, not notions of picturesque beauty, guided the subdividers of borderland areas south of Chicago. Rectilinear street grids, narrow lots, tiny houses jammed against one another became the norm. And writers like Chamberlin and Johnson discerned the long-term effect. In the borderlands of Chicago, thousands of people understood what Fisher glimpsed in West Philadelphia. Much of what agents advertised as borderland appeared nothing more—and sometimes less—than urban. By the 1890s, as the southern reaches of the city became a vast industrial zone crossed by thousands of trains, railroad passengers no longer admired the wildflowers and prairie homes beyond their windows. Instead they marveled at the immense steel mills, grain elevators, and factories that overpowered the rows upon rows of single-family houses that made up the southern edge of Chicago.[13]

Chamberlin saw no future for Chicago residents other than life in the borderlands, and he decided that even workingmen's families would move, and soon. "The rapidity with which Chicago workers are now flocking into the suburbs to live" convinced him that "the fact is thoroughly established that ninety-nine Chicago families in every hundred will go an hour's ride into the country, or toward the country, rather than live under or over another family, as the average New Yorker or Parisian does." Cheaper train fares and new forms of transportation would accelerate the migration of mill and factory workers, he determined, but so also would rising expectations of elbow room. "Turned loose in the country, where land is plenty and cheap," the newcomers "will not lose sight of the principal object of their going outside of the crowded city, viz.: plenty of room and the pure air, the freedom and the 'chance to grow,' which come with this boon." Some families will "put up" with a single lot, but most will "indulge" in one or more acres, requiring the settling of some 125 square miles of borderland territory between 1873 and 1883.[14] However optimistic Chamberlin's statistics, however colored by real estate boosterism, *Chicago and Its Suburbs* points at the growing attachment to borderland living among factory-worker families, families often unable to afford it, but hoping—and expecting—to afford it someday. Chamberlin understood, however vaguely, the growing, deepening understanding in Chicago that every family has a *right* to borderland space, a right to live away from South Chicago, a right to own a cottage almost magically beautiful, a right to the mysterious "chance to grow" unavailable in the city they expected to leave.

George Templeton Strong remembered Brooklyn as it had been, a village surrounded by farms, a place as nonurban as he could imagine.

Sunshine and spring lured George Tem-
pleton Strong from his urban responsibilities on April 10, 1858. The thirty-eight-
year-old New York City businessman wandered with a friend out to the borderlands, or where the borderlands once had been, "among the remote regions of
Southern Brooklyn, near Gowanus and the place where was of old the Penny
Bridge." Like Nathaniel Willis perhaps, Strong found the inner city unfit for the
splendid weather, and rather than forcing down his heart and struggling onward
with business, he sought fresh air and picturesque views. His walk failed. "The
growth of that region is marvelous," he confided to his journal. "A great city has
been built there within my memory. The compact miles of monotonous, ephemeral
houses which one overlooks from the Greenwood Cemetery ridge impress me as
does some great reef half bare at low tide and dense with barnacles." But Strong did
not dismiss the vast residential enclave as unimportant in the larger scheme of
things. "Each is a *home*," he mused, each with its "domestic history and prospects,"
and "each is an epitome of human life within each shabby domicile."[1] Brooklyn had
indeed grown, grown far, far beyond the wildest expectations—or fears—of the
first pioneer commuters riding twice daily the Brooklyn ferry that linked city and
borderland. And in the eyes of Strong, who loved, most of the time, the glamor of
Manhattan, the immense growth beyond the river seemed unfit, shabby even
though new, an immense failure.

Sidney Fisher glimpsed the reason for the failure on a long pleasure trip to two
country estates at Geneseo, New York. He delighted in the immense new house of
one of his friends, situated in a private "park" of four hundred acres with an
extensive view of the lowlands beneath the ridge, and he marveled still more at the
house of another, "large, old-fashioned, of frame painted white, in cottage style,
with deep piazzas" and other virtuous charms, chief among them a "livable home-
like look." His friends had both carefully shut off the approach of the village of
Geneseo, however, one by buying up "several lots on each side of the road between
his wall and the street," the other by acquiring two lots, each about four or five
acres, on either side of the road leading away from the village. In 1848, Geneseo was

a typical village, a string of structures running half a mile along both sides of the street, a place to be kept at a distance by wealthy adherents to the borderland credo of Downing, Willis, and others. "At any little village in New York, even at Geneseo, are well-stored shops and artisans in abundance who can minister to the wants not merely of comfort, but of elegant refinement," Fisher wrote, concluding his long diary entry in a rambling, wondering way. "The canal brings everything from New York. They can build you a house with every modern convenience and improvement, make every sort of carriage and harness, paint, paper, and furnish in excellent style almost anything that can be got in town."[2] Mid-nineteenth-century borderland life, indeed even the leisured rural life Susan Cooper extolled, required no sacrifice of urban refinement, for city delights might be purchased in any village touched by railroad tracks. Refinement originated in the desires of educated people, families guided by horticultural and other periodicals, perhaps, or by the example of acquaintances, not in the values of villagers. But although the materials of refined taste could be purchased in villages, from village retailers and craftsmen fully conversant with them, they did not reshape village architecture and layout. The very shopkeeper who sold the neutral house paints called for by Downing painted his own house a glaring white. The same carpenter who erected asymetrical houses for borderland clients built a box for his family. Clearly Brooklyn might have grown differently, just as West Philadelphia or the innermost suburbs of Chicago might have evolved differently, for the information and raw materials existed, even in villages like Geneseo, where people could purchase—often at the same price— things different from those pronounced shabby by Strong and Fisher.

Horsecar and (in the 1880s and 1890s) streetcar "suburbs" deserve another designation, for suburbs they were not, except in fitful pipedreams. In the first years, when speculators outside Philadelphia, Chicago, and other cities bought farms and gentlemen's estates, subdivided them into grids of unpaved streets and rectangular lots often only thirty by ninety feet, and enticed city governments to lay water and sewer lines, the landscape scarcely changed. Indeed, even as the first families moved into the one- and two-family frame houses, the vast areas still in agriculture or subdivided but still unbuilt strengthened the illusion of country. But as Chamberlin so clearly perceived in his study of Chicago and its environs (what he so precisely designated *suburbs*), fate predestined the innermost subdivisions to become urban residential neighborhoods. At the edge of every major city, mid-nineteenth-century land speculators thrust an essentially urban fabric over hitherto borderland landscape. Above all, rectilinear street patterns—adopted not only for ease of surveying and for maximizing the number of square or rectangular lots, but because subdividers envisioned their effort as urban in an age that equated urbanity with straightness—announced the reaching forth of urban form.[3] The first come-outers delighted in the long views from the most desirable hilltop locations, looking out over truck farms, harbors, and rivers—and sometimes over noxious industries banished by city governments into the environs—wholly unaware that houses-to-be on the parallel streets would close off vistas forever. Domestic architecture, too, whispered of deep-rooted urban visions. Many speculators erected identical houses on the narrow lots, marching them down the rectilinear streets of West Philadelphia or Humboldt or Brooklyn. Usually the houses stood apart from each other, but the scattered appearance of row housing, brick-built and in all features identical with that constructed far nearer city centers, accented the tacit assumption of urbanity. Miniscule grounds, front lawns extending three feet from the sidewalk (or sidewalk-to-be), back yards ten by thirty or forty feet, with luck receiving enough sunshine for a few flowers, vegetables, and perhaps an apple tree, without luck forever in partial shade, mocked the directives of horticultural societies and periodicals.[4] And scattered everywhere, multiple-family housing started families wondering.

Apartment houses vexed American understanding well past the turn of the century, and their spread into subdivisions of one- and two-family houses did not escape unnoticed, although it attracted less inquiry than the gradual proliferation of "French flats" near downtown areas—the precedent-wrenching proliferation that informs so much of William Dean Howells' 1889 novel, *A Hazard of New Fortunes*. Brooklyn prompted Strong to think of barnacles. Most Manhattan housing prompted one 1874 *Scribner's Monthly* author to compare New Yorkers to "hermit crabs, in other creatures' shells, suiting their lives to dwellings that do not fit them." In the opinion of the essayist, thousands of families unable to find decent housing "are driven to the surrounding country to build up Jersey and all the regions round about," largely because speculator carpenters and masons erect only "rows of houses as uniform in style and finish as if made by machinery, and as uniformly unsuited to the needs of their expected occupants." Far too expensive and far too large for increasingly smaller middle-class families, the four- and five-story row-houses lead to orgies of subletting that turn homeowners into boarding-house keepers, wives into drudges, and children into the streets for privacy—and turn single people, newlyweds, and childless couples into hermit crabs like the Marches of Howells' novel, who search desperately for a sensible flat like those they remembered from "their European days." The essayist argues that all sorts of ills originate from the flight of middle-class families to the frame houses of Brooklyn and other nearby places; their departure deprives the city of intelligent, honest, industrious voters, for example, encouraging the political corruption that forces away still more virtuous families. But many ills befall the departing, he asserts, most of whom feel the deprivation of "the privileges of recreation, social life, and culture which concentration makes possible," a deprivation unmitigated by the delights of genuine borderland life. In arguing that "the doubtful advantages of the suburbs are rather for those whose shorter hours of business allow them time to go and come without trespassing too much on the hours of rest," the author of "New Homes of New York" apparently has in mind places like Brooklyn, not the borderlands of Westchester. The author makes a strong case for intelligently designed, well-built apartments for working- and middle-class families and attacks the "British" prejudice against living over or under another family.[5] The anonymous essayist discerns in New York exactly what Chamberlin discovers in Chicago: middle-class and better-off working-class families move to the residential rings—or to the borderlands—not always by choice but often by necessity, to find decent, affordable shelter, not to enjoy country pleasures.

In the fringe areas at the edges of the urban fabric, apartment housing at first appeared like row housing, here and there, without seeming pattern. Since hundreds and sometimes thousands of speculators developed the regions abutting the legal limits of cities, building proceeded haphazardly. Outside Boston, for example, subdividers in financial difficulty or anxious to finish selling a set of lots often subdivided one or two lots into very tiny plots fit only for three-family houses, the wooden "three-deckers" known across the industrial northeast. The tall, closely ranked buildings had an immediate visual impact, dwarfing nearby trees, blocking the views that remained, shading adjacent yards and streets, and imposing an overwhelming, very urban massing on the larger arrangement of houses. Until the last years of the nineteenth century, families settling in the new neighborhoods accepted the three-family structures, possibly because multi-family buildings were relatively few. As land prices rose and three-deckers and other multiple-family housing became far more prevalent, however, purchasers of single-family houses in new subdivisions insisted on legal protection against them. Developers offered restrictive covenants assuring purchasers that no such housing, or nuisances like saloons, would be erected. Such covenants speak volumes about the new recognition of property values and urban context. They tell, too, of concerns about privacy, and they reveal the incredible spread of industrial and commercial enterprise into urban residential areas. But most of all, they speak of a growing appreciation of country pleasures—including the simple pleasure of viewing picturesque scenery. As housing or stores appeared on every vacant lot, as every supposedly unbuildable tract sprouted structures, as rising prices prompted developers to erect apartment houses, inhabitants of the new residential districts agitated for controls to growth, for "zoning."[6] While urban in origin and still city-minded enough to call for annexation to adjacent cities with their excellent public schools, fire and police protection, and parks, these people had enjoyed the remnants of country just long enough to notice the obvious detriments of tall, multiple-family structures, of straight streets that limited views, of fragments of yard too small for children's play.

The horsecar and especially the electric streetcar lines that linked the residential neighborhoods to downtown ran outward too, easily whisking inhabitants away to as yet "undeveloped" or "unimproved" country, making them painfully aware that they lived without the joys of genuine city life and without the pleasures of borderland residence. In the new residential zones that characterized most U.S. cities by 1900, people called the electric vehicles *streetcars,* for they clanged along paved streets running into the hearts of cities, or at least to ferry landings or bridge terminals opening on downtowns. Beyond the new residential zones, in the countryside not yet acquired by speculators and subdivided by capital-poor, urban-minded developers, Americans called the cars *trolleys* and thought of them differently. Away from the constrictions of pedestrian and dray traffic and freed from public rights-of-way, the silent cars hummed along, linking village with village, farm

In its first moments, the urban residential ring struck many prospective purchasers as positively borderland-like.

Once developers erected rows of houses, the first families arrived in the residential rings were subjected to restricted views, much street traffic, and a dozen other decidedly urban unpleasantries.

William Dean Howells and others remarked not only the crowded horsecars and, later, electric cars serving the residential ring, but the difficulties confronted by women riders in particular.

with farm, and—importantly—connecting inhabitants of the new residential zones with open country. Traction companies extended their radial and circumferential lines into sparsely inhabited regions partly to forestall competition from other firms and partly in expectation of eventual traffic, when the country "grew up." Most cars leaving downtown at the end of the day terminated at the outer edge of some new residential zone, often only six miles or so from their points of origin; the motorman stopped his car, the conductor reversed the trolley poles, and the car began cruising cityward again. The few cars which ventured beyond, however, especially on summer evenings, carried residential-zone pleasure riders enjoying afterdinner travels. On summer weekends, the cars carried families on picnics, in search of farm-fresh vegetables, on long, silent, swift rides to escape the heat, on excursions to view the "country seats" or "estates" of families residing in the borderlands.[7] Very cheap fares and reasonably frequent service educated the riders in remarkable ways.

So also did a growing number of journalists, acute observers like Henry A. Beers, who scorned the "limbo or ragged edge" that was neither city nor country. His 1894 *Suburban Pastoral* focuses on the city fringes of chemical and oil works, glue and soap factories, railroad shops and roundhouses, tenement blocks and failing farms, fringes like Chicago's south side. "Land, which was lately sold by the acre, is now offered by the foot front," he notes, "and no piece of real estate is quite sure whether it is still part of an old field or has become a building lot." Developers have begun marking out the widening of country roads into "boulevards"; a row of street lights straggles across the fields; far off, a horsecar, the "moving outpost of civilization," carries a solitary fare past "ragweed and daisies" to the end of the line. Beers, and many of his contemporaries, found much to ponder in limbo: "a smart new corner grocery in red brick," "rows of little new wooden houses" facing across the new street "a decayed farmhouse" bereft of all but a few cows grazing in fields crossed by the paths of men seeking shortcuts to car lines.[8] Picturesque landscape lay beyond the city-to-be space, so puzzling to analyze in its half-empty complexity, its utter rawness.

George Templeton Strong could not quite identify the source of his displeasure with Brooklyn; words like *monotonous* and *shabby* strike oddly, given the machine-made appearance of so many Manhattan residential streets and the gross shabbiness of much of the city. Of course, Strong remembered the vanished borderland countryside of Brooklyn, and that memory surely shaped his 1858 springtime conclusions. In a similar way, the trolley-riding residents of the streetcar residential zones experienced the borderlands a few miles from their closely packed houses. Brooklyn and the other areas compared badly with both the few fine urban residential neighborhoods and the many borderland regions. They compared badly because they sprawled like immense villages. Residential zones not only flowed outward from cities. As Fisher and Chamberlin observed, one of the great lessons in interpreting the growth of the Philadelphia and Chicago zones lay in understanding the significance of nearby borderland villages and the main roads leading to them from downtown. Even as subdividers marked off land just beyond city limits, others cut up land

Electric streetcars brought much traffic along major streets crossing the residential rings, in time creating strips of commercial development that defied precise designation.

The remnants of a shattered glass negative reveal the disorder that had evolved along one streetcar line in the Boston residential ring by 1900, a disorder characterized by dilapidated buildings half-adapted to new uses, a web of electric wires, and a lack of street trees.

New streets laid out in Parallelogram P[
opened into country, or so the first visito[
thought.

In the first years of the new century,
observers other than H. A. Caparn
discerned the comedy and desperation
apparent in Parallelogram-Park-like real
estate developments. This 1906 Life
cartoon, "From Our Airship," depicts th[
near chaos around the railroad station.

around the nearest villages, certain that horsecar or streetcar lines would arrive immediately. Sometimes the confidence of speculators bordered on the ludicrous; in 1880, one builder was so certain of instant growth near the village of Meeting House Hill in Dorchester, a few miles outside Boston, that he erected thirty-five brick rowhouses. Years passed before the neighborhood filled with single-family frame houses.[9] But the double growth, outward from city limits and from village edges, confirmed the long-term national dislike of village form; the speculators so imbued with city ideas did everything on a village scale. The straight, treeless streets, narrow lots, and frame houses jammed together indiscriminately with manufacturing enterprises derived from the American village as much as from the mid-nineteenth-century industrial city. A narrow street of perhaps fourteen frame houses standing isolated in a recently subdivided farm, meeting at right angles a wider road along which passed an occasional horsecar or streetcar, what else could such a construct screech to the educated reader of *The Horticulturist* or Willis' *Rural Letters* or *Country Life* or *Countryside* than "village"?

Surely the lack of trees confirmed the views of ramblers like Strong. For two decades after the speculators left, the subdivided fields and meadows often boasted few or no trees. Frame houses thrust upward everywhere, their massing unrelieved by towering oaks or elms and the streets they faced unshaded by poplars or maples. Developers did sometimes set out saplings along the straight residential streets, but the puny specimens did little to soothe the irritated sensibilities of visitors clearly aware of picturesque aesthetics and certain that the residential neighborhoods lacked all borderland beauty. Indeed, row housing might have struck visitors as more gentle on the eye, since many urban residential streets lacked trees. But detached, wooden houses without trees? Such structures existed only in villages.

In 1906 one magazine contributor summed up three decades of barnacle building. "Parallelogram Park—Suburban Life by the Square Mile" indicts a "suburban, cheap-residence park" of forty- by eighty-foot houselots facing a grid of narrow, straight streets running away from a road traversed by electric cars. "It is cheap with the cheapness of dullness, ignorance and indifference," H. A. Caparn told his *Craftsman* readers, a place "neither city nor country, nor can it ever supply the place of either." Caparn condemns the streets too narrow for traffic and the neighborhood's distance "from the center of things" as distinctly un-urban characteristics, but he also lambasts the lack of privacy. Urban row housing and urban manners offered greater family and individual privacy than this place of detached houses "huddled together on mean little lots all the same size and shape, all running the same way, so that neighbors can almost shake hands out of opposite windows." After weighing the place against the standards of urban and rural beauty and finding it wanting, however, Caparn makes a crucial discovery. "It can not even be suburban," he continues in a passage defining his terms with precision, "for it is too like a stunted town and has almost nothing essential of the country." He continues by describing the spatial characteristics of genuine suburbs as they appear to a commuting man—"flexible lines and surfaces, an air of rest and freedom, a respite from the tyrannical rectangularity of the street and the monotony of the windows of

As builders erected the first houses in Parallelogram Park thoughtful visitors noticed the alarming downgrading of lots and the dikelike sidewalks bordering sunken roads.

Parallelogram Park residents soon realized that little of country beauty dignified their new community: houses nearly touched each other, and housewives enjoyed no outdoor privacy at all.

his factory or office"—and stresses the importance of large lots. A back yard ought to allow for a clothesline, a "real" vegetable garden, flowers, and father–children play. Urban amenities—"sewers, electric light, and city water"—in comparison are far, far less significant in raising profits for land developers, he asserts, than is outdoor private space. Parallelogram Park might have been different, and more profitable to its developers, he argues, if the lots covered more space. Larger lots would increase block size and reduce the number of intersections and road footage, thus diminishing initial outlays for water and sewer mains. Caparn figures and sketches convincingly enough, suggesting how a better rectilinear residential neighborhood might be laid out and built at the same cost, but he concludes as pessimistically as the *Harper's Monthly* editor who wondered at rectilinear street layout sixty years before. Having heard about a large tract of land surveyed into lots so tiny that purchasers had to acquire two in order to erect houses, lots "which have sold like soda water in July at exorbitant prices," he doubts the power of magazine articles to overcome the effect of "clever and lavish advertising" on the minds of city residents desperate for quality, single-family housing and offered few choices by developers.[10] Caparn, like Strong and Fisher before him, knew the incredible spread of the village-like places. But unlike his predecessors, Caparn also knew the power of photography, and he illustrates his article with incredibly detailed, haunting photographs of muddy streets edged with plank sidewalks and saplings, of gaunt utility poles leaning over snow-covered lawns, of the desperate appropriation of unbuilt lots as temporary back yards, of housewives separated by clothes poles and ten feet of uneven grass. More than his prose, the images portray a sort of gigantic village of barnacle-like houses and wretchedly straight streets, a place absent not only from the old borderland literature but from the emerging one of "real" suburbs and "real" suburban life.

IV Borderland Life & Popular Literature

Cozzens understood the perplexity with which mid-nineteenth-century borderers often confronted farm animals, and he knew particularly clearly farm animals' penchant for coming indoors.

VISIONS

In 1906, Frederick Coburn discarded nine-
teenth-century notions of city and urged World Today readers to discover the transformations wrought by railroad, trolley line, mass-circulation newspaper advertising,
and telephone. His "Five-Hundred-Mile City" not only identifies beyond doubt a vast
new concurbation stretching between New York City and Boston, it also discerns the
awesome implications of borderland growth.

Beyond the village-like residential rings surrounding most major cities lay the
homes of the railroad commuters, homes not organized about streetcar lines and
speculator-contrived street grids but focused on stations strategically located on steam-
road lines radiating from downtown termini. In the early years of engine-driven flight,
Coburn glimpsed what aeronauts soon unthinkingly accepted; and although he
focused his analysis on the environs of New York City, he nonetheless knew the
national implications of his findings. Soon, he argued heatedly, enormous reaches of
landscape will look like the region from Newark to Boston.

"Commutation books are sold in surprising numbers to Greenport, ninety-five
miles from New York," Coburn writes. "Both sides of Long Island Sound are being
lined with series of well-built suburbs of the metropolis." Unlike many authors of
articles in mass-circulation periodicals, Coburn marshaled "statistical as well as
visual confirmation" of his findings, ferreting out the tendencies recorded by the
Federal census (which showed suburban regions growing at a faster rate than cities)
and buried in railroad-company reports. Moving with a certainty born of turn-of-the-
century faith in statistics, Coburn charts the post-1890 growth of Westchester County
villages, of the three Connecticut counties lying closest to New York City, of the New
Jersey counties lying on railroad routes "between Gotham and the big city between the
Delaware and the Schuylkill," and of areas of Delaware and Maryland formerly
"distinctly rural." Chamberlin and other "boosters" of specific cities had noted the
growth of railroad suburbs, but Coburn reshapes their arguments not only by distinguishing between old, chiefly residential zones—using West Philadelphia as an
example—and the new, distant borderland ones, but also by struggling to define a new
sort of domestic landscape unlike the now-urban residential neighborhoods established
in the 1865 to 1895 horsecar and streetcar period.

"What were formerly distant country towns are gradually filling up with commuters," Coburn asserts, after presenting his statistical evidence. But to define, let alone designate, the character of spatial change accompanying the population shift transcends the power of numerical analysis and finally defeats him. In announcing that "the semi-suburban, semi-rural character which thirty years ago belonged to Brookline, Milton and Medford has lately been acquired by such places as Lincoln, Maynard, North Wilmington, Hingham and Scituate," and offering no before-and-after illustrations, Coburn not only jerks his national readership from the precision of population figures to the vagueness of terms like "semi-suburban" but expects it somehow to know the landscape of Milton, Lincoln, and the other Massachusetts places over a thirty-year period. Confusion, deep-seated and nearly masked by detail, mars the conclusion of his argument.

What is the significance of the immigrant farmers he finds pioneering on "land from which the Yankee agriculturalist can not wrest a living"? Some of the newcomers, whom he identifies as Italians, Poles, Greeks, and Scandinavians, among many other nationalities, hold mill jobs "which are now only forty minutes away by trolley" and work their smallholdings part-time. Others farm full-time, shipping their fruit, poultry, and other produce by interurban railway express, and shop by telephone—their department store merchandise arrives the next day by trolley express. The part-time immigrant farmers, caught up in the same wave of after-work agriculture—usually market gardening or poultry raising—that drew so many native-born working- and middle-class families to the borderlands, occupy space Coburn scarcely describes, although he locates it "ten or twelve miles out of town."

Or what of the year-round summer people he discovers far out along the railroad and trolley lines they once used to reach summer homes? Coburn traces the process of first building, then enlarging a "bungalow or diminutive unplastered cottage," the lengthening "summer season" reaching into November, the growing popularity of winter sports, the spread of quality public schools into the regions once known only for their summertime pleasures, and, not least important, the difficulties of supporting two dwellings in times of economic uncertainty. But about the winterized structures he says almost nothing, implying only that they compare favorably with the best "suburban" architecture and siting.[1] Could closely packed, flimsily built cottages in time comprise a landscape semi-suburban and semi-rural?

Coburn's prescient article unwittingly displays the immense difficulties confronting turn-of-the-century observers of borderland landscape. As Chamberlin knew in the mid-1870s, indeed as Maxwell understood in Cincinnati a decade earlier, numerical data taken from census reports, real estate records, and railroad company statements demonstrated the progress of borderland growth, and offered thoughtful inquirers—and investors—opportunities to discover patterns. But statistics, even the far more accurate and complete statistics of the early 1900s, offered little insight into the visual transformation of the immense regions lying beyond the ring of residential neighborhoods surrounding almost every American city.

Coburn's "Five-Hundred-Mile City" not only thrust to the very center of a gigantic social and spatial transformation. It also heralded the downgrading of visual *analysis as a means of studying that transformation. All the precision of statistics, all the supposed accuracy of statistical extrapolation overwhelmed the dedicated scrutiny of Downing, Fisher, Strong, and other nineteenth-century borderland walkers. After 1900, expert analysis of the borderlands, the places often designated suburbs or metropolitan regions by a growing legion of professionals, depended increasingly on the collection and arrangement of statistics and the making of maps demonstrating differences in household income or property tax rates or average lot sizes. Popular analysis departed from the statistical mode, however, and focused on the most unquantifiable subjects—the coziness of houses, the excitement of gardening, the dignity of church buildings, the relative beauty of trees, and perhaps most importantly, topography. These subjects filled the pages of magazines like* Suburban Life *and* Harper's Monthly, *returning again and again to early-nineteenth-century notions of picturesque beauty, village tawdriness, and domestic virtue, and entrancing the individuals moving beyond the urban residential and industrial zone into commuter country, the domain of the women and children of the heights.*[2]

15 ❧ ADVOCATES

$\mathbf{B}$uilding in the 1880s into a flood of articles, books, and even poetry that nearly overwhelmed publishers in the 1890s and succeeding decades, the literature of the borderland good life mirrored and shaped turn-of-the-century middle-class thinking. In urban newspapers increasingly focused on metropolitan readerships, in general interest magazines and in new, narrowly aimed periodicals like *Country Life* and *Suburban Life,* in short stories and novels, readers discovered not the quantitative description and analysis Coburn favored, but a qualitative, almost lyrical one.

"How could we spare them—our dogs—for are they not part and parcel of the suburban household?" asked Henry Cuyler Bunner in an 1896 collection of his magazine essays entitled *The Suburban Sage: Stray Notes and Comments on His Simple Life.*[1] As a long-term editor of the humor magazine *Puck,* Bunner had had ample opportunity to poke fun at middle-class families moving into the railroad-laced borderlands of New York City, and particularly into northern New Jersey, but he teased gently and carefully. With wit and precision, he examined commuting etiquette, house hunting, lawn making, dog rearing, and a host of other borderland customs, for he took them seriously too. He found his material around his home, the New Jersey borderland Eden of Nutley, and on the trains and ferry boats on which he commuted. Perhaps more than any other writer of his era, Bunner addressed the incredible complexity of life in the borderland places far distant from the limbo-like urban fringes he scorned to label *suburban.*

Bunner wrote during the maturation of a forty-year-old genre, one begun by Alice Cary on the heights above Cincinnati and nurtured by a collection of competent, enthusiastic authors. Frederick S. Cozzens, R. B. Coffin, and William Dean Howells in particular laid the framework embellished by Bunner and his contemporaries. As early as 1855, Cozzens grasped the cultural significance of railroad commuting and borderland living in describing the adventures of a fictional family in the borderlands.

"The Sparrowgrass Papers, or Living in the Country" appeared as a *Putnam's Monthly Magazine* serial. Written in a blend of letter and diary format, and emphasizing spatial description and dialogue over plot, the long series details the adventures of the Sparrowgrasses, an educated, upper-middle-class family tired of the dirt and turmoil of New York City and recently arrived in the borderlands. Most episodes focus on good intentions gone awry. In the first, for example, disorder arrives in the form of unlabeled vegetable seed packets; all the careful garden planning with which the couple intend to occupy an evening vanishes when they recognize their utter inability to identify seeds by sight. Compared with an invasion by pigs, however—"the most villainous looking pigs rooting up" the pea-patch— the seed mix-up pales. The family dog is released to run off the pigs, but instead it drives the "ringleader of the swinish multitude" into the parlor. Thus the Sparrowgrasses learn something of the complexities of borderland life, a life in which they fumble as ludicrously as any bumpkins newly arrived in the city.[2]

The Sparrowgrasses are city people. Cozzens makes plain their total lack of firsthand experience with country things. His series of sketches presents, perhaps for the first time in American literature, a young married couple that knows only city things. "Living in the Country" originated in an immense cultural change. By 1855 New York City sprawled over enough territory that children might grow up wholly unaware of rural Westchester; within twenty years, indeed, Horatio Alger regularly depicted young boys as ignorant of anything beyond the East River and The Battery.[3] Cozzens perhaps exaggerates the restricted childhoods of his hero and heroine, but he explicitly emphasizes their idealistic, almost simplistic attachment to virtuous borderland life. Mr. and Mrs. Sparrowgrass, while inexperienced in life beyond the city, nevertheless know enough of the shadows of urban living to move themselves and their young children away to a place of possible perfection.

In all innocence, the Sparrowgrasses blunder again and again, extricating themselves from one crisis only to stumble into another. The husband buys a riding horse, for "it is a good thing to have a saddle-horse in the country." Aware that his former city life scarcely required a saddle horse—indeed, city traffic makes pleasure riding unpleasant—he dreams of early morning rides along the winding roads beyond his new house, and so acquires a nag from a unscrupulous dealer. The horse tramples the hybrid roses, lima beans, and other plants lucky enough to have survived the pigs, and after Sparrowgrass discovers that the beast is blind in one eye and heaves and stumbles, he rents a carriage to see if the animal is better suited to driving. The pleasant drive through rural Westchester County ends in catastrophe as the horse slips sideways, wrecking the rockaway and frightening Mrs. Sparrowgrass and the children. Badly shaken and more thoughtful, the Sparrowgrasses persevere, failing at raising pears, losing the rowboat rented for a day's riverine pleasure, and yet somehow enjoying each misadventure.[4]

"The Sparrowgrass Papers" rises far above simple humor. Cozzens' narrator, Sparrowgrass himself, grows wiser as the sketches progress, acquiring a balanced view of borderland life. "Thank Heaven for this great privilege, that our little ones go to school in the country," he remarks at the beginning of one later sketch. "Not in the narrow streets of the city; not over the flinty pavements; not amid the crush of crowds, and the din of wheels; but out in the sweet woodlands and meadows; out in the open air, and under the blue sky." Cozzens so neatly mimicks the content and tone of so much early nineteenth-century sentimental anti-urbanism that the real focus of the sketch acquires a chilling power. He describes Sparrowgrass arriving home on the commuter train, spying a crowd of people on the bank of the river beyond the station and his house, and learning of the drowning of a young boy. "What a desperate race Sparrowgrass ran that day, with the image of each of his children successively drowned, passing through his mind with the rapidity of lightning flashes!" On the little beach the commuter spots a stricken woman—not his wife—crying. Launching his own boat, he helps in locating the corpse. Sundown finds Sparrowgrass wondering at the splendid sunset, cavorting dogs, and singing birds, and at the oddly "quiet and orderly" children. "They had turned over an important page in life and they were profiting by the lesson."[5] Just a short distance from the schoolhouse, in the midst of the sweet woodlands and meadows, lurked a river that killed.

Slowly, then, the Sparrowgrasses grow wiser. After two experiences involving petty theft, a confrontation with the farmer–fence viewers who side with the pig-owner against them, and incidents like the drowning, the family no longer stares innocently at borderland life. But gradually come successes. "It is a good thing to have an agreeable surprise, now and then, in the country," the narrator remarks, and by the close of the series the surprises are chiefly agreeable, albeit small pleasures. Autumn means not only colors like a "fringe of fire" from sumacs and other trees, but a family learning to know the identities of wildflowers along the edges of roads and meadows. After false starts and assaults by the pigs and the half-demented saddle horse, the vegetable garden produces a bounty of muskmelons and watermelons, a fine crop of potatoes, and the probability of an excellent tomato harvest— assuming a late frost. Mrs. Sparrowgrass, at first frightened of every borderland responsibility and activity, acquires certainty during the daily absences of her husband, and finally deals with the crazed horse herself. As the nights grow chilly, the Sparrowgrasses congratulate themselves not only on owning a fireplace but on having had the foresight to acquire andirons and a supply of well-seasoned firewood.[6] If not yet "old settlers," no longer are they innocents in a rather tricky Eden.

Eleven years of in-migration did nothing to ease the trickiness of the borderlands beyond the rapidly growing city of New York. In 1866, R. B. Coffin chronicled the adventures of another family of innocents moving away from urban difficulties into the country crossed by commuter railroads. His *Out of Town: A Rural Episode* strikes a tone different from that of Cozzens' *Putnam's Monthly* sketches, however. Cozzens assumed readers interested in borderland life but essentially unfamiliar with its possibilities, let alone its surprising predicaments; he continuously reached backward into early nineteenth-century romanticism for allusion and metaphor, and even further, into the Country ideology. Coffin knew the changes wrought in one decade, and he aimed his novel at a knowing reader, one intimate with the big-city difficulties—and delights—of New York and familiar with the possibilities implicit in railroad timetables.

The Grays move from the city when they lose their lease on a rowhouse; new rents seem exorbitant, and they resolve "to save money by purchasing a place in the country." In the brief first paragraph of the first chapter, Coffin neatly summarizes the arguments of Bates, Trotter, and Downing, noting that the family was "thoroughly disenchanted with town-life," having spent ten years "amidst brick walls and street-flagging, without getting, in all that time, a whiff of country air, or a sight of a blade of grass, save what the city parks afforded." They had also begun to worry about their physical health, especially that of Mrs. Gray and the children. While the narrator (again the husband) suggests other reasons "which I will not particularize," the six-sentence paragraph makes exquisitely clear that the Grays are essentially urban creatures being forced from the city by high living costs and physical foulness.[7]

If the Grays cannot have a civilized, affordable city, they will have the borderlands, the "country" as Coffin designates it. The second paragraph, a distillation of the nonfictional advice of Downing and many others concerning the best ways of choosing a borderland community, darts from the convenience of commuting to the quality of its schools and physician to the purity of its water supply. But it subtly implies that the residential zone ringing the city—Brooklyn, for example—lies beyond contempt, indeed in a kind of limbo, exactly as George Templeton Strong perceived it. Although the Grays cannot afford to rent a multistory Manhattan rowhouse, they can certainly afford commuting costs and even a maid in their new location. They want far more than a tiny wood house on a postage-stamp Brooklyn lot. And they get it, and its accessory adventures.

The "little woodbine-clad cottage" in which Coffin sets the novel becomes at once Mrs. Gray's domain; the grounds—several acres in extent—become the province of her husband. In the beginning, Mr. Gray arrives home each evening to find whole rooms of furniture rearranged; his wife, determined to find the most efficient, pleasant uses of interior space, continually disorients him, prompting him to consider "someday" adding on a wing, or at least a room to serve as a parlor.[8] Adjusting to indoor domestic space leads at once to his considering the uses of the space outdoors; soon the Grays realize that they can entertain outdoors, which was impossible in their former accommodations; they can even swing hammocks in the orchard when too many overnight guests arrive. But "settling in" leads to one adventure after another, some not as easily resolved as the issue of entertaining outdoors. The icebox, too large to fit through the kitchen door, must be dismantled and reassembled; the furnace, an invention mistaken by some passersby as a gigantic Civil War souvenir, squats on the front porch for days while awaiting contractors commissioned to dig a wider entrance into the cellar. Three months pass while the Grays settle in, in which they name the house Woodbine Cottage and discover that the supposed woodbine may be honeysuckle. Mrs. Gray superintends the activities and plans additions to the structure; Mr. Gray rushes back and forth to the city and begins gardening.

Gradually, and with greater sureness than the Sparrowgrasses, the Grays adapt, and suddenly Mr. Gray realizes that he wants to stay home. "Since I have come into the country I find myself continually seeking reasonable excuses for not going into town every day." First he takes off a day to plant his half-acre garden, which he accomplishes only after many rest periods and swallows of iced punch, strawberries and cream, and cigar smoke. When his newly acquired hens scratch up his corn, he hires an old-timer to replant it; after all, he is a busy man. But business is sometimes only busyness, he determines, and one Saturday he neglects to "report at that the granite building in Wall Street" and remains at home, "ostensibly to do a little weeding, but really to recruit my exhausted system,—exhausted by a too close application to governmental work."9 Slowly but definitely, the Grays turn away from urban amusements, preferring the delights of their house, grounds, and surroundings. And gradually too, Mr. Gray takes home-life concerns into the city, becoming a commuter toting different values and bundles.

After confronting local poultry growers, for example, Mr. Gray purchases several hens at a New York specialty market and puts them in a large wicker basket, which he stows beneath the seat he occupies in the homeward-bound commuter coach. Already he is a seasoned commuter; having chosen a seat on the shady side of the car, and having covered the empty adjacent seat with "the various packages and newspapers which a dweller out of town is accustomed to carry with him whenever he goes home" in order to keep it unoccupied, he settles back to read *The Atlantic*.10 Unfortunately an elderly woman sits beside him, strikes up a conversation about the wicker basket, and finally prompts him to open it to show off his prize hen—just as the train sweeps into the Harlem Tunnel. In the dark, the hen panics and escapes, flapping onto the woman, then about the car, and setting off a near riot before flying out the door as the train passes through Yorkville. Somewhat frightened (the brakeman saves him from falling down the steps of the car) and very embarrassed, Mr. Gray arrives home minus not only the prize fowl but the exorbitant price he paid for it—and encounters the derision of Mrs. Gray, who argues for the value of simple, country-purchased hens.

Out of Town chronicles the family's growing attachment to borderland life largely by describing misadventures as complex as any Cozzens imagined. The Grays go fishing, equipped for everything but rain; they celebrate Independence Day on their own, discharging fireworks with unanticipated results. They suffer inroads by their neighbors' roosters, which eat ripening tomatoes, and by "a lot of miserable little, brown-paper-colored bugs," which eat melons. Their goat refuses to be milked, runs away, and winds up in the pound. And yet the family masters each difficulty, often with less trouble than beset the Sparrowgrasses, and adventures further.11 As the novel proceeds, Mr. Gray becomes ever more preoccupied with his home life; "work" begins to mean not his efforts on Wall Street but his efforts in and around his house. Moreover, the family grows increasingly independent, experimenting with goat-owning rather than simply buying milk, for example, and realizing the extent to which urban families rely on experts.

Once the Grays learn that no police department watches over their persons and possessions, their fear of burglary grows stronger by the night. Thus one night, when suspect noises awaken them, Mr. Gray can do nothing but hand their new-

Away from the supposed protection of the New York City police, the Sparrowgrass family discovers the difficulties of sleeping in a place ripe for burglary, and the even greater difficulties of defending their home themselves.

R. B. Coffin argues that children need contact with the natural world in order to become healthy, well-educated, and well-balanced adults. In this illustration, the plants, telescope, and dog combine to reinforce his argument.

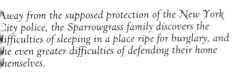

Farm animals bedevil the new boarders in Coffin's Out of Town too.

born baby into his wife's arms, put on his robe, and grab his "Colt's revolver" from the dressing-table drawer. After a stealthy creep downstairs, a loud noise so unnerves him that he accidentally discharges the pistol, terrifying his wife into screaming "murder!" from an upstairs window, and causing him to stumble through the pantry door, which locks behind him. In the darkness, beset by half a dozen stray cats maddened by terror, Gray fires again, and realizes, with sinking heart, that his neighbors, rushing to his house, are firing into the howling darkness. Now thoroughly panicked and smothered with flour, he attempts to surrender by flinging his cocked revolver through the window and against a tree, which causes it to discharge next to a would-be rescuer. Finally, after much yelling—and caterwauling by the stray cats earlier attracted to the food behind the open pantry window—the neighbors restore the peace. "But all's well that ends well, and though some of us were materially frightened by the events of the night, yet, after we had assembled together in the library, and had related our several experiences, and a bottle of California hock had been opened," the narrator recounts, nerves relax, and the Grays and their neighbors pass "the remainder of the night undisturbed by burglars or the fear of them."[12] The Battle of the Borderlands, fought and won by volunteers, only strengthens the family's confidence in itself.

Out of Town concerns pioneering as much as any contemporaneous novel about Minnesota or California or Wyoming. In learning about gardening and rearing poultry and goats, in mastering angling, in overcoming the fear of living without police officers, the Grays grow independent and learn to feel supremely confident of their abilities to surmount unknown obstacles ahead. They learn to scorn those weaklings dependent on experts, on hired help, and, perhaps, to scorn the flimsiness of urban marital arrangements and behavior. Coffin, like Cozzens, emphasizes the equality of husband and wife; and indeed, in both the novel and the serialized sketches, the wife shows not only superior common sense but marked financial skill and independence of thought. Mrs. Gray frequently pokes fun at her husband's pronouncements, and clearly her plans, had they been followed in the beginning, would have prevented many disasters. Just as married couples defending log cabins and sod houses depended on each other to help repel Indians, desperadoes, and locusts, and to make decisions in the absence of the other, so the Sparrowgrasses and the Grays enjoy noteworthy equality if separation of responsibilities.

In the late autumn, after the adventure of the cat-burglars, Mr. Gray totals the production of the family garden. Appearing in the novel as a list typeset in the format of so many nineteenth-century how-to-garden books, the record demonstrates the Grays' modest success. Cabbages, pumpkins, fifteen bushels of potatoes, carrots, beets, and other vegetables testify not only to the productiveness of the garden but to its large size. Gray enumerates sweet corn, popcorn "for the children," and yellow corn for the fowls. While Mrs. Gray is not satisfied with the bounty and remarks that her husband enjoyed the help of a farmer who assisted in replanting the corn (after depredations by birds) and in harvesting the potatoes, her husband delights in the autumn harvest and recalls the produce harvested and consumed throughout the summer. Keeping an orderly garden means much to Mr. Gray, who apparently finds it not only a source of genuine if occasionally stressful pleasure, but the most public emblem of his success in borderland living.

But while the vegetable garden provides spatial order and pure food, pure air, and pure exercise, it is the larger borderland landscape that continuously enchants both the Sparrowgrasses and the Grays. After cataloguing his harvest and drinking some October ale with his wife, Mr. Gray finds that the rain has ceased, and he ventures down to the Bronx River, whose banks are still accessible to a knowing walker. "A thin veil hung over the water, and the trees bordering its banks loomed spectrally through the fog, their slender limbs bare of leaves, and their trunks moist and slimy," he notes. "Not a sound arose to break the silence of the scene, and the very water of the stream lay under the fog with a sense of weight, as it were, upon its bosom." Mr. Gray finds the scene "one of gloom" and sadness, and he is happy to regain the "warmth and light" of his house.[13] His late afternoon walk led not simply into ordinariness, however. Along the Bronx he enjoyed what no urban resident could—outdoor privacy and silence in the presence of healing nature.

As New York City expanded in population, the urban residential zone overwhelmed the half-agricultural, half-afforested landscape in which the Grays fought burglars, chased goats, and grew grapes, and in which Mr. Gray delighted in solitary walks in restrained wilderness. Mountains, deep forest, and distant seashores enticed those nineteenth-century city dwellers prosperous enough to vacation and anxious for the supposed redemptive experience of wilderness solitude and for its aesthetic taste-sharpening. Borderlands offered less extensive and less grand wilderness to be sure, but as Haskell understood in laying out The Ramble in Llewellyn Park just a short commute from New York, only a little acreage long ago abandoned by slovenly farmers sufficed to delight the solitary walker, particularly the walker too poor to afford train tickets to northern Maine or the Sierra Nevada. Sparrowgrass on horseback, Gray on foot represent a recurrent image in borderland writing—the walk into a landscape at least as interesting as virgin wilderness, if not more so.

William Dean Howells emphasized "the pedestrian tour" in a number of magazine pieces he collected in 1898 as *Suburban Sketches*. His volume shares many concerns with Beers's *Suburban Pastoral,* particularly the notice it takes of the rubbish characterizing the region shifting from the borderland once traversed by Elias Phinney and railroad commuters to a residential district slowly crossed by passengers aboard horsecars and electric streetcars. But the rubbish, equal to any strewn about by slovenly farmers half a century before, fascinates rather than repels. "Here and there in the vacant lots abandoned hoop-skirts defied decay; and near the half-finished wood houses, empty mortar-beds, and bits of lath and slate strewn over the scarred and mutilated ground, added their interest to the scene."[14] This, the third sentence in the volume, presages an entire chapter devoted to a solitary walk through landscape in flux, a landscape about which Howells feels strongly indeed.

Howells—or rather the narrator, although the voice of the author is scarcely hidden—walks north from his mansard-roofed house on the "Avenue," away from a neighborhood of railroad commuters encroached upon by streets of close-ranged houses filling with horsecar commuters. He passes a small bridge spanning a railroad cut covered with trees and briars "and suggesting a quiet water-course" and swings off along the right-of-way into a manufacturing zone of vast brickyards, a village and a former farmhouse inhabited chiefly by Irish immigrants, a half-abandoned tavern with "wide-spreading cattle-pens" and great barn all threatened with replacement by "the predestined French-roofed villa," and a railroad station from which a train pulls away. "It has left the city and the suburbs behind, and has sought the woods and meadows," the narrator muses from the bridge over the rails, implying that the train seeks the country in order to achieve the speed that distinguishes it from horsecars. "But Nature never in the least accepts it, and rarely makes its path a part of her landscape's loveliness," he continues. Its passengers alighting at the residential zone station, the commuters— "suburbanly packaged, and bundled, and bagged, and even when empty-handed somehow proclaiming the jaded character of men that hurry their work all day to catch the evening train out, and their dreams all night to catch the morning train in"—lead the solitary tourist homeward, into the "vast quiet and monotony of the street itself."[15] As circular in argument as the tour it describes, the essay reveals a profound—and somewhat confused—reorientation of middle-class American culture.

Sparrowgrass, Gray, and Howells' narrator enjoy nature and natural scenery, but enjoy it best when built form punctuates it. Cozzens, Coffin, and Howells extol the wonderful diversity of borderland landscape, partly by juxtaposing it against the crowded confusion of downtown, the dreary monotony of the urban residential zone, and the starkness of wholly rural areas. Implicit in their works, and in the works of contemporaneous observers of borderland life, is a turning away from any gushing acceptance of wilderness or untouched natural scenery and toward an aesthetic of diversified landscape, an aesthetic of the intriguing, not simply the picturesque. Only Howells tenders any explicit inquiry into the change. His narrator notes that the brickyards might be perceived through the eye of an American tourist in Egypt; that the village of Irish immigrants, had it been sited in Italy, would attract "aesthetical" interest; that the lack of "sentimental association" caused by so much new building and other recent change deflects traditional romantic notions. Yet the narrator sees, however vaguely, the artistic possibilities in the overlays of landscape, musing about the historical items in the crossroads second-hand store, in the old farmhouse inhabited by immigrants. Nevertheless, diversity must be controlled, lest it grow as uncontrollable as urban diversity. "The householders view with fear and jealousy the erection of any dwelling of less than a stated cost, as portending a possible advent of Irish; and when the calamitous race actually appears, a mortal pang strikes to the bottom of every pocket."[16] So long as the immediate surroundings of the borderland family remain perfectly picturesque, a walk into nearby intriguing space provides more pleasure than a walk into farmland or woods. In *Suburban Sketches* lies half-formulated a landscape aesthetic—and a "lifestyle"—as potent for twentieth-century middle-class readers as the writings of Susan Cooper and her contemporaries were for nineteenth-century inquirers.

William Dean Howells shared Sidney Fisher's fascination with horsecars, and later with electric trolleys, finding their impact on borderland women particularly intriguing.

The narrator of Howells' *Suburban Sketches* soon learns that within a few miles of his borderland house lies an extraordinary range of places, including the shabby housing of newly arrived immigrant laborers.

More than perhaps any other nineteenth-century American writer, Henry Cuyler Bunner grasped the spatial and social implications of the railroad lines reaching across borderland space.

As an adolescent, Bunner watched the spread of factories and row housing across upper Manhattan, and the specter of the industrial city devouring woods and fields never left him.

At the close of The Runaway Browns the adventurous young couple returns exhausted and wiser to their borderland house, which stands waiting like a refuge in the storm of late nineteenth-century urban frenzy.

Henry Cuyler Bunner articulated the new landscape aesthetic and indeed a sort of credo of borderland living that far transcends anything offered by his predecessors or by Howells. Bunner wrote prolifically and wrote from experience; had he not died in 1896 at the age of forty, he might have created a comprehensive philosophy of metropolitan life, one phrased in fiction and satire.[17] What he did produce in the 1890s is as significant as the work of Andrew Jackson Downing.

His 1892 book, *The Runaway Browns,* sets the tone for most of his later writing. An almost plotless collection of sketches, the little book traces the adventures of a newlywed husband and wife determined to find the adventure so lacking in their brand-new "suburban" life. "Here, just outside their very gate," it seemed to them, "was a great world of action and event going on its entertaining way, while their life was as humdrum as an unbroken routine could make it." And so the Browns run away, blundering into one trying misadventure after another and within a week growing wholly weary of excitement, urban and otherwise. The close of the novel finds them, at six in the morning, hiking from a railroad station "into a broad cheerful street with taller trees along the edge of the roadway, and with a row of low, spreading-roofed cottages on each side," a street on which "every house stood in a large generous patch of lawn or garden." Their street, their grounds appear almost sacred, dignified with blooming roses, ampelopsis climbing "over half the house," with "scarlet runners on the sunny side." The husband, feeling "that some religious ceremony was needed," takes off his hat. The wife moves "among the flowers, caressing them with the tips of her fingers, patting their heads, and touching their cool cheeks as though they had been so many children."[18] Excitement, glamor, adventure pale against the sanctity of home.

His fervent love of New York City and especially of its literary society never erased Bunner's love of nature, and indeed the spread of the city, and particularly of rows of speculator-built "sham" houses for "poor people of moderate means" into decrepit agricultural regions in time turned him against urban life. His piercing attacks on the "tawdry little," "smug, mean little" houses—the houses George Templeton Strong also loathed—"tricked out with machine-made scroll-work and insufficiently clad in two coats of ready-mixed paint," derive from his love of the landscape, slovenly farms and all, of the borderlands around New York, the borderlands Mackenzie, fifty years before, claimed were perfect for picturesque villa parks. "From Tiemann's to Tubby Hook," an essay in an 1896 collection entitled *Jersey Street and Jersey Lane,* chronicles the progress of barnacle-like residential streets and laments the erasing of Manhattan Island colonial farms, country forges, gentlemen's estates, and other relics of the pre–Civil War years. Around present-day 125th Street, Bunner assures his readers, he and his boyhood friends knew that "five minutes' walk would take us into a country of green lanes and meadows and marshland and woodland." And one day, he spied in the woods "something that stood awkwardly and conspicuously out of the young woodgrass—a raw stake of pine wood, and beyond that, another stake, and another; and parallel with these was another row, marking out two straight lines, until the bushes hid them."[19] Soon came a straight boulevard, and the end of the woods.

Bunner claims that in 1895 he visited the locale after an absence of many years and found it "checkered and gridironed with pavements and electric lights," crossed by the elevated railroad, and covered with "great, cheerless, hideously ornate flat buildings." Decisively, Bunner labels the place "a demoralized suburb," indeed "a cheap, tawdry, slipshod imitation of the real city—or perhaps I should say, of all that is ugliest and vulgarest, least desirable, and least calculated to endure, in the troubled face of city life." Nothing remained of the picturesque quasi-rural scenery he recalled so vividly. Nothing suggested anything of the wonderfully energetic city downtown. In his eyes, the urban residential zone—what Caparn called Parallelogram Park—failed as part of the city fabric, failed even in being suburban. It was demoralized and demoralizing.

Bunner was perhaps the first American scrutinizer of borderland beauty and lifestyle to grow up in the borderlands and to see them swallowed not by the city proper, but by the monotonous city residential zones. His anger derives in part from the loss of his boyhood haunts, the shattering of the theater of childhood. Another essay in the volume makes clear the only solution he ever discovered, a solution for himself and for his own children.

"A Letter to Town" parallels the arguments of many essays by Nathaniel Parker Willis, but it begins with another indictment of the residential zones, "those abominable and abhorrent deserts of paved streets laid out at right angles, and all supplied with sewers and electric light wires and water-mains before the first lonely house escapes from the house-pattern books to tempt the city dweller out to that dreary, soulless waste which has all the modern improvements and not one tree." Against the "cheap back-extension of a great city," Bunner juxtaposes a place severed from every urban amenity except for "the railway's glittering lines of steel." The landscape engenders a "green awakening" in the new commuter's heart, for all that "the perfect silence" at first seems "somewhat lonesome" and even frightening. "Then your children keep running up to you with strange plants and flowers, and asking you what they are; and you find it trying on the nerves to keep up the pretence of parental omniscience." Self-reliance originates in firing the suburban furnace, in tending the garden—"for these stories of suburban gardens where nothing grows, are all nonsense"—in abandoning a lease for a mortgage.[20] Implicit in the essay is not only a definition of *suburban* linked only to large-lot borderland communities miles distant from cities and "back-extensions," but a wealth of details Bunner develops into entire chapters of *The Suburban Sage*.

Nutley, New Jersey, a commuter haven only fourteen miles from New York, blossomed after 1872, when a branch of the Erie Railroad linked it with Hudson River ferries. It achieved a sort of literary fame when Bunner, Frank Stockton, and other important turn-of-the-century authors chose it as their home.[21] In Nutley, the Bunner family enjoyed firsthand adventures that became literary material for its head. Bunner built a little log cabin for his daughter, erected thirteen different kinds of fence on the family land, and kept a dog, two cats, white Cheshire pigs, a parrot, driving horses, "a rich and powerful voiced donkey," an Egyptian lizard, and two opossums.[22] He delighted in driving his urban visitors in a great open barouche, in

"Johnny-jumper!" he says, scornfully, when you have hazarded a guess out of your

meagre botanical vo- cabulary: "Why, man, that's no Johnny-jumper, that's a wild

Borderland living confronted city-bred parents with difficult questions, Bunner argued, questions involving the identities of flowers and the names of insects.

Bunner agreed with Coffin on many subjects, including the happy consequences of the nervous businessman's encountering on his borderland walk not only nature, but even a virtuous farmer in touch with traditional matters.

Most of Bunner's borderland families discover not only the trials and rewards of growing flowers, shrubs, and trees, but the maddening intricacies of dealing with nurserymen and other experts.

facing neighborhood emergencies alone when all other men had entrained for the city, in watching the antics of families discovering, or as in his own case, rediscovering, borderland vexations and joys.

In *The Suburban Sage: Stray Notes and Comments on His Simple Life*, Bunner immortalized the blossoming of Nutley and the tentative explorations of its newcomers. Published in 1896 in book form, many of the chapters had previously appeared in *Puck,* and all take at first glance a humorous approach to borderland life. But a seriousness underlies the humor, along with a sureness that the Nutley neighbors are pioneers in a massive shift away from urban living. The chapters range over a score of issues from bicycling to borrowing, from architectural design to building contractors, from golf to religion, from dogs to the snickers of families still resident in cities, from reasons for walking to the snobberies implicit in railroad timetables. Bunner's breadth of vision undoubtedly originates in his acute awareness of the burgeoning nonfiction literature on suburbanization, but his clarity of insight seems as much a result of firsthand experience in Nutley as it does in his love of language.

One phrase best indicates Bunner's sharpness of insight. His use of *metropolitan city,* a phrase he may have coined, structures much of his book, and demonstrates his advance beyond the thinking of Cozzens, Coffin, and other nineteenth-century borderland authors.[23] In 1896, Henry Cuyler Bunner understood as clearly as Coburn or any other scrutinizer of census and cartographical data that old notions of urban form and city life no longer described a new reality of space and feeling. *The Suburban Sage* offers an exquisite vehicle with which to explore the turn-of-the-century borderland places that most Americans soon came to designate as properly "suburban."

Pride in maintaining—and maybe even designing—houses and grounds characterizes almost all of Bunner's borderland families, especially young couples aware that caring for the home is about all the work they share.

Marking out the rooms of their future houses delights many of Bunner's couples, especially those unaware of scale, cost, and time.

Bunner's borderland men take immense pride in learning new technologies; here the male members of a dinner party have adjourned to the cellar to study furnace problems.

Late nineteenth-century borderers learned to borrow and loan—for most families needed a diversity of gadgets to finish houses, make gardens, and create lawns, and most, after buying real estate, had very little free cash.

Along with so many other nineteenth-century observers of borderland life, Bunner scrutinized the social dynamics of the commuter platform, noting almost unthinkingly how frequently shopping-bound wives accompanied husbands aboard the local.

*Traditional values, including traditional
domestic architecture, order all of Bunner's
books about the outer suburbs, for all that
his characters lead pioneering, innovative
lives.*

*Achieving home-ownership awes many of
Bunner's young married couples, like this
one devoting an evening to gazing at their
heaven-on-earth.*

16 ❧ FROSTING

"I was much struck by the quantity of uncleared forest which extends up to the immediate neighbourhood of Boston," remarked John Robert Godley, an Englishman traveling through New England in 1843. "The road between Boston and Lowell (the most frequented in New England) is bordered for the most part by a wilderness which does not bear, apparently, a trace of man's proximity."[1] Struck though he was, Godley inquired carefully, learning that almost all the forest was second-growth, and that it spoke volumes about slovenly farming and the westward and southward migration of industrious farmers. What Godley found outside Boston other mid-nineteenth-century travelers discovered everywhere along the eastern seaboard. Once beyond the prosperous truck farms ringing east coast cities—farms including those that eventually gave New Jersey the nickname Garden State—they rode into the sleepy, slovenly, ever more afforested regions like Westchester County and Orange, New Jersey. By the 1890s the scrubby trees had matured, and few real estate speculators needed the vision of Llewellyn Haskell to perceive the picturesque possibilities implicit near so many stations half an hour or more beyond the urban residential ring. *Forest* and *Woods* repeatedly entered the nomenclature of American commuter towns—Lake Forest, Forest Hills, Forest Grove, Woodland are only four examples—and the woods shaped the popular perception of what constituted "real suburbs." As Cozzens, Coffin, Howells, and Bunner knew, turn-of-the-century borderland residents cherished trees.

Wilson Flagg addressed the borderland love of trees not only by detailing the characteristics of specific species, but by philosophizing about borderland forest in general. His *Halcyon Days,* an 1881 collection of essays, builds on the strengths of his *Year Among the Trees* and rams home not only the framework of the borderland forest aesthetic, but its details too. It presents a whole theory of aesthetics, one tailored particularly to late nineteenth-century borderland readers anxious not so much to learn what distinguishes the picturesque from the sublime, but to be assured that borderland landscape epitomized beauty. Flagg's essays, appearing

The Old Oak, Hampstead, N. H.
30 feet in circumference

Nineteenth- and early twentieth-century Americans delighted in trees, especially ones of great age or beauty of "historical associations."

regularly in *The Atlantic Monthly* and other general audience periodicals, reassured indeed.

No other turn-of-the-century critic inquired so painstakingly into the view from the heights. Flagg dismissed the notion of roughness implicit in so many definitions of picturesqueness, and instead focused on the effect of uneven, especially rocky or preciptious terrain covered with trees and smaller plants. Such terrain pleases all educated people, he argued, simply because it offers an intriguing diversity of plants and a useful topography. On the one hand, he directed attention at a typical "craggy precipice, rising thirty or forty feet out of a wet meadow," an elevation crowned by a grove of pines or birches, with an understory of whortleberry, spiraea, bayberry, and sweetfern, and dignified on its slopes with mountain laurel perhaps, some projecting oaks and beeches, and where wet, with ferns, and elsewhere with lichen. No plant he lists speaks of the older, agriculture-based landscape aesthetic; indeed, the plants indicate only infertile or exhausted soil. Pines and whortleberries meant nothing to the farmers Susan Cooper scorned; they meant scarcely more to early nineteenth-century women botanizers exercising their minds and bodies by looking chiefly at flowers. Instead, Flagg argued that viewing his example precipice and similar terrain might put observers in mind of "various scenes and incidents of romantic adventure." That alone made it valuable.[2] On the other hand, however, lay the real importance of such terrain. Flagg reserved his enthusiasm not for looking at the tree-covered precipice but for looking *from* it.

"Abrupt situations," he concluded, offer wonderful advantages "both for prospect and for pleasant secluded retreats." The vegetation and rocky outcroppings on his typical precipice provide a hundred places from which to view the landscape beyond, beneath, and simultaneously another hundred locations suitable for hiding, for withdrawl. Europeans know little of this peculiarly American experience. "Unaccompanied by the melancholy that attends us on surveying a wide scene of ruins," Americans sharing "a distant view of a fertile and prosperous country" instead enjoy "a sense of cheerful exaltation." In the late nineteenth century, Susan Cooper's dreams of witch-hazel wands replacing American rural scenery with medieval landscape no longer appealed to middle-class needs. Flagg understood the fascinating intrigue of contemporary American space, the view of cities, towns, railroads, and the like, the mix that enticed Howells.

But he knew too how easily the view disturbed, for all that he never explicitly addressed the realities of industrialization and urbanization. The trees framing the view of the urban industrial or residential zone indeed make the vista into a picture, softening the subject by softening the frame, lightening the urban shadows by diffusing rural light around the edges. At times, however, the frame fails, and the vista and its unnerving connotations come too near the observer. Then the viewer steps back, into the seclusion of the trees and rocky nooks, and finds the suddenly disturbing view vanished. Seclusion, which Flagg repeatedly coupled with solitude, informed much of his thinking; he argued that while glen, valley, forest, and even pasture offer varying degrees of individual freedom and seclusion, "the word 'park,' on the contrary, savors less of nature than of the city, less of beauty than of decoration, less of romance and poetry than of taste and artifice."[3] Susan Cooper might stand in a hilly near-wilderness and imagine a medieval landscape. Flagg looked out at urban space, and when threatened, stepped back into a medieval hilltop retreat, just as Howells did, just as everyone in Llewellyn Park did.

Trees did more than frame borderland vistas, whether across the valleys around Cary's Cincinnati or across the roads ridden by Fisher. They spoke eloquently not only to nineteenth-century botanizers—especially women familiar with such essays as Harland Coultas' 1859 *Godey's Lady's Book* article, "Observations on the Growth of Trees"—but to the ever more confident philosophers of the American way of life, at least those musing in the borderlands. Skyscrapers, great bridges and tunnels, sprawling industrial zones, and express trains all emblematized national greatness, manifest destiny, the triumph of capitalism, and earthly progress through mastered technology, but many turn-of-the-century families understood more clearly the raw strain of continuous improvement, of constant enlargement, of growing complexity. They feared nervousness and nervous breakdown as intimately as early nineteenth-century families dreaded cholera and other diseases supposedly urban in origin.

By 1910, thoughtful Americans understood at least the new language of illness associated with great cities, industrialism, and technological advance. Agoraphobia, claustrophobia, mysophobia, and other illness entered the national consciousness as varieties of nervousness, but their precise causes and symptoms, let alone cures, remained vague indeed. "The great curse of American civilization today is that we are living too much on our nerves," argued Samuel McComb in *Everybody's Magazine*. "Not a day passes but we hear of some man prominent in the professional or business world driven into premature retirement because of a nervous breakdown."[4] Filled with case studies and potential cures ranging from posthypnotic suggestion to electric shocks, McComb's "Nervousness—A National Menace" claimed that a combined failure of moral and psychical faculties alone explained the rising tide of businessmen terrified of elevators or railroad cars; of men and women desperately fatigued but unable to sleep or unrefreshed by prolonged sleep; of prosperous, physically healthy adults beset with trembling hands, fleeting visions of suicide, and emptiness of heart. In novels like E. J. Rath's *The Nervous Wreck* and *Too Much Efficiency,* in hundreds of articles in general circulation magazines, and in periodicals aimed especially at the wives of men susceptible to it, Americans learned of nervousness, its prevention, and its cure.[5] Moral and mental failure coupled, not simplistic "back to religion" or "eschew worldliness" diatribes, inform the literature of nervousness. As McComb (a clergyman operating a nervousness clinic in his large urban church) so persuasively argued, along with so many others, nervousness attacked the union of soul and mind, not soul or mind alone. And outside of counseling and electric shock, only forest vacation or woodland residence seemed likely to rejoin what twentieth-century progress has sundered.

Vacationing, and especially camping in the Adirondacks, the Maine wilderness, or the Rocky Mountains seemed a certain preventative and a likely cure, for vestiges of transcendentalism, however warped, endured to shape the literature of nervousness. In the first American manual of sport camping, *Woodcraft*, George Washington Sears summed up the psychospiritual argument:

> For brick and mortar breed filth and crime,
> With a pulse of evil that throbs and beats,
> And men are withered before their prime
> By the curse paved in with the lanes and streets.
>
> And lungs are poisoned and shoulders bowed.
> In the smothering reek of mill and mine
> And death stalks in on the struggling crowd—
> But he shuns the shadow of oak and pine.

In 1884, Sears addressed only a handful of readers interested in getting beyond the resort hotel, into a canoe or onto a trail, and his interpretation of urban illness emphasized moral depravity and physical sickness—in terms Ely Bates and Thomas Trotter might have understood—not nervous decay. Within two decades, however, *Forest and Stream* and other new "outdoor" magazines chronicled the astonishing rise of hiking, camping, "nature education," hunting, bird-watching, and nature study, sports and other activities interesting millions of urban and borderland folk—although not farm families and others resident in wholly rural or wilderness areas—worried about nervousness and slowly beginning to understand the meaning of "recreation." As Benjamin F. Leggett argued in his 1906 *Out-Door Poems*, "All the woods of April show / Widsom we should heed and know." Knowing the woods, knowing the taxonomy of trees and Latin terminology, no longer mattered. "Seed and root and fibre fine," Leggett continued, "Have a message half divine."[6] Hearing and digesting that "half divine" message recreates the congruence of soul and mind. In the woods, according to the savants of nervousness, even the most harried businessman might grow whole again, and he needed no botany to do it. Henry James understood the effect; by Easter time, he wrote in *The American Scene* in 1907, the well-to-do of New York City had fled, leaving behind the city he condemned as "some colossal set of clockworks, some steel-souled machine-room of brandished arms and hammering fists and opening and closing jaws."[7]

If forest vacationing sometimes prevented or cured nervousness, permanent residence among trees struck reformers as an even better alternative. Trees, and the understory of shrubs and flowers, injected spirituality into everyday life and so strengthened the soul, as Flagg argued as early as 1871 in an *Atlantic Monthly* essay tracing the ways woodland flowers "awaken every agreeable passion of the soul."[8] The awakened, strengthened soul in turn balanced the mind taxed by business, by trivia, by everything new. Between 1890 and 1915, the national preoccupation with nervousness heightened the value of trees immeasurably.

Throughout the nineteenth century, reformers argued that trees clean city air of impurities, that indeed they function as the "lungs of the city." Experts disagreed about the exact process by which trees purified polluted air, but most city dwellers understood immediately how effectively they shaded sidewalks in summer and

Treeless city streets reinforced the love of commuters for the sylvan delights awaiting them at the opposite end of their daily lives.

Everywhere in cities, and especially in the urban residential ring, street trees suffered in collisions with wagons and especially from being used as hitching posts.

deflected autumn and spring winds. Street trees, especially mature ones, softened adjacent architectural form and delighted aesthetes familiar with romantic and picturesque doctrines. Despite the worries of fire insurance companies and the continual difficulties of maintenance, trees graced urban residential streets long before nervousness captured public attention. Yet even as nervousness spread and the curative powers of trees received ever sharper scrutiny, street trees began disappearing from eastern and midwestern cities.

In 1908, a *Good Roads Magazine* essayist summarized the decline of urban street trees, piling example upon example to confirm what many pedestrians suspected. Urban inventions waged war on trees, sometimes almost deliberately, sometimes surreptitiously. Telephone, electric, and street railway companies, lamented Albert D. Taylor, "disfigure trees which have been the pride of a community for years" by cutting branches away from cables.[9] Tree butchery by wire-stringers frequently preceded tree murder by electrocution: live wires chafing against limbs during wind storms often ignited whole trees. Moreover, the companies frequently connected guy wires to trees, either damaging them severely at once or injuring them just enough to foster disease. Leaking gas mains killed trees far more slowly, but equally certainly, and the paving of gravel roads damaged root systems or prevented rain from watering adjacent trees. Injured by horses gnawing on their bark, by drays bumping against their trunks, and by such natural causes as ice storms, turn-of-the-century urban street trees grew deformed and withered, and their numbers dwindled. Street-widening efforts often doomed even the healthiest specimens, as city engineers felled whole rows of trees in order to adapt pavements to double tracks for streetcars, carriages and wagons, bicyclists, and horseless carriages. A wholesale withering of urban street trees, coinciding perfectly with an outpouring of reform literature glorifying the moral-spiritual-psychical power of trees, directed the attention of city folk, nervous and otherwise, at the leafy borderlands beyond the treeless residential zone.

Suburban Life extolled the value of trees. Issues from 1907 demonstrate beyond doubt the power of the pro-tree lobby, which unwittingly directed attention at the city trees for which Taylor felt such concern. In April, for example, a clergyman asserted that "a noble grove of pines is more apt to remind me of their Maker than a sky-scraper, even if the stones and brick clay of which it is built did come originally from God's country." Francis E. Clark insisted that "just to see things grow, seems to make the soul grow with them," and he directed the attention of readers of "Why I Chose a Suburban Home"—a regular feature of the magazine—at the maple and the chestnut.[10] In "Tree Seats and Balconies," another April author suggested that readers think carefully about building platforms around and in large trees, to enjoy not only the view and cool shade but "the songs of the birds and the soft whisper of the waving branches."[11] As a place for outdoor sleeping, treehouses offered not only soothing sounds, but relief from many low-flying insects. Love of trees extended beyond individuals and families to entire borderland families. A February author, in another regular feature entitled "Suburban Betterment," described the successful efforts of a "Tree Protectors' League," when a gas company began extend-

Demands for electric communication and power often doomed roadside trees, making borderers and others aware of the fragility of sylvan beauty.

Borderers anxious to have sizable trees invest their new houses with dignity sometimes purchased the services of nurserymen specializing in transplanting large specimens.

ing its lines, to "dictate just where the pipes should be placed, in order to avoid all risk of injury to the beautiful elms and maples that line the roadsides." Equally splendid results were obtained when the association forced a streetcar company interested in double-tracking its route to follow the league's rules of beauty, not mere engineering.[12] Quite clearly, trees mattered, and in November, an essayist made clear the rapidly rising status of tree-owning.

"Chicago's Most Unique Suburb" is introduced by a lengthy and revealing subtitle: "Kenilworth Was Laid Out in the Virgin Forest and Not a Tree Has Been Needlessly Sacrificed." F. E. M. Cole lavishes praise on the "beautiful little suburban town," finding every detail enchanting. From the "low-lying stone depot half hidden in vines and shrubbery and gay with flowering plants," to the "low, rambling building, nestling under a mighty elm" that serves as a community hall, to the houses, built by people committed to "disturbing as few of the original trees as possible" and growing to love privacy-giving hedges, everything is delicate, refined, and perfectly picturesque. Away from the built areas lingers "a miniature wilderness" of "great trees of oak, elm and ash, many of them covered with Virginia creeper, wild grape, and bittersweet"; they are the habitat of rabbits, squirrels, and a startling diversity of birds. None of the houses, Cole insists, is particularly expensive by standards of cities and other borderland places, but the overall "setting of tree and flower" is priceless—and a powerful stimulant to further improvement. Gas and electric lines run underground, and after a successful battle with the electricity company, the families of Kenilworth are struggling with the newly arrived telephone company against "unsightly poles and objectionable wires." With its two churches, elementary school, high school building, and incredibly swift, frequent train service to downtown Chicago, Cole argues, Kenilworth is near perfection, a place where large trees have been left in the middle of winding streets, a place that "gives a new lease of life and helps prepare the mind and body for the world's business battles." Within the simple, moderately priced houses surrounded by trees and hedges, urban tensions are dissipated, families grow closer, and the bobwhite and whippoorwill enliven the evening quiet, strangthening soul and mind.

Design, not accident creates such places, Cole and his contemporaries assured readers of *Suburban Life* and other borderland-oriented magazines. Kenilworth excluded by law all manufacturing plants, livery stables, powerhouses, and commercial greenhouses. It prohibited all houses "constructed below a stipulated price" and insisted that every house be set back at least forty feet from the edge of the street on a lot of at least one hundred foot frontage. Cole argued that such restrictions produced "a uniformity which is very pleasing," but he meant less a social homogeneity than an aesthetic one. Natural vegetation, not built form, dominated Kenilworth, not only masking the rather run-of-the-mill domestic architecture but emphasizing the values of its families. An appreciation of the seasons, fresh air, and above all the invigorating influence of the woods brought people to Kenilworth and led them to subordinate their houses and public buildings to trees and to protect their right to enjoy their happiness—whatever the assaults of gas and electricity companies.

Subordinating architecture to existing or intended vegetation clashed not only

Bunner knew the importance of trees, and street trees in particular, in the hearts of borderers. In this *Suburban Sage* illustration, one family has protected its prize with a wrought-iron fence.

North of Chicago along mainline commuter routes, Kenilworth offered perhaps the epitome of the frosted residential landscape, something instantly apparent to anyone stepping onto its station platform.

Kenilworth houses nestled in wooded nooks as delicately beautiful as any imagined by Susan Cooper or Nathaniel Willis.

with American tradition but with the tenets of urban modernity. Pioneers and farm families had long built symmetrical, white-painted houses as soon as circumstances permitted. Such houses, and the other buildings of the farmyard, announced the triumph of humanity over forest and prairie wilderness. As Downing so well knew, the attachment to such stand-out buildings survived long after the pioneers. Sixty years after Downing and his contemporaries lamented the propensity toward white-painted structures, reformers still chastized the mass of Americans. But by 1902 the ever more powerful love of sylvan beauty—and the strengthening distaste for living in cities increasingly built of everything but wood—made the task more easy. Families moving to the borderlands had already committed themselves to experiment, precisely as Cozzens, Bunner, and other writers knew, and they frequently experimented with integrating their houses into wooded sites. "Chameleon-like, the house should take the color of its surroundings," advised Claude Bragdon in a 1902 *Country Life* article aimed at "people of moderate means" and stressing practical solutions to specific problems. "If it be among trees, it may appropriately be stained gray, like the tree-trunks, and the blinds painted a leaf-green, with white sash, perhaps, to give interest and variety." The body color should be "a restful, neutral tint" and bright colors must always be avoided; stain rather than paint ought to be used for every surface except sash and doors, perhaps. Bragdon and his fellow advice givers addressed a reform-minded audience, one closely attuned to the virtues of naturalness. Out of their many articles emerges an implicit image: the borderlands, not the working agricultural regions and not the city (and especially not the urban residential zones), are stained, not painted. "Stain is better than paint from an esthetic standpoint." Bragdon continued, "because it does not obscure the grain and enhances the natural beauty of the wood, penetrating and becoming part of it—and improving with the lapse of time instead of becoming gray and shabby as paint does."[13] City people might fight air pollution by continuously repainting their houses and might advertise their allegiance to progress by experimenting with bright colors—and in the urban residential zones they might distinguish their houses from one another by experimenting with unique colors and patterns—but borderland families by and large committed themselves to a different aesthetic, one grounded in a natural palette and after the turn of the century sometimes suggesting the sheathing of roof and walls with natural-colored wooden shingles. The borderland aesthetic was grounded as well in a growing love of domestic privacy.

In the first years of the twentieth century, families in Kenilworth and other suburbs tentatively enclosed parts of their land, withdrawing behind fences and hedges just as their stained houses blended into a background of foliage, itself withdrawn from the city. While the movement from city to borderland resulted from a host of concerns, some clearly recognized by the movers, some scarcely consciously sensed, the withdrawl expressed in so many tall hedges and trees derived from a preoccupation with privacy.

With the twentieth century arrived a new concern with self-defense, with protecting self and family from intrusion. Certainly the metropolitan daily newspaper, given over, in the words of one 1905 *Harper's Weekly* commentator, to "the

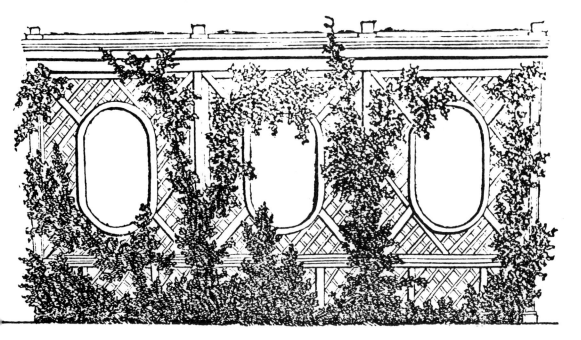

Outdoor privacy preoccupied borderers as early as the antebellum years, when Downing offered suggestions for "a partially inclosed veranda."

Outdoor privacy also preoccupied many physicians and other experts writing in magazines aimed at borderers. Here trees and vines not only cool a small patch of ground, but offer some visual screening too.

interests of petty gossip, mean curiosity, and idle scandals," kindled a desire for reserve in some of the very people who delighted in its probings.[14] To be exposed in the newspaper, according to turn-of-the-century writers, meant forfeiting family secrets, meant being stripped, if not naked, at least to one's underclothes. But a greater cause of the new preoccupation lay in urban crowding and urban technology. Only the urban rich had indoor space enough to be alone, mused a 1914 *Forum* author, and even they had to endure servants; the poor and the middle class had more cramped quarters, and everyone suffered the thronged streets. Middle-class businessmen slowly learned that each working day "is punctuated with casual and often quite unnecessary interruptions" and that home life guaranteed little better. "We have all become so accessible, by telephone, by telegraph, or by post," argued Robert J. Shores, "that we are at the mercy of almost anyone who chooses to make a demand upon our time." While the rural family might welcome the Bible salesman as a pleasant interruption, the urban businessman or housewife, bombarded constantly with visits and calls from salesmen and others, grew at first annoyed, then angry. Shores recognized the long-term effect of the daily newspaper and benevolent societies upon the urban resident: "He has impressed upon him, through the press and by word of mouth, his responsibility for all the poverty, vice, ignorance, and crime that exist in the world today."[15] And once made to feel responsible, the conscience-stricken reader quickly learned that he could do very little about the problems he had difficulty understanding, and so he withdrew into his family circle, dreaded the ringing of the telephone, and considered borderland life.

And yet even in the borderlands, individual families withdrew from strangers and their neighbors, albeit in subtle ways countenanced—in time—by nearly everyone. Until well into the 1920s, borderland withdrawl from strangers meant simply setting the house well back from the street, preferably far enough back so pedestrians could not see into windows, curtained or not. Fences, hedges, and other defenses, including high foundation plantings, struck nearly everyone as un-American, what long-ago Jacksonians might have called Federalist. Indeed, only the rare critic condemned the typical borderland street edged with trees and lawns sweeping uninterrupted up to houses, and more important, sweeping along parallel to the street itself. "I never admire one of these thoroughfares without amazement at the householders who can freely throw away half their land and all their privacy in order to make a boulevard of an indifferent highway," confessed a 1912 *Atlantic Monthly* writer. H. G. Dwight argued that he would sacrifice the "'front lawn' on the altar of public opinion," then erect "a hedge so thick and so high that my neighbors would have to go to some trouble in order to take observations of my affairs."[16] Dwight well understood the scandal his remarks would cause. The prevailing sentiment against hedges, fences, and other blocks to vision originated in supposedly "American" notions of equality and uniform behavior. Edward Payson Powell had summarized the sentiment against "exclusivity" twelve years before in *Hedges, Windbreaks, Shelters, and Live Fences,* quoting one horticulturist as the final word: "My own opinion of hedge fences is that they do not add to the attractiveness of the country. If allowed to grow high they hide the landscape, and give an air of exclusiveness that is un-American."[17] The horticulturist, Powell, and other savants argued that screen hedges and fences not only implied the presumed superiority of families planting or erecting them, they restricted the pleasant views supposed the right of all travelers. Perhaps even more important, the screens suggested eccentric private activity, if not worse, within their walls. Yet by the beginning of the new century, borderland observers like Cole noticed hedges and fences appearing everywhere.

Surely the "pointers" Bunner satirized prompted many families to withdraw ever further from the street. Low weekend fares on trains and interurban trolleys brought many city people into suburbs for relaxed pedestrian tours. Bunner loathed them, for they stared at houses, grounds, and inhabitants. "Though their dress proclaims them from the city, they loiter and gawk like country folk; and they stare at everything they see about them like people wandering through a waxwork show." Many brought box lunches, eaten "in the railroad station, to the great disgust of the station agent," and in time they learned that real estate agents would drive them around in carriages, hoping to sell them houses.[18] But many others simply came for a walk along tree-lined streets, to see something of the great borderland experiment informing so much metropolitan and national literature; and had they only walked, and perhaps not pointed so sharply, Bunner and other homeowners might have tolerated them. Unfortunately, they also talked, in the loud voices of city people inured to street noise. Their voices carried, and borderland families disliked their criticisms of lawns, color schemes, and architectural styles. In the years just before the automobile age, borderland areas on direct rail or trolley lines from urban residential zones became pleasure grounds for city folk bored with city parks and perhaps contemplating the purchase of a lot or existing house. Their weekend visits prompted many, many plantations of evergreen hedges.

So also did minor nuisances. However much borderland families legislated against slaughterhouses and saloons, foundries and chemical works, they eventually realized that neighbors would sometimes breach the etiquette of niceness. Outdoor laundry-drying irritated many turn-of-the-century authors more than perhaps any other rudeness. The typical borderland resident, according to one aroused critic writing in the 1902 *Architectural Record,* "has a much less commendable want of reticence about some of his domestic arrangements—such, for instance, as the drying of his laundry—which are not either interesting or seemly objects of public inspection."[19] Inventors soon patented collapsible shields that housewives could erect around clotheslines, but householders adjacent to yards lacking such devices—and families particularly concerned about neighbors' viewing their underclothes—began erecting more permanent barriers. Yet screening clothes-yards and such other issues as the placing of doghouses to shelter the animals Bunner and *Dog Fancier* and other turn-of-the-century magazines extolled—really explain little of the planting craze that swept the borderlands after 1910.

Outdoor recreation, especially the spontaneous kind, prompted much of the planting. Farmers had long honored the wonderful microclimatic effects of carefully

Stately trees attracted not only day tourists into the borderlands, but also photographers like C. S. Luitwieler, whose Old Settler *won a 1900* Photo-Era *contest.*

A businessman at work, getting exercise and shaping privacy simultaneously.

Although walking and golfing are the best outdoor exercises, a man can derive both pleasure and profit caring for his garden and grounds

sited hedges: in deflecting or stopping cold winds, in trapping sunlight, in shading ground from summer sun, hedges and hedgerows contributed substantially to farm economy. As early as the 1840s, Downing advised borderland families to learn from farmers the extraordinary climatic improvements that followed the planting of tall hedges.[20] Sixty years later, the borderland preoccupation with physical and mental well-being caused families to spend more and more time outdoors, on their own property, exposed not only to the eyes of "pointers" but to wind, cold, and glaring sun. Edward Payson Powell and other reform-minded landscape architects, horticulturists, and magazine columnists responded to complaints of "unusable grounds" by insisting on hedge-planting, especially the planting of evergreens. "When the day is bitter outside, the moment I step into my drives between my arbor-vitae hedges the climate becomes comfortable," Powell remarks in his book on hedges. "Under the lee of protecting hedges, December not seldom gives me a dandelion," and birds tarry in the wind-free sun-traps. While Powell extols the visual delights of red-barked dogwood, high-bush cranberry, and barberry, he emphasizes that only interplanting among evergreens leads to a weather-improving hedge. His "Sunlight Catcher," a curving, eight-foot-high hedge of arbor vitae facing south toward a similar hedge twenty-five feet away, traps all winter sunlight in a bowl wholly protected from north and west winds. An "invigorating retreat" in November, December, and March, the sun-trap is visually appealing as well, for in it "stands a great barberry bush, that all winter is so red that you can warm your fingers by it."[21] Graced even in near midwinter by thriving green grass and dandelion blossoms, and in very early spring by violets, it demonstrates beyond doubt the usefulness of evergreens in creating nearly magical nooks and corners in northern houselots.

Sun-traps in winter, leafy recesses in midsummer, more open nooks and alleys in spring and fall all appealed to a developing borderland love more of spontaneity than of nature alone. In 1860, Wilson Flagg argued that *spontaneity* designated an aesthetic appreciative of indigenous vegetation, the volunteer trees and other plants that often arranged themselves in more picturesque ways than anything formal gardeners might create.[22] When Powell published *Hedges,* however, spontaneity referred far more to the *use* of borderland grounds. Central Park in New York City, along with other urban parks, catered to deliberate users, men—and more important, perhaps, women—who determined to visit them, dressed themselves for the walk along public streets, and entered decidedly public realms not especially well designed for use in harsh weather. Even the wealthiest city resident knew that "stepping out for some fresh air" or a brief walk meant donning attire and attitudes fit for publicity. In the first decades of the twentieth century, borderland families finally and completely understood the implication of large lots and evergreen hedges. Not only did the hedges create microclimates accessible throughout the year on moment's whim, they shielded their owners from the eyes of strangers and neighbors—and thus from the dictates of propriety and fashion.

In a chapter entitled "The Woman's Corner," Powell captures and explicates the powerful effects of hedges and the forces prompting families to plant more and more of them. Because woman "does the hardest task—the fretting, nerve-wearing work," he asserts, she "has a right to such retreats, sheltered from the sun, and peculiarly her own." After 1900, women recognized that nervousness, stress, and fatigue not only struck their husbands, but reached into the home. The decreasing availability of servants and the arrival of demanding "labor-saving" machines con-tributed to the problems scrutinized in women's magazines, but the ever-increasing responsibilities placed upon borderland women by modernizing society undoubted-ly contributed more. Powell argues, therefore, that borderland women ought to have outdoor nooks in which to sew and do other chores free from the gaze of neigh-bors—"a delicate housewife hates to proclaim to all the world the condition of the family wardrobe," he remarks in arguing for laundry-drying yards screened from passersby and neighbors. But, far, far more important, they need nooks in which to relax, with friends, children, and alone. In describing a circle of arbor vitae some fifteen or twenty feet in diameter and grown together overhead, with the inside branches trimmed upward to about fifteen feet, Powell describes a retreat contain-ing a little table, a hammock, "a small, plain writing-desk, and half a dozen hard-wood chairs that will endure the rain." Here a woman may entertain friends, find "a charming enclosure for a baby," and seek solitude "where she can work a little, rest a little, think a little, and sleep in a hammock if she likes."[23] In concluding that his book will have done some good if it convinces a few housewives to sleep one hour every afternoon, Powell places it squarely in the center of the great debate concerning women's right to spontaneous freedom from housework, to freedom to develop individual loves from botany to fiction.

Large lots and high hedges together offered that freedom to borderland women. A few accessories helped. In the first decade of the new century, the Hough Shade Corporation responded to the double-barrelled concern for microclimate modifica-tion and privacy by advertising its Vudor Porch Shades, thin-slatted linen blinds hung on twine cords, with two slogans: "How To Cool a Hot Porch" and "She Can Look Out, But You Can't Look In." Most of the advertisements emphasized the second theme. *House Beautiful* readers were told that "passers-by cannot see through them, though you can look out. This affords privacy, and you can serve luncheons or lounge in negligee on your porch without fear of observation."[24] Hedges helped far more than porch blinds, however, for they enabled borderland housewives to step outdoors with no concern for personal appearance, to enjoy outdoor invigoration year round, and to hide eccentricities from neighbors. To read or doze outside on washday meant risking the criticism of neighbors in the urban residential zones where second-story windows opened on postage-stamp backyards. To relax, to re-create oneself, to study German grammar outdoors secure from censorious eyes struck the borderland readers of early twentieth-century women's magazines as heavenly—and perfectly possible.

The rush to outdoor privacy through the careful siting of hedges and trees reshaped the backdoor borderland landscape after 1900, and soon the effects spread to front lawns as well. Lack of personal and family privacy became the new urban evil, one addressed regularly in popular periodicals. In 1907, for example, *The*

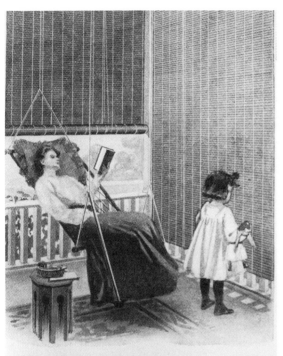

"She can look out, but you can't look in."

These shades are made of Linden wood fibre and str

Manufacturers devised many contraptions intended to supplement the screening and cooling effects of trees and hedges, often advertising them by showing a woman relaxing, not working, secure from public observation.

Trees, especially conifers, not only softened the seasons but screened family gatherings from the eyes of the public, and even from the eyes of neighbors.

Independent published "Suburban Cottages Versus Flats," a scathing condemnation of middle-class apartment houses. "Flat life is not home life, for home life is strongly individuated, and to some extent constitutes a unit by itself," declared the author in words and tone reminiscent of John Ware's indictment a half century earlier. "The consciousness of contiguity is always an annoyance." Perhaps the juxtaposition of social classes grated on the strained nerves of middle-class city folk; perhaps the newly arrived immigrants taxed traditional social expectations. But more likely, the tinkling of a badly tuned piano, the drifting scent of burning liver, the squalling of miserable infants made apartment life, except for the rich, increasingly wearing on already strained men and women. Public parks, too far away and too populated for frequent, almost instantaneous visits, offered little relief to women and children needing spontaneous recreation. "Meanwhile the tide which set in countryward is moving with accelerated activity," the anonymous essayist continued. "The middle classes especially desire less publicity and more retreat." In accepting the cultural impact of "country home books" in reawakening traditional American values—"it is very hard work to root out of human nature a longing for handfuls of violets and goldenrods, for beech nuts and daisies"—and in identifying the utter failure of the urban residential ring as the hope of the middle classes, the essayist precisely defined suburbs.

"The word *suburbanism* means at the present day something a good deal larger than it indicated twenty-five years ago," the writer concludes. "It takes in something more than the suburbs," covering a region "from five to twenty-five miles, or even more from dense population." The last phrase carries vast importance. In his or her mind, true suburbs begin *beyond* the urban residential ring served by streetcars, beyond the West Philadelphias, five miles beyond the "dense population," not five miles beyond downtown. There live people most of whom "own from one to ten or even twenty acres of land," people who enjoy garden and orchard work, people whose "homes are quite up to date as to windbreaks and hedges and shrubbery," people who "are learning how to be natural and simple." There live people blessed with hard-earned indoor and outdoor privacy, a privacy announced by trees.[25]

Trees and tall hedges became the frosting of the early twentieth-century borderland—or "suburban"—cake. Increasingly beautiful and soothing to city people watching street trees wither and die, increasingly eloquent in the dialogue of traditional religion and nature worship, ever more clearly announcing the social stability and timeless values of their owners, borderland trees, and especially evergreens, veiled the lives of borderland families. Shielded by trees and by hedges, by large lots and curtained windows, borderland families enjoyed the privacy utterly necessary to the development of the American—and, perhaps, the human—spirit. Francis E. Clark unwittingly hit upon the significance of the trees and hedges in 1907, when he mentioned one way city people distinguished the commuter at evening time. "His friends are said to know him by the bundles which his capacious arms bring out of the city every night," the commuter noted. "But if he is the happy possessor of a long green bag, he can stow away in it anything from a turkey to a half-pound of peppermints for the children, or a bunch of catnip for Tabby, and no one through its

Large lots and dense foliage gave Kenilworth residents, and other inhabitants of the frosted borderlands, some relief from the lack of urban privacy regularly attacked in mass circulation magazines, such as this one announcing "The Joys of City Life."

opaque sides can get a glimpse of the details of his domestic economy or econom-ics."[26] Trees and hedges, like the long green bag, created a defense against mass society, a *nook* in Alice Cary's terminology, a defense within which flourished, like the simple grass and dandelions within Powell's Sun Catcher, spontaneity, diver-sity, simplicity, tradition, invention, and a host of other values many women and men came to honor. Love of nature endured in the borderlands, but the love enfolded and masked the ever more powerful love of outdoor privacy, of visual separation from pointers and other strangers, of stepping back from views of facto-ries and cities, of spontaneous enjoyment of outdoor space.

17 ❧ IMPROVEMENT

For Clark, for Cozzens, for the hundreds of thousands streaming along city streets to the great urban terminals sheltering rows of commuter trains, evening meant the daily return to commuter country. "It is an inconvenient world, this distant, darkened, unmapped country of the Commuter," mused Dallas Lore Sharp in 1910. "Only God and the Commuter know how to get there, and they alone know why they stay." In the early decades of the new century, in magazine articles like his 1910 *Atlantic Monthly* pieces, "The Commuter and the 'Modern Conveniences,'" and in *The Hills of Hingham* and *The Lay of the Land* and other books, Sharp became the preeminent observer of borderland living. Not only tracing great transformations in national affairs—the shift to assembly-line work in factories, the growing power of advertising on young, white-collar employees, the perfecting of the motor car—and integrating them into his understanding of borderland living, but discerning too the seemingly insignificant details that illuminated the innermost recesses of the borderer's psyche, Sharp addressed not just a borderland audience, but a determinedly urban one too. "Can Heaven, beside the Commuter, find out the way there?" he asked his *Atlantic* readers. "You are standing with your question at the entrance of the great terminal station as the wintry day and the city are closing, and it is small wonder that you ask if God knows whither, over the maze of tracks reaching out into the night, each of this commuting multitude is going." Sharp decided in favor of borderland life—he commuted twenty miles each way, five or six days a week—but perceived its limitations far more precisely than did Henry Cuyler Bunner.

To commute meant to carry bundles, in the anonymous green bag favored by Francis E. Clark perhaps, but more often in paper wrapped with twine or boxes tied with string. "The bundles I have carried!" Sharp exclaims. "And the bundles I have yet to carry! to 'tote'! to 'tote'"![1] Through the gates of the great metropolitan terminals flowed not only a human throng but a collection of bundles so diverse and so numerous that city people, waiting patiently for a cross-country limited to arrive or depart, could only wonder. Wherever the commuters went at nightfall, the parcels and boxes and bundles accompanying them implied that their destinations lacked retail businesses.

Now and then writers boasted of storeless, or nearly storeless places. F. E. M. Cole delighted in reporting that Kenilworth sheltered only one store among its magnificent trees, and turn-of-the-century mapmakers employed by fire insurance companies frequently explored settlements as uncommercialized as any on the frontiers of Oklahoma or Montana.[2] "Purely residential" spaces heartened "pointers" and other prospective borderers disgusted with the urban juxtaposition of stores, factories, stables, taverns, and housing, desperately anxious to locate in places permanently free of noxious activities.[3] Families newly arrived in such pristine locales simply assumed that husbands would carry home anything urban stores did not send out by express, and the vast literature of early twentieth-century borderland living demonstrates the swiftness and completeness with which assumption became reality.

Consider the example of John Preston True, also an *Atlantic Monthly* author and self-confessed "commuter," who published in 1908 his account of bee-keeping ten miles outside New York. After planting his grounds with raspberries, strawberries, grafted pears, and other delicacies, he looked about at different ways of raising livestock and settled on bee-keeping as "the crowning luxury of all." But he did not buy bees and hives in the borderlands, or even in the rural regions beyond; instead he found a beeman "right in the busiest heart of the city," where Sparrowgrass found his poultry dealer. Two stories up, "with a swarm of carpenter-shops, blacksmith-shops, and other mechanics round about," True discerned a steady stream of bees flying to and from a window, and inside the building he found a small shop manufacturing hives. There he acquired bees, hive, smoker, and assorted other paraphernalia and went home to tell his doubting wife that the adventure had begun.

Of course he carried nothing. "In due time," he explains. "the hive appeared, by express, and was carried up into the front attic. The expressman seemed unusually glad to make delivery."[4] True wrote in an age graced by express companies, by the great Adams, Wells Fargo, and Railway Express firms to be sure, but by ten thousand local ones too, individually owned and operated businesses absolutely essentially to borderland existence. Taken utterly for granted by their customers, they surface repeatedly in the literature of borderland growth. Almost never, of course, do authors describe the routine activities of express companies—bringing to back doors and then to their proper rooms furniture, applicances, bicycles, and other bulky items bought the day before in city stores or two days before from telegraph-order firms or ten days earlier from mail-order houses. Instead, the writers focus on the delivery of furnaces as massive as that which troubled the Grays' neighbors, giant patent iceboxes, pianos, growling dogs, and angered, buzzing bees.

The local railroad station served as a portal opening not only on the borderland community around it but on the railroad trains speeding to and from the city. Early twentieth-century borderland families understood the significance of the station gateway, as did railroad corporations, and families, usually through "improvement societies" or municipal government, combined with railroad management to secure tasteful structures surrounded by small parks and gardens. "Stepping from the train, after a thirty minutes' ride from Chicago, one is impressed with the beauties of the low-lying stone depot half hidden in vines and shrubbery and gay with flowering plants," remarked Cole of one particularly handsome commuter station. "Passing through the stone archway, the beauty of Kenilworth makes itself manifest, for this is really Kenilworth's front door."[5] As any housewife in Kenilworth or every other borderland community knew, however, the depot functioned as a back door too.

After the commuters had departed for the city, an outbound train paused at the station to unload mail and "express" onto the large wheeled carts rolled out from the baggage room by the station agent. The local postman then carried the mail to an office in his house or store—in the years before rural free delivery the Post Office delivered no mail to rural houses—and the local expressman loaded the crates, barrels, and boxes onto his wagon and set off to deliver them to back doors. One deceptively simple operation masked a complex system of retailing; it worked so well that few contemporaneous authors scrutinized it or its effects. Had they done so, American metropolitan life might have retained the efficiency and grace that delighted borderland families.

Borderland housewives expected almost every purchase to be delivered into their kitchens, sometimes put away. Icemen delivered blocks of ice directly into iceboxes; milkmen, often operating from local farms, placed milk on top of the ice. Along the curving roads, according to set schedules, came the competing butchers, fishmongers, vegetable sellers, and other vendors of food. In the early years of any borderland settlement, the lack of such vendors or the existence of only one in each speciality irritated families accustomed to urban diversity and resulting improve-ment, via competition, in quality and price. But the tradesmen quickly arrived in the borderlands, for they understood that the newcomers represented not only an affluent clientele but one whose notions concerning health and happiness prompted the purchase of first-class produce. "The butcher's wagon rattled merrily up to our gate every morning; and if we had kept no other reckoning, we should have known it was Thursday by the grocer," enthused William Dean Howells. "We were living in the country with the conveniences and luxuries of the city about us."[6] Nor did the necessity of purchasing beef or bananas require the housewife to remain at home, for many tradesmen trusted by their customers not only delivered ordered meat and produce to empty houses, but also put away the purchases, entering unlocked kitchens and opening icebox doors. Borderland women, after all, had things to do outside their houses.

Along with walking in the woods, bicycling, and visiting in gardens shielded by hedges, borderland women shopped in cities. Railroad corporations understood the need for mid-morning inbound trains and for trains leaving the city in the early afternoon; such trains carried women to urban stores and shops, particularly to the retail invention of the age, the department store. City shopping, for all the problems of crowds and dirty streets, at least partly satisfied the growing need of American women—borderland and urban—for self-determination.[7] In the department store, in the streetfront shop, women decided what to buy. There, along with other women and free of all but the half-forgotten admonitions of absent husbands, women made up their minds, and in that decision-making they enjoyed some taste of the larger independence they craved. To shop in a large, anonymous store or small, cozy shop, whether alone or with a friend or two, to satisfy oneself that each purchase represented the best value at the best price; to lunch in a tearoom or restaurant, perhaps with her husband, perhaps with friends, perhaps alone; to return before children arrived home from school—such was the tiring, sometimes exhausting, and often exhilerating experience that informs so many articles in periodicals directed at women readers. And to return home on a hot summer day or frigid winter afternoon carrying an envelope of dress patterns perhaps, or a new watch, knowing that the next day the expressman would deliver the other purchases to one's back door, that was only the way of things, something so ordinary as to scarcely deserve mention.

Advertisers exploited women's new role as shoppers and increasingly recognized them as decision-makers. Newspaper and magazine advertising by national manufacturers cemented the concept of the "brand-name" item, telling women over and over to buy no brand until they had examined the one advertised. Across post–Civil War rural America, small-town storekeepers felt the repeated blows of such advertising; women wanted to buy no sewing machine until they had tried a Singer, for example, and storekeepers learned the expense of stocking several brands of every appliance, every type of canned fruit, every dress pattern; they watched in horror customers venturing to the nearest big city to comparison shop. Borderland women scrutinized not only brand-name advertising but all the department-store advertising in the newspapers delivered in the early morning or brought home by husbands in the evening. And, very frequently, they ventured "to town."

"It is one thing to live on a city street, just around the corner from a well-stocked grocery," begins "Buying the Supplies for a Suburban Home," a 1906 magazine article aimed at women readers living "ten miles from a lemon." Helen M. Winslow points out that borderland housewives shopping "in town" have an enormous advantage over apartment dwellers. Their large houses provide space to encourage, indeed almost to dictate, saving money by buying in bulk. She describes the usefulness of a cold, dry fruit-and-vegetable storage cellar—it permits the wise housewife to buy potatoes, onions, and other necessary produce at cheap autumn prices and keep them until the following July without spoilage. Winslow offers the simplest advice to women who have a pantry or "preserve closet": "Groceries? Buy them in quantities of the large grocers in the near-by cities. You can get them at a discount in that way and be sure of always having something in the house to eat." To be sure, some things keep badly. Buying a barrel of flour or a fifty-gallon drum of kerosene is economical, but acquiring a barrel of sugar almost always leads to ants. Winslow's article emphasizes bulk purchase—she even advises buying thread and other sewing notions by the dozen—not only to save money, but to save visiting the village store. "I would not want to be understood as advising my readers to buy

The borderland commuter station bustled only twice each day, but that bustle indicated to women and children alike something of the city activity just down the track, the activity that entices Bunner's young couple to run away.

This illustration from Bunner's Jersey Street and Jersey Shore is one of the first depicting what by mid-nineteenth-century was a common practice— the borderland woman and her child waiting for the evening commuter train.

Women's attempts to improve the lives of their families often began in apartment-house kitchens, when young wives first began calculating how to afford borderland houses, and culminated in the large-scale effort to beautify commuter-stop villages.

everything in the large cities," she concludes, seemingly suddenly aware of the import of her lengthy essay. "One should patronize the local merchant in one's own town and suburb whenever possible to do it as cheaply and with as good results." But in again warning readers about the "rather ancient" produce and high prices on all but a few dry-goods items, "Buying the Supplies" returns to its praise of urban stores and bulk shopping.[8]

Urban retailing combined with the efficient express system to stifle commercial development in the borderlands. In twine-tied packages or long green bags, husbands regularly brought home small, low-cost items—new scissors or catnip or baking powder—that they purchased during lunch-hour walks. Shopkeepers and railroad companies worked diligently to make "toting" simple. A department-store customer could request an item to be delivered to the terminal "parcel room" before the evening rush hour; there for a token fee the railroad company stored it until the commuter called for it on his way to the train platform. Moreover, the railroad corporations leased terminal retail space to cobblers, watch repairers, bakers, candy sellers, florists, and other specialists devoted to serving the commuters who passed by the concourse shops twice each day; one 1911 *Country Life* writer remarked that his "local bookshop" stood smack in the concourse of a great terminal far from his home but wonderfully convenient for browsing and buying.[9] Only a rare borderland community supported a jeweler, a florist, or even a cobbler; contemporaneous business directories make clear the overwhelming retail dominance of the cities.

Commercial development proceeded slowly in the borderlands, therefore, and its tentative, almost fitful progress once again directed public attention at the American village. Between 1880 and 1930, borderland families confronted the enduring shabbiness of the shops and other businesses—and houses—remaining from the nearly vanished agricultural era, now huddled about a depot serving commuters.

When Warren Manning published his "History of Village Improvement in the United States" in a 1904 issue of *Craftsman,* most Americans understood the reform movement as one focused on rural areas. His article emphasizes the pioneering efforts of Downing, Willis, and other mid-nineteenth-century writers in awakening farmers' and villagers' interest in beautification, especially in roadside tree planting and the clearing of rubbish from village backyards and vacant lots. At first reading, the *Craftsman* essay places the village improvement movement squarely within the larger rural improvement or "country life" movement in which so many turn-of-the-century reformers participated.[10] The country life movement focused the efforts of Theodore Roosevelt, the American Academy of Political and Social Science, agricultural reformers like Liberty Hyde Bailey, and other individuals and associations, but by 1910 a divergence of interests had begun to separate genuinely agricultural efforts from those of borderland people. Indeed, Manning's article displays a subtle fuzziness of thinking: while its text emphasizes rural efforts and challenges, its illustrations demonstrate a concern with commuter regions. As a landscape architect, Manning understood that the bulk of improvement would occur where people had the greatest commitment and the most funds. He also perceived that families intensely interested in creating picturesque home grounds might combine to tailor entire communities—and require professional assistance.

A subtle shift in language marked the division. A powerful faith in environmental determinism continued to imspire those reformers convinced that improving the physical environment would necessarily "elevate" rural social life. Adherents to the country life movement continued to speak of village or rural "improvement" exactly as George E. Waring, Jr., had used the term in 1877 in his *Village Improvements and Farm Villages,* a collection of essays reprinted from *Scribner's Magazine* and based on a single premise: "the shiftless village is a hideous village."[11] Making the village attractive, in Waring's estimation, would undoubtedly improve its inhabitants, exactly as Downing had argued decades before. But borderland families thought differently, and articles addressed to them reflect the difference. Since borderland families understood their lives to be already improved, what the depot and its immediate surroundings needed was "beautification" confirming and advertising the wonderful life announced in seats, grounds, and tree-lined roads.

Yet borderland families remained caught up in the larger "improvement" effort simply because so many lived in quasi-agricultural areas dotted with enduringly ugly villages. Early twentieth-century reformers now and then attempted to unravel the complexities that so frequently deflected improvement or beautification efforts, but their essays reveal the same fuzziness that flaws Manning's. In 1905, for example, Frederick Law Olmsted, Jr., published his attempt at solving the puzzle. His "Village Improvement," an *Atlantic Monthly* article, consists mostly of a lengthy "fragment" from the writings of his famous uncle, the designer—with George Waring—of Central Park in New York City. Written around 1885 or 1890, the fragment recalls the "bare, bleak, cheap, utilitarian structures" and other ugliness of the American village of the 1840s. Olmsted condemns the successors of Andrew Jackson Downing for focusing on "decorative beauty" in their improvement of the physical environments of so many such places, rather than gently improving natural beauties and eliminating the worst blemishes. In using the example of the clipper ship—which causes both "a high-bred lady and a dull, low, degraded, and sodden seafaring laborer" to become "animated at the same instant by the same impulse of admiration" of its beauty—the elder Olmsted asserts the democratic rightness of simple, practical beauty. His nephew and the inheritor of his landscape architecture firm traced the subsequent "energetic spasm of Village Improvement," which accomplished "first and best" the removal of litter, but thereafter perpetrated catastrophes of decoration ranging from the setting out of "bad-colored" rubbish barrels to the erection of pseudo-Italian fountains nearly everywhere it gained support. But what better might be done? The younger Olmsted offered very little advice to rural villagers, and even less to borderland families residing a mile or so from a scruffy commuter stop. "The only safe procedure, when one goes a single step beyond the neat and orderly provision for generally recognized practical necessities of the village," he determined, "is to look fairly and squarely into the future, to adopt a definite and comprehensive plan and policy" against which every proposed change must be judged.[12] How such a plan and policy—the one presumably graphic, the other written—might be conceived, the article leaves unanswered.

By whom the policy should be created, however, had been answered much earlier. "At the outset it is to be said that the organization and control of the village society is especially woman's work," opined George Waring in 1877. Women had the habit of "good housekeeping" already, and the improvement movement "calls for a degree of leisure which women are the most apt to have." More important, however, Waring declared that "it will especially engage their interest as being a real addition to the field of their ordinary routine of life."[13] Contemporaneous documentation strongly suggests that farmwives and other women lacking much leisure time contributed far less to the country life movement than did the women of borderland families. Mary Caroline Robbins, in an 1897 *Atlantic Monthly* essay, "Village Improvement Societies," focuses on the "essential femininity" of the movement—emphasizing, as did so many other writers, that Mary Hopkins had founded the effort in Stockbridge, Massachusetts, decades earlier—but confines her examples chiefly to borderland places. "There is something about it congenial to the feminine temperament," Robbins declares of the movement. She argues that it offers women the finest possible opportunity to order the larger landscape as precisely as they order their houses, and then to beautify that larger landscape just as they do their own gardens. But Robbins is far more hard-headed than Waring, noting that "village improvement is thus the offspring of the cities, and in most cases it is paid for and engineered by those who have enjoyed city advantages." Among such urban advantages she includes not only physical amenities like water, sewer, and gas mains, but the chilling awareness of sterility and decay in urban residential zones. The borderland woman aware of the gross ugliness of Staten Island—once a "beautiful and healthy region" but now "defiled" by "dram-shops and factories"—she argues, will understand that village improvement by beautification is no whimsical pastime, but a vitally urgent effort at turning back city evil. Words like *defile* in the women-authored literature of village improvement suggest a half-conscious connection between the defiling of home and community and the defiling of a woman herself. Borderland women may or may not have connected the two, but their arguments make clear their understanding of village beautification as something more than skin deep.

Robbins argues that a moral necessity underlies borderland beautification efforts. Planting street trees, for example, dries up the stagnant water that contributes to malaria; scouring lots and roads of rubbish and manure likewise strengthens community health. Preserving shrubs and vines along curving roads saves a "picturesque wildness" that strengthens the place's "artistic sentiment." In arguing that women ought to expand their efforts from beautifying the home for the sake of the tired businessman and children—essentially the argument of the middle decades of the nineteenth century—to embracing the whole residential community, Robbins amplifies the echoes of Susan Cooper, hinting that borderland women can almost magically transform whole landscapes. Of course, the borderlands needed little improvement. Families moved to them, after all, in part to enjoy existing picturesque beauty and better ways of living. But in asserting that the typical improvement society should be divided into committees overseen by a board of managers, "one half of whom may be women," Robbins emphasizes that problems of ugliness, of potential defilement, exist, and that solid organization and money—and husbands—are required to solve them.[14]

Fragmentary evidence suggests that borderland women succeeded, at least in some places, in correcting ugliness. In the late 1870s, for example, the women of Montclair, New Jersey, organized the morning after hearing a lecture on village improvement. The Wednesday Afternoon Club, and in later years, the Woman's Town-Improvement Association, worked in a dozen committees, in frequent meetings, and with immense enthusiasm to tackle head-on minor and major problems. The women raised funds for hundreds of street trees, stopped the posting of advertisements on utility poles and the door-to-door distribution of flyers, ended the use of utility poles as stands for "nostrum vendors," and insisted on the enforcement of long-forgotten laws. Birdsley Grant Northrop reported in 1895 that he had been privileged "to hear the admirable, business-like reports given by the chairman of each of these committees."[15] His 1895 *Forum* article emphasizes that the organized women of Montclair had discovered not only their ability to beautify space, but some inkling of their political muscle.

By many names, afternoon clubs, improvement associations, garden clubs, women's clubs, the groups of women—and men, especially as financial backers—subtly changed the public appearance of borderland communities, especially those areas around commuter-station villages. In almost every instance, they tackled manageable problems, securing by public, collective action not only public good, but distinctly private good as well. Tree planting, rubbish collecting, street draining, and other efforts pleased everyone day after day, from the commuter striding to his morning train to the child bicycling to the woman hurrying home from a quick visit to a local store.[16] The women extended their loathing of slovenliness from their privately owned lots into the public realm, eliminating, or nearly eliminating, the vestiges of rural and village messiness that so irritated Nathaniel Willis and other early borderers so many decades before. But still they confronted the challenge of the village itself—the collection of structures in which the railroad corporation placed a station, or which in time grew up around the depot.

Maps made for fire insurance firms, and especially the wonderfully detailed ones made by the Sanborn Company, demonstrate not only the endurance of villages through the settlement of the borderlands, but their adaptation first to the railroad, then to nonfarming newcomers. Many borderland stations, even those along the stylish "main line" running west from Philadelphia or north from Chicago, boasted a spur track serving a hay and grain dealer, and sometimes a coalyard too. Borderland families required feed for their horses and other livestock and fuel for their furnaces; such bulky freight defeated the best efforts of teamsters and traveled cheapest by rail anyway. Often the feed dealer operated a hardware store on the street side of his structure, slowly altering his stock as full-time farming vanished before gentlemen farming, gardening, and lawn-making. Near many coalyards, frequently along the same spur track, prospered a small lumberyard providing the framing and finish timber for the houses and outbuildings erected by the newcomers. Together, depot, freight house, feed mill, coalyard, and lumberyard, along with a few houses sheltering owners and employees, often constituted all the structures of a village or "crossing," a small commercial place focused on the intersection of a country road and a railroad right-of-way. Sanborn Company investigators often found more structures, of course, and carefully recorded the existence—and flammability—of moribound and prosperous small factories producing chairs, tacks, incubators, and a thousand other products, along with the houses in which their owners, managers, and employees lived.[17] A well-traveled road or small manufacturing operation frequently sustained a general store and post office, and sometimes such additional retail establishments as a tavern or a blacksmith shop, all essentially unchanged from the 1840s.

The changing population of the borderlands added remarkably little to many train-station villages; the efficient express system and the husbands' long green bags simply stymied retail development. In the early days of lot sales, one or two real estate agents might erect small offices, which in time came to shelter modest commercial operations like barber and bicycle shops and promised just enough business to encourage the feed dealer or nearby farmer to open a horse-and-carriage livery. Most of the few new businesses smacked of the twentieth century. The drugstore announced the change in occupancy best. Going by a hundred names (often Station Drugs), the drugstore heralded the end not only of folk medicine remembered by Lincoln-trained botanizing women, but of many patent remedies too. With its rows of medicines, its soda fountain, its "notions" counter, the commuter-stop drugstore bespoke not only the continuing concern with health that fueled the early twentieth-century rush to the borderlands, but also the continuing borderland love of urban delights—ice-cream sodas being among the most important. Along with the so-called "variety store"—which sold in more polite arrangements the newspapers, periodicals, and tobacco products offered in urban "news agencies," along with perhaps more feminine goods like greeting cards—the general store, the drugstore, and the peddlers of food satisfied most of the wants of families in daily touch with urban stores.

Sanborn Company maps, often updated every ten years in order to provide insurers with reasonably contemporary information concerning the structural material and contents of town buildings, reveal the gradual diversification of village retailing that accompanied the peopling of picturesque, formerly agricultural places. Meat and produce peddlers sometimes settled down, opening stores while retaining home delivery services; local express agencies moved from wagons and back-yard quarters into store-front locations. Undertakers, upholsterers, "hardware and plumbing" dealers, and stationers built their own modest structures or rented space in the one wood or brick "block" erected by some local investor. Banks, too, often in brick structures, appear on Sanborn maps in the early years of the new century, announcing the increasing economic independence of communities incorporated as boroughs, towns, villages, hamlets, or townships but lacking the broad retail base—

and almost invariably, the saloons, emblems of degradation—of rural small towns. Borderland train-stop villages lacked more than saloons, of course. Conspicuous by their absence from Sanborn Company maps are local newspaper publishers, large dry-goods stores, furniture suppliers, offices of physicians, dentists, attorneys, and other professionals, jewelery and florist shops, and often even bakeries and shoe-repair shops. Quite clearly, borderland families lavished very little discretionary income on village merchants. Not infrequently the Sanborn Company reported a particularly dangerous fire hazard—vacant stores. City goods and city services glistened too near.

Early twentieth-century writers understood something else about the borderland villages, especially those new villages lacking any old-fashioned manufacturing and wholly dependent on retail activity. Borderland families, perhaps especially borderland women, disliked retail activity and kept it in its proper place, near the station. Even in handsome but quite built-up borderland places like Mount Vernon, New York—by 1907 an incorporated city whose "few manufacturing industries," in the words of one visitor, "are grouped along the railroad tracks, quite removed from the business and residential portions of the town"—families insisted on a clear separation of business and residential districts. "No business has been allowed to creep into the best residential district," H. W. Mathews assured the readers of *Suburban Life*, "so that one may walk or drive for long distances, seeing only these beautiful residences with an occasional church or school building."[18] And only those businesses "necessary to feed and clothe and properly house the inhabitants" comprised the village near the station. No longer did borderland families worry much about the vast manufacturing complexes snaking through urban residential zones miles down the tracks. In the first decades of the twentieth century, they devoted their attention to a handful of stores.

In 1915, Frederick L. Allen argued in the January issue of *House Beautiful* that "our cities and towns and countryside are in appearance undeniably shabby," chiefly as a result of crushing industrialism and gross ignorance of simple beauty. Allen focused his attack on industrial zone housing, on summer resorts, on the shipping docks in Hoboken and East Boston; about the borderlands he says little explicitly, but his conclusion directs attention at the train-stop village. Allen, along with many other writers of his moment, rediscovered the English village beloved of Hawthorne, Melville, and Olmsted, and rediscovered it without the skepticism of James Fenimore Cooper. "In the average American town the artist finds practically nothing to delight the eye," he asserts, dismissing the notions of intrigue that preoccupy William Dean Howells' *Suburban Sketches* narrator. "For every picture which the place offers, the most unpromising French or English village would offer a dozen." With its smooth lawns, well-tended hedges, spectacular flower boxes everywhere, the English village overwhelms the American visitor, even the visitor from handsome borderland landscapes dotted with tawdry train-shop villages. "The Village Improvement Societies and the 'Clean Up and Paint Up Weeks' have made a beginning," Allen concludes, but only "the slow and painful process of educating people to see the difference between the beautiful and the ugly" will improve the entire built landscape.[19]

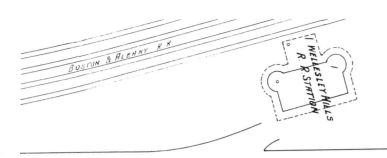

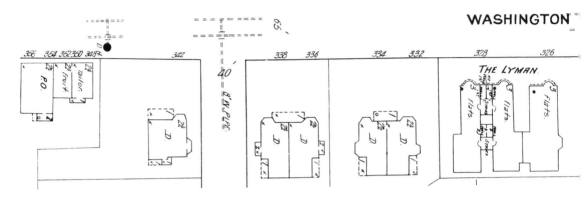

Late nineteenth-century Sanborn Company maps suggest how few businesses stood near most commuter-train stations. Here only a tailor, fruit store, and post office offer any commercial activity.

From the time of Susan Cooper into the 1930s, the English countryside of thatched-roof cottages and tree-lined, narrow lanes remained the epitome of landscape beauty for well-educated, American borderland women.

Allen wrote out of a growing disgust with much modern commercial building, a disgust that found expression in many popular periodicals. An 1899 *Atlantic Monthly* writer argued that the "quiet expression" of the few good buildings in the United States—Dutch colonial farmhouses, eighteenth-century Harvard College dormitories, and a handful of others—"ought to furnish a useful lesson to our rising architects." Charles C. Moore stated his case simply: "excellence of design and the mellowing touch of time" made such buildings, which he admitted were not "beautiful examples of architecture," nevertheless "entirely agreeable objects to look upon." However complex the popular and professional debate concerning the form and appearance of urban commercial structures—one which ranged from the height of skyscrapers to the Gothic revival to brilliantly colored terra-cotta materials to the importance of contiguous trees and other plants—in the borderlands the Old World village, and especially the Tudor English village, reappeared as the standard by which American train-stop villages should be evaluated.[20] As magically as the medieval English landscape Susan Cooper invoked, the sixteenth-century English village returned as the antidote to twentieth-century commercial ugliness.

Borderland families delighted—sometimes honestly, sometimes smugly—in the picturesque, simple, "natural" beauty of their houses and grounds, finding their homes, and communities of homes, a proper check against rampant industrialism, urbanism, capitalism, and a host of other threats that ruled space and life beginning at the depot doorstep. Confining those forces to the railroad track and its ancilliary structures began to preoccupy borderers sometime in the 1890s, if articles appearing in special interest magazines offer a correct indication. In 1907, for example, a *Suburban Life* author pleaded for "color harmony" not only in the houses of the "poor or middle classes" but in communities inhabited by the rich. In arguing for neutral, natural colors, A. E. McCrea did little more than parrot the aesthetics Downing championed seventy years before, but in fastening on the sinister effects of railroad-company color schemes, McCrea sliced deeply into the borderland distrust of large-scale corporate capitalism. "It is astonishing how infectious the house-painting spirit is," she noted. "The fever often starts at the railroad station buildings, and the predominating color used can be seen scattered over the town for many blocks." The corporate color schemes or "liveries," particularly the "brilliant reds and yellows," reflect only a "cheap advertising" McCrea found difficult to connect with the otherwise "splendid railway systems."[21] But what appalled her was the unnerving willingness of uneducated, small-town people to appropriate the colors for their own houses. Such people need guidance, she concluded, almost as much as well-to-do borderland families unaware that harsh, jarring colors contribute as much to stress as urban noise. The only right way to achieve a sensitive, honest, spirit-strengthening physical environment, consequently, lay in harmonizing the colors of all structures in a neighborhood. Implicit in the brief article, implicit in so many other articles addressed to borderland readers, is the absolute necessity of selecting not only the colors of nature, of time-mellowed English villages, and of pre-industrial American common building, but colors that connote nothing of corporate capitalism.

Improvement societies soon transcended their first efforts and slammed head-long into changing the appearance of train-stop villages. In community after borderland community—those places many authors precisely identified as "true suburbs"—the societies convinced railroad corporations to dignify the right-of-way with tasteful stations and handsome station gardens, arguing that such stations would entice more and more homeseekers (and fill more coaches) while serving as properly handsome portals on handsome towns.22 In Kenilworth, in Mount Vernon, in Brookline and Wellesley outside Boston, in Scarsdale outside New York, in a hundred places in the eastern half of the country, corporations discovering the profits in commuter service heeded the wishes of improvement associations, sometimes even anticipated them. But achieving low-storied, modestly colored, finely planted depots scarcely satisfied the associations, for (except in a few accomplished places like Kenilworth) a handful of unhandsome stores lay between the handsome station and handsome home grounds.

Commuters hustling to morning trains or strolling homeward noticed the stores, of course, but women, the inhabitants of the borderlands, scrutinized them, found them wanting, and determined to improve them. Improvement associations attempted to commute the utter obviousness of commercial enterprise, not by closing the stores, but by dressing them in feudal or colonial garb, by making their appearance support the alternative way of life announced by fine gardens, tall trees, and factoryless landscape. Nothing, the women argued, must compromise the shaping power of the borderland landscape.

"Arrived at the village station on a wintry evening, when the gloaming is punctuated by the cheery household lamps, shining here and there like golden stars, through the leafless trees, the man going home has again an advantage in that he returns to a house and not to a fraction of one," argued Margaret E. Sangster in a 1901 *Collier's* article devoted to borderland commuting. The commuter "speeding across country in a comfortable railway coach, has a seat, and his paper, and agreeable company," of course—"come-outer" delights alien to the city executive jammed in a streetcar. But the important delights lie just beyond the depot, delights that make him feel "that the fourteen or eighteen or twenty miles between his office and his home are a mere nothing, and that the home seems the more sacred and sweet that there is a decided separating wedge of solid distance between it and the place of the daily grind." Sangster's essay implies that only professional men, men who work in offices, enjoy such rewards, and that such men need not only the miles of separation from "the grind" and the sacred home in frosted space, but relief from commercial structure. "When the winds are holding a jubilee, and the white blanket of the snow folds over the fields, when every branch and twig are powdered with silver or coated with ermine, the suburban town is beautiful as a dream and charming as a scene in fairyland."23 Sangster's fairyland, as free of commercial intrusion as the feudal scene Susan Cooper imagined from her elevated nook, was the goal of the borderland improvement society, the destination of Sharp's commuters hurrying to the trains running toward stops frosted, if not with snow, at least with trees and pre-big-business-era store-fronts.

V The Planned Residential Community

Olmsted and Atterbury understood the visual and social
importance of borderland station-stop areas, and they devoted
much time to designing the gateway to Forest Hills Gardens.

❧ RESTRICTIONS

Francis H. Bulot intended nothing special in presenting his 1916 American City *article to a readership of city managers and engineers, real estate promoters, and urban planners. Concise, factual, almost stark, the text and photographs offer a glimpse at Shawnee Place, a brand-new residential subdivision located within the city limits of Fort Wayne, Indiana. "Developing a Restricted Home Community" appeared in November, part of a genre focused on an increasingly popular sort of real estate development, the engineered, precisely restricted configuration of single-family houses on small lots.*

Shawnee Park consisted of forty-six lots, each with 40 feet frontage along the street and reaching back 140 feet. A piece of "bowl-shaped" land just less than nine acres, after careful draining, became the stage on which the Wildwood Companies created its model residential neighborhood. "The architectural treatment is free from repetitions of designs or preponderance of styles so often found in 'Builder's Row,'" Bulot states. "Careful study of building sizes, heights, grades, sky line, harmony of color and texture of building materials has given a charm to the surroundings, has developed an air of comfort, and created a community spirit." The Wildwood Companies sold a stable future, too. Restrictions written into every deed limited use of the property and specified the siting of houses "relative to the front and side streets" and the number of residences per lot. "In general," the engineer concludes, "those things which make for a well-contented community and protect the many against the whims of the few are to be found in these restrictions." Having gracefully sited the lots, houses, and improvements like asphalt pavements, cement walks, shade trees, and shrubs (each marked with a species identification tag), having legislated the future physical character of the place, the Companies did only one thing more. It established a "neighborhood association" to "inaugurate and manage" such activities as garden contests and celebrations.[1] Its investment recouped and profit made, the Wildwood Companies moved on.

Nothing of borderland form or living characterized Shawnee Place. Planted firmly within city limits, the development lacked even superficially the right to the word suburb. *A solid, tasteful, lower-middle-class urban neighborhood, it reflected its* inhabitants' increasingly sharp dislike of most urban residential zones, "Builder's Row" in the jargon of its creator and advertiser. It also represented the fleeting love of mandated permanent perfection, the love of restrictions Nathaniel Hawthorne knew in Rock Park nearly a century before.

Articles of Agreement Regulating the Use, Holding, and Enjoyment of the Rock Park Estate in the County of Chester dates from 1837. Minutely, almost fanatically detailed, the document first introduces restrictions upon the use of the carriage drives and walks, specifying that "no carts, wains, or waggons shall be permitted to use or pass over the same" except when carrying building materials to abutting lots. The agreement continues by prohibiting brick making; by specifying the square footage of land necessary to allow a householder to erect a stable, the materials from which houses must be made, the setback distances of structures; and by forbidding any trade, business, or profession, other "than the learned professions" such as medi-cine or teaching (and then for not more than six students), to be carried on within the grounds. Purchasers might erect no walls or fences, especially board fences, above three feet in height; they must keep their structures in good repair, and they may share the common water supply.[2] The document is timeless. No one could buy property in Rock Park without agreeing to its restrictions, and the association of householders, while able to alter the code after following a complex and deliberately time-consuming process, oversaw its enforcement. The Rock Park restrictions indeed seem set in stone.

Shawnee Place and Rock Park responded to the same loathing of disorder, partic-ularly disorder that destroyed a family's investment in its land and house. "The whims of the few," Bulot termed such disorder, and his readers understood his import. Every urban residential zone displayed by 1916 the catastrophic results of mixed-use devel-opment, of horrors that made inharmonious paint schemes almost unnoticeable. Fami-lies in the zones began to specify what they wanted, and authors began to repeat their desires—and demands—in print. They wanted fresh air, solid "church and school privileges," a place "where their children could have an opportunity to romp and play with an abundance of room and in the right sort of atmosphere," in the words of one 1907 Suburban Life writer. "To put it in a different way," H. W. Mathews con-tinued, "they sought a city of homes."[3]

For the rich, for the well-to-do, for the lower middle class willing to commute, for the working-class families willing to relocate to the service villages growing up around commuter-train stations, the borderlands offered those things and more. But by the beginning of the twentieth century, especially around New York City, the commute had become almost impossibly long, and real estate developers began experimenting with the memories of Llewellyn Park and other constructs one 1851 Cincinatti writer designated suburban villages. The developers projected "communities" of single- and multi-family houses on new sorts of lots, places of country and tennis clubs, of "com-mon" lands, of perfectly harmonized, perfectly restricted form, places without train-stop village ugliness, without any slovenliness at all.[4] On Long Island, outside Cleveland, and in a handful of other places, developers and professional designers offered an alternative vision of borderland life.[5]

In October, 1914, Samuel Howe mused at length on the example of Forest Hills Gardens, explaining to readers of the lead article in *House Beautiful* that the real estate development in Queens represented what Americans had learned from German "garden cities," and especially from Krupp and Essen. "We, as a nation, are thinking, changing, growing. We are learning," he concluded after praising the creation of the Russell Sage Foundation and its architect and landscape architect. Howe thought he had glimpsed the future in the rolling countryside of Queens. Something other than large houses and broad lots on curving roads would characterize subsequent twentieth-century borderland development.

Yet something disturbed him, something so tentative, so subtle that it only implicitly appears in his conclusion. In Krupp and Essen, in Roland Park outside Baltimore, and in Whitinsville and Hopedale in Massachusetts, he found "bright, cheerful houses, well arranged, well trimmed lawns, hedging carefully cut," with an "admirable" overall effect compounded by "distinctly joyous" roads. The garden cities, the future developments patterned on Forest Hills Gardens, would be nearly perfect, peculiarly happy arrangements of space and structure. "Some people might like to think of the garden city as a tiny principality, presided over by a strong personality," Howe decided, "who, in some subtle manner, at times humorous and again defiant, but always good natured, endeavors to extract from everyone so fortunate as to be within its boundaries, the natural good and worth-whileness of each character, so as to make of this neighborhood a pleasing page in the history of the locality."[1] In one long sentence following his brief paen to Essen and Hopedale, Howe all unwittingly put his finger on the terrible tension that contorted the long-term impact of Forest Hills Gardens.

In the first, wonderfully optimistic years of planning and ground-breaking, no one realized the tension implicit in the text and drawings, and soon apparent on the 142-acre farm in Queens. A spate of booklets, leaflets, and newspaper advertisements explained the thinking of the Russell Sage Foundation so thoroughly, so logically, that apparently no one saw any more deeply than Howe. What had begun as the private passion of Mrs. Russell Sage quickly became a chief interest of the foundation she established in memory of her husband. An English-like garden city, providing rental and owner-occupied houses for families able to afford twenty-five dollars "and upward" a month for shelter would rise in borderland Queens.

As *Forest Hills Gardens*, the first explanatory pamphlet published by the Sage Foundation Homes Company, makes clear, the foundation aimed at larger issues. Of central importance in the mind of the foundation, the "educational purpose" shaped nearly every component of the scheme. Simply put, the foundation intended to build a wholly profitable housing development that would demonstrate to the most callous developer of residential-zone and borderland housing the greater profits to be realized from new arrangements of streets and structures, from new building materials, and from integrated beauty. If it succeeded, "people of moderate income and good taste, who appreciate sympathetic surroundings, but are tied close to the city by the nature of their occupation" would "find some country air and country life within striking distance of the active centers of New York."[2] Those people in search of "country" residence and the thousands of expected visitors— "pointers" with something unique at which to point—would force private developers to reach new levels of residential design and new levels of profit.

The foundation moved quickly after purchasing the farm, as quickly as any private developer, but it moved according to its fundamental pedagogical purpose. At once it organized a design team around two men, landscape architect Frederick Law Olmsted, Jr., and Grosvenor Atterbury, an architect of equal reputation. The two designers worked intimately with the financial management group assembled by the foundation, which was determined to create a place reflecting perfectly the emergent "scientific principles" of town planning. Of far greater importance, however, the two designers committed themselves to explaining in writing the rationale behind every detail of the immense project. *Forest Hills Gardens* is only the first of their many descriptive efforts.

In a lengthy chapter entitled "The Landscape Work," Olmsted explains that "three important principles in city planning" underlie the overall scheme of the development. The first, that main thoroughfares "should be direct, ample, and convenient no matter how they cut the land," explains the position of three main streets, two 80 feet wide and one 125 feet wide, aligned with the tentative gridiron street plan New York City intended for Queens—if and when the urban residential ring arrived. Second, but not at all less important, all other roads must be "quiet, attractive" residential streets, not "fantastically crooked," but laid out "so as to discourage their use as thoroughfares" and kept narrow to increase the area of lawns and front gardens. About his wide streets Olmsted says scarcely anything, but about "the cozy, domestic character" of those created from his understanding of the second principle he is eloquent. In Forest Hills Gardens "the monotony of endless, straight, windswept thoroughfares which represent the New York conception of streets will give place to short, quiet, self-contained and garden-like neighborhoods." The collection of neighborhoods organized around the quiet streets focuses on "parks and public open spaces," the creatures of the third great principle—the absolute necessity of parkland—derived as much from European and American city planning theory as from village improvement work. Olmsted emphasizes that the location of the site, adjacent to the five-hundred-acre reserve called Forest Park, makes "wholly needless" any large park within the development. Instead, scientific planning dictates not only a three-and-one-half-acre "green" within view of the railroad station, and two much smaller parks, but two other sorts of parklike places. Behind the groups of houses, instead of private back yards, will blossom "enclosed private parks" shared by abutting families. "They cannot be used for active, noisy games of large boys nor will they be open to the general public or to loafers, but will provide places where the smaller children of the block can get room to play instead of being forced out onto the streets." Intended for the exclusive use of abutting families, the enclosures seemed almost as unique as the wholly designed "Station Square," which Olmsted, with Atterbury, developed "as a single composition," displaying a perfectly seamless style of architecture and planting within a space precisely designed for pedestrian, train, and carriage traffic. "It is treated with a regard for the pleasure the residents may derive from its use that is impossible in the individualistic development of business centers usual even in the most costly and most fashionable suburban districts," Olmsted asserts, alluding to the inharmonious commuter-train-stop villages that irritated so many borderland families.[3]

Olmsted assumes knowing readers, and he writes little more about his views on avenues and streets and on a handsome station area of planned depot and shops. But about diminished private back yards and the creation of semi-private enclosures he writes at some length, for he knew his innovations, however scientific, clashed with concepts of privacy drawing city families to borderland living. Essentially, he explains that "some of the lots" in Forest Hills Gardens, "being intended for homes of moderate size, are made shallower than the customary New York lot on which the deep, badly lighted tenement house was developed," while others are of "usual" or greater depth.[4] Shallow lots provide more room for the experimental semi-private spaces, of course, but those very spaces, he assured prospective buyers, increase the value of adjacent homesites. Olmsted argues strongly, not only because he knew that private developers must be convinced of the profitability of innovation, but because he understood the wariness with which many "pointers" would approach Atterbury's architectural forms.

Atterbury understood that caution from the beginning. "Yet the apparently anomalous fact remains that a supposedly model town is being built largely of contiguous houses in more or less continuous rows directly adjoining plowed fields," he argues in his chapter of *Forest Hills Gardens,* immediately following Olmsted's lengthy explication. Atterbury pleads with his readers to consider the arrangements of houses in terms of "small groups," not with the connotation of "block" in "its ordinary dreary and hopeless sense."[5] If readers could only understand the exquisite final product of scientific town planning and unified architecture, they would instantly accept the innovative arrangements.

The foundation intended to construct ten different groups of buildings in Forest Hills Gardens. Around the railroad station—which the Long Island Railroad erected according to foundation specifications—would grow up the three- and four-story structures housing "stores, offices, and a restaurant, and in the upper stories small non-housekeeping apartments both for men and women." Away from Station Square would rise row houses, two-family houses, and single-family houses containing from four to twelve rooms, all built of the same materials and in the same harmonious style, texture, and color. From the outset, the foundation intended to control architectural development completely and planned to build the Station Square structures and some houses itself. The first hundred purchasers of lots received free architectural plans and specifications for their houses, an offer the foundation made "not only in order to stimulate the early improvement of vacant lots but to maintain a high standard of design and construction in the buildings erected." Not every purchaser had to retain Atterbury, but every would-be builder needed the approval of the master architect before beginning construction. In a sort of deliberate haste, therefore, Olmsted and Atterbury drew up their plans and specifications and began work.

Through a series of newspaper advertisements, immediately collected in a booklet entitled *A Forward Movement in Suburban Development*, the foundation explained that its advertisements "ought to be classified as publicity," not as advertising at all. The outpouring of notices, leaflets, announcements, and booklets, many with identical titles, focused attention on town planning issues certainly, but in the end, for all the protests of the foundation, they emphasized lot sales. Over and over, the "publicity" boasts of finely paved streets and walks, of underground utility arrangements, of excellent water and sewer mains, "all installed along modern scientific lines." It boasts of highest-quality planting schemes providing, "in addition to shade and foliage, a touch of color throughout the year" and trumpets the preservation of the mature oaks, beeches, and dogwoods native to the site. "Forward movement" meant "masonry construction of all buildings" to obtain "the lowest insurance rates yet promulgated for any outlying district of New York City" and to retard maintenance costs; it meant unique designs for street-lamp poles and other public-way furniture; it meant the building of churches, a country club, and a school—and it meant restriction.

No previous borderland real estate development carried such tight restrictions, both explicit and implied. "Every lot is restricted," the foundation assured interested families. "The Gardens IS NOT and never will be a promiscuous neighborhood. Every safeguard has been provided to preserve its character and integrity." In 1911 the foundation codified many of its restrictions in its *Declaration of Restrictions,* a lengthy document keyed to detailed maps of the site. After six years of development, the foundation had a fairly clear idea of what to exclude, and the excluding required a massive paragraph ranging from brass foundries to crematories, hog pens to cesspools, making ink to producing cream of tartar, dynamite manufactories to sugar bakeries, and from tanning to soap-preparing. The paragraph covered practically every industrial activity and most agricultural ones. It excluded all but one- and two-family houses on individual lots, private garages more than one story in height, and any " 'block' of buildings more than two hundred and fifty (250) feet

The inn offered a striking vertical element in the larger expanse of Queens, and its details, like those of the adjacent streetlight, emphasized the feudal and natural bases of Forest Hills Gardens architecture.

Station Square storefronts emphasized not only the Old World, pre-industrial architecture that characterized the entire development, but the importance of mature trees in making structures appear old.

in width or length."[6] It restricted almost everything, including the distance houses were to be set back from streets, the building of fences and walls, the location of automobile garages, the placement of front steps, oriel windows, and utility poles, and the use of private lanes opening into the semi-private enclosed spaces. Moreover, the document spells out the right of the Foundation Homes Company—the subsidiary formed actually to build the place—to enter private space to cut grass and to provide other planting maintenance on semi-private land. All of the restrictions only complement those written into every deed and make clear the overriding effort to create a totally homogenous place.[7]

In its preliminary information for purchasers, the foundation extended its effort at social control, stating bluntly that no one might rent or buy who could not produce references concerning his "character and business." Such restriction derived from the intent to create "a homogenous and congenial community," and about it the foundation spoke bluntly: "It is essential to the commercial and social success of the undertaking that prospective buyers should not only be responsible and reliable but that they should be congenial neighbors to other residents." Although already sensitive to criticism that its educational work seemed not to be focused on providing high-quality housing for workingmen anxious for borderland life—a goal that intrigued Atterbury perhaps more than any other member of the development group—the Foundation nevertheless proceeded effectively to restrict residence in Forest Hill Gardens to middle-class white Protestants.[8] Everything was to be homogenous at the start, it assured inquirers, and would remain so forever.

Contiguity of living undoubtedly reinforced whatever contemporaneous racist, anti-Semitic, and anti-immigrant biases originally fostered the social restrictions the foundation established. Olmsted, Atterbury, and other foundation spokesmen knew that Forest Hills Gardens required families to live in houses set closer together than typical in the borderlands, to share semi-private and public spaces, and to be thrust upon each other by a distinctive, almost unique street plan.

Certainly the typical group of houses posed social problems from the start. For all the dominant Gothic-Tudor style, for all the harmonious color, texture, and planting, the pairing of two single-family houses with one two-family "double" house radically shifted traditional arrangements of front and back yards. The double house faced the street, set back across a very broad lawn; on either side, like the top and bottom arms of a capital E, the two single-family houses faced each other, each presenting an end to the street. Four families thus shared one large front lawn and three rather small back yards, one of which—behind the double house—opened directly on semi-private space, two of which opened on the back yards of the single-family houses of the adjacent groups. Outdoor privacy thus nearly vanished at the drawing-board stage.

Visitors, and particularly expert observers mightily intrigued by the design experiment, rarely noticed the social problems implicit in the arrangement of houses and the juxtaposition of house types. The overall scheme of things, and particularly the integration of plantings with a wholly harmonious architecture, simply overwhelmed them. even during the first construction stage. In 1912, for example, Louis

Atterbury's row housing offered little outdoor privacy, but it did feature roll-up clotheslines.

In their first years, the "groups" of two detached houses and one double house struck many observers as utterly novel, perhaps because trees and hedges had not grown enough to offer privacy from passersby.

Graves assured readers of *Building Progress* that Forest Hills Gardens seemed like make-believe, something utterly unlikely to be in the same hemisphere as "prosaic Brooklyn" and "the Astoria gas-making plant," something that belonged "somewhere near the Rhine." Everything, from the "medieval tower" half-hidden by scaffolding in Station Square to the first occupied houses, was wholly harmonious. While the "whole outlay seems a trifle bizarre" at first, an automobile tour quickly made clear the wonderfully inventive minds at work.

Graves fastened on the actual construction materials to illustrate the care lavished on the development. In "a sort of factory or test house" the designers worked out ratios of stucco and ground tile to achieve the perfect reddish hue, cast and tested concrete beams used in some structures, and built upon the original findings of the New Jersey laboratory that tested materials for fire retardance and other qualities. "From the artistic side," Graves asserted, "perhaps no one feature has received more minute attention than has the composition of the stucco." Indeed, Olmsted and Atterbury struggled constantly to unify texture and color. They smashed roofing tiles and mixed them with tinted cement to pave sidewalks and make curbs, for example, ensuring a graduated palette from ground to skyline. They worked to integrate brick color with plantings and with tinted stucco, roof tiles, and sidewalks. Their originality, and above all their completeness, impressed Graves, as it did W. F. Anderson, who assured readers of *The Brickbuilder* the same year that the designers had hit upon a wonderfully practical, low-cost way of harmonizing texture and color. He thought so much of the stucco tinting that he published the formulas with his essay.[9]

A decade after its beginning the development began to attract widespread attention. No longer did magazine writers have to trust only the magnificent drawings made by Olmsted and Atterbury, drawings reproduced in *American City* and other periodicals, or the muddy, debris-strewn site itself.[10] As early as 1914, Samuel Howe illustrated his *House Beautiful* article with full-page photographs of sideyards, the Station Square tea-room facade, and the entranceway to a single-family house, along with many other smaller images. "They are just plain every-day views taken with a camera," Howe argued, and the simple photographs reveal a very complex, mellow place, "full of shade and shadows, of interesting detail, and unexpected views, all interesting in color." Howe claimed that the foundation had provided an exquisitely beautiful place, one that grew more beautiful every year and that grew in an absolutely predictable way, a place where families *knew* who their future neighbors would be. Without realizing it, Howe and other post-1914 visitors to Forest Hills Gardens wandered into the first deliberately photogenic residential development built in the United States. Howe gasped at the similarity of finished structures and arrangements of structures to the "attractive," "ambitious," "highly colored" drawings he had seen exhibited five years earlier.

Forest Hills Gardens was not pretty as a picture, therefore. It *was* the picture. Howe and others described it as a painting: "The woodwork is often white, and at times of a dark, richly-grained oak, coated with creosote, which goes admirably with the bricks, which are often small and dark, and never seem to have that ugly new, yellowish-red tinge which we think of as a brick color."[11] The designers had succeeded on a new level of subtlety, not only building in a Gothic-Tudor or German-Tudor or "medieval" style but aging the buildings from the start, giving an appearance of traditional stability to an otherwise innovative housing arrangement. Olmsted planted brilliantly, using newly set-out specimens to complement the mature trees on the site, to give very quickly—indeed only ten years after ground-breaking—the appearance of a nearly mature planted form. Nothing might have pleased Susan Cooper more than Forest Hills Gardens, sprung up overnight, in the medieval style.

Surely it pleased magazine writers addressing the public interested in borderland living, in houses, in town planning, just as it pleased experts addressing design professionals. In 1915, for example, Mary Eastwood Knevels assured *American Homes and Gardens* readers that Olmsted had vanquished the ugly service yard with "its flapping clothesline, prominent garbage can, and deplorable ash heap." In Forest Hills Gardens clotheslines reeled in when not in use, and they stretched out to poles disguised as flower arbors. Service uses consumed only a few square feet of space. All other land flowed into beautiful lawns and gardens enjoyable from within living rooms and from outdoor vantage points as well, and wholly integrated into a larger scheme. A year later, Charles C. May told readers of *Architecture* that the "picturesque" place already showed signs of charming weathering and claimed that it represented the epitome of wholistic American landscape design.[12]

Yet by 1916 writers addressing public and professional audiences began to discern, or at least to notice unconsciously, flaws beneath the ever more beautiful surface. Their hesitancy, their unwillingness to look closely at some of the features of Forest Hills Gardens previously extoled, and the place of their articles within the larger literature focused on the development suggest a nascent sense not of failure, but of trouble ahead. After 1915, authors began emphasizing the architecture of its houses, particularly the single-family houses, rather than the overall development, and they began turning away from prose analysis to photographic praise.[13] Even Charles C. May introduced his generally favorable piece with a caveat sounding a new note: "It has become trite to make the Russell Sage Foundation development at Forest Hills the subject for pages of rhapsodic eulogy. Much of what has been written has been marked by fulsomeness rather than by discrimination." Something was out of joint.

A continuing tension between publicity and privacy now and then puzzled observers otherwise delighted with everything about Forest Hills Gardens. Aymar Ambury blundered into the question in a 1916 *House Beautiful* piece entitled "Co-Operative Building." After explaining the wonders of the "groups" in Forest Hills Gardens and stating that "even at best a back yard is not an agreeable outlook"— something he claimed English town planners had realized in a revolutionary moment—he asserts that American real estate developers had misread the American character. "They are inclined to say that the people are too individualistic and decline to enter any community arrangments," he determines. "This is hardly a correct answer, since nobody who is not full of the dog in the manger spirit would

Before the custom-designed stucco weathered, before the
saplings matured, the houses of Forest Hills Gardens appeared
only slightly different from those of many other borderland
real estate developments. Note the fake shutters on the double
windows, for example, and the scruffy lawns.

For all their attachment to naturalistic design, Atterbury and
Olmsted often set houses at right angles to very straight streets
and sidewalks, lessening the charm of both architecture and
planting.

Nothing better indicates the ability of trees to soften new-
built structures than the background woods evident in this
photograph of a Forest Hills Gardens "group."

decline to do something for his neighbor, if the doing of it helped him also." Yet for all his concern with group action, his confrontation with issues of plumbing reveals his uncertain view of American individualism.

Given the contiguity of Forest Hills Gardens house groups, why did Atterbury provide each with an independent heating system, plumbing system, and so on? Why not communal electric systems? Why not experiment with communal kitchens? In Embury's time, a number of thoughtful feminists had suggested the last experiment as utterly sensible, and Atterbury had erected nonhousekeeping apartments at Station Square. Embury did not avoid the obvious questions, but his confrontation proved virtually fruitless. Joint systems, even a joint heating system, would fail because "people who have been living in apartments have become so little self-reliant and so utterly dependent on the janitor and the city, that it is very doubtful if they could get along together in running a little private manufacturing plant."[14] Embury did not explain how people determined to control their own furnace would fare in an outdoors over which they had almost no control.

Social homogeneity might decrease the friction implicit in the novel arrangements of houses, especially if most newcomers arrived straight from the very private apartment-house world eight miles away in Manhattan. Only Graves, the observer chiefly interested in brick and mortar, thought to investigate the seemingly homogenous population filtered through applications and references. He found the "character of the population" intriguing—"illuminating" in his words—but he fails to explain why, or even why his listing of occupations ends his article on the subject. Of the purchasers of lots in Forest Hills Gardens, 22 percent were "salesmen and clerks" and another 15 percent, "merchants and managers"—apparently the very sort of heads of household the foundation hoped to attract. But "architects and artists" made up another 11 percent, "teachers and educators," 12 percent, and engineers 7 percent; when combined with totals for physicians, lawyers, advertising agents, and several other occupations, Graves's tallies suggest that the development appealed very, very strongly not only to well-educated husbands but to husbands in future-oriented professions like engineering and especially those favoring visual methods—architecture, advertising, and others. Graves concludes nothing about his occupational breakdown, but clearly Forest Hills Gardens spoke to a particular sort of householder, one involved in "creative" work, if creative means producing new things rather than maintaining systems. So few "railroad officials" bought in the development, for example, that Graves simply lumped them with "others."[15] Too much can be made of Graves's list, but the very fact that he made it and presented it to his readers suggests that at least one observer knew Forest Hills Gardens might not appeal to all prospective buyers.

Dealing with visitors other than journalists very quickly concerned the homeowners' association of Forest Hills Gardens, for the annual tennis matches attracted throngs to the "club" nestled in one corner of the development. At first the road system Olmsted designed worked perfectly; much of the crowd arrived by rail and simply walked from the handsome station. But as more and more people arrived each year by motor car, the limitations of the entire development scheme became glaringly apparent, even to favorably disposed observers. Simply put, Olmsted planned for the horse, not the motor car. Not only did the groups of houses provide almost no space for garages, let alone driveways, the cozy streets made curbside parking nearly impossible. The common stables did little to alleviate the growing demand for garage space, and while owners of some single-family lots found it possible to jam in a one-car garage, many families began learning that Forest Hills Gardens seemed better suited to a rapidly vanishing horse-and-carriage era. The three broad streets quickly reflected the changing traffic pattern, for by 1916, instead of carrying pleasure-seeking carriage riders, they were commuter routes. Charles May argued that "a walled town in America would be perhaps insulting to the genius of our institutions," but he stressed the suddenly apparent, wholly accidental usefulness of the immense Long Island Railway embankment defending the development on one side.[16] Olmsted's "scientific principles" quickly appeared anachronistic; not only had the designer scarcely provided for automobile parking within the development, he had enticed daily streams of automobile traffic across it, streams which soon rivaled the tournament-day lines of a few years before.

How quickly residents understood the problems posed by a jewel-like, totally "finished" residential development remains unclear. By 1915 they had plunged into amateur ornithology, retaining an expert to discover what birds might be attracted to the place and how, then beginning regular winter feeding. But aside from the need to erect some nesting boxes, the bird-watching craze provided little opportunity to shape space, and the inhabitants of the Gardens appear to have devoted their energies to tennis and other organized sports and to church-going.[17] Mrs. Russell Sage certainly facilitated the last; in 1915 she donated funds for the Church in the Gardens, and four years later the Atterbury-designed structure stood complete, even to what its architect called "a quaint and picturesque roof with truncated gables," adding to its "informal, old-world character."[18] Apart from squabbling about the placement of automobile garages, the residents apparently did little to change their outdoor surroundings or even to accept responsibility for them. In the Gardens, built form, even the church building, appeared from above, like something vaguely feudal, vaguely European spawned by Susan Cooper's witch-hazel magic wand. From their beautiful if static form, the residents first looked smugly out at lesser places, then viewed with alarm the spread of a very ungardenlike urban residential zone around their island. Suddenly the Gardens began to strike observers not as a prototype, but as a failed experiment.

Just prior to 1920, two years before its homeowners formed a syndicate and bought the entire property from the Sage Foundation, Forest Hills Gardens vanished from the pages of popular and professional magazines. It stood incomplete, although residents assumed otherwise as trees and shrubbery matured and brick, tinted stucco, and tile weathered as perfectly as Atterbury hoped. In 1924, one family acquired a large lot fronting the Village Green, a lot smack in the center of the development and from the beginning specifically intended by the foundation for apartment-house use. From 1929 to 1944, the family and its architects fought valiantly to build a large multi-family structure in "the Old World vogue." The foundation no longer dictated building; the homeowners' association enforced the restrictions established long before. When the six-story "Leslie," complete with

The designers of Forest Hills Gardens knew that many would-be purchasers insisted on single-family houses, and they provided many, but they ignored the growing popularity of the motor car and often omitted space for garages.

The Church in the Gardens fit precisely into Atterbury's overall architectural scheme, and as a gift of Mrs. Russell Sage, it fit precisely into the traditional practice of industrialists, who provided church buildings for workers in their company towns.

In East Hampton, Atterbury designed a single-family house much like those he later designed in Forest Hills Gardens, but the borderland family rejected his conception of formal grounds and set about shaping space on their own.

underground garage, stood finished in 1944, the cozy streets had been overwhelmed by a structure totally out of scale in the development. The completion of the building confirmed the fears of its long-term opponents: Forest Hills Gardens had no capacity to absorb change, be it hundreds of parked cars or one large apartment house, without badly marring its jewel-like perfection.[19] As early as 1920 it had become a noble but mistaken trial, yet one with enormous educational value for the thousands of commuters whose trains roared past on the elevated four-track embankment.

Forest Hills Gardens taught commuters over the years something about the wholly designed place nearly unable to accept change, of course, but it spoke more clearly, if perhaps more softly, of something Samuel Howe suspected in his 1914 *House Beautiful* essay. Forest Hills Gardens indeed looked like some "tiny principality, presided over by a strong personality"—it looked like a new-model company town.[20] Atterbury might have suspected at least something of the public reaction. In the years before he designed the structures of Forest Hills Gardens, he had made a fine reputation as a designer of single-family houses in the borderlands, and at least one commission should have taught him something about the American propensity to shape some personal space. In East Hampton, at the far tip of Long Island, Atterbury designed a "cottage," complete with servants' rooms, that was in exterior appearance and material much like the single-family houses he built in Forest Hills Gardens. His clients built it exactly as he designed, but they utterly spurned his meticulous plans for formal gardens and other surrounding beauties. "The imagination of the architect is known to frequently overreach the owner's willingness to execute a design, however attractive it may be," Atterbury admitted to readers of a 1903 issue of *House and Garden*.[21] His photographs clearly reveal his clients' love of a naturalistic, informal home landscape and imply their desire to shape something of the space they inhabited. The Russell Sage Foundation gave Atterbury and Olmsted the chance to make a perfect place for homeowners uninterested in shaping outdoor space at all. About the deeper implications of such a chance, neither designer appeared to care.

Only company towns had hitherto provided such opportunities to build beautiful but wholly static places, and after his work for the Sage Foundation, Atterbury built two company towns, one in Massachusetts and one in Tennessee. Although a part-time borderer—he lived in Southampton, Long Island, during the summer months—Atterbury never adequately understood that the forces drawing middle-class families to the borderland were the same as those inspiring the upper-class borderland families who regularly retained him, and that the corporation-owned, worker-inhabited company town, whatever its physical appearance, grated on the nerves of visitors and inhabitants alike. Forest Hills Gardens, soon surrounded by the residential and commercial sprawl of Queens and cut through by automobile traffic, whispered "company town" to railroad commuters looking up from newspapers as they raced homeward to the borderlands shaped by speculators more in touch with American individualism than with German town planning and its "scientific principles."

19 🌿 SHAKER HEIGHTS

Speculators succeeded where philanthropy failed. Eight miles east of Cleveland, on the heights overlooking the city, two developers risked their fortunes in a large-scale, absolutely for-profit borderland residential undertaking. A quarter-century after they began, educated people everywhere in the United States knew at least the name of their creation, and millions touched by mass-circulation periodicals had seen its stylish face photographed again and again. At the outset of the Great Depression, Americans understood the achievement of Shaker Heights as the epitome of planned "community building."

They knew too the Van Sweringen name, for the two brothers who built Shaker Heights fascinated financial experts and journalists and mesmerized the general public, for all that they employed a public relations expert to keep their names out of the press. Oris Paxton Van Sweringen and Mantis James Van Sweringen, born in 1879 and 1881, moved like titans through 1920s financial circles, enveloping themselves in mystery and striking fear into potential competitors. In 1930 the brothers owned or controlled a number of railroads, among them the Chesapeake & Ohio, the Missouri Pacific, and the Erie, and they had given Cleveland a multistory skyline second only to those of Chicago and New York. Commended in national magazines for transforming their city from "an overgrown country town into a real metropolis," for giving it a union station second to none, for amassing and directing capital with an uncanny sureness, "the Vans," as readers knew them, owed their success to residential real estate development.[1]

At the turn of the century, the brothers abandoned their bicycle repair shop, visualizing achievements as great as—if different from—two other Ohio bicycle repairers, the Wright brothers. Technical innovation entranced the Wrights, who understood with crystal clarity the driving force of American technological experiment and the potential market for flying machines. The Van Sweringens followed the lure of finance, and they grasped the significance of the vast movement to borderland space as clearly as the Wrights foresaw a movement into the air. The Wrights extrapolated from the machinery of the bicycle; the Van Sweringens extrapolated from the destination of so many weekend cyclists, including the bloomer-attired women Bunner depicted in *Suburban Sage*.

After abandoning their repair business, the young brothers made a down payment on several residential lots in Lakewood, part of the urban residential ring growing so quickly around Cleveland. In later years the brothers successfully masked their past, but surviving evidence suggests that this move was wholly a speculation and a failure. For two years afterward, the bankrupt brothers did business in the name of their sister, evolving the first of the two principles that subsequently guided all their real estate activities. In Lakewood the Van Sweringens learned to avoid all involvement with low-income buyers, apparently because such marginal customers lacked the funds to act quickly on their decision to purchase—and the resulting cash-flow crises had destroyed the brothers' miniscule reserves. Their next effort demonstrated their resolve. They bought a sizeable tract in Cleveland Heights, creating a subdivision of large lots on North Park Boulevard. Profits realized almost at once, the brothers moved farther away from the city, to Fairmount Boulevard, and offered large lots again. In Cleveland Heights the men formulated their second principle, emphasizing the invaluable significance of first-class rapid transit for commuting husbands. During their Fairmount Boulevard operation, they enticed the Cleveland Electric Railway Company to extend its trolley route past their lots. The spectacular rise in property values mirrored what Sidney Fisher had witnessed in West Philadelphia and along the Germantown road, and it provided the profits that capitalized the Van Sweringens' Shaker Heights venture.[2]

A perfect correlation of supply and demand favored the brothers in 1905, just as they plunged into their daring effort. Cleveland had remained small well into the nineteenth century; as late as 1850, only about 17,000 people called it home, and fewer called it a stopping place. Westward-moving families bypassed it, even after the completion of the Ohio Canal, and rail travelers looked forward to Chicago, not the de facto capital of the old Western Reserve of Connecticut. Not until 1852, when a sailing vessel brought six barrels of iron ore from the upper peninsula of Michigan, did Cleveland investors consider ironmongery. They soon brought ore from Minnesota, Canada, and Michigan, transshipped it inland to Warren, Youngstown, and Pittsburgh, and began firing it in Cleveland itself. Pennsylvania coal and iron combined with northern ore to project the lakeport into a yeasty and stinking industrial realm, enriching thousands of Cleveland families and attracting tens of thousands of workers. In 1900, some 362,000 people, including the two bicycle repairers, lived in the sprawling confusion.[3] Blackening the sky with smoke, a smoke in which Clevelanders delighted—at first—the steel industry eventually directed attention at the borderlands east and south of the city, the destination of weekend cyclists.

Some of the most picturesque countryside lay east of the city, five hundred feet above lake level and, by some quirk of nature, almost always free of the odor of industrial activity eight miles away. In Warrensville, one of the original townships of the Western Reserve survey, time stood nearly still, at least on the fourteen hundred acres of prime land owned since 1822 by The United Society of Believers in the Second Appearing of Christ. One of the most distinctive of the "come-outer" sects, the "shaking Quakers" or Shakers had found their site by divine inspiration.[4] Fusing Old Testament, Tree of Life, and manifest destiny thinking, the Shakers settled on the lofty acreage, calling it "The Valley of God's Pleasure," apparently using *valley* to suggest a sort of shelter from secular troubles.

In time it became a shelter indeed. As they did elsewhere, the Shakers formed a commune, restricted those who might live among them, and began shaping the land. They built dormitories, barns, and workshops, cleared immense fields, and eventually supported—chiefly through agriculture but also by manufacturing worldly items like hair dyes—about three hundred members. Only rarely bothered by religious persecution, the Warrensville commune prospered even as it declined in membership. Its prohibition of sexual intercourse meant that the sect could grow only by making converts, and in the decades after the Civil War, its attractiveness was diminished by secular rationalism and other forces, and membership shrank. In 1888 only twenty-seven members lived on the vast site, still farming, still dancing away their sins, still enjoying their grist mills and the three large, beautiful lakes that powered their wheels.

A year later the society elders sold the site to a Buffalo land development company, and the surviving members moved to other communes. By 1904, the Van Sweringen brothers had become sales agents for the land. Within a year, they owned options on some of the acreage; a few months later, the brothers acquired the rest of the site and began subdividing it into large lots.

While the two developers knew that sluggish sales would result in bankruptcy, they knew too that only the highest quality project would entice upper- and upper-middle-class families away from residential neighborhoods close to downtown Cleveland. Consequently they mounted a public relations campaign unparalleled in the history of borderland development, publishing an array of pamphlets, newspaper advertisements, leaflets, and broadsides, almost always stunningly illustrated. The literature prepared at their direction glorifies the single-family house on a large site and denounces the insidious, family-wrecking effect not only of living close to factories, but of living in or even *near* apartments or residential hotels—and of living near blacks and other people forbidden to buy into their development. A proper home, a home useful in cementing family ties and elevating the spirit of parents and children, must be meticulously sited, designed, and constructed: "Good taste calls for well-designed residences that combine the things that make for comfort and convenience with the things that make for beauty."[5] While they never settled on a precise name for their hilltop project, in pamphlet after pamphlet, the Van Sweringens formulated a sort of secular religion of the home, using the "come-outer" Shaker philosophy as a touchstone, explicating their distrust of apartment houses as forcefully as they championed the virtues of single-family residences.

Not every single-family house found favor in their eyes, however. "We do not believe that bungalows or houses of any similar type can have a proper setting in a built-up section, such as Shaker Heights is destined to be," they determined, "so we have thought it necessary to exclude all buildings of that character from our property." *Shaker Village Standards,* one of the booklets detailing the restrictions the brothers placed on purchasers and architects, implies that bungalows and like structures belong in wholly agricultural regions, not in an immense area given over to picturesque beauty. Nor do merely decorated residences belong there. "No so-called Dutch Colonial houses may be created by building a cornice on the gable ends of a Colonial house or other houses of similar design," it continues. "It is not too far a cry to that Queen Anne era, when towers and arches were as numerous as the sacred niches of a Buddhist temple. Then again there are those horribly ugly examples of the Age of Cast Iron and the Brownstone Period, which should make the intending home-builder of today sufficiently wary."[6] Both Van Sweringens identi-fied—and exploited—the growing concern of educated Americans familiar with architectural innovation. While much experiment struck the educated public as "tasteful," much more did not, causing families to find refuge in proven styles like the medieval or Tudor favored by so many reformers and dignifying Forest Hills Gardens, or enticing them to escape to a place forever governed by traditional form reflecting pre-big-business-era lifestyles and values.

After banning all manner of styles and details and specifying the traditionally accepted forms that ought to characterize Shaker Heights, the brothers mandated that no house could be erected unless an architect had designed it. "Without the guidance of a competent architect, imagination may easily run to the freakish in residences," they noted. But they distrusted architects too. Announcing from the very beginning of their vast undertaking that "we cannot approve plans prepared by amateurs or unqualified persons," they also insisted that prospective builders retain "a graduate architect, or one whose qualifications warrant, and whose drawings express, a thorough, technical knowledge of the highest and best in architecture, together with the ability to combine materials and prescribe color schemes that will proclaim the finished result as the work of a trained and competent hand."[8] While they frequently stated that their concern lay only in a fierce desire to protect purchasers from the heartbreak of living adajcent to a freak, the brothers also seem to have realized the incredible fragility of trying to begin a "tasteful" development from scratch. One or two ugly or tawdry houses could halt sales instantly. And so the Van Sweringens sharpened their instructions, insisting that house plans submit-ted for their approval include all elevations, all floor plans, detailed color schemes, enlarged details of important features like front entranceways, "cornices, and other special features that need to be detailed to insure the right result," and a complete cross-sectional drawing specifying the height of stories. They further mandated "a full-dimensioned plot plan no less than one-eighth of an inch to the foot, showing that the house and garage can be placed upon the lot without a violation of the restrictions."[9] They warned that any would-be designer or builder disputing their interpretation of his plans must stand ready to defend the drawings before the local chapter of the American Institute of Architects.

In their own way, the Van Sweringens attempted to exercise as much control over Shaker Heights architecture as the Sage Foundation exercised over Forest Hills Gardens. But instead of employing a master team of one architect and one landscape

SHAKER
VILLAGE
Standards

From the beginning, the Van Sweringens knew the importance of both gently restricting architectural design and encouraging Shaker Heights purchasers to explore the range of their own creativity.

architect, the developers followed a restricted market approach. Certainly their statements and restrictions demonstrate their uncertainty about the willingness of architects to make traditionally tasteful—rather than originally spectacular—residences, as well as a canny understanding that few prospective builders and their architects would go through the immense trouble and expense of preparing complicated, highly finished plans of houses so tawdry or freakish as to fail examination. Insisting on architect-designed houses and on immensely detailed drawings simply boosted the price of any house built in Shaker Heights, ensuring the "tastefulness" of the place immediately, and into the future.

Shaker Heights architects worked under two sorts of restrictions. One type, usually presented in charts specifying mathematical ratios, derived perhaps from the brothers' early experience with machinery and from their allegiance to legally enforceable, "business-like" documents, the language of annual reports and financial ledgers. The other, which they expressed at length in graceful prose, derived from a genuine thoughtfulness about turn-of-the-century urban residential neighborhoods and the future of family life in the borderlands. Capitalists though they were, the Van Sweringens understood something of the problems bedeviling upper- and middle-class families, and they insisted that, as well as producing a stunning profit, Shaker Heights would meet pressing, vitally important moral, aesthetic, cultural, and spiritual needs. Every bit as reformist and environmentally determinist as the Sage Foundation, the brothers set about creating a "come-outer" place almost as utopian as the old Shaker commune.

In the charts, the developers detailed their restrictions almost to the decimal point. One, entitled simply "The House," traces the ratios of lot frontage to house width, specifying not only the widest possible house but the narrowest, and accounting also for the width of accessory structures, especially porches. Marginal notes instruct architects thinking about houses with tapering sides or multiple porches.[10] Other charts detail garage dimensions and the placement of such new-fangled structures on lots, including specifications for the distance of detached garages from rear lot lines. Marginalia reveal the sophisticated thinking behind the numbers; asterisks direct attention to special restrictions on corner lots and other unusual circumstances. Designated, defined, and graphed, the restrictions appear almost all-encompassing.

Yet the brothers knew that such ratios and other numerical arrangements required philosophical support, clearly explained reasons for their being. That knowledge produced pages of detailed prose focused on seemingly insignificant subjects that the brothers carefully showed opened on matters of first interest. "The coal bin should be readily accessible from the driveway, and the furnace should be near the coal bin," they remarked in an essay entitled "The Basement." Since "basements are usable in proportion to the light and air in them," design rules in Shaker Heights are "intended to provide for each house more light and air than is usually provided in other communities."[11] In order to have light and air in efficient basements, and basement windows easily accessible to coal wagons and motor trucks, architects must plan carefully not only the inner arrangement of windows, bins, and furnaces but the relation of basement windows to sunlight, prevailing breezes, and driveways. One of the chief evils of lake-level Cleveland underlay the Van Sweringen fascination with light, airy basements. Air pollution—even in basements—had no place in Shaker Heights, and architects practicing there should know it.

"The kind of house one builds determines the nature of the purchaser," they asserted in the environmental-determinist spirit of their age. "A good vacant lot is much better for any neighborhood than a poorly designed house."[12] They wrote, therefore, about their understanding of good design, about driveway location and planting details, about why ridge lines should be no more than sixteen feet above the second story and entrances on the front rather than sides of houses, about the prohibition of visible concrete block in Shaker Heights. About roofs and stonework they wrote in detail, displaying most clearly their philosophy of twentieth-century family life.

Roofs do far more than shed water in the Van Sweringen understanding. "It is the roof, more than any other part of the house, that is outlined against the sky, and which by its symmetry, its display of lights and shadows or its contrast of color with the rest of the building, promotes interest, arouses enthusiasm, and suggests comfort and contentment." The brothers insisted on "harmonious" roofing, stating bluntly that tile roofs do not belong on colonial-revival houses "and, therefore, we cannot approve them for buildings of that type." Harmony of roofing extended between houses too: the brothers permitted no tar-, composition-, or asphalt-shingle roofs, for such materials have "neither character nor beauty." They likewise forbade "artificial stone," specified that "all stone work shall be Briar Hill or Bedford limestone, or sandstone, of an approved local variety," and announced very specific restrictions concerning brick: "No buff-colored brick shall be used in any event, and no light-colored brick such as gray or white brick, or vertical-cut brick shall be used without the written consent of The Van Sweringen Company." Even mortar received scrutiny; the brothers mandated mortar of natural cement or light buff color and warned that "dark-colored" mortar could not be used without written consent.[13] The pages upon pages of reasonable reasons behind meticulous rules certainly derived from the same love of color harmony that inspired village-improvement adherents like McCrea, but the restrictions originated also in a powerful conservatism concerning family stability.

All of the Van Sweringen prose is informed by an almost religious belief in the capacity of a tasteful larger landscape of domesticity to strengthen family spirit already heartened by tasteful home interior and grounds. Advertising although it might be, the literature clearly connects with the issues of its day and with its intended audience. Booklets like *The Heritage of the Shakers* demonstrate the Van Sweringen familiarity with the post-1880 literature of borderland life as the only proper life for families financially tied to cities. Running through it and other pamphlets are whole streams of related ideas that together reveal the brothers' understanding of the "moral" effects of picturesque, domestic landscape. "The charm of many a house is enhanced on approach, by a glimpse of china or beautiful furniture, through the drapery-framed vista of a full-length window," they explain in defense of stipulations involving "full-length" windows, not "high-up or casement sash," on some ground-floor sides. *Charm* becomes an important key word in the Van Sweringen prose, focusing the brothers' hoped-for overall effect. Shaker Heights was to be a charming and a charmed place, as magical as Susan Cooper's witch-hazel landscape, as beautiful as Margaret Sangster's wintertime fairyland. "All that conserves home-spirit is cultivated; that which is inimical to it is barred," the brothers asserted.[14] But they knew that fine houses on fine lots alone would not succeed. Charm came from larger arrangements too.

Unlike the Sage Foundation concept of Forest Hills Gardens as a totally harmonized whole, the brothers conceived of Shaker Heights as a whole created almost entirely by beautiful houses on beautiful lots oriented toward connective streets. The larger arrangment of ways concerned the Van Sweringens much less than the design of individual houses, and about as much as what they called "conveniences." Since the site lay five hundred feet above the surrounding topography, the building of some amenities like sewers proved remarkably easy; and by 1910, extending other utilities from the city was much cheaper and easier than it had been only a decade earlier. In an early publication entitled *Questions and Answers Regarding Shaker Heights Village*, the brothers advertised "electric arc" street lamps, water and sewer mains, storm drains, pavements, curbs, and stone sidewalks; natural gas, electricity, and telephone lines were also among "the city conveniences" that made Shaker Heights so livable immediately. But a 1914 "Map of the Property of The Shaker Heights Improvement Company" depicts only several paved streets. A color key identifies "streets in which improvements are completed, including macadam pavement, stone sidewalks, water mains, storm water sewers, and sanitary sewers," distinguishing them from streets in the process of improvement. The map reveals the importance of access roads, the near gridiron arrangement of part of the larger pattern of ways, and the relative unimportance of parkland. Shaker Heights Park, nearly three hundred acres of unimproved land, stood nearly disconnected from the improved roads.[15] Quite evidently, the brothers had devoted almost every borrowed and earned cent to finishing roads and installing utilities, not to orchestrating the appearance of the larger landscape.

On October 27, 1911, the development extending some six-and-one-half miles incorporated itself as Shaker Village, boasting an assessed tax value of $2,525,800, much of it unsold land owned by the Van Sweringens. For all its natural beauty and urban conveniences, for all its fresh air, and for all its restrictions promising generations of stable tastefulness, sales of lots in the new municipality were sporadic. Access to downtown Cleveland remained wretched, as the Cleveland Railway Company refused to extend its line to the property. Its president, smarting over the scant profits received from extending track to the brothers' last site, called such speculative lines "bleeders, not feeders."[16] Lack of rail access struck the Van

Sweringens as the last obstacle remaining between them and immense profits, and so they determined to build their own high-speed trolley line.

Down Kingsbury Ravine to the center of Cleveland seemed the only feasible route, albeit expensive. They acquired two-thirds of the right-of-way quickly, but then they ran into resistance from the New York, Chicago, and St. Louis Railroad Company, which refused to share its right-of-way into downtown Cleveland. The firm valued its assets highly—Vanderbilt had nicknamed it The Nickel Plate Road and the name became quasi official—and simply stymied the Van Sweringen effort. For several years, therefore, electric cars to Shaker Heights rumbled through city streets before reaching the private right-of-way along which they raced. In one way, the urban route proved useful; the trolleys traversed the black section of the city along East Thirtieth Street, picking up maids employed at the end of the line. A second route soon replaced the first but proved little faster. *The Shaker Heights Subdivision of Shaker Heights,* another booklet advertising in its title the brothers' continuing confusion about the exact name of the place, appeared in 1914 to confront the commuting time head-on: "running-time to down-town is about thirty-five minutes," the Van Sweringens confessed. In 1914, fifteen miles an hour struck everyone as too slow, and street-running electric cars seemed too much of an urban inconvenience.

In a fit of capitalist courage, therefore, the brothers mortgaged themselves and bought a controlling interest in Nickel Plate stock. By 1916 the Shaker Heights electric cars rocketed along, following a wholly private route. The Van Sweringens devoted much attention to beautifying the right-of-way, not only by plantings, but by locating simple yet attractive stations at focal points throughout the development, a design device reassuring commuters that theirs was an electric railroad with distinct stops, not a streetcar line. Advertising an exclusive, high-speed commuting route paid immediate dividends: lot sales and housing starts boomed. Between 1919 and 1929, purchasers erected an average of 300 new houses a year, and nearly every house cost what many Americans considered a large sum indeed. In 1924, the Van Sweringen Company noted that the 556 houses projected to be built in 1925 would together cost about $9.1 million. Such success provided the brothers with a very large fortune—one observer estimated their 1926 income to be about $5.6 million from all aspects of the Shaker Heights project—and by 1929 the property they had acquired for $1 million was worth eighty times as much.[17] Sticking to their two principles had payed off.

In 1926, the brothers expanded their operation. They began development of an adjacent four-thousand-acre site, which they referred to (usually) as Shaker Country Estates, and they decided to offer only very large lots, from six to ten acres. In *Peaceful Shaker Village* they noted that the lots "are six hundred feet above the smoke and turmoil of the city, in the midst of clean sunshine and abiding peace. Yet, with the extensions of electric express service, they will be but thirty to forty minutes from the Public Square" downtown. The promotional literature aimed only obliquely at wealthy families wanting large lots. Its real focus lay on small-scale

As important as the big, four-square, resoundingly American house is the two-car garage at the back of its lot.

Shaker Heights houses reflected not only the rising love of American-style architecture, but concerns with good health, as evidenced here in the day and sleeping porches.

Trees mattered a great deal to early Shaker Heights residents, and many constructed houses around existing trees. Here a driveway curves past two clumps of trees to a two-car garage beyond.

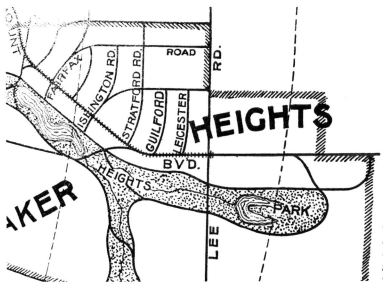

The developers knew both the importance
of large parks—not the tiny ones that
characterized Forest Hills Gardens—and
good trolley car commuting, and their maps
emphasize both.

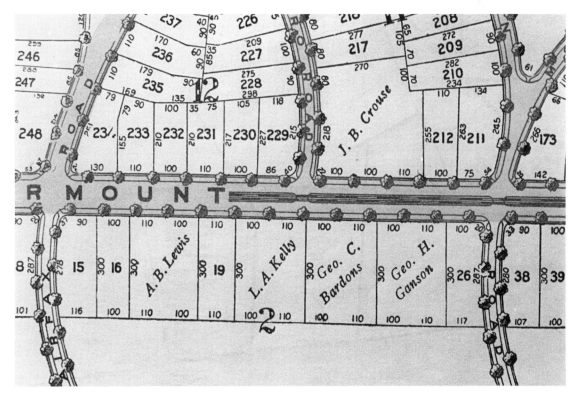

Street trees, curving roads, large lots, and a
right-of-way for high-speed trolley cars all
figure prominently on this detail from a
map published by the Shaker Heights
Improvement Company.

investors willing to speculate, in ways remarkably similar to those of 1880s Chicagoans, on future appreciation. "What you are doing, then, is buying land comparable to the 100-foot sections of present Shaker Village, at wholesale prices."[18] Given the wonderful rise in real estate values in the older Shaker Heights territory, the founding of churches, schools, and a country club there, and the brothers' determination to restrict the new development as tightly as the old, putting money into acreage to be someday subdivided and sold struck many investors as safer than putting it into stocks and banks. For families who bought land and built houses on the large pieces, the investment proved delightful too.

The Country Estates orientation suggests that by the mid-1920s the brothers had learned the rich preferred to live further from Cleveland that Shaker Heights. In the 1920s, the brothers themselves moved from Shaker Heights to giant estates many miles beyond, in the rural areas just being discovered by borderers. Middle-class families continued to buy, however, attracted not only by existing and potential attributes, but by the stability the Van Sweringens advertised more strongly as the decade advanced. As early as 1920, however, the brothers no longer devoted much attention to their massive development project. Buying into a railroad had whetted their appetite for more speculation in railroad firms, and struggling to find a suitable terminal for the Shaker Heights cars prompted them to build first a union railroad station in Cleveland, then other massive commercial structures. They sold off land in the Country Estates section to raise capital for more railroad ventures, but by 1933, when Depression-era Shaker Heights land sales brought in only sixty-five thousand dollars, their forty-million-dollar debt to J. P. Morgan became impossible to repay, and the last of their Shaker Heights land passed into other hands.

In 1929 Shaker Heights seemed almost perfect, a larger, infinitely more durable construct than Forest Hills Gardens, if not so jewel-like. In that year F. A. Cushing Smith told the readers of *American Landscape Architect* that just east of Cleveland lay "a home community resembling something the imagination might conjure as a place in which to live." His sumptuously illustrated article, "The Glory of Shaker Village," traces the history of the site and the Van Sweringen development effort and describes the rapid transit line, school system, and soothing scenic effect of a place dignified only by single-family houses on curving roads. It also explores the Van Sweringen understanding of city growth. On the one hand, Smith points out that manufacturing spearheads urban expansion, and that the factories spilling into urban residential zones in Detroit, New York, Boston, Chicago, and other cities drive families "toward that fringe of green that will always be the ideal setting for the home." Only the "protective restrictions in force for a century" can assure thoughtful families that industry will always remain distant. On the other hand, Smith emphasizes that commercial development serving suburban families can also destroy a "community of homes," and so the Van Sweringens created Shaker Square just within the Cleveland city limits. The "gateway" to Shaker Heights "is being developed as a shopping and apartment center" focused on a "central motive" of six acres devoted to retailing. Smith's description of Shaker Square suggests that the Van Sweringens glimpsed more than the retailing needs of Shaker Heights. The commercial development reflected only a little of the early twentieth-century love of medieval- and Tudor-revival borderland village architecture; it included only one Old World structure, "an English Tavern." Everywhere else, the brothers followed a pronounced, rousingly American colonial motif. "Harmonizing Georgian architecture, and of Colonial brick construction, with white shop fronts, entrances and cornices," the buildings housing bank, shops, theater, and other businesses stood thirty-five feet back from the curbs of elm-lined streets.[19] While the commercial activities condemned it to an urban location, Shaker Square clearly reflected an emerging commitment to applying late-eighteenth-century American architecture to retail structures, and it displayed a deepening understanding of the transformation of train-stop villages into automobile-focused retail nodes. The gateway to Shaker Heights took its form not from Old World sources or contemporary urban forms like the massive towers the Van Sweringens built downtown, but from nostalgia for an age shoppers perceived as golden, the same age from which the brothers derived their concepts of borderland home, home life, and landscape.

Forest Hills Gardens and Shaker Heights reflect something of the range of the early twentieth-century planned residential development. Clearly the borderlands, even that borderland of plowed fields suddenly within the legal limits of Queens, permitted residential arrangements other than the kind typical across the United States—single-family houses on reasonably large lots fronting curving or straight roads haphazardly leading to villages and commuter depots. And yet before the 1950s Forest Hills Gardens produced almost no progeny, while Shaker Heights produced many, although none so extensive.

Certainly its village or company town appearance haunted Forest Hills Gardens despite the best efforts of its backers and designers. Indeed, Forest Hills Gardens grew up in the borderlands as simultaneously familiar and alien, and always slightly distrusted.

By 1910, Americans had wearied of "typical" company towns, the ramshackle conglomerations of houses, detached and otherwise, clustered like flies about one or more factories sited in some rural area far distant from stores not owned by the company. Mining and lumbering towns struck Pullman-car passengers as hideously barren; even the permanent installations around textile, steel, and other mills seemed impossibly ugly. Despite a growing reliance on professional designers, the great industrialists learned that company towns mysteriously begat strikes, and the better the master plan, the worse the strike. Even Pullman in Illinois, designed by an architect and a landscape architect charged with creating a city of distinctive housing, athletic fields, and shops along with railroad-car factories, witnessed brutal clashes between strikers and the guards and soldiers representing the company. In Pullman, arguably the home of such innovations as the shopping mall, industrialists and thoughtful observers learned the dismal shortcomings of environmental determinism applied to urban design for worker control. Harmonious, sanitary, affordable housing and surroundings did not necessarily make for contented workers.

Here and there amateur industrialists succeeded, albeit on a small scale. From the early 1860s onward, the Cheney family created a handsome industrial village in

South Manchester, Connecticut, attracting eventually the scrutiny of reformers, architects, industrialists, and essayists writing for mass-circulation periodicals. Around their mills lived the six brothers, each in his own house, in grounds "laid out like a park," in the words of one 1872 *Harper's Monthly Magazine* writer. Beyond the brothers' houses lay groups of single-family, two-story "cottages," all "designed with an artistic taste" and with great regard for high-quality plumbing and "plenty of light." No expert advice informed the brothers' design decisions. They built widely separated groups of houses in order to keep different immigrant groups away from each other, "thus avoiding any possible turmoil which might grow out of petty discords." They forbade the keeping of cows and hens and encouraged the occupants to create flower and vegetable gardens, but in the end they simply built for their employees slightly smaller versions of the old farmhouse in which they had grown up. The *Harper's* writer wondered why other industrialists failed to follow such straightforward policies, if only for the clear financial rewards flowing from a happy work force renting high-quality houses. South Manchester seemed almost too good to be true, a sort of expanded eighteenth-century New England town that somehow solved the problem of "industrial organization." As the decades passed and more visitors—some from Europe—arrived to see the wondrous simplicity, as more essayists discovered "contented labor," the brothers may have wondered at the fuss.[1] After all, they had only improved the landscape in which their father had begun business at the close of the eighteenth century, and they had avoided all European principles and styles.

Most American industrialists, as well as designers intrigued by large-scale town planning, looked overseas for guidance in building company towns. Usually they looked to England, and especially to Bourneville, the rural home of the Cadbury cocoa- and candy-making company. George Cadbury moved his manufacturing operation from the slums of Birmingham simply because he thought "that the worst of human ills follow the unwholesomeness of city life." American civic and industrial reformers discovered Bourneville around the year 1900 and praised it without limit. Somehow they missed the deeper forces explaining the undertaking—starting with Cadbury's come-outer Quaker faith, which countenanced physical separation from urban evil—and focused chiefly on the appearance of the place. On 480 acres, Cadbury had erected housing for some thirty-five hundred people, laid out cricket fields, football grounds, and all sorts of parks, erected libraries, gymnasia, and hospitals. "The many picturesque features at Bourneville, the woodland walks, the embowered nooks and the charming pleasure grounds afford delight," wondered Annie L. Diggs of the place that attacted pleasure parties from everywhere in England.[2] Diggs's contemporaneous *Cosmopolitan* article is only one of many American essays extoling the English "garden city," and like most it focuses on Bourneville as the best example of what might be accomplished in the future, even in the United States.

Garden city proved a difficult designation, however, since clearly many of the best examples in Britain and elsewhere prospered only as dormitory towns. Hellerav, which John T. Klaber told readers of his 1914 *Architectural Record* article

The Cheneys' "industrial experiment" at South Manchester, Connecticut, succeeded partly because workers lived in houses resembling those inhabited by the owners.

Mature trees and pleasant paths and roads attracted many visitors to South Manchester and pleased the factory workers employed there.

In the evening, factory workers and their families walked the sylvan streets of South Manchester, enjoying not only the handsome grounds of the single-family houses but a refreshing change from the industrial order of the factory.

English company towns often provided design details for American proponents of wholly planned borderland communities. Here in Cadbury's company town is a potential origin of much of Atterbury's architecture in Forest Hills Gardens.

Annie Diggs found in Bournemouth and other English planned towns the perfect solution to American borderland growth. She said little about the feudal architectural style, however, and even less about the lives of women in the model towns.

Many turn-of-the-century English "garden cities" provided tiny parks like those Olmsted designed for Forest Hills Gardens, not larger wooded areas such as those called for by so many American reformers.

was both a garden city and "a German housing development," existed as a first-rate residential experiment four miles outside Dresden, but it was scarcely a city.[3] Designed according to the guidelines of the Deutsche Werkstatten, a cooperative manufacturing furniture on the site, Hellerav in all its tinted stucco, tile-roof glory spoke of the prosperous medieval village increasingly important in pan-German mythology, not of the medieval cities Imperial planners worked so hard to rebuild according to scientific principles.

The merest glance at the photographs illustrating Diggs's and Klaber's articles demonstrates the origin of Grosvenor Atterbury's Forest Hills Gardens architecture. From Bourneville and Hellerav, Atterbury took the stylistic components that became German-Tudor facades, and he took a whole philosophy too. In "Model Towns in America," a handsomely illustrated *Scribner's Magazine* article of 1912, he explicitly links Forest Hills Gardens with company towns like Pullman, Whitinsville in Massachusetts, and even Gary in Indiana. "Model Towns" contains a lengthy explication of his intentions for Forest Hills Gardens, as well as a particularly detailed explanation of his groupings of one semi-detached house with two single-family ones.[4] Atterbury's terminology reveals far more than his sketches, for he speaks of the "beneficent monarchy" that forces purchasers to consider the options of the novel groupings. He also reveals the potential for change in the overall design scheme, about which the Sage Foundation said little. The semi-private courts, he asserts, are so planned that a majority of abutters can vote to abolish any one of them and their rental fees. After such a vote, the foundation would run a new street through the site and sell the new streetfront lots either to abutters or to the general public. Not only is Forest Hills Gardens under the control of a benevolent despot, its novel spaciousness lies constantly at the mercy of any majority deciding that the enclosures and gardens "do not pay." In the end, it appears that Atterbury desires an extension of the beneficent monarchy over the entire United States, providing the opportunity to plan centrally and professionally not only the borderlands, but cities as well.

In the same July issue of *Scribner's,* Frederick C. Howe, a prolific American authority on city planning and urban reform issues, waxed eloquent on the subject of English garden cities. Howe emphasized the static perfection of Letchworth and other "garden cities" or "model towns" all "designed with the utmost care by the best of architects and in harmony with the village idea." He found the building restrictions admirable and concluded that "the beauty of these garden cottages with their stuccoed walls and gray and orange tiles, with porches and projecting eaves, compels one to question if ordinary house-building is not a neglected art and whether we are not on the threshold of a new development in domestic architecture."[5] Assuring his readers that Forest Hill Gardens fitted perfectly into the larger European philosophy, Howe predicted that soon cities would undergo revolutionary transformation. In one way, Howe predicted accurately. Within two years, European cities underwent artillery and aerial bombardment.

The Great War deflected interest from model towns, especially German ones. By 1917, when Atterbury was planning Indian Hill, a company town near Worces-

*Hellerav and other German planned communities impressed
some American observers before the Great War, but their
density made them unpopular as models in the United States,
even for industrialists building company towns.*

*Few American company towns achieved the quiet, relaxed
beauty of South Manchester, although the housing built in
Hopedale, Massachusetts, came near it, partly because of the
frosting of trees.*

*Atterbury admired the overall scheme of Gary, Indiana, but
he said remarkably little about the monotonous effect of large-
scale repetition of straight streets and nearly identical houses.*

ter, Massachusetts, in which workers demanded single-family houses from the architect, few American borderland families respected much of European model-town thinking.[6] A civilization turned barbarous elicited only pity, not respect for scientific principles suddenly outmoded by automobiles and seemingly incapable of adapting to other immediate changes. The 1920s witnessed a few reasonably successful company town ventures, most notably Kohler in Wisconsin, and intermittent pleadings from design professionals that they now better understood the automobile, change, and individualism. But clearly Shaker Heights, the gently restricted, resoundingly American solution had triumphed over the German-Tudor experiment.[7] And even Shaker Heights struck many would-be borderland families as too much the creation of beneficent monarchy.

Company towns turned thoughtful Americans away from almost every sort of "garden city," "model town," and "planned development," and even as Howe, Diggs, Atterbury, and others praised the European examples, contrary arguments appeared in popular periodicals. "The most successful attempts at industrial social betterment in our country are those farthest removed from the suspicion of domination or control by the employer," Eugene J. Buffington concluded in "Making Cities for Workmen," a lengthy *Harper's Weekly* piece of 1909. "Fresh in the minds of all of us is the failure of the Pullman Company to maintain its authority over the village affairs of Pullman, Illinois, near Chicago." Against the great thrust of model-town thinking ran the emerging working-class devotion to building-and-loan associations that enable working people to buy land and build houses beyond company town limits. The associations, along with cooperative savings banks, reiterated the moral value of the owner-occupied "home" and implicitly renounced the company town, however beautiful it might be.[8]

The catastrophe at Pullman and the failure of so many other well-intended company towns tainted the efforts of designers and developers striving for perfectly harmonized, homogeneous, "finished" industrial and residential developments. Between 1890 and 1917, developers learned to trust their intuitive sense of the emergent American love for a *little* stability, a *little* harmony, and *much* room for individual adaptation to change. Near Baltimore between 1891 and 1910, for example, a development company employed the Olmsted firm to plan and oversee Roland Park, a large-lot residential effort modeled on Riverside outside Chicago, with a nod to Llewellyn Park. While never as well known as Forest Hills Garden or Shaker Heights, Roland Park demonstrates the growing "Americanness" of the upper-class "planned" residential preserve.[9]

The Olmsted designers linked their Baltimore work directly to the creation of Riverside, a planned residential community begun in the late 1860s. For many reasons, among them its swampy site distant from Chicago and its rather novel arrangement of carriage drives, Riverside grew very slowly, and even Everett Chamberlin found little of note in it, citing in his *Chicago and Its Suburbs* the "litigation and financial embarrassments" plaguing Riverside's progress.[10] But the senior Frederick Law Olmsted persisted in hs vision of a place marrying city and country. In promotional pamphlet, *Riverside in 1871, with a Description of Its*

Improvements, he argued that the Riverside homeowner enjoyed more than fresh air and sunlight: "He has plenty of elbow room, and can dig to his heart's content, raise his own fruits and vegetables, keep his own cow, and even make his own butter. And he can do all this without the sacrifice of the urban comforts which long use has made a necessity to him."[11] In emphasizing that every lot had space for a barn and for "the cultivation of trees, shrubs, flowers, small fruits" and other plants, Olmsted emphasized his understanding that families would want to shape their own space, to adapt it to change, to farm as gentlemanly as any Federalist, albeit on a smaller scale.

Olmsted's thinking no longer ruled when his firm accepted the Roland Park challenge; Frederick Law Olmsted, Jr., handled most of the work.[12] But clearly the tradition of Riverside endured, for Roland Park consisted almost entirely of large single-family houses. It was a place that mightily impressed Waldon Fawcett, who described it in 1903 for readers of *House and Garden.* According to Fawcett, the developers quickly learned that would-be purchasers wanted street frontage not of fifty but of seventy-five feet at least, and they immediately redesigned the site. The developers gently restricted building, rigorously enforcing only house setbacks. Fawcett understood that the developers hoped "to insure architectural harmony in as great a degree as is practical," but that they had no wish "to dictate to property holders what style of architecture shall be followed in the provision of houses or which materials shall be employed." In consequence, Roland Park architecture ranged from Queen Anne to English cottage styles, from colonial revival to Dutch colonial to "domestic Gothic," and the community even included "entirely shingled" houses that Fawcett found "unique." Aside from the one block of stores built in "picturesque Flemish architecture" like the "beautified" retail structures in so many other turn-of-the-century commuter villages, Roland Park exhibited no "official" architectural appearance, only a vital diversity of architectural styles and a population actively gardening.[13]

Roland Park from the beginning echoed urban rather than rural traditions. Its developers forbade the private stables that the Riverside promoters loved, and lot sizes were far smaller, perhaps because many Roland Park buyers had grown up accustomed to Baltimore row houses and saw Roland Park lots as positively extensive. Not until 1911, when one Roland Park homeowner successfully broke them to build a driveway and a garage, did the general restrictions arouse much opposition. Indeed, the developers understood restrictions as rules not to dictate quality design but to stymie freakish "anomalies." By 1910, Roland Park existed as a handsome residential neighborhood within the city limits of Baltimore, a gentle contradiction to designers smitten with European notions of wholly harmonized, wholly static garden cities.

The younger Olmsted somehow lacked the cultural acuity that his senior almost always displayed. Upper-class residential preserves followed the precedents of Llewellyn Park, Riverside, and Roland Park, becoming either summertime retreats—like Cushing Island off Portland Harbor in Maine—or extremely expensive enclaves like Tuxedo Park and Belle Terre outside New York.[14] In the enclaves the rich moved with few restrictions, trusting to good sense and good manners. In the middle decades of the twentieth century, designers like the younger Olmsted forgot the essence of the handsome enclaves, forgot that they originated not from strict design guidelines, but from the gentlest of restrictions agreed upon by homogeneous populations educated in similar ways by similar schooling and reading.

After the Great War, Forest Hills Gardens, Shaker Heights, and even Roland Park spoke far less persuasively to families seeking escape from the urban residential ring than did the far older tradition of rural living. The import of the wholly planned residential development struck home long before inhabitants of Forest Hills Gardens learned the heartbreak and expense of repairing houses built entirely of unique materials no longer available anywhere.

In the first decade of the new century, mass-circulation magazines aimed at middle-class readers published a wide range of articles focused on the transformation of the borderland and on the mindset of the people whose trains raced past Forest Hills Gardens into distant Long Island. In a 1903 *Cosmopolitan* essay, for example, Waldon Fawcett catalogued the advantages of living on the edge of farming country, not the least being the wonderful physical exercise provided by gardening, important given the "current allegiance to athleticism." In arguing that "the walk to the station cannot take the place of the exercise to be had in digging, planting, and weeding in a garden—exercise which involves almost every muscle of the body," however, Fawcett only touched upon the significant limitations of living in "a house in a park" in which the grounds have been wholly shaped at the start. "One never cares quite so much for a place which has been mapped out and finished by strangers, and may be the exact duplicate of a hundred others." Fawcett understood the ever more powerful need of many Americans to shape house and grounds on their own, to personalize the structures turned out by architects—and, by implication, builders—"regardless of the spice of diversity" designed in at the start. The essay concludes with a fervent assertion that "the suburban home has been instrumental in disclosing to many men and women the pure enjoyment which may be derived from tilling the soil." In the borderlands beyond the urban residential ring, "the smallest of these miniature estates affords surprising opportunities for the office-weary business man who finds keen relaxation in experimenting with a garden, and for the woman to whom floriculture affords a genuine diversion." Certainly the owners of "vast suburban estates finding vent in scientific forestry, highly specialized fruit-raising, dairying, and the raising of blooded stock" may improve the nation's agriculture, but it is the family on the acre of land which improves national culture.[15]

Personalizing family space indoors and out became the theme of writers in dozens of magazines. In 1906, an essayist argued in *The Craftsman* that speculator-builders owed it to the purchasers of their houses to install no planting whatsoever, but to leave as undisturbed as possible the indigenous vegetation "of the wilderness," trusting the new owners to improve it themselves.[16] In the same year another writer told readers of *Popular Science Monthly* that behind the "sentiment" prompting many families to live in the country "is an unerring instinct which leads

In the years after designing the houses in Forest Hills Gardens, Atterbury designed houses in the company towns and learned that in Indian Hill and elsewhere, early twentieth-century American factory workers wanted nothing of European models—they wanted single-family houses and lots of trees.

Gardening in private space entranced businessmen worried about lack of exercise, adulterated food, and urban stress.

us back to contact with the soil and to communion with nature, to a simpler and less artificial kind of living."[17] To be sure, periodical authors now and again poked fun at the supposedly simpler life revolving around garden- and lawn-making, but almost all such articles appearing between 1890 and 1920 display only the gentle satire of a 1910 *Everybody's Magazine* piece, "Why Pay Rent?" Eugene Wood mocked the newcomers arriving in speculator-built places of "fresh air and sunlight and green grass, and a garden," noting especially the seductions of the nurserymen who show up before the new residents have even connected gas lines and proffer illustration books "printed on glossy oilcloth in the most ravishing colors known to art." Whatever their "resolve upon Spartan simplicity," the newcomers plunge into ordering hydrangea bushes, crimson ramblers, two hundred strawberry plants, and sapling shade trees, wholly unaware of the complexities involved in arrange-ment and planting but absolutely delighted in independent action.[18]

They ordered carpentry tools, too—often the wrong ones, to be sure, according to magazine experts writing in the early years of the new century, but in the finest of American spirit. Jared Stuyvesant enumerated the essential woodworking tools in a 1910 *House and Garden* article entitled "Why You Should Have a Workshop and How," one of many essays he and his contemporaries aimed at professional men newly arrived in borderland houses. With simple tools, Stuyvesant argued, any patient executive might not only respond to the "impulse to make minor repairs or additions about the house when the need of these appeared" but enter into a genuinely restorative avocation "bringing work of a kind entirely different from that which occupies your work-day hours." Household repair, however, matters very little to the professional man, in Stuyvesant's final analysis; "the real joy of craftsmanship lies beyond that, in actual creative work."[19] Implicit in his long, straightforward article is the barest glimmer of realization that office work, even for the most successful of businessmen, offered little creative outlet as the century advanced.

Other magazine pieces appearing in 1910 illustrate the range and depth of the genre that soon competed on equal footing with gardening columns. *Country Life* published a long article about wintertime woodworking for the harried executive, in which Julian Burroughs focuses his argument on the increasingly nervous state of businessmen. "The joy of using edged tools is not only a great training for the brain as well as the body, but it is a most sane, wholesome exercise, adding to one's resources, health, and self-mastery," he determines. "It has a great future, it is a lesson in conservation, it will help to bring us to a more simple, less artificial life, it will open new and inexpensive ways of enjoyment and self-expression."[20] Mixed in with his advice about seasoning lumber and preparing stains is a sketchy picture of new problems confronting the commuting professional. Responsible fathers, for example, can use the basement or backyard shop to teach sons about patience, thoroughness, and self-discipline, sharing with them not only companionship but the fruits of learning a craft together. Moreover, in this way fathers can offer some insight into the values and great enterprises of generations preceding the urban, industrial one. Burroughs recommends dragging logs from woods or from rivers and

Much of the nineteenth-century fascination with borderland living derived from the determination of young couples to shape domestic space together, to share some sort of meaningful work.

Nurserymen descended on newly arrived borderers, often bringing seed and tree catalogues on moving-in day.

Tools Of Quality

Hardware Of Quality

A Handsome and Useful

Christmas Gift

The only thoroughly practical

Combination Bench and Tool Cabinet

Consisting of a solid oak, brass-trimmed, highly finished cabinet, with work-bench and vise: a complete assortment, 95 in all, of the **finest quality standard carpenters' tools.**

Complete, as illustrated above, $85.00

We make also the following outfits in polished oak, brass-trimmed Wall-Cabinets, shaped like a suit-case, but larger, with same grade of tools as above :

No. 47, 21 Tools, $7.50   **No. 53, 36 Tools, $15.00**
No. 52, 24 Tools, $10.00   **No. 54, 40 Tools, $20.00**

Our prices are f. o. b. New York, giving the best tools made (instead of cheap tools and paying the freight). *Special Tool Outfit Catalogue, No. 2046, illustrates and describes all five outfits. Send for copy.*

THE "TOURIST AUTOKIT" is made up of the very best selected tools obtainable, and is the highest type of repairing outfit for road use. The "Tourist" is especially arranged with reference to its quality and utility, and embodies every possible permanent and emergency value that can be included in a kit of this size. "Tourist Autokit" Circular, No. 2045, sent on request.

We issue many special catalogues, among which are the following: No. 2108, Wood-Carvers' Tools. No. 2109, Venetian Iron and Tools.

Hammacher, Schlemmer & Co.

Hardware, Tools, Supplies and Piano Materials   NEW YORK, SINCE 1848
Fourth Ave. and Thirteenth St., Block South of Union Square

This 1906 Suburban Life *advertisement speaks to men and women not only anxious to explore the creativity accompanying woodworking and home repair, but to men and women with the space, usually in a basement, for such an array of tools.*

The turn-of-the-century businessman in his cellar, like the 1850s businessman on his farm, relaxed by exploring a world apart from his office.

We are pioneers in the sale of high-grade tool outfits for
Order direct (we have no agents) o

HAMMACHER, SCHLEMMER & CO., N
HARDWARE. TOOL

In the cellar on stormy winter nights, the businessman might teach his son something of craftsmanship, sharing the time so precious to the commuter father.

shaping them into lumber, and he joins Stuyvesant in suggesting the old farm shop as a prototype of a well-ordered workplace graced by simple, cared-for tools used by virtuous, dignified men. A *Suburban Life* piece, far more pedestrian, tells the "handy man about the house" that household repair work not only saves money but imparts a deeper, truer interest in the house he inhabits.[21] Painting screens, unsticking doors, even replacing a broken windowpane contribute to the family budget, but more importantly to family stability and happiness. Almost always the magazine essayists focus not on the farmer or craftsman intimately familiar with tools from daily work, but on the "brain-worker" confronting the subtle evils of job-related stress.

Until well into the 1920s, the articles largely ignored women, except as the beneficiaries of new closet shelves, china cabinets, and porches. But during the Great War the first suggestions appeared that borderland women ought to know something of household repair and ought to demand from architects, builders, and repairmen sensible, labor-saving design and construction. Unlike the utopia-minded reformers envisioning communal kitchens and laundries, periodical writers like Marion Harland, who conducted a "school for housewives" column syndicated in newspapers, focused on small changes that would make housekeeping easier and far less time-consuming.[22] Much housekeeping advice directed to borderland women assumes houses with large rooms adaptable to personal needs and implies that the handyman husband might reshape such domestic space precisely. Fitting the new shelf to his wife's height, building the china closet "comparatively contiguous to the table set in the middle of the floor," and continuously adapting kitchen and other rooms to the housekeeping inventions that appeared so rapidly—and of course building every sort of outdoor improvement from clothesline poles to garden arbors—struck authors as the job of husbands.[23] By the 1920s, however, columnists had begun urging women to learn more about tools themselves, building on their century-old experience of using gardening implements. Florence Taft Eaton's "Equipping the Toolhouse" asserts that one's garden tools become "after long and affectionate use, really personal possessions" and deserve not only careful arrangement but a modest, attractive toolhouse.[24] Eaton's *House Beautiful* article of 1926 dovetails perfectly with a series by Gladys Beckett, "The Handy Woman About the House," featuring specialized, detailed information. Her January essay, "Be Your Own Electrician," pushes far beyond replacing blown fuses into the mysteries of rewiring electric percolators and irons or simplicities like installing a new plug on a worn cord.[25] Beckett and other women emphasized one message over and over again: Women in the borderlands often live far from carpenters, electricians, and even handymen husbands much of the time, and as courageous members of a great experiment in living, they ought to fear nothing in and around their houses. Apartment women summon janitors, the columnists assert; modern borderland women grab the correct tools and fix things themselves.

Moreover, borderland women strengthen their marriages and inspire their children by tackling projects with their husbands. In the first years of the new century, article after article recounts the joy of joint effort. Male and female magazine writers alike agreed that couples should build benches and partitions and greenhouses together not only to save money, and not even because such projects often require more than one pair of hands, but because jointly shaping domestic space shapes happiness too. In "Twenty Miles Out: Indiscretions of a Commuter's Wife," a 1925 *House Beautiful* series describing the dozens of joint projects undertaken by a newlywed couple nearly ignorant of tools and techniques, the anonymous author makes clear the sheer joy to be had from home repair.[26] A heavy rainstorm finds her husband on the leaking roof, and endangered by drooping electric lines; and she beside him, a rubber boot on each hand, ready to knock him from electrocution. Together they determine that an old automobile license plate will patch the leak, and when proven successful in their creativity and effort, they sit on the shingles delighting in the sheer joy of shared repair.

Handymen husbands and handywomen wives—and handy couples too—found immense encouragement in the advertising of hardware companies. Simmons Hardware of St. Louis and New York, for example, wholesaled the "Keen Kutter" line of woodworking tools, telling readers of *Country Life* and other borderland journals that "the desire to 'make something' is just human nature" and that having fine tools "in the home is not only a joy but an economy."[27] Perhaps the Stanley Company of New Britain, Connecticut, advertised most effectively, however, moving in the early 1920s from producing high-quality tools for professionals and amateurs to publishing as well. *How to Work with Tools and Wood: For the Home Workshop,* a 1927 clothbound, photograph-illustrated volume nearly two hundred pages long, reflects the firm's awareness of the burgeoning tool market in borderland places. Anonymously authored by a man confessing to a lifelong love of the smell and feel of both new lumber and very old furniture, *How to Work with Tools* fastens at once on the essential rightness of a family man's knowing how to "humor a furnace fire, fix electric lights, or grease the chassis on a car"—and build nearly anything from wood. The book offers few projects.[28] Rather it moves precisely and quickly from simple issues like planing, using sketches of a cat's fur to explain woodgrain direction, to setting mitre boxes and making dovetail joints. And clearly it addresses borderland men, professionals owning large cellars for workshops, who wear vests and ties while holding chisels. Equipped with the tools and plans advertised in its final pages, the borderland man might make birdhouses, flat-bottomed rowboats, garden seats and trellises, and, of course, the massive workbenches so essential to everything.

More than a concern with nervous tension suffuses much of the do-it-yourself literature published before 1940. Surely the tired "brain-worker" might save money doing his own repair and building projects, and surely he might transmit valuable traits to his helper sons and daughters; and he might strengthen his marriage by sharing with his wife the learning, the failures, and the successes of handiwork. Surely the "new woman" of the twentieth-century borderlands might grow in unexpected ways through mastering woodworking and metalworking tools. And surely the man and woman who shape their house and grounds might acquire a deeper love of structure and space. Such arguments float everywhere in the vast literature published in *Country Life* and *Popular Science* and a thousand tool-company-sponsored do-it-yourself leaflets and books.[29] But something else drifts beneath the prose.

Perhaps the official closing of the frontier in 1890 sparked the thinking, perhaps the developing love of American antique houses and furniture directed it, perhaps the mounting concern about the "Americanness" of city life urged it on, but by the 1910s the do-it-yourself movement had acquired the slightest flavoring of patriotism. After all, so many essayists argued, most Americans had always built their own houses and barns, had felled their own trees and split their own shingles, had whittled spoons and fitted pails. In the borderlands of large lots and roomy cellars, and soon garages, professional men might remain in touch with an essential element of American character lost to office work—the making and remaking of built form—and transmit it to sons and even daughters. The borderland houselot offered in its vegetable garden and flower beds, in its solitary fruit tree and spreading lawn some traces of rural landscape and, according to so many writers, some opportunity for rural virtue. The house itself offered something American too—the proving ground for men and women equipped with imagination, tools from Simmons or Stanley, and room enough down in the cellar or in the back yard for a china closet or gazebo under construction.

And the wholly planned places like Forest Hills Gardens, even places like Shaker Heights and Roland Park, subtly spoke of a different tradition, even a dangerous one, as 1920s writers began to assert.

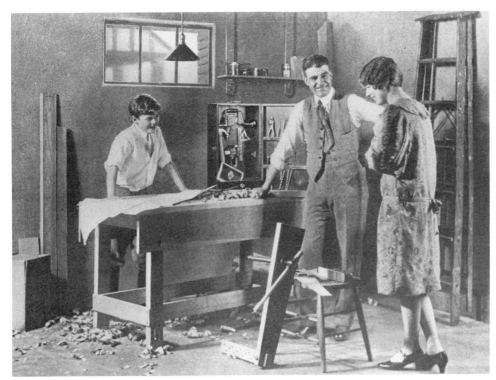

The Stanley Tool Company told 1920s fathers not only how to build things, but where, with whom, and for whom.

In the years between 1890 and 1940, the basement of the single-family house appears repeatedly as the warm, private, secure alternative to the urban YMCA or playground, a place where boys learn skills, not sports.

*Borderers in the Pacific Coast states knew
that the mountains lay only a short distance
beyond the houses of the urban residential
rings.*

*Hillside houses overlooking immense vistas
lured West Coast city families into the
foothills.*

*The forests of Washington and Oregon
offered stunning possibilities to borderers
trained in the east coast art of tree
appreciation.*

Before Atterbury's tinted brick and stucco weathered, long before Olmsted's planting matured, Forest Hills Gardens began to connote more than the intriguing intimacy of company town design and model suburb planning. As early as 1912, one writer glimpsed the essential easternness of so much design-profession thinking about borderland growth. Forest Hills Gardens grew provincial, almost obsolescent.

Elmer Grey titled his 1912 *Scribner's* article as precisely as he argued and illustrated it. "The New Suburb of the Pacific Coast" suggests that all the borderlands of California, Oregon, and Washington share a fundamental likeness of intent immediately visible to any discerning visitor. "The East has been an experimental station for the West in the matter of suburb planning; and this is fortunate," he argues, for "haphazard" borderland development would ruin "some of the most beautiful scenery in the world." The beauty of that scenery attracts people to sites an hour or more distant from cities, luring them up mountainsides for housesites offering "the finest view." Beauty orders Grey's article, surfacing in explications of the ways orange groves and "villas" remind visitors of Spain and Italy, in explanations of road alignment, in analyses of the devotion paid by architects and builders to ancient oaks. Scale seems at first unimportant. Only the illustrations and a few random comments suggest otherwise.

Pacific Coast borderlands demonstrated indeed their creators' learning from eastern prototypes. In many instances lots were far, far larger, perhaps due, at least in southern California, to the openness—and consequent lack of privacy—of a landscape of thinly scattered trees. But away from Beverly Hills and a half dozen other smaller-scale places, the borderland residents delighted in large hillside lots offering immense views; and in the rainy northern borderlands, blessed with immense stands of deciduous and coniferous trees, the reasons become clear. West Coast borderers knew of the spread of urban form everywhere in the eastern borderlands, and around Seattle, San Francisco, and other cities, they settled far, far beyond what they dreamed would ever be the outermost reach of barnaclelike residential and industrial zones. Moreover, almost from the start the borderers moved to preserve the forested views across the valleys beyond their hillside windows. As Andrew Jackson Downing had directed in 1847, they sought natural wood to make their new western houses seem as old as the trees, to make nooks from which to admire views of forest. Around Seattle and Spokane, for example, borderers preserved not only street trees, but existing forest through which roads might pass in the future. A few examples of ugliness, especially surrounding Tacoma, spurred the efforts of borderers well aware of what Sidney Fisher learned so long ago on the banks of the Schuylkill—no matter how beautiful its grounds, a borderland house facing an industrial view lost its ability to restore the psyche.

Another factor made west coast borderlands different from their eastern predecessors. By 1912 Grey grasped the power of the automobile in shaping borderland space. Not only did the west coast borderers live almost wholly free of commuter-train schedules, they lived free of railroad-track real estate developers like those Henry Cuyler Bunner satirized. Able to choose the best sites without regard for accessibility to train depots, they forced their powerful automobiles up slopes and across valleys, then forced county and municipal governments to improve roads. Around Portland, for example, Grey discovered "the manner in which streets have been zigzagged and wound up the sides of hills of great height, following the natural contours, and the steep sides utilized for building purposes." The layout of the new roads was possible because there was no need to spare horses pulling carriages and drays, but it derived from the overwhelming devotion to perfect views. Almost all, if not all, of the borderland places Grey describes he visited by automobile, and his language, in even the most casual of phrases, marks his view as wholly modern, "thoroughly up-to-date" in the parlance of his era. He remarks on needing a camera at every turn to do justice to the scenery, on how a particular house "seems welded to the landscape." "The automobile glides over smooth hard roads that are virgin soil, while on either side, where the surface has not been disturbed, it is like a well-kept lawn."[1] His is the voice of the new century, the century not of blacksmithing and riveting but of welding, the century just discovering the automobile borderlands.

Everywhere in the Pacific Coast borderlands Grey glimpsed the transformation of borderland growth. "Railroads and steamboats have now become so numerous that all classes, from the humblest mechanic to the wealthy banker, can have their homes in the country, reaching them in about the same time, and as cheaply, or nearly so, as they could ride from the City Hall to the upper part of the city," the architect Henry Hudson Holly told readers of *Harper's Monthly* in 1876. "It is not an occasion for wonder, then, that there are so many ready to avail themselves of this rapid transit, and that we see studded along the lines of our railroads picturesque and cheerful homes, where the heads of families are not only recuperating from the deleterious effects of the confinement of city life, but are, with the aid of fresh air and wholesome food, laying the foundation of greater strength and increased happiness for their children."[2] In 1876 Holly forecast the outline of borderland growth for a half century. But by 1910 his forecast no longer applied to the Pacific Coast borderlands. There, and elsewhere, even his words had new connotations. *Mechanic* meant an automobile repairman, the specialist so essential to borderland life outside Spokane, Portland, and San Francisco, and within a few years equally important in the Long Island borderlands Fitzgerald depicts in *The Great Gatsby*.

After 1900 American magazines begin recording the adaptation of borderlands to the automobile. Advertising may have helped shape editorial policy. By 1907 manufacturers of automobiles, tires, and motoring accessories were purchasing much space, especially in borderland-oriented periodicals like *Suburban Life*. But clearly the borderlands adapted well to early automobiling. "There is not unalloyed joy in motoring through crowded city streets, with narrow-minded policemen in unexpected places," argued Hilda Ward in a 1907 *Suburban Life* article; "but coursing over the wide stretches of macadam road in the small settlements, motorists find much to attract them in the way of pretty scenery, adequate hotels, country clubs, handsome residences, and withal a sheet-anchor ready for the engineer in the shape of telephones and repair shops." Ward's "The Automobile in the Suburbs from a Woman's Point of View" heralds the new force sweeping away the borderland organizing element that Holly so clearly perceived. "The automobile has caused the word 'suburb' to carry miles further than it used to," Ward states bluntly, "until now it has come to signify to the motorist almost any place where gasoline may be readily obtained." Ward and many other women writers make clear that among the transformations wrought by the automobile, the change in the lives of borderland women was scarcely insignificant.

Ward lists many delights obtained from her car, everything from the freedom of having the car all day after dropping her husband at his commuter station to the special healthfulness of wintertime motoring (in all seasons, she claims, automobiling "is soothing to the nerves" and "apt to make one sleep soundly and eat particularly heartily") to driving children on outings. "Out in the suburbs are the true Happy Hunting Grounds of the motorist," she decides. But the greatest delight lies in learning.

Not only can the modern woman learn to drive the automobile. She can learn to repair it, at least most of the time, savoring the joy of the "feminine brain" mastering mechanism. "There is no more delightful way of spending one's hours than in learning to run and take care of an automobile," Ward determines, and she suggests that the "whole family devote the winter evenings to a careful study of the subject of motor-cars and acquire an intimate knowledge of the mechanism, and how to care for their own machine."[3] Borderland roads offer the quiet, space, and freedom from scornful observation so necessary to women learning to drive. But "learning" transcends learning about the machine, about cranking and loose connecting rods. It means learning about the larger landscape, exploring every lane and way. In 1840 the borderland woman savored the mastery of botany, delighting in the excuse science provided for long exploratory walks. In the late 1900s automobiling entered the writing of borderland women in a nearly identical way, epitomizing the freedom borderland life offered adventurous women.

Articles like Ward's did not escape the attention of men, and particularly that

A combination of equitable climate and good road maintenance made automobile commuting both pleasant and reliable in California, Oregon, and Washington.

Cranking Up for a Spin on a Frosty Day

Borderland women learned the pure joy of the motorcar on uncrowded roads—and the even more exhilarating joy of motoring away from husbands and other men.

of observers of borderland growth. "The automobile gives one the country, not merely the suburbs," Eugene A. Clancy warned readers of *Harper's Weekly* in 1911. "There is no longer the necessity of attaching oneself to a railroad station, nor even to a village. You may stake your claim wherever you please." By *country* Clancy meant regions beyond sensible distances from borderland commuter stations, places twenty-five to fifty miles from urban centers. And he realized that old ideas, the ideas Holly so cogently expressed, had faded before the reality of Pacific Coast borderlands reached chiefly by automobile roads. "An amusing feature of the new idea is its nerve-racking effect on the country real-estate man. One might say his Bible and his faith have been torn from him." No longer can he safely speculate on land easily reached from new commuter stops. "He knew and had to deal with but one species of urban outcast—the predestined commuter."[4] No longer predestined by railroad-track alignments, the new commuter, exactly as Ward knew, might settle nearly anywhere.

In the 1900s and 1910s few writers had the prescience of Holly. They extolled freedom from timetables and real estate men, freedom to live in houses far distant from cities, to live in houses atop hills that would wind any horse. They examined the Pacific Coast borderlands and saw nothing of the unpredictable sprawl that would accompany the popularization of the automobile. And they failed to understand that cities would soon fail motorists anxious for pleasant drives, for long, glorious afternoons with engines in fourth gear, for coursing through the country.

VI ❧ Arrivals

Few photographers captured the scale of the San Francisco fire, but this image succeeds, in part by juxtaposing refugees and their meager possessions with a city burning to the ground.

Urban fires, explosions, and earthquakes left parts of many
American cities resembling vast graveyards. Here an
illustration reveals the rubble of Boston after a major
nineteenth-century fire.

Photographs in mass-circulation magazines convinced many
Americans that urban form and urban society might crack at
any moment, precisely as San Francisco cracked, making
refugees of its citizens.

By 1917, large-scale warfare had trans-
formed, albeit subtly, the magazines aimed at borderland residents. To be sure,
editors published articles about war gardens and "poultry-yard patriotism," advocating using petrochemical fertilizer only for vegetables, not flowers. But a deeper, stronger undercurrent reshaped editorial content as the Great War reshaped the
European landscape.

An anonymous woman glimpsed something of the current, and in a 1917 issue
of *Countryside* described her growing understanding of the essential fragility of
major American cities. In "Why Is a Suburb?" she relates a dream of destruction, a
dream of the "City Spirit" that she fears. "I woke up one morning on the twelfth
floor of a Fifth Avenue hotel, and as I looked out of the window I saw—and that
sight is still real to me now—the city lying in ruins." The aftermath of destruction,
the city "a chaos of fallen granite and skeleton steel," leads her to wonder about the
mindset of people, especially well-off people, who live in cities and "mock" the
commuter.[1] Her article is a sort of reverie, an intensely evocative series of set-pieces,
mostly visual images, flowing from dream insight. In a few paragraphs it explains the
new, or heightened, perceptions that in time encouraged so many people to leave the
city and the urban residential ring.

Whoever she was, this writer knew the growing perplexity and vague fear
with which European intellectuals after the turn of the century had begun to view
the sprawling city. She understood, too, the growing complexity of machinery.[2] Her
references to Maupassant and to cities as "monstrous, machine-made creatures"
order her initial argument, but her comments about an earthquake in Jamaica focus
her theme. "All of them," she says of the inhabitants of the borderlands reached by
train, the places of big gardens, strutting hens, and individual expression in house
color, are "in the bottom of their hearts, *afraid* of the City." Urban form is fragile—
and potentially lethal. The "towering apartment buildings which so effectively cut
off the sunshine from our millionaires' homes" can tumble into bits. What explains
the dream, the nightmare vision of falling granite and tottering steel?

Certainly educated Americans knew of urban destruction, of fires like the one in 1886 that leaped from warehouses to destroy a hundred of the finest houses of Galveston, and of earlier fires like that which spurred the settling of Chicago borderlands. They knew too, at least in New York City, the continuous thunder of dynamite toppling obsolescent buildings. "The commonest of New York noises is still, as it was when I first knew the city fifteen years ago, the roar and tremor of dynamite blasting," reported one Englishman in 1911. "One rushes to the window at the first explosion with a mind-revolving disaster."[3] Americans also knew—and women especially regularly and repeatedly condemned—the incredible shaking racket of street traffic.[4] But the leveling of San Francisco by earthquake and fire proved modern urban fragility beyond doubt. Writers like Jack London provided eyewitness accounts and riveting photographs for *Colliers* and other national magazines struggling to describe, let alone analyze, the catastrophe. "All the cunning adjustments of a twentieth-century city had been smashed by the earthquake. All the shrewd contrivances and safeguards of man had been thrown out of gear by thirty seconds twitching of the earth-crust," London wrote of the immediate destruction. But it was the subsequent burning that transfixed him, watching first from a boat offshore, then from the streets thronged with people fleeing in the utter silence of deep trauma, with men dynamiting structure after structure, with cavalrymen urging continuous retreat, watching the phenomenon that had no name. "It was dead calm. Not a flicker of wind stirred. Yet from every side wind was pouring in upon the city. East, west, north, and south, strong winds were blowing upon the doomed city," London wondered. "The heated air rising made an enormous suck. Thus did the fire of itself build its own colossal chimney through the atmosphere." Near the ever-widening center of the fire, the draft "was often half a gale, so mighty was the suck"; everywhere the smoke rose, for three days making a "lurid, swaying tower" visible a hundred miles away, casting "mauve and yellow and dun" colors over the flaming city.[5] London settled on the word *volcano* to designate the blazing core. He did not know the word *firestorm*.

Yet however powerful the specter of such physical destruction, something far stronger produced the fear the author of "Why Is a Suburb?" discerns.[6] The toppling of towers and bridges quickly becomes a metaphor for the collapse of social and economic order, for the end of traditional virtue. She argues that from the wilderness or distant rural areas—where she has lived "for months a hundred and fifty miles from any human habitation—the city is "merely absurd, ridiculous." Mountain wilderness is not pure—she notes that her wilderness locale had "its own grimness, even its ghosts," and things that even Indians feared—but her residence there at least offered some thinking distance from the city, a distance that sparks her increasingly critical appraisal of urban form and life. The city is not, she determines finally, ridiculous, but rather incredibly dangerous, for in it fundamental values, the values of the early Republic, totter. Its order is one of money-making, of machines and systems of machines grown beyond personal or public control, of an individualism-smothering "public opinion." And at any moment that order can run amok.

Other writers knew the potential for social cataclysm. At the end of his book

Education, Henry Adams describes New York in 1904, arguing that "power seemed to have outgrown its servitude and to have asserted its freedom" and that "the city had the air and movement of hysteria, and the citizens were crying, in every accent of anger and alarm, that the new forces must at any cost be brought under control."[7] Two years later Henry James witnessed the frenzied dash for streetcars, the mad crossing of streets he subsequently recorded in *The American Scene.* And James—like the anonymous *Countryside* essayist a decade later—remarks the fading sense of history in the city. "There is not, outside the mere economic, enough native history, recorded or current, to go round."[8] In the frenzy, according to James, urban Americans forget to consider, forget to think, forget their traditions. In "Why Is a Suburb?" the anonymous writer advances the argument a step further, asserting that borderland families fear the destruction of a whole way of life and its replacement by chaos. "We are called Suburbanites and Commuters, and people shrug their shoulders when we have to leave the theater or the dance to catch the last train home," she concludes. "Little do they realize that in the thousands who scatter every night from New York by tube and train and ferry-boat, the real traditions of America are still alive." *Tradition* and *virtue* order her magazine article, and *fear.*

The Great War changed the American understanding of city living. Zeppelin bombing, heavy artillery, and perhaps above all, poison gas assault entered the minds of all reading Americans, and never left. Throughout the 1920s and 1930s, magazines published scores of articles on new weapons and new tactics, and most identified cities as prime targets. The public remembered the war, remembered that thirty-six different poison gases had floated over Europe, and remembered the carnage and destruction of Ypres and Verdun. Armistice Day commemorations kept vivid the memory and the knowledge, and by the mid-1930s officers of the Chemical Warfare Branch had begun assuring readers that even large-scale gas attacks would kill few city residents. After all, argued Major Adrian St. John in a 1934 *Literary Digest* article seeking to set straight the erroneous arguments made in magazines like *The Independent* and *World's Work* and *The Nation* and *Nineteenth Century,* "gassing large cities is a rather silly idea" because "war is an organized business and not just a mad riot of uncontrolled activities," and few countries could afford the large fleets of planes necessary to gas anyway.[9] Besides, mustard gas settles along the ground, and astute New Yorkers would need only to climb up several stories to escape it. About the gas settling into subways the major said nothing, and his article appears to have allayed few fears. Within a year, Liddell Hart, in a *Harper's* essay entitled "Would Another War End Civilization?" explored the potential horror of mustard gas attacks in major cities, and more articles followed his.

Clearly the author of "Why Is a Suburb?" wrote from fear, from all sorts of fear. But clearly too she wrote not as a product of the nineteenth century, not as Adams and James, but as a "modern woman," one aware, for example, of the power of advertising. Her choice for living in the suburbs, she explains, "is upheld by these most modern of all artists and all writers—the advertisers. It is not to the city-dweller that they make their appeals. The radiators which bring warmth and happiness to father and mother and all the family are pictured as in the suburban home." Vaguely, indirectly, she identifies the fears, the growing value of "tradition" against modernism, the skill of advertising agencies in identifying markets and shaping campaigns. "I live in a Suburb as a protest—a protest against the City," she exclaims. In her mind at least, to live in the outer suburbs meant living not only in stable, traditional space, but living away from the city of mustard gas, earthquake, and humanity-riding machines. It meant choosing sides in a widening split.

Only inferno *accurately designates the aftermath of the San Francisco earthquake.*

23 ❧ SPLIT

In 1935 real estate developers knew of the change, knew more bitterly, more clearly than any other professional group, including the architects who struggled onward, pursuing a dream hatched in Europe and every day less suited to the Republic.

One periodical chronicled the change. The young *National Real Estate Journal* knew not only that the boom years of the 1920s had ended, but that 1920s thinking no longer applied in the straitened circumstances of the Great Depression. In article after article, it advised its chastened, often terrified readers that modern thinking, and especially modern European thinking, would create only further havoc. Land development in the borderlands must proceed according to traditional wisdom, it asserted, or it would not proceed at all.

"Realtor Experts Give Pointers on Successful Home Building" epitomizes the new awareness. The developer-builders agree on one point above all else: the modern style of house, what one Oklahoma City man calls "modernistic or extreme," suits no one. "Under the guise of doing something new and modern, you are liable to have extremes of design that may not only be unusual at this time but actually offensive ten years hence," cautions a Kansas City developer who suspected that the modern style appealed at least sometimes to architects "not entirely capable of handling the old styles and on the lookout for something new in which they may express their ability." Over and over, experts from around the country ask whether "the present modernistic trend will be in vogue twenty years from now" and wonder whether "the buying public will adopt or accept modernistic architecture as compared with traditional architecture."[1] No developer in the symposium argues against improvement. New kitchen appliances, they claim, strike many would-be purchasers as absolutely essential and ease the marketing of houses in difficult economic times. But all agree that traditional construction materials and time-tested amenities like fireplaces add far more value than the novelties of the new style.

New Deal experts seconded the developers. In another 1935 *Journal* article, Perry Wilson, one of the regional directors of the Federal Housing Administration,

Was 1929 Berlin the new utopia? Clearly the rows of new apartment buildings announced newness, but a newness perhaps unwelcome in the United States.

suggests that small houses on large lots of land make sense for economic reasons alone. "During the recent depression, numerous families throughout the nation found they had displayed excellent judgment in building their homes upon sufficient land so that part of it could be used for gardens, poultry runs, or other purposes that would assist when the industries in which they were employed were forced to shut down, or when their income, otherwise, was materially reduced," he determines. The financial advantages of such miniature farms add to "untold opportunities for improved mental and physical health" and lay the "foundation of a true home."[2] But besides large lots, traditional architecture, and especially neighborhoods of harmonized architectural styles, produce—along with careful planting—the spatial beauty that makes families happy. Air conditioning and other technological wonders are welcome, but only so long as they remain unobtrusive. What matters most is tradition.

Ten years earlier tradition counted for far less, and indeed the borderlands had become known in national periodicals and in the "new" magazines as bastions of reaction. Consider "The Suburb De Luxe," a 1920 *Atlantic Monthly* piece by Edward Yeomans. An angry, satirical attack on the residents of Toppington, a fictious borderland place far from New York, the essay focuses on men who commute in club cars, playing cards "while the train rushes through more and more inferior suburbs as it approaches the city." Toppington, writes Yeomans, "is part of the two per cent who own sixty per cent of the wealth of the country," and it "is actually reptilian in its hissing anger against the opponent of orthodoxy." Change terrifies the commuters and their shopping-bound wives, for it spells the end of the comfortable life of pleasant houses, travel, and "flowing sentimentalism."[3] But such change is precisely what Yeomans wants for the country.

The *Atlantic Monthly* article belongs to a genre as yet unnamed, although its authors retain the designation provided by Gertrude Stein, the Lost Generation.[4] In new magazines like Mencken's *American Mercury, Broom,* and a dozen other periodicals, a loosely connected group of writers continued and deepened the condemnation of "business civilization" begun decades earlier by William Dean Howells, Hamlin Garland, Robert Herrick, and other writers. More stridently than their predecessors, they lambasted the sterile, pompous lives of so many small-town midwesterners and other adherents to old-fashioned ways. Many of the writers, too young to recall clearly the many triumphs of Progressive politics and the accomplishments of its rural cousin, Populism, focused their anger on two reforms: the prohibition of liquor and the restriction of immigration. Prohibition struck many young urban writers as not only painfully intrusive but impossibly outdated; moreover, many discerned anti-urban and anti-Catholic strains in what they condemned as the triumph of rural preachers and small-town busybodies. Immigration restriction struck the young writers as nativistic and anti-Semitic, and as an attack on what so many sophisticated residents of New York and other eastern cities saw as a yeasty ethnic mix. But the writers hated most what they saw as smug satisfaction in "American" ways, not only in the rise of business as the shaper of daily life and national culture, but in the unwillingness of most Americans to learn the lesson taught by the Great War—that all old things needed reexamination, even the national myth, even the American landscape.

Of all the new generation of writers, perhaps Van Wyck Brooks and Lewis Mumford dealt most incisively with the links between culture and landscape. Along with so many young intellectuals of his time, Brooks acquired at college a withering scorn of almost all American culture, and especially the cultures of the Puritans, the frontier, and business. In *Seven Arts* articles like his 1916 "Enterprise," he describes "the fag end of a great cross-town thoroughfare" that crosses the "frayed edges of the town," a zone like "the outskirts of some pioneer city on the plains of the Southwest." The zone is village-like, he determines, and he wonders "how many thousand villages, frostbitten, palsied, full of a morbid, bloodless death-in-life, villages that have lost, if they ever possessed, the secret of self-perpetuation, lie scattered across the continent." Villages and countryside, and indeed almost every part of every American city, lack the grace of Europe; the Puritan turned pioneer turned businessman prefers "the lowest rung of the ladder of spiritual evolution," choosing money-grubbing over all else. Brooks remembers his boyhood borderland home, Plainfield in New Jersey, as a barren "suburb of Wall Street" and finds nothing redeeming in other American places. Only Europe knew grace.

In *The Golden Day: A Study in American Experience and Culture,* Mumford argued in 1926 that the whole of American culture had originated in the fragmentation of European life following the Reformation, and that "the movement into backwoods America turned the European into a barbarian." Along with Brooks and other contemporaries, Mumford determines that "Puritan, pioneer, and businessman came to exist through the breakdown of Europe's earlier, integrated culture," and that in the New World each type developed to an "extreme." About the links between the pioneer, who wantonly destroyed the wilderness while losing all memory of European cultural richness, and the businessman, who wantonly consumed natural resources and capital while caring nothing for religion and art, Mumford has no doubts whatsoever. With the exception of examples set by a handful of heroic men, the Republic offers nothing of a usable past to thoughtful Americans trying to "escape from this sinister world" to something finer. "We must rectify the abstract framework of ideas which we have used, in lieu of a full culture, these past few centuries."[5] Almost everything would have to be constructed from scratch.

In *Sticks and Stones: A Study of American Architecture and Civilization,* Mumford scrutinizes what had been built and finds it almost wholly the creature of business civilization. "Scarcely any element in our architecture and city planning is free from the encroachment, direct or indirect, of business enterprise," he remarks after cataloguing the "forms of business" spreading outward from urban office and retail districts. Sometimes, he argues, architects do know best; many integrate the best of classical and modern form into buildings that improve human life. More and more frequently, however, the architect surrenders to the financier, and nowhere is the surrender more abject than in the office tower. Narrow city streets make skyscrapers little more than street-level facades decorated with mundane doorways into elevator banks. "One need not dwell upon the way in which these obdurate, overwhelming masses take away from the little people who walk in their shadows any semblance of dignity as human beings," Mumford asserts before concluding, "it is perhaps inevitable that one of the greatest mechanical achievements in a thoroughly dehumanized civilization should, no doubt unconsciously, achieve this very purpose." From a distance, the towers appear "like the fairy stalagmites of an opened grotto," but close up they "have precious little to do with the human arts of seeing, feeling, and living, or with the noble architectural end of making buildings which stimulate and enhance these arts." Everywhere about him, Mumford finds the landscape of the dictator businessman—a sprawling chaos of engineering technique intended only to maximize profit. Given the barrenness of American culture and its gross ignorance of European innovation, little else might be expected, although Mumford still hoped. "Sooner or later we will learn to pick our way out of the debris that the dwarfs, the gnomes, and the giants have created," he notes in the last sentences of his book, but he offers no schedule, for he knew of worse problems.[6]

In the urban residential ring—the "fag end" Brooks discovered, albeit slightly less industrialized—Mumford discerned a catastrophe in the making more threatening to human happiness than the skyscrapers rising in so many cities. "The great mass of modern houses are no longer framed for some definite site and some definite occupants; they are manufactured for a blind market," he exclaimes. Made of precut timber and standardized components by a "machine process" that "has created a standardized conception of style," the residential-ring house announces that "the designer, whether he is the architect, the owner, or the working contractor, works within a tradition whose bearing lies beyond him." Families who accept the machine process live in "those vast acres of nondescript monotony that, call them West Philadelphia or Long Island City or what you will, are but the anonymous districts of Coketown." Families who reject the process and its standardized products choose the "superficially vivacious suburbs" where the landscape retains some vestige of naturalness and charm.[7] Sticks and Stones confirms the predictions of Sidney Fisher. West Philadelphia is not a suburb but a drab extension of the city, a place beneath the contemptible residential rings satirized in Sinclair Lewis' Babbitt, a 1924 novel Mumford praises as perfectly accurate.

Sinclair Lewis worked within the Lost Generation genre, tasting success in 1920 with his Main Street, an inquiring exposé of habits and values in a small midwestern town. Main Street was the equal of any Seven Arts or other "little magazine" cariacature. Lewis struck again four years later in Babbitt, a long novel ordered about the narrow life of a real estate developer in a small city. George Babbitt specializes in subdividing and developing residential-ring land, and he does so in a bumbling mix of technological fixation, profit maximization, artistic ignorance, and public spiritedness. "When he laid out the Glen Oriole acreage development, when he ironed woodland and dipping meadow into a glenless, orioleless, sunburnt flat prickly with small boards displaying the names of imaginary streets," says Lewis early in the novel, "he righteously put in a complete sewage-system." Yet throughout the novel Babbitt yearns vaguely for something better than his profit-based life. He tries to offer that something to his family, in part by living in Floral Heights, a new residential community beyond the reach of streetcar lines, to and from which he commutes in an open car. The hilly land, twenty years before "a wilderness of rank second-growth elms and oaks and maples," still pleases Babbitt, who delights in the remaining undeveloped woodland and "the fragments of an old orchard."8 From his open car he sees the apple leaves and cherry blossoms, hears the robins, and drives cityward to convert similar land nearer the rising towers of Zenith into streetcar-laced "homesites."

What else could Babbitt do? Bereft of any aesthetic tradition and submerged in the maelstrom of profit, the realtor could only plunge on, and doubt. Of course the new generation offered the example of Europe, in magazines like *Creative Art*. In 1929 appeared "A Modern Utopia: Berlin—The New Germany—The New Movement," a handsomely illustrated article typical of so many of the two decades after the Great War. "Germany is already full of Houses of the Future," argues the author, because in Germany "the Intelligentzia take over the powers and functions which formerly belonged to a military class." The Intelligentzia make architecture into politics, seeking no longer to build structures and complexes of structures that reflect national culture, but to direct the life of the people. Given full power by a reformist state, the architects create rows of identical apartment buildings "that make magnificent street perspectives." "Struck by the vision of an ultra-mechanical art," they use technology to decorate structure with the "impression of an industrial Grimms' fairy tale." While the author worries a little about the "certain bleakness" of the new architecture, in the end he affirms its absolute usefulness: " 'Half-timbered Elizabethan' conceptions cannot stand the strain of modern life: and we must study the Utopian methods of the new Berlin carefully in order to produce something of value which need not, and indeed ought not be the same."9 Deftly, almost offhandedly, the author dismisses all the efforts of Grosvenor Atterbury in Forest Hills Gardens, making the Sage Foundation's "forward movement" into something hopelessly outdated. Others did too, and by the middle of the 1920s, sophisticated denunciations of American culture and traditional European built form had spilled from the pages of the new periodicals into mass-circulation magazines.

In 1928, for example, Christine Frederick published "Is Suburban Living a Delusion?" in a February issue of *Outlook*. Her first paragraphs give readers her answer. For "the more sophisticated and individual types" of people, "the suburb is sometimes utterly intolerable, and nearly always a disappointment." By *suburb* Frederick understood a sweep of territory, everything from the outermost of urban residential rings to railroad-commuter towns, like the fictional Toppingham, more than a hour distant from New York City to even more distant places accessible only by motor car—the "station wagon" designed to meet trains at borderland stations, the car in the title of Faith Baldwin's novel. All such places suffer from two sorts of weakness. First, life in them proceeds according to the "neighbor and hereditary social basis of the small town"; a family makes friends not according to interests but simply according to spatial proximity. Away from the city they find the intellectual narrowness and continuous nosiness that Lewis discovered along Main Street. Indeed, Frederick hopes that Lewis, whose *Babbitt* "proves he is chosen of the gods for the task," will write a novel satirizing the "gorgeous panorama of naivete and 'boobery'" of life between downtown apartment buildings and farms. Moreover, the built environment of the suburbs not only defeats families' attempt to discover the joys of nature, but produces incredible amounts of work unknown to residents of modern apartments. The single-family house means tending the furnace and making repairs, until, finally, it makes "slaves out of its occupants." In the end the "little gingerbread attempts to achieve difference are so palpably hollow and unsuccessful" that "only the *bourgeois* can see beauty and spacious living in these serried rows of homes." In the great city the mechanized apartment house provides privacy while allowing tenants the chance to grow beyond the need for spatial uniqueness, and the diverse urban population offers people the opportunity to make friends according to interests and the freedom to express their own individuality. The supposed "coldness" of New Yorkers is the wonderful proof "of social emancipation and modernness," and all sophisicated people knew it.[10]

But Ethel Longworth Swift did not know it, and as she told *Outlook* readers two months later, she considered herself sophisticated enough to see through Frederick's assault. After living in two European capitals and "the two largest cities of America," she and her journalist husband moved to the borderlands of New York, to a place "neither especially fashionable nor yet notably unfashionable." There her family discovered that friendships are made according to interest—she does not know the name of her neighbor two hundred feet away—and that the borderlands are filled with intriguing intellectuals, among them professional women taking time from their careers to stay home with young children, whose only common idea is that the natural world has significant value. "We moved to the suburbs so that we and our children might be near to the grass and the trees," she states, and she catalogues the natural pleasures her family finds spontaneously—ranging from the elms shading the front door, to the crooked ledge of gray rock covered with wild ferns, to the 75-by-125-foot garden she tends herself. Shaping the outdoor environment delights her family. Her son builds "a hut from packing-boxes in the sumach bushes of the vacant lot next door," her daughter builds a cigar-box birdhouse to lure bluebirds, and everyone shovels snow. "We have tramped the countryside for miles about," she writes. "We have grilled steaks on wooded hills and have built our camp-fires in the snow, and we have thanked heaven that the suburb gave us a chance to do so." Swift catalogues urban problems too, pointing out that her husband's forty-minute commute to downtown takes less time than people who live in the city often spend getting to the same downtown place. She reminds the reader that "in the city small children cannot be permitted to go far from home alone, a state of affairs which hinders the development of the spirit of independence" Frederick values so highly. Swift concludes that philistines and boobs can be found in cities, small towns, and suburbs alike, and that every person makes his or her own circle of friends. The outer suburbs offer something of older ways and immersion in the natural realm. Those who love a hike in the snow, who watch for the first "furry signals of the pussy-willow," who on hot summer afternoons hear the crickets, "thank that enterprising realtor, Babbitt, for the suburb."[11]

Only once in the two lively articles does spirit give way to sarcasm. Frederick fleetingly condemns the "neat colonial lives" of the families resident in the tidy houses on manicured lots.[12] Her phrase is significant indeed, for by 1928 the urban avant garde perceived the awesome power of a new force in American culture—one based in the borderlands but already reaching for the heart of urban intellectual life.

The first years of the twentieth century witnessed a renewed interest in the colonial past, an interest that moved beyond the recognition and preservation of historic artifacts like Mount Vernon into a love affair with antiques. Brooks loathed the interest, arguing that "old American things are old as nothing else anywhere in the world is old, old without majesty, old without mellowness, old without pathos, just shabby and bloodless and worn out."[13] But Virginia Robie in *The Quest of the Quaint* and Robert and Elizabeth Shackleton in *The Quest of the Colonial* and *The Charm of the Antique* championed antique collecting as a low-cost way to reach back to the values of a simpler, better America and to avoid the despair of living surrounded by machine-made artifacts. "In addition to the actual grace, the actual beauty" of an antique object, the Shackletons claim, "there is the charm of association with an interesting past." And equally important, they emphasize again and again, is the search at rural auctions and city secondhand shops—the sort of store at which Howells' *Suburban Sketches* narrator pauses to finger old-time items—for desirable chairs or hand tools or mirrors. Antiquing gives purpose to rides in the borderlands and beyond, and repairing the antiques oneself provides a relaxing avocation.

In the end, however, acquiring antiques is both financially sound and a sophisticated cultural statement. "As a matter of fact, it is actually cheaper to furnish one's home with the fine and charming things of the past than it is to furnish with the comparatively unattractive furniture of today," the Shackletons assert in *The Charm of the Antique* before demonstrating the "simplest arithmetic" that proves their contention.[14] Moreover, the value of old furniture can only rise as the antique-collecting movement grows; new furniture loses its value almost immediately. Implicit in the financial logic lies another message, one that eventually ordered most of the books and articles focused on the conversion of junk into objects of value. The antique is usually handmade and always evocative of a better era, one predating the rise of business civilization, mass-produced goods, massive urbanization, and a host of other complex problems.

By the early 1920s the love of antique furniture had begun shaping attitudes toward houses, particularly old houses. Family after family moving into the borderlands determined to restore ancient farmhouses rather than demolish them to make room for new structures. Families awakened to the values implicit in antiquing transformed them into values of landscape aesthetics; the pro-antique movement taught the love of the unmatched "set" of chairs or dining-room furniture, and its partisans quickly condemned streets of identical, or "look-alike," or "carbon copy" houses. Many borderland families unable to acquire antique houses insisted on

In The Charm of the Antique, *Robert and Elizabeth Shackleton argue for the value of pre–Civil War "country" things, including old houses and old gardens.*

Early twentieth-century authors advised motorists to scrutinize the rural landscape. With luck, the borderers might find antique chairs standing on decrepit front porches.

By 1920 the old house, and especially the house dating to the colonial era, became a stock illustration in books emphasizing the value of American antique furniture.

The Shackletons loved pre-industrial handicrafts as much as Atterbury and Olmsted loved the architecture of medieval Europe, but the Shackletons emphasized American antiquity, not foreign.

Carrick's "next-to-nothing house" is small, simple, and above all, old.

A WORKER AT AN OLD-TIME HAND-LOOM; AND

A MAKER OF OLD-TIME BRAID-ED RUGS.

For all her love of pre-industiral virtue and simplicity, Carrick valued outdoor privacy too.

owning old-looking new houses. Even Lewis' Babbitt lives in a "green and white Dutch Colonial house," one of three on his street alone. Old or revival-style houses furnished with antiques not only pleased cultured taste but provided secure refuge from an increasingly tormented world. Such is the argument advanced in *The Next-to-Nothing House*, a 1922 tour de force by Alice Van Leer Carrick, an intellectual absolutely devoted to the exploring the past—on a tight budget—and using full-page photographs to advance her arguments. "In those late-eighteenth-century days, when Democracy was something more than a mere name, no doubt farmer and farm hands alike ate in this long, low-ceilinged room," writes Carrick of her lovingly restored kitchen in her lovingly—and cheaply—restored little house.[15] Like Swift and Mumford, Carrick is suspicious of architects, remarking that the up-to-date rugs called for by one well-known designer wear far worse than old, handmade ones, especially in a house inhabited by three children forever running in from muddy fields. The practicality of the old house, the livability of the old furnishings, the incredible toughness and beauty of both cause Carrick to suspect all that is new.

Carrick shares with Lewis and Mumford a deep suspicion of 1920s national culture. One night, when Babbitt is preparing for bed, Lewis scans the activity of the Zenith region, noting the humming factories, a conference of union officials, and the death of a Civil War veteran who had never ridden in an automobile, never seen a bathtub, and who believed "that the United States is a democracy."[16] Yet while Lewis, Mumford, Frederick, and so many other writers looked to Europe and to the future for guidance to a better life, Carrick and the other devotees of antique collecting looked backward into the American past.

Even as the most influential of historians continued to trace the evolution of pioneer into businessman and condemned the "politics of acquisition," even as Charles and Mary Beard published volume after volume of their history of the United States as a promise twisted by corporate capitalism, a handful of investigators began publishing the results of their precise, backward scrutinizing. Constance Rourke led the way. In *American Humor: A Study of the National Character* she flatly contradicted Mumford's assertions in *Golden Day*, marshaling evidence that overwhelmed the "pioneer as barbarian" theory. "This study has grown from an enjoyment of American vagaries, and from the belief that these have woven together a tradition which is various, subtle, sinewy, scant at times but not poor." In following the development of folk and popular traditions, in emphasizing regional identity, Rourke in *American Humor* and other books introduced the Lost Generation writers to their own rich past. "A consistent native tradition has been formed, spreading over the country, surviving cleavages and dispersals, often growing underground, but rising to the surface like some rough vine." In books on John James Audubon and Davy Crockett, then in *American Humor* and *The Roots of American Culture*, Rourke brilliantly demonstrated her contention that "for the rather hazy, popular theory as to the destructive nature of the pioneer, another, simpler reading of the record can be substituted."[17] With developing power, regionalists of national stature began condemning the Lost Generation view of things as ignorant and provincial, and younger historians began deciphering the meaning of the westward

Simple fireplaces attracted more and more urban apartment dwellers as the twentieth century advanced: wood fires bespoke naturalness, tradition, and coziness, and implied a borderland woodlot (or at least a borderland woodpile).

Carrick's entrance hall, stark and almost barren, introduces her argument that newlyweds might furnish a borderland house as cheaply with antiques as with new furniture.

experience.[18] In *The Attack on Leviathan: Regionalism and Nationalism in the United States,* Donald Davidson condemned the poverty of homogenized, urban-east-coast-written history and the simplicity of so much contemporaneous political theory, while in *The Frontier in American Literature* Lucy Lockwood Hazard concluded her analysis by musing on the potential, untapped riches inherent in the pioneer-businessman tradition. By 1937, when Andrew Wyeth sold every painting in his first show, even the most Europe-oriented intellectual knew the power of the still unnamed movement.

Very quickly the new movement created its own journals. One of the earliest and most wide-ranging, *Antiques,* trumpeted the call to American art and values even as its staff tried to understand the motives and directions of the movement. "The student of men and things may find food for thought in recent, seemingly instinctive, manifestations of growing national, or historical, consciousness among the people of America," it editorialized in 1922, just two years before the New York Metropolitan Museum of Art opened its new wing of American antiques. The new consciousness existed as strongly in recently settled parts of the country as in the Old South and New England, and it focused more strongly on simple, "close to the soil" items than on those that displayed "the polite influences of aristocratic English life." The new movement appeared not only anti-European but anti-upper-class as well; it fixed on old regional identities and on the "simple life" of farms and small towns. "It is no belittlement of Wallace Nutting, or of his *Furniture of the Pilgrim Century,* to urge that his book is rather symptomatic than causative of this eagerness," the editor decided.[19]

Wallace Nutting had indeed identified something, and his output of books demonstrates both his perceptiveness and his uncanny ability to tap a still unfocused energy. Nutting did more than publish books on early American furniture and describe his attempts at restoring an ancient, run-down house. In a lavishly illustrated series of monographs entitled States Beautiful, he portrayed the retired rural landscape of the northeastern states.[20] In *Pennsylvania Beautiful* and *Massachusetts Beautiful* and his other volumes, he succeeded with his camera as Wyeth succeeded with his paintbrush, carefully depicting the longevity and beauty of landscape untouched by industrialization and urbanization—the old-fashioned sort of landscape Robinson had found decades earlier in Westchester, a landscape no longer connected with agricultural backwardness. In *Photographic Art Secrets,* Nutting told novices how to "touch out" utility poles from negatives and perform other tricks to make beautiful images of otherwise only nearly beautiful places. In selecting a deliberate mix of natural scenery and aged agricultural objects ranging from wagon wheels to tottering stone fences, Nutting helped create a landscape aesthetic of incredible power, one eventually popularized by the Eastman Kodak Company and other photographic equipment manufacturers—and almost always fixed in the far borderlands.

Nature study supported the new movement focused on antiques, American culture, and borderland landscape, sharpening its anti-European, anti-urban, anti-business bias.[21] Bird watching in particular raised doubts in people's minds about the long-term impact of urban life, especially when the amateur ornithologists remarked the certainty with which close-packed structures united with the English sparrow and starling to drive out native American birds. Grosbeaks, bluebirds, and other species retreating before the miles of cement and tenacious immigrants from Europe became conspicuously in their absence from urban residential zones, despite the best efforts of bird conservation societies in Forest Hills Gardens and elsewhere. Immigrant species not only did not sing but failed to destroy the insects loathed by amateur gardeners. Almost imperceptibly, a note of warning entered the writings of popular naturalists. However much James Buckham protested in *Where Town and Country Meet* that native birds and other wildlife still frequented the borderlands, amateur observers noted the English sparrows along roadsides, the empty bluebird houses, and the arrival of Dutch elm disease and other alien nuisances. If immigrant birds drove out native species, if immigrant blights destroyed the American trees gracing the borderlands, might not immigrant people overwhelm Americans of English, German, and Irish descent, Americans already weakened by stressful, urban lives given over to business?

The question proved difficult to answer, for it harbored vexing issues of tradition and modernization. In "Shenandoah, the Best Type of Iowa's Small Towns," a 1906 *Suburban Life* article, Henry Field asserted that a handsome built environment reflected a traditional, healthy, decidedly American society. Field wrote in the admiring tone Timothy Dwight and Andrew Jackson Downing reserved only for prosperous, devout, neat early nineteenth-century New England towns. "There is no race problem in Shenandoah—no colored people and no foreign population. There are no slums, no tenements, no double houses, and no shacks." Every house depicted in Field's photographs might please Carrick, and in the final analysis, Shenandoah turns out to resemble the best of borderland residential communities. "It is neither a village nor a city, being big enough to have all the comforts of the latter, and small enough to enjoy freedom from its drawbacks."[22] Clearly Field sees the presence of blacks or immigrants in large cities as a "drawback," but his is no snap racist or xenophobic diatribe. Rather it is a measured inquiry into a question that grew more troubling by the year. If both the Lost Generation urban intellectuals and the Shackleton–Carrick–Nutting borderland school agree that twentieth-century business civilization is a fraud, what else happens to rural blacks and European peasants arriving in large cities than an absolute travesty of acculturation? By the 1920s the question vexed not only the virulently anti-immigrant, anti-Semitic, racist authors, but thoughtful writers speculating about the acculturation lessons offered by national advertising and big-city life. Samuel McChord Crothers, in a 1927 *Atlantic Monthly* article, "A Social Survey of the Literary Slums," argued that "the Manhattanese School" had not only mistaken New York City for an entire nation, but had so embraced urban culture that it could make precious little sense of that culture within a broader context. "To see a modern city aright, one must be able to look at it as he looks at a great mountain, or a stormy sea—with a certain detachment."[23] For the young urban intellectual and, even worse, for the newly landed immigrant, the large city provided no vantage point, and in time,

Readers of Craftsman *learned how to "bring old houses up to date" without sacrificing their American distinctiveness or destroying their old trees.*

In Shenadoah, Iowa, and in so many other small midwestern towns scorned by New York City "highbrow" critics, readers of borderland magazines learned that traditional virtue still held sway.

Twentieth-century amateur ornithologists learned to avoid main roads in favor of the half-abandoned wagon paths that still sheltered native birds resisting the inroads of immigrant starlings.

Crothers implies, the urban resident forgets the vastness of the spaces beyond his crowded street.

The final twist in the argument appeared in early 1930s magazines, even in the very bosom of the debunkers, *The American Mercury*. "There is a growing feeling among thoughtful people that the modern large city as an experiment in human association is turning out badly in many respects," one author began. "Even the well-to-do are encountering increasing difficulty in getting sufficient space—either indoors or out—to be comfortable and to maintain any degree of privacy in their lives." In arguing that cities would continue to grow in size and density until physical movement became impossibly difficult, Warren S. Thompson demonstrated that urban growth, especially fast, disorderly urban growth, lined the pockets of many groups, starting with "all those who own real estate or deal in it" and ending with the professional boosters, the writers of industry-attracting advertisements employed by city governments and chambers of commerce. "We are so constantly and so exclusively being told what a fine thing it is to have our city grow that most of us never stop to ask: Fine for whom? or to inquire what this growth means from the standpoint of national economy and individual welfare." Very, very subtly, in two long, tightly reasoned articles, Thompson implied that the intellectuals forever glorying in big-city life and scorning life everywhere else had somehow fallen into the mindset of the very business civilization they denounced, and that architects embracing the new forms employed them almost always for the businessmen in charge. Everyone, and especially immigrants and children growing up in the great cities, needed far more unbiased information if they were not to swallow whole the business-spawned bait of urban bigness and excitement, if they were not to live less able to evaluate urban life and form as well as rural or small-town or borderland Americans. "That the vast majority of people crowded together in our large cities today can find much enjoyment in the daily routine of living is unbelievable. The lack of space alone makes life hideous for the majority of them and the feverishness of their activity in their leisure time is the natural consequence of such congested living," Thompson determined. "Once the use of leisure becomes associated with jazz and a generation has grown up which believes it is enjoying life because it moves fast and far," the quest for "the tapping of the human resources in our population" is lost. Only when "we make it possible for people to have a little elbow room and a chance to enjoy some privacy" can the quest resume.[24] Thompson wrote incisively, having for immediate background recent articles like Frederick Lewis Allen's "Suburban Nightmare"—a 1925 *Independent* essay lashing out at the encroachment of urban form and urban frenzy into borderland space—and Lewis Mumford's 1926 *Harper's* piece, "The Intolerable City: Must It Keep on Growing?" But perhaps Thompson wrote too out of dawning self-interest, as one of a handful of urban intellectuals suddenly aware that urban hurry, radio and phonograph music, advertising, cinema, and lack of quiet, elbow room, and privacy threatened not only the primacy but the very existence of the "serious" print media through which he and other urban intellectuals advanced their thinking.

By 1934 even Malcolm Cowley, one of the self-confessed Lost Generation, had begun wondering about the rural childhoods of so many of his urban friends. "The country of our childhood survives, if only in our minds, and retains our loyalty even when casting us into exile," he finally decided. "We carry its image from city to city as our most essential baggage."[25] But as the memory of a country childhood dimmed, did the forces Thompson decried have more and more effect? Would urban intellectuals scorn the new cultural aesthetic taking ever stronger root in the borderlands, emerging like Rourke's rough vine to challenge the sophisticated urban aesthetic born in the years around the Great War? Would the generation divorced, at least in its own mind, from American business civilization find itself somehow thrust aside by a new movement owing nothing to European sophistication and little to American urbanity? Would jazz and advertising and nightclub drinking and metal furniture constitute everything left of avant-garde promise? Would traditional, regional thinking and building supplant the modern, international movement?

As early as 1929, readers of *Creative Arts* learned one answer. In "Wood or Metal?" John Gloag briefly summarizes the introduction to American life of very high-quality, decidedly modern metal furniture created by German designers. "What may be called Robot modernism" has improved, certainly, Gloag argues, but it still expresses an "utter inhumanity." American stamped-metal furniture, especially when painted to resemble wood, is ugly, but the modern German furniture is simply brutal. Gloag determines that metal furniture may be suited to the "office" but that "there does not appear to be any case for substituting metal for wood in furniture that is designed to give convenience and harmony to a home." Deftly coupling modern metal furniture and modern glass-and-steel building, Gloag condemns all such "machines for living in" as "grimly misleading," part of an aesthetic that converts human beings into mechanisms. Against the traditional softness of wood, Gloag finds the German metal style fit only for robots at work, not Americans at home.

Within a year, readers of *Fortune* learned from a massive advertising campaign by Wood Office Furniture Associates that metal is unsuited for the workplace too. Wood furniture is "warm and friendly to the touch" and available not only in simple desks and chairs for clerical staff but in "period suites for executives" desiring "charming" upper-echelon offices "dignified through the 'natural' beauty of wood."[26] No longer did antique collectors alone prize wood furniture. Suddenly it appeared in the van of a movement grown infinitely more powerful, but a movement still without a name, without a cohesive identity, and still scorned by Lost Generation opinion-makers.

Financial panic, then depression coupled with the rising horror of Fascism to strengthen the Americanist school, which by the middle of the 1930s recalled the old Country ideology and reassured borderland residents that traditional- and regional-style houses, long rambles in songbird-filled woods, antique and reproduction-antique wood furniture, and representational painting had as much worth as any "international style" big-business office tower, nightclub evening, chromed-tube chair, or piece of abstract art—perhaps even somewhat more. Exactly as the chastened realtors suspected, prudent home-buyers considered "modern" houses, but almost always bought or built traditional ones.[27] In 1938, among pages describing the rising evil in Germany, *Life Magazine* published articles on new houses; by the end of the year, when Berlin struck most Americans as nothing like utopia, the first buyers of *Life* plans had begun erecting their houses all over the country. All but one was so distinctly traditional that Carrick herself might have moved in, antiques and all.

In 1945 infantrymen lining the troopship rail looked ashore with educated eyes. Everywhere around the harbor stood closely ranged wooden buildings, the mix of three-deckers, tenements, two-families, and single-family houses in which Bostonians and residents of the urban residential ring had lived for decades. The men shuddered and talked. They saw wooden houses with asphalt-shingled roofs. A single airborne incendiary attack might finish the whole place. The sergeant from the borderlands never forgot the lesson of that landfall, the recognition that Boston would "go up like kindling."[1]

Of course within three years or so the understanding had deepened into horror. A 1948 *New Yorker* columnist casually quoted a Los Alamos scientist as saying that Broadway made the world's best atomic bomb target.[2] While the actual destructiveness of the weapon remained a mystery to all but the GIs who had seen the Japanese rubble, the import took hold. "The subtlest change in New York is something people don't speak much about but that is in everyone's mind. The city, for the first time in its long history, is destructible," worried E. B. White in 1949. "A single flight of planes no bigger than a wedge of geese can quickly end this island fantasy, burn the towers, crumble the bridges, turn the underground passages into lethal chambers, cremate the millions."[3] White mourned the loss of vitality, the advent of a new tension potentially as lethal as bombing, a tension worse than that Henry Adams had mourned nearly half a century before.[4] "The cylinder had exploded," Adams wrote of urban power outgrown its servitude, "and thrown great masses of stone and steam against the sky."[5] But as the prescient *Countryside* essayist had envisioned in the midst of the Great War, the explosion seemed always about to come, and to White and others, the atomic age city seemed almost like a jostled bomb, about to explode. By the late 1940s, the dread expressed by the anonymous essayist had deepened, had spread, and had fueled a great migration to the suburbs, to the borderlands, and to rural regions supposedly far from ground zero. In California, the warm, sunny land settled by so many discharged veterans educated by fire-bombed cities and by Hiroshima and Nagasaki, the flight from ground zero was fastest.

Fear of physical destruction masked the growing threat of social cataclysm, of rampant industrialism, of monopoly capitalism, of marketing forces gone wild. Late in the nineteenth century, magazines directed to borderland readers began attacking, however obliquely, the distortion not of urban life particularly, but of big-city living. Only rarely did editors suggest how the great cities of the Republic might change for the better. Indeed, the magazines conveyed a sort of bemused scorn of such essentially cosmetic reforms as the "city beautiful" movement and the efforts at political housecleaning that captivated so many city dwellers. In 1905, for example, the editors of *Suburban Life* argued bluntly that "country life magazines are the product of the last five years"; they derive their strength from "actual experiences of men and women who have been through the experimental period and have won out successfully," and they differ from previous generations of agricultural and "horticulturist" magazines by taking a far broader view of the meaning of borderland life.[6] Implicit in the argument is not only the notion of victory—hard-won "come-outer" victory earned in individual or family terms—and the possibility, indeed the probability, of gaining and maintaining some semblance of control over physical surroundings and day-to-day events. Also implied are the dramatically worsened physical conditions for the urban businessman, for the middle-class city family not yet won over to come-outer thinking.

Between the 1880s and the 1930s thousands of intellectuals labored to explain what Julian W. Brandeis explained in a 1911 *Country Life* article. In "A Rational Scheme of Living for the Commuter," the physician proposed a complex prescription for the urban ills, and especially the nervous temperament, Trotter had diagnosed so many decades before. Essentially the "first and most important resolution for the suburbanite to inscribe upon his tablet is, 'I resolve to live in the country entirely, not half the time in the country and half the time in the city.'"[7] By this Brandeis meant not only rarely visiting the city "for an evening in town after return from business" but a sort of mindset or worldview firmly grounded in borderland or "country" values and unchanged during city hours. Brandeis and the other early twentieth-century authors who offered similar proposals emphasized that siting house and family in the tree-frosted borderlands, that flower gardening or raising hens, that nature tramping or carpentry would not alone save the commuter's spirit. Only if the commuter bought into the city each day a set of values different from those ruling the city would he be saved. Only if the come-outer remained steadfast would he triumph. Whether he would save the city no longer mattered.

Landscape and living in sight of it become incredibly important in the turn-of-the-century argument for borderland salvation.[8] To live in a place still visually dominated by hills, trees, and other natural forms, to interact with nature through gardening, carpentry, poultry-raising, and other avocations, is to deal with force apart from business, to know laws other than economic, to constantly relearn seasonal cycles, timelessness, and humility. "The city breeds strange illusions that we often mistake for realities," asserted Richardson Wright in 1922. "The city offers a competition based on material possessions and ruled by exacting modes that change from day to day. The forces of the city are forces of noise."[9] But Wright entitled his book *Truly Rural: Adventures in Getting Back to Earth* and suggested that the restorative landscape lay not only beyond the urban residential ring but beyond the leafy suburbs reached by long-distance commuter trains, beyond even the zone in which a night in town after return from business was out of the question.

Truly Rural was certainly not the first book to argue that salvation lies in living in genuinely rural space, but it marks the growing fascination with noncommuter living that characterized a small segment of 1920s borderland writing, a genre that swelled with the rise of "back-to-the-land" thinking in the Depression. As early as 1925, Frederick Lewis Allen outlined the range of the fascination in an *Independent* article. He concludes "Suburban Nightmare," an angry condemnation of the spread of urban residential zones across beautifully variegated borderland landscape, with a paen to Vermont, a place free of "urban improvements."[10] With that genre and the migration that accompanied it, a new chapter in the peopling of the nation opened, along with a new perspective on borderland space.

And now the problem grows thornier. The back-to-the-city movement appears to slow, and a back-to-the-suburbs movements appears to develop. Realtors around the nation confirm suspicions raised by watching the newcomers to the borderland place in which this book took form. Yuppies are abandoning the city, moving away from the astronomical rents that cause *The Village Voice* to wonder about the longevity of the New York City cultural community, away from the crime that appears to grow less tolerable as victims turn thirty, away from a place new parents suddenly and decisively determine is not the best environment for children.[11] They arrive embarrassed, half-ashamed of deserting the city that so evidently needs reform-minded people, half relieved that some fragment of natural order has returned to their lives. As Jerry Adler points out in his 1986 *Newsweek* article, "The Return to the Suburbs: Boomers Are Behaving Like Their Parents," a change of enormous implication is underway, something beyond the capacity of mere census data to relate.

That change involves nothing different from those wrought by the atom bomb, or even earlier by the fear of the city out of control. It involves something that informs an entire recent issue of *New Criterion*, a New York journal of the arts.[12] Devoted to "New York in the Eighties," the special issue collects a multiplicity of views about the contemporary city and its contemporary artists. Despite the optimism that informs so many of the articles, an optimism bordering on the boosterism distrusted as early as the 1920s, a terrible tension haunts the issue. "Nowadays I see New York as a steel engraving embodying the falling moral stance of a nation. Its skyscrapers crowd ever closer and higher, a naked temptation in this era of the bomb," writes novelist Hortense Calisher. "At their windowed bottoms, which are crammed with every provender, the homeless lie, more blatantly than in the days when they were confined to the Bowery." Architectural critic Ada Louise Huxtable condemns the tyranny of real estate developers, arguing that New York City architecture is no longer an art, only the skirting of power. And art historian Barbara Rose traces the impact of "development" on artists, watching the numbing

After seeing the rubble of German cities, the borderland sergeant married, had children, and bought a house farther into the borderlands, away from ground zero.

EXTEND YOUR HOME
TO ALL YOU OWN

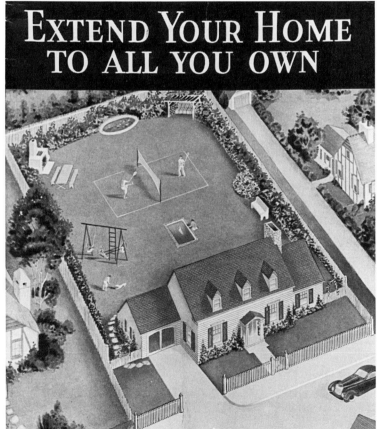

From the Depression on, outdoor privacy has increasingly preoccupied Americans living on large lots, as this 1930s advertisement suggests.

However the critics joked, 1950s Americans remained committed to the love of shaping space, even the tiny yards of the postwar automobile suburbs.

exodus of working artists from Soho and other neighborhoods. "Most of the American artists I know whose work I admire live in small towns in New England or the South," she concludes. "Today, New York is the place where Madison Avenue meets Wall Street and the values of advertising, marketing, speculation, and manipulation prevail, along with the morality of the 'bottom line.'" Other *New Criterion* essayists share such views. While admitting that "for those of an impeccably agrarian orientation, New York has alway been one of the Cities of the Plain," Samuel Lipman, music critic for *Commentary,* concludes that "one would hardly want to say that life in New York these days is comfortable." Something, however vague, has worsened. "We should not be surprised that along with the desire of many people to live in what can never be more than a finite amount of space go all of the afflictions of city life: traffic, social tensions, and everywhere an underclass, sometimes merely apathetic and sometimes actively hostile to what they see as the privileged life going on around them." Comfort is gone.

Whatever the contemporary tension, be it recognition of the atom bomb or a weariness borne of overbuilt urban infrastructure or something Thomas Trotter found so long ago in London, it now stimulates study. As Stanley Milgram argues in an incisive 1970 article in *Science*, the "atmosphere" of very large cities may indeed produce a sort of psychological "overload," apparent only to those new to city life or returning from visits to nonurban places.[13] For the latter, the conscious perception fades after only a few days, making exceedingly difficult any empirical study by psychologists. About commuters, especially those resident in the borderlands, Milgram says nothing explicit, but his precise argument implies that the commuter moves through the large city more aware of the "distinctive, frenetic atmosphere" than urban residents. That atmosphere, according to two physicians, Edward A. Charlesworth and Ronald G. Nathan, often results in unhealthy stress. In *Stress Management* they point out the as-yet scarcely studied stress originating in contemporary urban life, a subject of increasingly frequent newspaper comment that is only now being addressed by scholars. Whatever the tension, it helps energize the reexamination of the old borderland of the come-outers, the country of the commuters, the region lost for decades in the swirl of post–World War II suburbanization, the region still half-hidden by the "frontier" paradigm. Who was the woman on the heights looking down at the children and the city? Who was the man on the 4:45, green bag and seed catalogue in hand? Who if not believers in witch hazel?

Witch hazel, that hardy shrub beloved of Susan Cooper, blooms in winter, its showy yellow flowers bright against the snow. On a February morning it calls into question all the bleakness and beauty of winter, all the starkness of white. Infrequently noticed, let alone prized in summer, in time of cold it acquires immense power to reorient values.

Women notice it more frequently, more deeply than men, perhaps. Maybe they always have, as Susan Cooper, Alice Cary, and the anonymous *Countryside* essayist suggest. When Mary Cruger published *How She Did It: or, Comfort on $150 a Year* in 1888, she argued incisively that only the borderlands provided a refuge for the single woman anxious to build her own house, live graciously but very inexpen-

From the 1840s to the present, the stresses of urban life, and especially of urban business, have prompted men to move to the borderlands.

New Vigor for Overworked Nerves

Mary Cruger's house, small and simple and furnished with old items, and book demonstrated to her readers that in the borderlands single women might live more freely and more comfortably—and much less expensively—than they could in cities.

THE HOUSE THAT FAITH BUILT.

sively, and above all live free of the dictates of urban custom and urban fashion. For $1444.08 Faith Arden builds her private cottage on a rocky, tree-frosted rise, and on a scant income lives comfortably, if not free of difficulties with slovenly farmers and piercing winter wind.[14] Cruger uses statistics and prices as sharply as Maxwell uses them to analyze the borderlands of Cincinnati, but she uses the name of her central character to advance her concept of the practical, attainable utopia for thoughtful women. "Faith Arden" connotes not only the intense, come-outer-like, nearly religious faith that drives the woman away from urban shadows and business attitudes toward a comfortable, graceful place. It also implies the importance of the open forest, the old woods of northern Warwickshire, west of Stratford-on-Avon, the woods of *As You Like It*. In the open woods, Shakespeare's old duke tells his lords, all dressed for the moment as foresters,

> . . . this our life, exempt from public haunt,
> Finds tongues in trees, books in the running brooks,
> Sermons in stones, and good in everything.
> I would not change it.[15]

Faith Arden changes nothing either, once she discovers the balm of borderland landscape and borderland living.

The enduring power of borderland landscape between the early nineteenth century and the beginning of World War II suggests that many women and men understood more by *commuting* and *country* than train schedules and pastures, and hints also that the cities of the Republic failed to provide an urban fabric as joyous, as restorative as that found by borderers a few miles beyond. However hard to define, borderland landscape endured as the standard by which millions judged urban form and found it insufficient as human habitat. And if contemporary studies indicate accurately, it endures to this day, a sort of attic in the national superstructure, a place of calm, a place of older things, a heights to visit when downstairs all is commotion, all noisy busyness.

NOTES

PREFACE

1. The phrase is, of course, Sam Bass Warner's. See his *Streetcar Suburbs,* the pioneering and enduring model work in the history of American suburbs.
2. Holly, *Country Seats,* p. 21.
3. Definitions of urban form receive much revision nowadays. The definition *semi-suburban* recently advanced by Professor Roger Courtenay in his landscape architecture theory courses at the University of Virginia is particularly fruitful: "It is an area of single-family homes (thus fairly low density), within walking distances of community services, small retail stores, etc., but not (necessarily) of work."

INTRODUCTION

1. Chaucer, *Canterbury Tales,* in *Works,* p. 249. On the suburbs of medieval Canterbury, see Urry, *Canterbury,* pp. 185–190; see also Braudel, *Structures,* pp. 487, 503–524.
2. Platt, *English Medieval Town,* pp. 38–40; see also Hoskins, "Elizabethan Provincial Town," esp. pp. 40–51.
3. Nashe, "Christ's Teares," *Works,* II, 148.
4. Shakespeare, *Henry VIII,* V, iv. This notion of "rabble" endured, of course. See "Glance at the Suburbs."
5. As an example, see Morrow, "Downsizing the American Dream." See also Stilgoe, "Suburbanites Forever."
6. See Masotti and Haddon, eds., *Urbanization of the Suburbs* and the works cited in the bibliography issue of *American Quarterly* 37 (1985), edited by Zane Miller.
7. Josephson, "Frontier," esp. 77–78. On the frontier, see, for example, Billington, *Far Western Frontier;* Bartlett, *New Country;* Fahey, *Inland Empire.*
8. On "leafy" suburbs, see, for example, Singer, "Funny Money," 90.
9. Signs of this appeared earlier, of course: see, for example, Bookwalter, *Rural versus Urban* and Carlton, "Urban and Rural Life."
10. On the back-to-the-farm movement, see Fritts and Gwinn, *Fifth Avenue to Farm;* Peterson, *Forward to the Land;* and Perrin, *Second Person Rural* and *Third Person Rural.* See also Peterson, ed., *Cities are Abnormal.* For the contemporary viewpoint, see issues of *Mother Earth News* and *Country Journal,* as well as a new magazine, *Country.* On advertising, see Bright, "Of Mother Nature and 'Marlboro Men.'" For general background, see Gavignaud, *Le Révolution rurale.*
11. Willis, *American Scenery,* I, 106. At least one early nineteenth-century observer decided that railroads would cause a mass out-migration from U.S. cities: see Caldwell, "Thoughts on the Moral and Other Indirect Influences of Railroads." On "countryside" today see Schauman and Adams, *Assessment Procedure,* and Adams, *Nature's Place.*

12. Of course, many wives may have followed husbands unwillingly, as Kolodny suggests in *The Land Before Her*. On the migration in general, see Handlin, *The Uprooted;* on migration within the United States, and especially on those "left behind," see Barron, *Those Who Stayed Behind.*
13. Bradford, *Of Plymouth Plantation,* pp. 23–28. See also Bloomfield, *Opposition.*
14. Morgan, *Puritan Dilemma,* pp. 40–41. See also Bebb, *Nonconformity,* and White, *English Separatist Tradition.*
15. Bradford, *Of Plymouth Plantation,* p. 25.
16. Mather, *Magnalia,* I, 69–76.
17. Palfrey, *History,* I, 131, 146–147.
18. Adams, *Epic,* p. 31. See also his *Founding,* pp. 118–138, and Beard, *Basic History,* pp. 16–17.
19. On the errand, see Miller, *Errand,* pp. 1–15, and his *Orthodoxy,* pp. 153–156; Gay, *Loss,* pp. 29–31; and Bozeman's excellent essay, "The Puritans' 'Errand into the Wilderness' Reconsidered."
20. On the vague doubts, see Bartlett, *New Country,* pp. 38–58.
21. Tocqueville, *Democracy,* p. 283.
22. Cooper, *Notions,* I, 71–73.
23. Twain, *Huckleberry Finn,* p. 328.
24. Bartlett, *Glossary,* pp. 92–93; Haliburton, *Nature,* I, 216–217. Haliburton, a widely known Nova Scotian commentator on American custom, cites Bartlett's quotation of Evans' *History,* pp. 212–215. Lincoln, *Cap'n Eri,* esp. pp. 35–52, marks the narrowness of early twentieth-century Cape Cod come-outers. See also Mead, *Lively Experiment,* pp. 109–112.
25. Olson, *Logic,* pp. 1–65 and passim; Mead, *Lively Experiment,* p. 110.
26. Pomfret, *Poems,* pp. 1–7. On this concept in English literature much has been written, of course. Particularly insightful is Johnstone, "Turnips and Romanticism." For background on the theme, see Marx, *Machine in the Garden.*
27. Curtiss, "They Are Moving," esp. 75–79.
28. Hawthorne, "Footprints on the Sea-Shore," *Twice-Told Tales,* p. 504. Bremer, *Homes,* I, 47, and passim.
29. On the commanding view, see Rosenthal, *Constable,* pp. 75–77 and passim.
30. Hooker, *Application,* pp. 53–54. See also Meyer, "American Religion of Vision." I am grateful to my colleague Stephen Thernstrom for information regarding the dearth of contemporary historical writing about American middle-class buying power, mortgage availability, middle class versus middle income, and so on. This small galaxy of subjects must be one of the most potentially intriguing, yet oddly enough it remains unstudied. For an example of contemporary confusion regarding "middle-class" buying power, see the UPI wire story, "Middle Class Threatened."
31. Baldwin, *Station Wagon Set,* p. 3.
32. I have written recently about contemporary suburbs and borderlands: see Stilgoe, "Suburbanites Forever," "Hobgoblin in Suburbia," and "The Suburbs."
33. "Cambridge as a Place of Residence." See also "Mistakes of Suburbans."
34. Scholars have of course traced the linking of urbanization and changing attitudes toward landscape and landscape painting. See, for example, Harris, *Artist,* pp. 119–120, and Brown, *Dutch Landscape,* pp. 26–29.
35. On newspapers as a guide to past landscapes, see Stilgoe, "Treasured Wastes: Spaces and Memory."
36. On screens, see "Mosquito Window Screens"; Hutchinson, "How Doth the Little Bug Fly"; Howard, "Menacing Mosquito"; "Rolup Screens"; "Banish the Garbage Can Nuisance"; Douglass, "Summer Use of the Screen." Much, much more needs to be done in understanding the social consequences of such seemingly minor innovations as screens. As an example of what can be done, see Arsenault. "End of the Long Hot Summer."
37. On bicycles, see, for example, Bushnell, "When Chicago was Wheel Crazy"; Baxter, "Economic and Social Influence of the Bicycle"; Harmond, "Progress and Flight"; and Sargent, "Exercise and Longevity." The brief heyday of the "safety bicycle" has received very little sustained scrutiny from contemporary scholars, but contemporaneous periodicals suggest that bicycling transformed urban attitudes concerning the scale of a summer outing and may have changed attitudes toward landscape too.

38. For a sampling of such articles, see Hitchcock, "Joys of Being a Farmer," and Sadler, "The Suburban and the City Child." See also Stickley, "Craftsman Movement."
39. See, for example, three *Ladies Home Journal* pieces: "Summer Windows"; Talmadge, "Under My Study Lamp"; Ashmore, "Side Talks."
40. See Thompson, "Servant Question," for a turn-of-the-century attack on male-designed (and especially male-architect-designed) houses. The relation of the rising feminist movement to the architectural profession remains nearly unstudied, but contemporaneous sources suggest that many women distrusted male designers: see Tryon, "Reflections of a Housewife."
41. Gardening was *moral* too: see "Moral Influence of Gardening." The relative morality of different recreational activities throughout the nineteenth century and into the twentieth deserves study, since morality often dictated what activities might occur on Sunday (gathering wildflowers) and what might not (swimming, automobiling). Contemporaneous fiction and nonfiction articles, the latter chiefly in women's magazines, convince me that this subject is more important than it seems at first.

VIEW

1. Maxwell, *Suburbs of Cincinnati*, p. 9.

1: WITCH HAZEL

1. Willis, *American Scenery*, II, frontispiece; see also II, 41, 363, 529. On the view from the heights, see "Lines Written on Prospect Hill" and "Village Teacher: One Morning."
2. Willis, *American Scenery*, II, 561.
3. Stilgoe, *Common Landscape*, pp. 205–207.
4. Tichi, *New World, New Earth*, pp. 172–175 and passim.
5. On the picturesque, see Salerno, "Picturesque"; Price, *Essay*; Knight, *Landscape*; see also Hawes, *Presences*; Richards, "Lake George" and "Susquehanna"; and "Niagara" and "Legends of Trees."
6. Cooper, "Dissolving View," in *Home Book of the Picturesque*, p. 81.
7. Ibid., pp. 89, 91–98; on the "magical view" see also Lincoln, *Village*, p. 18.
8. Cooper, *Rural Hours*, pp. 84, 88; *Putnam's Monthly* received the book very favorably (see "Rural Objects") as did *The Horticulturist* (see "Review of *Rural Hours*").
9. Cooper, *Rural Hours*, p. 83.
10. Thoreau, *Miscellanies*, pp. 182–183; see also "Wild Scenes."
11. Cooper, *Rural Hours*, p. 51. See also Ruggles, "Picturesque Farming."
12. Hentz, *Lovell's Folly*, pp. 5–6.

2: BOTANIZING

1. Willis, *Rural Letters*, pp. 106–108, 169, 133.
2. Ibid., pp. 15–19, 52, 53.
3. Olmsted, *Walks and Talks*, pp. 58–59.
4. Hawthorne, *English Note-Books*, p. 185. See also Abrams, *Natural Supernaturalism*, pp. 96–117.
5. Hawthorne, *Our Old Home*, pp. 68–69; on the invisiblity of the rural poor, see Barrell, *Dark Side*.
6. Cooper, "American and European Scenery," in *Home Book of the Picturesque*, p. 52.
7. Melville, *Redburn*, p. 209; more than many other Americans of his era, Melville discerned the poverty and power implicit in the British countryside; see, for example, pp. 210–215.
8. Hawthorne, *Our Old Home*, pp. 70–71.
9. Stilgoe, *Common Landscape*, pp. 137–138, 149–170, 202–208.
10. Cooper, *Rural Hours*, pp. 104–111.
11. Emerson, "Home," *Early Lectures*, 3:25.
12. Cooper, *Rural Hours*, p. 104.
13. Ware, *Home Life*, pp. 3–18.

14. Willis, *Rural Letters*, p. 186; the meaning endured in popular usage: see, for example, "Cottage at Nutley" and "Suburban Cottage."
15. Downing, *Rural Essays*, p. 51.
16. Breck, *Flower-Garden*, pp. 29–31.
17. Tuckerman, "Essay," 38 and passim.
18. Beecher, *Plain and Pleasant Talk*, pp. iv–v. Beecher's comments on flowers are quoted in Howard, *Life*, pp. 116–118. For similar remarks of the period, see Parkman, *Book of Roses*, p. 7 and passim; and "The Flower Girl." On Parkman, see Whitehill, "Francis Parkman."
19. Howard, *Life*, p. 116.
20. Lincoln, *Familiar Lectures*, pp. 13–15.
21. Keese, *Floral Keepsake*, pp. 101–112. See also "The Flower Forget-Me-Not"; for a mid-nineteenth-century article aimed at farm women, see "Floral Dictionary."
22. Hale, *Flora's Interpreter*, esp. pp. 3–14; see also Waterman, *Flora's Lexicon*. For an example of the link between Christmas annuals and floral dictionaries, see the advertisement for Hale's book in *Lady's Almanac for 1861*.
23. Hawthorne, *Scarlet Letter*, p. 225.

3:SHADOWS

1. Willis, *Rural Letters*, pp. 179, 225–252. The best study of eighteenth-century cities is Bridenbaugh, *Cities in the Wilderness*, esp. pp. 55–93; see also Boyer, *Urban Masses*.
2. Emerson, *Early Lectures*, II, 273, see also "Dress." For an excellent analysis of the home-as-refuge concept, see Halttunen, *Confidence Men*, esp. pp. 33–53.
3. Bates, *Rural Philosophy*, pp. 5, 257, 209–223, vii (rpt. Philadelphia: Hopkins, 1807).
4. Ibid., pp. 123, 130, 333–338.
5. Trotter, *View of the Nervous Temperament*, pp. 55–57, 63–64 (rpt. Troy, N.Y.: Wright, 1808).
6. Chapin, *Moral Aspects*, pp. 252–253.
7. Condie and Folwell, *History*; for a fictional account, see Lippard, *Monks*; see also Ehrlich, " 'Mysteries' of Philadelphia." On urban corruption, see Griffith, *History*, esp. pp. 63–96; and "Democratic Principle," esp. 13–14. The most casual reading of *New York Times* stories suggests that Manhattan women confronted rudeness regularly and that rural men found such treatment shocking; see, for example, the 1858 letter to the editor, "Insulting Women in the Streets."
8. "World of New York," 659.
9. Rosenberg, *Cholera Years*, pp. 4, 28, 143, 172, 210, and passim.
10. "World of New York," 659, 661, and passim. See also "Consumption." On American urban epidemics, see "History and Incidents of the Plague." On suburban health, see Fisher, "Ten Commandments."
11. "World of New York," 662. See also "New York Central Park" and Wheeler, "Unofficial Government."

4:PARKS

1. Hawthorne, *English Note-Books*, pp. 72–73; see also Forster, "An American"; Rush, "An American"; Hubbard, "Commuter Country"; on Liverpool poverty, see Melville, *Redburn*, pp. 180–215.
2. Hawthorne, *English Note-Books*, pp. 170–171.
3. Ibid., pp. 259–263.
4. Mackenzie, *American in England*, I, 229–232; see also I, 217–235. I have seen only the London edition of this work, which appeared a year after the American one.
5. Olmsted, *Walks and Talks*, pp. 55–56.
6. Daniels, "Villa Parks," 495–496; see also Archer, "Country and City."
7. On Haskell, see Swift, "Llewellyn Park"; Davies, "Llewellyn Park"; Wilson, "Idealism"; Pierson, *History*, II, 306–307.
8. Pierson, *History*, II, 289–293.

9. Quoted in Davies, "Llewellyn Park," 143.
10. Theodore Tilton writing in *The Independent*, May 26, 1864, quoted in Davies, "Llewellyn Park," 143. Pierson, *History*, II, 307–308. Davies, "Llewellyn Park," 143; Swift, "Llewellyn Park," 327. I have personally examined the view from Eagle Rock; contemporary smog diminishes it.
11. Davies, "Llewellyn Park," esp. 144; Pierson, *History*, 2:307–310; Swift, "Llewellyn Park,"; Wilson, "Idealism."
12. Quoted in Davies, "Llewellyn Park," 147; see also Downing, *Landscape Gardening*, pp. 567–571.
13. Quoted in Wilson, "Idealism," 147. Wilson, "Idealism," 147. "Llewellyn Park," 227. See also Swift, "Llewellyn Park" esp. 331.
14. "Landscape-Gardening," 248; see also "Growth of Cities."

5:HEIGHTS

1. Cary, *Clovernook Tales, Second Series*, pp. 13 and passim. For an excellent analysis of Cary's place in the literature of frontier writers, see Kolodny, *The Land Before Her*, pp. 178–189. For an 1852 nonfiction account of borderland Cincinnati, see "Environs of Cincinnati."
2. Cary, *Clovernook Tales, Second Series*, pp. 14, 57–59 and passim.
3. For Maxwell's biography, see Greve, *Centennial History*, II, 43–50.
4. Maxwell, *Suburbs*, p. 14.
5. "Camp Meeting."
6. Maxwell, *Suburbs*, p. 14.
7. Ibid., pp. 26–52, 66. For other descriptions, see Kenny, *Illustrated Cincinnati*, pp. 300–342 and Goss, *Cincinnati*, II, 527–533.
8. Maxwell, *Suburbs*, p. 128.
9. "*Rural Hours*: By a Lady," 231.
10. Maxwell, *Suburbs*, p. 106.
11. Cutting, *Suburban Whirl*, esp. pp. 149–176.

6:PROSPERITY

1. Willis, *Hurry-Graphs*, pp. 129–133. Not every reader enjoyed Willis' books and articles; see "Mr. Willis's Prose."

7:SLOVENLINESS

1. Robinson, "Day." On apple-stealing, see also "Proposed Remedy."
2. "Good and Bad Farming."
3. "Farmer Snug and Farmer Slack." On New Jersey farmers, see "Six Samples"; see also "Portrait"; Mitchell, "Farmer's Homestead"; Downing, *Rural Essays*, p. 400; "Pitchfork."
4. Dwight, *Greenfield Hill*, pp. 120–131. Cobbett, *Year's Residence*, pp. 3, 141–142.
5. Robinson, "Farmer's Error," 348.
6. "Development of Character." See also "Shiftless Farmer"; "Exhortation"; "Farmer and Storekeeper"; "Farms, Farm Houses, Water"; "Causes of the Embarrassments of Farmers."
7. "Modern Farmer"; see also "Science of Agriculture" and contemporaneous issues of *Mechanic's Advocate* and *American Mechanic's Magazine*.
8. Colman, "Address"; see also "Farming Life in New England."
9. Carmichael, "Why the East"; Bidwell and Falconer, *History*, p. 89; on general background, see Danhof, *Change*.
10. "Deleterious Effects"; see also Drake, *Historic Fields*, p. 99, and Wilder, "Agriculture," 323–324.
11. "Supposed Effects."
12. "Destroy Your Weeds"; "Look to Your Weeds."
13. Partridge, "To Our Farmers"; see also "Agriculture."
14. "Large and Small Farms"; see also "Liquid Manure."

15. "Economic Cultivation."
16. Ketcham, "Manures," 464–465 and passim.
17. "Farming and Gardening"; see also "Farm of G. G. Howland" and Durand, "Grounds of Farm Houses."
18. "Farming and Gardening."
19. Fowler, *Journal,* pp. 25–28; see also Bidwell and Falconer, *History,* p. 381.
20. "Stock on Long Island," 195 and passim.
21. Fowler, *Journal,* p. 32; Fowler used wage and land-price figures to support his claims. Throughout the first half of the nineteenth century, agricultural experts struggled to demonstrate the incredible profits possible in market gardening around New York City. Against the incredulity of farmers and other readers, they marshaled detailed balanced sheets; see, for example, Harold, "Cultivation of Asparagus."
22. Lewis, "Long Island Farming" (September 1847); Lewis, "Long Island Farming" (December 1847); Young, "Long Island Farming"; see also Dwight, *Travels,* III, 212–214.
23. Lewis, "Long Island Farming" (September 1847).
24. Gookins, "Culture of Rural Taste"; see also "Study of the Beautiful" and Yeoman, "Old Colony Memorial."

8:VILLAGE

1. Dwight, *Greenfield Hill,* p. 33. See also Dwight, "Greenfield Hill." On villages in general, see Schultze-Naumberg, *Dorfer,* and Taylor, *Village and Farmstead.*
2. Langland, *Piers Plowman,* pp. 3–4.
3. See Stilgoe, *Common Landscape,* pp. 43–58, 202–208.
4. Freneau, *Poems,* pp. 213–225.
5. "Our Neglected Poets," 298–304. On the regional use of the word *town* see Dwight, *Travels,* I, 156; see also Stilgoe, *Common Landscape,* pp. 44, 57.
6. "Some Recollections," 192–196.
7. Bushnell, "Age," 113; Lemon, "Early Americans"; Henretta, "Families." On mechanics, see Bushman, *From Puritan to Yankee;* Brown, "Emergence"; "The Mechanick"; Hunter, "Relics." On village industrialization see also Wood, "Elaboration"; Zelinsky, "Pennsylvania Town"; Marks, "Rural Response."
8. Spafford, *Gazetteer,* p. 176. See also Gordon, *History,* pp. 99–101, and Darby, *Tour,* p. 47.
9. Gordon, *Gazetteer,* pp. 632, 714; see also pp. 635, 656, 658. The transformation continued: see French, *Gazetteer,* and Bidwell, "Rural Economy."
10. Barber, *Connecticut,* pp. 70–71. On the accuracy of Barber's "views" see Krim, "Graphic Landscapes."
11. Barber, *Historical Collections of New Jersey,* pp. 244–245.
12. Barber, *Historical Collections of Massachusetts,* pp. 243–246.
13. Wood, "Elaboration," esp. 341–352.
14. "Fire," 120; see also Gage, *History,* pp. 427–429; see also "Farms, Farm Houses, Water"; Adams, *Address,* pp. 10, 13; *Heritage,* pp. 249–266 and passim; Rawson, *Forever,* p. 198.
15. Adams, *Address,* pp. 10–14. See also Chelsea Fire Dept., *First;* Hancock, *Emigrant's Five Years,* p. 318. On urban street trees and insurance, see Watson, *Annals,* I, 222–223, and Lockwood, *Gardens,* I, 338. The destruction of houses by tree-fed fire in Bar Harbor, Maine, in 1947 illustrates trees' ability to communicate fire.
16. "Causes of Fire," 184; see also Dwight, *Travels,* I, 171, 311, and II, 231–232 (Dwight found Connecticut Valley town centers beautiful in part because their houses stood safely apart from each other); and "Farms, Farm Houses, and Water."
17. *Litchfield* [Connecticut] *Monitor* (June 29, 1803); see also Cushing, "Town Commons," esp. 92–93.
18. "Waste Places," 131.
19. Downing, *Rural Essays,* pp. 229–243.
20. Ibid., p. 238n.
21. Barber, *Connecticut,* pp. 389–393.
22. "Half an Acre," 14–15.

23. Dwight, *Travels*, I, 376.
24. Ibid., III, 80.
25. Ibid., I, 376.
26. Ibid., III, 231.

9: COUNTRY SEAT

1. Downing, "Multiplication," 9–11.
2. Wood, *Creation*.
3. Bailyn, *Ideological Origins;* Wood, *Creation;* Stourzh, *Alexander Hamilton;* Pocock, "Virtue and Commerce." On georgic poetry, see Rosenthal, *Constable*, pp. 47–71 and passim.
4. Parrington, *Main Currents*, I, 267–398; see also Howe, *Changing Political Thought*, esp. pp. 217–251.
5. On Federal-era domestic architecture, see Newcomb, *Colonial and Federal;* Ross, *Book of Boston;* and Lagerberg, *New Jersey Architecture.*
6. Thornton, "Moral Dimensions"; see also "Judge Quincy's Farm."
7. "Democratic Principle," esp 13.
8. Thomas, "Romantic Reform."
9. Bodo, *Protestant Clergy.*
10. Tichi, *New World, New Earth*, pp. 114–205.
11. Nash, *Wilderness*, p. 60.
12. Thoreau, *Journal*, II, 341–342.
13. Neufeldt, "Henry David Thoreau's Political Economy."
14. Baker, *Modern House Builder*, pp. 14–16.
15. Martyn, "How to Make," 222–225.
16. "Domestic Architecture," 31, 33, 34.
17. "Rural Scenery: The Thatched Cottage," 211 and passim.
18. "Country Houses on the Hudson River," 331; see also "Farm Houses."
19. Downing, *Architecture*, pp. 257–270. For an exceptionally perceptive analysis of the architectural design of Downing and Davis, see Pierson, *American Buildings*, pp. 270–431; this is a very significant study. See also "Country Dwellings" and Davis, *Rural Residences.* Much of Downing's thinking came from Britain, of course; see Slater, "Family, Society, and the Ornamental Villa."
20. Stilgoe, *Common Landscape*, pp. 159–170; see also "Farm Houses" and "Farms, Farm Houses, Water."
21. Baker, *Modern House Builder*, pp. 18–19 and passim.
22. Melville, *Great Short Works*, pp. 382–387.
23. Wordsworth makes his point throughout *Description of the Scenery.*
24. Downing, *Rural Essays*, pp. 252–259. On the styleless houses, see "Improving Old Houses." See also Weaver and Doucet, "Material Culture."
25. Stilgoe, *Common Landscape*, pp. 166–169; on Cincinnati soot, see "Color of City Houses"; on white-painted country houses, see Elliott, "Paint for Buildings," and especially Peabody, "Rural Architecture," 9–10.
26. "Country Residences—A New Plan."

10: GROUNDS

1. Jaques, "Landscape Gardening," 33–34.
2. Lydia Sigorney, "Horticulture," in *Godey's Lady's Book* (June 1840), 179.
3. Thornton, "Moral Dimensions" and "Cultivating the American Character." See also Goodman, "Ethics."
4. "President of the Massachusetts Horticultural Society."
5. Dearborn, *Address*, p. 9. See also Greenwood, *Sermon*, pp. 22, 33, and passim.
6. "President of the Massachusetts Horticultural Society," p. 15. See also Wilder, "Horticulture."
7. "New American Orchardist," 448.

8. Ibid., 447–449.
9. Downing, *Rural Essays*, p. 278.
10. Sherman, "Daniel Webster"; Seaton, "Idylls"; Wilson, *Where*, pp. 62–121.
11. "Farm of G. G. Howland."
12. Yeoman, "Old Colony Memorial."
13. Cobbett, *Year's Residence*, p. 3.
14. "Villa of Mr. Halsey"; see also "Country Houses on the Hudson River."
15. "Villa of Mr. Sargent"; for a popular-periodical article, see Lossing, "Arlington House."
16. For popular-periodical articles, see "Horticulture" (*Quarterly Review*) and "About Pear Trees." See also Gray, "Review" and Peabody, "American Forest Trees."
17. Flagg, "Old and New," esp. 538–539.
18. Stilgoe, *Common Landscape*, pp. 170–208.
19. "Laying Out Farms," 107.
20. Quoted in Greve, *Centennial History*, I, 349.
21. "Village Teacher: Favorite Occupation," 323.
22. Jaques, "Landscape Gardening," 34–35.
23. "Farm of G. G. Howland.".
24. Jaques, "Landscape Gardening," p. 34; see also "Complete Country Residence" and "Improving and Planting Grounds."
25. Flagg, "Spontaneity," 491.
26. Flagg, "Elm," 27; see also his "Oak," "Cherries," "Birches," "Poplar," and "Maples."
27. Hovey, "Virginia Fringe Tree"; see also his "Our Ornamental Trees."
28. "Ailanthus-Tree"; see also "Culture of Sumach."
29. Downing, *Rural Essays*, pp. 160–165.
30. Jaques, "Landscape Gardening," 35.
31. Holly, *Country Seats*, p. 25.
32. Flagg, "Old and New," esp. 536–539.
33. Flagg, "Treatment of Landscape," esp. 293–294; see also his "Landscape."
34. "Improving and Planting Grounds," esp. 32.
35. "Picturesque in Floriculture" see also Junius, "Remarks on Rural Scenery: The Cottage Garden."
36. "Notes on Some of the Nurseries."
37. Ibid., esp. 126–127.

11:MIX

1. Hall, Reminiscences," pp. 278–287.
2. "Town and Country," 249–250.
3. "Editor's Easy Chair," 129–130; on straight versus curved roads, see Daniel Drake, quoted in Greve, *Centennial History*, I, 349.
4. Bowen, *History*, p. 183.
5. Greeley, *What I Know*, pp. 87, 62, and passim.

PHINNEY

1. Binford, *First Suburbs*, pp. 86–87.
2. Monroe, "Elias Phinney " 70–71.
3. Colman, *Fourth Report*, pp. 193–199 and passim.
4. Drake, *Historic Fields*, pp. 98–99; Binford, *First Suburbs*, pp. 95–101.

12:PHILADELPHIA

1. Maxwell, *Run*, pp. 166–167.
2. Oberholtzer, *Philadelphia*, pp. 226–227.
3. Smith, *Philadelphia*, pp. xii, 14–19.

4. Oberholtzer, *Philadelphia*, pp. 326–330.
5. *Dictionary of American Biography*, VI, 411.
6. Fisher, *Philadelphias*, pp. 316, 327–328 and passim.
7. Bowen, *History*, p. 183; on horsecars, see Gloag, *History of Urban America*, pp. 147–148.
8. Day, *Historical Collections*, p. 75.
9. Fisher, *Philadelphia*, pp. 316, 327–328.
10. Stetson, "William Hamilton."
11. Eberlein and Hubbard, *Portrait*, pp. 447–454; Webster, *Philadelphia*, pp. 195, 218. See also Rosanthal, *History*.
12. Fisher, *Philadelphia*, p. 328.
13. Miller and Siry, "The Emerging Suburb."

13:CHICAGO

1. [Kirkland], "Illinois in Spring Time," On the growth of Chicago, see Wade, *Chicago*, and Hoyt, *One Hundred Years;* see also Monchow, *Seventy Years*, and the excellent forthcoming study by Marc Weiss, *The Rise of the Community Builders.*
2. Hancock, *Emigrant's Five Years*, pp. 257–258.
3. Fellmann, "Pre-Building Growth Patterns."
4. Abbott, "Necessary Adjuncts."
5. Sheahan, "Chicago."
6. Posadas, "Home in the Country."
7. *Our Suburbs*, pp. 5–11, 20–24.
8. Chamberlin, *Chicago*, pp. 204–205, 215, 223.
9. Ibid., pp. 434–435.
10. Ibid., pp. 215, 223, 236, 364–368; see also Davenport, "Sanitation Revolution."
11. Johnson, *North Chicago*, p. 8 and passim. On North Chicago see the excellent piece by Ebner, "In the Suburbs." See also Kirkland, *Chicago Yesterdays.*
12. Sheahan, "Chicago," 530–531.
13. Stilgoe, *Metropolitan Corridor*, pp. 75–103.
14. Chamberlin, *Chicago*, pp. 188–190.

14:BARNACLES

1. Strong, *Diary*, II, 396; see also McCullough, *Brooklyn.*
2. Fisher, *Philadelphia*, pp. 215–218.
3. Stilgoe, *Common Landscape*, pp. 99–106, 207–208.
4. Binford, *First Suburbs*, p. 42.
5. "New Homes of New York," 64–65 and passim; on apartment houses and their effects, see Barth, *City People*, pp. 45–53. Howells, *Hazard*, I, 64–98 and passim. Dislike of apartment houses sometimes orignated in arguments focused on the nobility of paying real estate taxes (something renters did only indirectly); for an example of such thinking, see Brackett, "Address."
6. Warner, *Streetcar Suburbs*, pp. 81–82.
7. Stilgoe, *Metropolitan Corridor*, pp. 287–310.
8. Beers, *Suburban Pastoral*, pp. 5–7.
9. Warner, *Streetcar Suburbs*, pp. 81–82. The developer was out of touch indeed, for as Warner remarks (p. 142), in those years "no amount of romantic ornament could make a cottage out of a city row house."
10. Caparn, "Parallelogram Park," 767, 770, and passim. "Editor's Easy Chair."

VISIONS

1. Coburn, "Five-Hundred-Mile City," 1256–1259 and passim.
2. Stilgoe, *Metropolitan Corridor*, esp. pp. 266–337.

15:ADVOCATES

1. Bunner, *Suburban Sage*, p. 130.
2. Cozzens, "Sparrowgrass Papers," 166–169.
3. Alger, *Ragged Dick*, p. 49.
4. Cozzens, "Sparrowgrass Papers," 299–302.
5. Ibid., 166–169.
6. Ibid., 629–633.
7. Coffin, *Out of Town*, pp. 2–3.
8. Ibid., pp. 4–6, 8, 10.
9. Ibid., pp. 34–35, 57, 78.
10. Ibid., pp. 45–47.
11. Ibid., pp. 67, 69–75.
12. Ibid., pp. 89–90.
13. Ibid., p. 98.
14. Howells, *Suburban Sketches*, p. 11.
15. Ibid., pp. 61–62, 65–66, 86, and passim.
16. Ibid., pp. 65–66, 71–72.
17. Few scholars have studied Bunner, and none has examined his place in the literature of the borderlands; see, however, Jensen, *Life and Letters;* Wells, "Henry Cuyler Bunner"; and Hutton, "Henry Cuyler Bunner."
18. Bunner, *Runaway Browns*, pp. 18, 208–213, and passim.
19. Bunner, *Jersey Street*, pp. 41–43, 56–57, 60–61.
20. Ibid., pp. 178, 181–182, 184, 190, 193.
21. Brown, *History*, pp. 52–53 and passim.
22. Jensen, *Life and Letters*, pp. 122–123, 168, and passim. See also Brown, *History*, pp. 54–58.
23. Bunner, *Suburban Sage*, p. 146.

16:FROSTING

1. Godley, *Letters*, I, 10–12.
2. Flagg, *Halcyon*, pp. 30–35.
3. Ibid., pp. 207–208.
4. McComb, "Nervousness," esp. 259.
5. Rath, *Nervous Wreck*. See also, of course, Beard's *American Nervousness*.
6. Leggett, *Out-Door Poems*, p. 31.
7. James, *American Scene*, pp. 87, 73.
8. Flagg, "Field and Garden," 275.
9. Taylor, "Care," 409 and passim. See also Solotaroff, "City's Duty"; Peets, "Street Trees"; Mitchell, "Trees." The street tree issue was debated at length in 1910 issues of *Park and Cemetery.*
10. Clark, "Why I Chose," 189. See also Haxton, "Why People Left the City."
11. Johnson, "Tree Seats."
12. Whiting, "What an Enterprising Improvement Society Can Do."
13. Bragdon, "Making of a Country Home." It is useful to talk with house painters; their sanding machines reveal layer after layer of paint. See also McCrea, "Color Harmony." On shingles, see "Page."
14. "Privacy"; see also Speed, "Right."
15. Shores, "Plea"; see also Adams, "Law"; Maxwell, "Lack"; Lee, "Dominance."
16. Dwight, "Gardens," 64; see also "Design for a Partially Enclosed Veranda." On laundry, see "Hill Dryer Co."
17. Powell, *Hedges*, p. 9. On "Americanism" see "Contemporary Suburban Residence" and March, "Fences."
18. Bunner, *Suburban Sage*, pp. 71 and passim; see also "Porch Shades."
19. "Contemporary Suburban Residence"; see also Barnes, *Suburban Garden.*
20. Downing, *Rural Essays*, pp. 357–358, 373.

21. Powell, *Hedges*, pp. 49, 93–94; see also McLeod, "Planting" and Hatfield, "Long-Lived Hardy Evergreens." See also "Hick's Hardy Evergreens" and McLaughlin, "Transplanting Large Trees."
22. Flagg, "Spontaneity." See also Burnett, "Four in the Open."
23. Powell, *Hedges*, pp. 102–104; see also Underwood, "Garden" and McFarland, "My Growing Garden."
24. "How to Cool."
25. On indoor privacy in relation to political freedom, see Arendt, *Human Condition*, pp. 63–64 and passim.
26. Clark, "Why I Chose."

17:IMPROVEMENT

1. Sharp, "Commuter"; see also Goodwin, "Commuter's Wife." Some men commuted by motorboat: see Martyn, "Era."
2. Cole, "Chicago's Most Unique Suburb."
3. The best guide to the study of commuter-train stops and the construction around them is the mapping done by the Sanborn Map Company.
4. True, "Beatitudes."
5. Cole, "Chicago's Most Unique Suburb."
6. Howells, *Suburban Sketches*, p. 12.
7. Barth, *City People*, is the best introduction; see also Boorstin, *Americans*, pp. 90–187. For a contemporaneous account, see "Suburban Prices." See also Atherton, "Midwestern Country Town"; Mather, "Littleton"; Veblen, "Country Town"; Fletcher, "Doom"; and Stilgoe, *Metropolitan Corridor*, pp. 215–218.
8. Winslow, "Buying." On one large grocery concern that delivered to borderland houses, see Crawford, "One Hundred Years." On railroad-terminal shopping, see "Our Bookshop."
9. "Our Bookshop."
10. Manning, "History"; Wilson, "Social Life" (the March 1912 issue of the *Annals* focused on rural life); Garland, *Son;* Carver, "Life"; Wyckoff, "With Iowa Farmers"; Bowers, *Country-Life Movement*.
11. Waring, *Village*, p. 12; see also Egleston, *Villages.*
12. Olmsted, "Village Improvement"; see also "Parks versus Villages."
13. Waring, *Village*, pp. 16–17.
14. Robbins, "Village"; see also Sedgwick, "Village Improvement." Other authors emphasized the role of women; see, for example, Northrop, "Work," esp. 104.
15. Northrop, "Work," esp. 101–102. See also Mathews, "Montclair."
16. Angell, "For the Good."
17. My conclusions here derive from prolonged study of Sanborn Map Company maps; on vacant stores, see also Sharp, "Commuter," 561.
18. Mathews, "Mount Vernon."
19. Allen, "Our National Shabbiness"; see also Crane, "Planning"; *Village Builder;* "America in Bloom."
20. Moore, "Materials for Landscape"; see also Macdonald, "Home District," and Hartt, "Beautifying."
21. McCrea, "Color Harmony." See also Ripley, "Village." Some paint manufacturers seconded McCrea's ideas: see for example, "Cabot's Shingle Stains."
22. On the railroad gardening movement, see Stilgoe, *Metropolitan Corridor*, pp. 223–245 and passim; see also "Railroad Station at Chestnut Hill."
23. Sangster, "Suburban Resident."

RESTRICTIONS

1. Bulot, "Developing." See also Taylor, *Satellite Cities;* Nichols, "Suburban Subdivision"; Parry, "Study."
2. *Articles of Agreement*, pp. 3–5, 7, and passim.

3. Mathews, "Mount Vernon." See also Cheney, "Zoning"; Nichols, "Housing"; Hoyt, *Structure.*
4. See, for example, Smith, *Overbrook Farms;* Hurd, *Principles;* Monchow, *Use of Deed Restriction.*
5. On suburban villages, see "Country Residences—A New Plan."

18:FOREST HILLS GARDENS

1. Howe, "Town Planning," 136.
2. Sage Foundation, *Forest Hills Gardens,* pp. 12–15. See also "Forest Hills Gardens" and "Garden City Platted."
3. Sage Foundation, *Forest Hills Gardens,* pp. 16–18; see also "Suburban Cottages vs. Flats."
4. Sage Foundation, *Forest Hills Gardens: Preliminary Information,* p. 13.
5. Sage Foundation, *Forward Movement.*
6. Sage Foundation, *Declaration of Restrictions,* pp. 2–3 and passim.
7. Sage Foundation, *Forest Hills Gardens: Preliminary Information,* p. 3.
8. On Atterbury's worries, see Sage Foundation, *Forest Hills Gardens,* p. 17, and Atterbury, "Forest Hills Gardens," 317.
9. Graves, "A 'Model Village' Under Way"; See also his "A 'Model Village' Run on Business Principles" and Anderson, "Forest Hills Gardens."
10. For the drawings, see "Forest Hills Gardens."
11. Howe, "Town Planning."
12. Knevels, "What the Suburban-Dweller May Learn"; May, "Forest Hills Gardens"; Embury, "Co-Operative Building."
13. For an article on single-family houses see, for example, "Recent Houses."
14. Embury, "Co-Operative Building." Cooperative kitchens were a proven success by this time: see Hayden, *Grand Domestic Revolution.*
15. Graves, "A 'Model Village' Under Way."
16. May, "Forest Hills Gardens," 163 and passim.
17. Knevels, "What a Suburban-Dweller May Learn." See also Quarles, "Protection."
18. "Mrs. Sage Gives Church." On the structure itself, see Atterbury, "Church."
19. "Forest Hills Gardens Sold." See also "Problem of Pressures." Atterbury had, of course, built an earlier tall apartment building on Station Square: see *Forest Hills Inn.*
20. Howe, "Town Planning," 136.
21. Atterbury, "Cottage and Garden."

19:SHAKER HEIGHTS

1. On the Van Sweringens, see "Two Young Men" and the article in the *National Cyclopedia of American Biography,* vol. A, 539–540; see also Lowenthal, "Case." The brothers worked hard to keep their biographies and interests hidden from public scrutiny. Haberman's excellent *Van Sweringens* contains only one chapter on the financial arrangements concerning the land speculation; otherwise it focuses on the brothers' railroad activities.
2. "Two Young Men."
3. Condon, *Cleveland,* pp. 188–193 and passim.
4. Frary, "Suburban."
5. Ibid., see also *Heritage of the Shakers.*
6. *Shaker Village Standards,* p. 3.
7. Ibid., p. 12.
8. Ibid., pp. 4, 10–12.
9. Ibid., pp. 6–9.
10. Ibid., p. 6.
11. Ibid., p. 13.
12. Ibid., p. 14 and passim.
13. Ibid., pp. 13–14.
14. Ibid., p. 14; see also *Heritage of the Shakers,* pp. 1–3 and passim.

15. *Questions and Answers*, pp. 1–4 and passim. See also "Map of the Property" and Pease, "Shaker Heights."
16. Frary, "Suburban"; see also "Shaker Heights for Sale."
17. Condon, *Cleveland*, pp. 190–192; see also *Shaker Heights Subdivision*, p. 16.
18. *Peaceful Shaker Village*. See also *Shaker Heights Subdivision*, pp 17–19.
20. Smith, "Glory," esp. 22–23. Smith's understanding of the process of urban growth is not, of course, unique; see, for example, Walker, "Wonders." For the Van Sweringen philosophy, see "How to Protect Yourself."

20:IMPORT

1. "Industrial Experiment."
2. Diggs, "English Garden City."
3. Klaber, "Garden City of Hellerav"; see also Mullen, "American Perceptions."
4. Atterbury, "Model Towns," esp. 28–29 and passim. In time designers began to think of planning the entire national landscape; see, for example, Manning, "A National Plan."
5. Howe, "Garden Cities," 6 and passim. For some of Howe's additional thinking, see his "Way Toward," "Dusseldorf," and "German and American City." He did write on company towns too: see his "Industrial Villages." See also Schott, "City's Fight" and Kaplan, "Andrew H. Green."
6. May, "Indian Hill." See also Veiller, "Industrial Housing."
7. See, for example, "Kohler Village" and "Town of Kohler," also "Kohler of Kohler."
8. Tompkins, "Working People's Homes."
9. Schalck, "Planning Roland Park."
10. Chamberlin, *Chicago*, pp. 415–416.
11. Riverside Improvement Co., *Riverside*, pp. 21, 9, and passim. See also Omsted, "Riverside"; Ramsey, *Olmsted*; and Olmsted Society, *Riverside*.
12. Schalck, "Planning Roland Park," 424; see also "Some Inexpensive Country Homes." On the earlier borderlands near Baltimore, see "Visits to Country Places." Purchasers of lots in Roland Park could, of course, buy two or more contiguous ones and thus site their houses more privately.
13. Fawcett, "Roland Park"; see also *Book of Pictures* and Doolittle, "Cost."
14. "Port Jefferson: Belle Terre."
15. Fawcett, "Suburban Life," esp. 310, 314.
16. Barnard, "Commercial Value," esp. 766.
17. Carlton, "Urban and Rural," esp. 256–257; see also Packard, "Developing a Suburban Colony."
18. Wood, "Why Pay Rent?" esp. 770; see also Ferris, "Suburban," and Davis, "Our Suburban Friends."
19. Stuyvesant, "Why You Should Have a Workshop," esp. 352. For other examples, see Clark, "Twenty Miles," and Hitchcock, "Joys."
20. Burroughs, "Joy of Edged Tools."
21. Griffith, "Handy Man"; see also Dearborn, "Bird Houses."
22. Hayden, *Grand Domestic Revolution*. See also "Beauty in Architectural Detail," Thompson, "Servant Question," esp. 525, and Tryon, "Reflections."
23. Harland, "Home-Made Efficiency"; other experts shared her views: Riley, "Running the Home"; Gaylor, "If You Can't Get Beef"; Arnold, "Thrift Talks."
24. Eaton, "Equipping the Toolhouse"; see also "Gardening Clothes"; "Right and Wrong Way"; Williams, "Wood"; "Planet Jr. Garden Implements"; "How to Build a Greenhouse"; Woolworth, "Matter of Wiring."
25. Beckett, "Handy Woman"; see also Rockwell, "War Garden"; "Garden in the House"; Tryon, "Reflections."
26. "Twenty Miles Out" [February], 158–159; see also "Study in Architectural Alchemy"; "Bringing an Old New England Home Up to Date"; Githens, "Farmhouse Reclaimed."
27. "Satisfaction of Good Tools."
28. Stanley Rule and Level Plant, *How to Work with Tools and Wood*. See also Dearborn, "Bird

Houses." On teaching children, see Jordan, "What Do Our Children Know?" and Wood-ward, "Suburban Woman."

29. See, for example, Seymour, "Economy"; "Woman's Poultry"; Whitman, *First Aid for the Ailing House;* Farrington, "Poultry-Yard Patriotism"; "New Word: 'Democracy' "; "Nature as a Landscape Garden."

21:COAST

1. Grey, "New Suburb," 36, 37, 40, 41, 45, and passim.
2. Holly, "Modern Dwellings," 856.
3. Ward, "The Automobile in the Suburbs," 269, 270, 271.
4. Clancy, "The Car and the Country Home," 30.

22:TREMOR

1. "Why Is a Suburb?" See also H. G. Wells's predictions concerning aerial bombardment, and especially the destruction of New York City, in his 1908 novel, *The War in the Air,* pp. 95–105, 243–245, and passim.
2. On the fear, see Fleming, "Roots," esp. 76–78.
3. "New York Revisited," 11.
4. For an example of women's hatred of street noise, see "The Suburban Woman and Her Neighborhood Clubs," 166. On this and other forms of urban stress, see also Beard, *American Nervousness* and Girdner, *Newyorkitis.* Such inquiries into urban stress deserve the most precise scrutiny today. Girdner, for example, was a physician as intrigued by urban illness as Trotter, and his speculations are of contemporary importance.
5. London, "Story," 22, 23, 26.
6. Smith, "Urban Disorder," esp. 94–95; this is an exceptionally important article.
7. Adams, *Education,* pp. 499–500.
8. James, *American Scene,* p. 346 and passim.
9. St. Johns "Will Gas Destroy Populations?" See also Allen, "Chemical Warfare"; Villard, "Poison Gas"; "Gas in the Next War"; Lewis, "Poison Gas"; Steed, "Future of Warfare"; "New Shelter."

23:SPLIT

1. "Realtor Experts," 42–44.
2. Wilson, "New Market"; see also "Higher Values." Advertising carried forward the tradi-tionalist argument; for examples of such advertisements, see Arkansas Soft Pine Bureau, "Let's Not Go Wrong on Fads in Home Building" and Conant-Ball Company, "The Colonial Touch in the Modern Home."
3. Yeomans, "Suburb," 105–107.
4. Susman's "Useless Past" is perhaps the most penetrating introduction to this issue. On the Lost Generation and business civilization, see Commanger, *American Mind,* pp. 246–276; Cowley, *Exile's Return,* esp. pp. 94–95; Beard, *Rise of American Civilization* and Aldridge, *After the Lost Generation.* See also Kazin, *On Native Ground.* For an example of the vague sense of pre-business-era virtue lost, see "In Praise of the Lumber Garret." In these brief paragraphs I make no attempt even to approach summarizing or analyzing in detail an incredi-bly important moment in American culture; nor do I address the issues of periodical literature and women readers Commanger discusses in *American Mind,* pp. 41–81 (and which should be read against Marchand's *Advertising the American Dream*).
5. Brooks, "Enterprise," 57–58; see also his "Culture of Industrialism" and *Scenes,* pp. 3 and passim. On Brooks's views, see Hoopes's *Van Wyck Brooks.* Mumford, *Golden Day,* pp. 58–59, 74–75, 282, and passim. See also Leuchtenburg, *Perils of Prosperity;* Muirhead, "Some Recent Books"; "In Praise of the Eighteenth Century."
6. Mumford, *Sticks and Stones,* pp. 158–159, 174–176, 238, and passim. See also Beard, *Ameri-can in Midpassage,* esp. pp. 3–115; Beard, *Rise of American Civilization,* pp. 166–210, 285–343, 663–800; and Beard, "Culture."

7. Mumford, *Sticks and Stones,* pp. 185–186. On Mumford's own living arrangements, see his *Green Memories.*
8. Lewis, *Babbitt,* pp. 45, 28.
9. Gaunt, "Modern Utopia?" 860, 865, and passim. See also Kahn, "Province of Decoration."
10. Frederick, "Suburban Living," 290, 291.
11. Swift, "Defense," 543, 544, 558.
12. Frederick, "Suburban Living," 290.
13. Brooks, "Enterprise," 60. Shackleton, *Quest,* p. 12.
14. Shackleton, *Charm,* pp. 89–91.
15. Carrick, *Next-to-Nothing House,* pp. 83, 10, 28, 46; see also Gillespie, "House."
16. Lewis, *Babbitt,* pp. 98–99. See Saylor, "Personality," for contemporaneous remarks on colonial reproduction houses.
17. Rourke, *American Humor,* pp. 10, 233, and passim and Rourke, *Roots,* p. 81.
18. Geselbracht, "Ghosts of Andrew Wyeth"; see also Kouwenhoven, *Made in America,* and Hoyt, "Haystack Loaves."
19. "Frontispiece." On the early history of antique collecting, see Stillinger, *The Antiquers,* and Kaplan, "R. T. H. Halsey"; see also "Boys and Girls"; Morse, *Furniture;* Singleton, *Collecting;* Axelrod, ed., *Colonial Revival;* Roberts, *Antiquamania.*
20. On the context of Nutting's work, see Stilgoe, "Popular Photography." For Nutting's rebuilding of an old house, see his *Massachusetts Beautiful,* pp. 246–269.
21. On nature study, see Schmitt's *Back to Nature* and Torrey, "My Real Estate." On bird watching, see Buckham, *Where Town and Country Meet;* Scoville, *Everyday Adventures;* and Mowbray, *Journey to Nature.* On immigration restriction see Leuchtenburg, *Perils,* pp. 126–127 and Solomon, *Ancestors.*
22. Field, "Shenandoah," 12–13. See also "Speaking of Antiques" and Raymond, "Study in Contrasts."
23. Crothers, "Social Survey," 327.
24. Thompson, "On Living in Cities," 200 and his "Future," 335. See also Wilson, "Wanted." and, on advertising, Marchand, *Advertising the American Dream,* esp. pp. 88–205.
25. Cowley, *Exile's Return,* pp. 14–15. See also Marx, *Machine,* pp. 354–365 and Brooks, *Writer,* pp. 144–145.
26. Gloag, "Wood or Metal," 49–51; "Wood Office Furniture." See also Mumford, "Economics."
27. On *Life* houses see "Eight Houses"; "Life Houses"; "Which *Life* House?" and "Pictures to the Editors."

24:LANDFALL

1. I base these sentences on information from my father, John F. Stilgoe, who remembers the landfall conversations clearly.
2. Lang, "Los Alamos," 86–87.
3. White, "Here Is New York," 44.
4. It also worried planners; see, for example, Coyle, "Twilight."
5. Adams, *Education,* p. 499; see also "Value of Arts."
6. "Mission."
7. Brandeis, "Rational Scheme," 22; Smith, "Country Catechism," and Brunner, "Influence."
8. Stickley, "Most Valuable"; see also Sharp, *Hills,* p. 100.
9. Wright, *Truly Rural,* p. 9.
10. Allen, "Suburban Nightmare." See, for example, the "back to the land" issue of *Country Life* (March 15, 1911) and Sharp, "Commuter."
11. "Artists, Writers, and the Fall of New York."
12. The *New Criterion* essays, individually untitled, appear in a "Special Issue" [Summer, 1986].
13. Milgram, "Experience," 1466.
14. Cruger, *How She Did It,* esp. pp. 10–81.
15. Shakespeare, *As You Like It,* II, i.

BIBLIOGRAPHY

Abbott, Carl. " 'Necessary Adjuncts to its Growth': The Railroad Suburbs of Chicago, 1854–1875." *Journal of the Illinois State Historical Society* 73 (Summer 1980), 117–131.

"About Pear Trees." *Putnam's* 7 (April 1856), 390–392.

Abrams, M. H. *Natural Supernaturalism.* New York: Norton, 1971.

Adams, Bill. *Nature's Place: Conservation Sites and Countryside Change.* Winchester, Mass.: Allen & Unwin, 1986.

Adams, E. "Law of Privacy." *North American Review* 175 (September 1902), 361–369.

Adams, Henry. *The Education of Henry Adams* [1918]. New York: Modern Library, 1931.

Adams, James Truslow. *The Epic of America.* Boston: Little, Brown, 1932.

———. *The Founding of New England.* Boston: Little, Brown, 1921.

Adams, John Quincy. *Address to the Members of the Massachusetts Charitable Fire Society.* Boston: Russell, 1802.

Adler, Jerry. "The Return to the Suburbs: Boomers Are Behaving Like Their Parents." *Newsweek* 108 (July 21, 1986), 52–54.

"Agriculture." *American Quarterly Review* 21 (March 1837), 1–17.

"Ailanthus-Tree." *Yearbook of Agriculture for 1855–1856.* Philadelphia: Childs & Peterson, 1856.

Aldridge, John W. *After the Lost Generation: A Critical Study of the Writers of Two Wars.* New York: Noonday, 1951.

Alger, Horatio. *Ragged Dick.* Ed. Rychard Fink [1866]. New York: Macmillan, 1970.

Allen, Frederick Lewis. "Our National Shabbiness." *House Beautiful* 37 (January 1915), 33–36.

———. "Suburban Nightmare." *Independent* 114 (June 13, 1925), 670–671.

Allen, R. S. "Chemical Warfare: A New Industry." *Nation* 124 (January 12, 1927), 33.

"America in Bloom: The Work of Country Garden Clubs, East and West." *Craftsman* 29 (November 1915), 144–151.

Anderson, W. F. "Forest Hills Gardens—Building Construction." *Brickbuilder* 21 (December 1909), 319–321.

Angell, Herbert C. "For the Good of the Neighborhood." *House & Garden* 25 (March 1914), 163–165, 234.

Archer, John. "Country and City in the American Romantic Suburb." *Journal of the Society of Architectural Historians* 42 (May 1983), 139–156.

Arendt, Hannah. *The Human Condition.* Chicago: Univ. of Chicago Press, 1958.

Arkansas Soft Pine Bureau. "Let's Not Go Wrong on Fads in Home Building." *American Home* 3 (February 1930), 495.

Arnold, Frank. R. "Thrift Talks from Back Yards." *Countryside* 23 (October 1916), 204.

Arsenault, Raymond. "The End of the Long Hot Summer: Air Conditioning and Southern Culture." *Journal of Southern History* 50 (November 1984), 598–628.

Articles of Agreement Regulating the Use, Holding, and Enjoyment of the Rock Park Estate in the County of Chester. Liverpool: Laces, Clay, Myers, 1837.

"Artists, Writers, and the Fall of New York." *Village Voice* 31 (August 6, 1986), 32.

Ashmore, Ruth. "Side Talks." *Ladies' Home Journal* 7 (June 1890), 10.

Atherton, Lewis E. "The Midwestern Country Town—Myth and Reality." *Agricultural History* 26 (July 1952), 73–80.

Atterbury, Grosvenor. "The Church in the Gardens." *Architectural Review* 9 (August 1919), 37–40.

———. "A Cottage and Garden at East Hampton, L.I." *House and Garden* 3 (April 1903), 213–214.

———. "Forest Hills Gardens, Long Island: An Example of Collective Planning, Development, and Control." *Brickbuilder* 21 (December 1912), 317–318.

———. "Model Towns in America." *Scribner's* 52 (July 1912), 20–35.

Axelrod, Alan, ed. *The Colonial Revival in America.* New York: Norton, 1985.

Bailyn, Bernard. *The Ideological Origins of the American Revolution.* Cambridge: Harvard Univ. Press, 1967.

Baker, Zebulon. *Modern House Builder from the Log Cabin and Cottage to the Mansion.* Boston: Higgins, 1857.

Baldwin, Faith. *Station Wagon Set.* New York: Grosset & Dunlap, 1938.

"Banish the Garbage Can Nuisance." *House and Garden* 53 (January 1928), 144.

Barber, John Warner. *Connecticut Historical Collections.* New Haven: Durrie, 1836.

———. *Historical Collections . . . of . . . Massachusetts.* Worcester: Lazell, 1844.

———. *Historical Collections of the State of New Jersey.* New York: Tuttle, 1846.

Barber, John Warner, and Henry Howe. *Historical Collections of the State of New York.* New York: Tuttle, 1842.

Barnard, Charles. "The Commercial Value of the Wild." *Craftsman* 10 (September 1906), 763–766.

Barnes, Parker Thayer. *The Suburban Garden Guide.* New York: Macmillan, 1913.

Barnes, R. L. *Twelve Miles Around Philadelphia.* Philadelphia: Barnes, 1858.

Barrell, John. *The Dark Side of the Landscape: The Rural Poor in English Painting, 1730–1840.* Cambridge: Cambridge Univ. Press, 1980.

Barron, Hal. *Those Who Stayed Behind: Rural Society in Nineteenth-Century New England.* New York: Cambridge Univ. Press, 1984.

Barth, Gunther. *City People: The Rise of Modern City Culture in Nineteenth-Century America.* New York: Oxford Univ. Press, 1980.

Bartlett, John Russell. *Dictionary of Americanisms: A Glossary of Words and Phrases Usually Regarded as Peculiar to the United States.* Boston: Little, Brown, 1859.

Bartlett, Richard A. *The New Country: A Social History of the American Frontier, 1776–1890.* London: Oxford Univ. Press, 1974.

Bates, Ely. *Rural Philosophy.* London: Longman, 1804.

Baxter, Sylvester. "Economic and Social Influence of the Bicycle." *Arena* 6 (October 1892), 578–583.

Beard, Charles A., and Mary R. Beard. *America in Midpassage.* New York: Macmillan, 1939.

———. *A Basic History of the United States.* New York: Doubleday, 1944.

———. "Culture and Agriculture," *Saturday Review,* 5 (October 20, 1928), 272–273.

———. *The Rise of American Civilization.* New York: Macmillan, 1930.

Beard, George. *American Nervousness.* New York: Putnam's, 1881.

"Beauty in Architectural Detail." *Craftsman* 27 (April 1915), 105.

Bebb, E. D. *Nonconformity and Social and Economic Life, 1660–1800.* London: Epworth, 1935.

Beckett, Gladys. "The Handy Woman About the House." *House Beautiful* 59 (January 1926), 70, 93.

Beecher, Henry Ward. *Plain and Pleasant Talk about Fruits, Flowers, and Farming.* New York: Derby & Jackson, 1859.

Beers, Henry Augustin. *A Suburban Pastoral and Other Tales.* New York: Holt, 1894.

Bidwell, Percy Wells. "Rural Economy in New England at the Beginning of the Nineteenth Century." *Transactions of the Connecticut Academy of Arts and Sciences* 20 (April 1916), 241–399.

Bidwell, Percy Wells, and John I. Falconer. *History of Agriculture in the Northern United States, 1620–1860.* Washington: Carnegie, 1925.

Billington, Ray Allen. *The Far Western Frontier, 1830–1860.* New York: Harper, 1956.

Binford, Henry C. *The First Suburbs: Residential Communities on the Boston Periphery, 1815 to 1860.* Chicago: Univ. of Chicago Press, 1985.

Blane, W. N. *An Excursion Through the United States and Canada During the Years 1822–1823.* London: Baldwin, 1824.

Bloomfield, Edward H. *The Opposition to the English Separatists, 1570 to 1625.* Washington, D.C.: Univ. Press of America, 1981.

Bodo, John R. *The Protestant Clergy and Public Issues, 1812–1848.* Princeton: Princeton Univ. Press, 1954.

Book of Pictures in Roland Park. Baltimore: Munder, 1911.

Bookwalter, John W. *Rural Versus Urban: Their Conflict and Its Causes.* New York: Knicker-bocker, 1910.

Boorstin, Daniel J. *The Americans: The Democratic Experience.* New York: Vintage, 1974.

Bowen, Daniel. *A History of Philadelphia.* Philadelphia: Bowen, 1839.

Bowers, William L. *The Country-Life Movement in America, 1900–1920.* Port Washington, N.Y.: Kennikat, 1974.

Boyer, Paul S. *Urban Masses and Moral Order in America, 1820–1920.* Cambridge: Harvard Univ. Press, 1978.

"Boys and Girls: An Invitation." *Antiques* 1 (June 1922), 243.

Bozeman, Theodore Dwight. "The Puritans' 'Errand into the Wilderness' Reconsidered." *New England Quarterly* 59 (June 1986), 231–251.

Brackett, J. Q. A. "Address." *Annual Report of the Massachusetts Board of Agriculture [1887]* 35 (1888), 110–115.

Bradford, William. *Of Plymouth Plantation, 1620–1647,* ed. Samuel Eliot Morison. New York: Random House, 1952.

Bragdon, Claude. "The Making of a Country Home: Hints on External Treatment." *Country Life in America* 2 (September 1902), 172–175.

Brandeis, Julian W. "A Rational Scheme of Living for the Commuter." *Country Life* 20 (August 15, 1911), 22–24.

Braudel, Fernand. *The Structures of Everyday Life: The Limits of the Possible,* trans. Sian Reynolds [1979]. New York: Harper, 1981.

Breck, Joseph. *The Flower-Garden.* Boston: Jewett, 1856.

Bremer, Frederika. *Homes of the New World: Impressions of America,* trans. Mary Howitt. New York: Harper, 1853.

Bridenbaugh, Carl. *Cities in the Wilderness: The First Century of Urban Life in America, 1625–1742.* New York: Ronald, 1938.

Bridges, Amy. *A City in the Republic: Antebellum New York and the Origins of Machine Politics.* New York: Cambridge Univ. Press, 1984.

Brigham, William. "Farming in New England." *Report of the Massachusetts Board of Agriculture* 3 (1856), 327–335.

Bright, Deborah. "Of Mother Nature and Marlboro Men." *Exposure* 23 (Winter 1985), 5–18.

"Bringing an Old New England Home Up to Date." *Craftsman* 29 (November 1915), 180–191.

Brooks, Van Wyck. "The Culture of Industrialism." *Seven Arts* 1 (April 1917), 655–666.

———. "Enterprise." *Seven Arts* 1 (November 1916), 57–60.

———. *Scenes and Portraits: Memories of Childhood and Youth.* New York: Dutton, 1954.

———. *The World of Washington Irving.* Philadelphia: Blakiston, 1944.

———. *The Writer in America.* New York: Dutton, 1953.

Brown, Christopher. *Dutch Landscape: The Early Years: Haarlem and Amsterdam, 1590–1650.* London: National Gallery, 1986.

Brown, Elizabeth Stow. *The History of Nutley, Essex County, New Jersey.* Nutley: Women's Public School Auxiliary, 1907.

Brown, Richard D. "The Emergence of Urban Society in Rural Massachusetts, 1760–1820." *Journal of American History* 61 (June 1974), 29–51.

Brunner, Arnold W. "The Influence of Surroundings." *Craftsman* 27 (March 1915), 562.

Bryant, William Cullen, ed. *Picturesque America; or The Land We Live In.* New York: Appleton, 1874.

Buckham, James. *Where Town and Country Meet.* New York: Eaton, 1903.

Buffington, Eugene J. "Making Cities for Workmen." *Harper's Weekly* 53 (May 8, 1909), 15–17.

Bulot, Francis H. "Developing a Restricted Home Community." *American City* 15 (November 1916), 533–535.

Bunner, Henry Cuyler. *Jersey Street and Jersey Lane.* New York: Scribner's, 1896.

———*The Runaway Browns: A Story of Small Stories.* New York: Keppler, 1892.

———. *The Suburban Sage: Stray Notes and Comments on His Simple Life* [1896]. Freeport, N.Y.: Books for Libraries Press, 1969.

Burnett, Vivian. "Four in the Open—Chronicles of a Summer Holiday." *Craftsman* 10 (September 1906), 775–783.

Burroughs, Julian. "The Joy of Edged Tools." *Country Life* 19 (December, "mid-month," 1910), 189–190, cxxxii.

Bushman, Richard L. *From Puritan to Yankee: Character and the Social Order in Connecticut, 1690–1765.* Cambridge: Harvard Univ. Press, 1967.

Bushnell, George D. "When Chicago was Wheel Crazy." *Chicago History* 4 (Fall 1975), 167–175.

Bushnell, Horace. "The Age of Homespun." *Litchfield County Centennial Celebration.* Hartford, Conn.: Hunt, 1851, pp. 107–130.

"Cabot's Shingle Stains." *House Beautiful* 23 (May 1908), xi.

Caldwell, Charles, "Thoughts on the Moral and Other Indirect Influences of Rail-Roads." *The New-England Magazine* 2 (April 1832), 288–300.

"Cambridge as a Place of Residence." Cambridge [Mass] *Chronicle* 2 (January 19, 1856), 2.

"Camp Meeting." *Gleason's Drawing Room Companion* 3 (September 11, 1852), 176.

Caparn, H. A. "Parallelogram Park—Suburban Life by the Square Mile." *Craftsman* 10 (September 1906), 767–774.

Carmichael, T. J. "Why the East Cannot Compete with the West." *Farmer's Cabinet* 11 (September 1846), 62–63.

Carlton, Frank T. "Urban and Rural Life." *Popular Science Monthly* 68 (March 1906), 255–60.

Carrick, Alice Van Leer. *The Next-to-Nothing House.* Boston: Atlantic Monthly, 1922.

Carver, T. N. "Life in the Corn Belt." *World's Work* 7 (December 1903), 4232–4329.

Cary, Alice. *Clovernook; Or, Recollections of Our Neighborhood in the West.* New York: Redfield, 1852.

———. *Clovernook Tales.* 2d ser. New York: Redfield, 1852.

"Causes of the Embarrassments of Farmers." *New England Farmer* 21 (July 13, 1842), 10.

"Causes of Fire." *New England Farmer* 4 (December 30, 1825), 184.

Chamberlin, Everett. *Chicago and Its Suburbs.* Chicago: Hungerford, 1874.

Chapin, E. H. *Moral Aspects of City Life*. New York: Lyon, 1853.

Charlesworth, Edward A., and Ronald G. Nathan. *Stress Management: A Comprehensive Guide to Wellness*. New York: Atheneum, 1984.

Chaucer, Geoffrey. *Works,* ed. Alfred W. Pollard. London: Macmillan, 1906.

Chelsea [Mass.] Fire Department. *First Annual Report*. Chelsea: *Citizen* Office, 1858.

Cheney, Charles H. "Zoning in Practice." *National Municipal Review* 9 (January 1920), 31–43.

Clancy, Eugene A. "The Car and the Country Home." *Harper's Weekly* 55 (May 6, 1911), 30.

Clark, Francis E. "Why I Chose a Suburban Home." *Surburban Life* 4 (April 1907), 189.

Clark, Grace McKenzie. "Twenty Miles from Boston." *Surburban Life* 7 (February 1910), 75–76, 81.

Cobbett, William. *A Year's Residence in the United States*. London: Chapman and Dodd, [1819?].

Coburn, Frederick. "The Five Hundred-Mile City." *World Today* 11 (December 1906), 1251–1260.

Coffin, Robert Barry. *Out of Town: A Rural Episode*. New York: Hurd, 1866.

Cole, F. E. M. "Chicago's Most Unique Suburb." *Suburban Life* 5 (November 1907), 283.

Colman, Henry. "Address." *New England Farmer* 10 (May 23, 1832), 356–357.

———. *Fourth Report of the Agriculture of Massachusetts: Counties of Franklin and Middlesex*. Boston: Dutton and Wentworth, 1841.

"Color of City Houses." *Western Horticultural Review* 1 (January 1851), 153–155.

Commanger, Henry Steel. *The American Mind: An Interpretation of American Thought and Character Since the 1880s*. New Haven: Yale Univ. Press, 1950.

"Complete Country Residence." *Register of Rural Affairs* 4 (1858), 21–35.

Conant-Ball Company. "The Colonial Touch in the Modern Home." *American Home* 4 (April 1930), 78.

Condie, Thomas and Richard Folwell. *History of the Pestilence, Commonly Called Yellow Fever, Which Almost Desolated Philadelphia in . . . 1798*. Philadelphia: Folwell, 1799.

Condon, George E. *Cleveland: The Best Kept Secret*. Garden City, N.Y.: Doubleday, 1967.

"Consumption." *New England Farmer* 1 (April 5, 1823), 283.

"Contemporary Suburban Residence." *Architectural Record* 11 (January 1902), 69–81.

Cooper, James Fenimore. *Notions of the Americans Picked Up by a Travelling Bachelor* [1828]. New York: Ungar, 1963.

Cooper, Susan Fenimore. *The Rhyme and Reason of Country Life; or, Selections from Fields Old and New*. New York: Putnam, 1855.

———. *Rural Hours*. [1850; rev. ed. 1887], ed. David Jones. Syracuse, N.Y.: Syracuse Univ. Press, 1968.

"Cottage at Nutley, New Jersey." *Scientific American* 76 (June 19, 1897), 395.

Coulanges, Fustel De. *The Ancient City* [1864], trans. Willard Small. Garden City, New York: Doubleday, n.d.

Coultas, Harland. "Observations on the Growth of Trees." *Godey's Lady's Book* 59 (October 1859), 344–347.

"Country Houses on the Hudson River." *American Agriculturist* 10 (November 1851), 331.

"Country Residences—A New Plan." *Western Horticultural Review* 1 (May 1851), 404–406.

Cowley, Malcolm. *Exile's Return: A Literary Odyssey of the 1920s* [1934; rev. ed. 1951]. New York: Viking, 1969.

Coyle, David Cushman. "Twilight of National Planning." *Harper's* 171 (October 1935), 557–567.

Cozzens, Frederick S. "The Sparrowgrass Papers, or Living in the Country." *Putnam's* 6 (August–December 1855), 166–169, 299–304, 392–395, 505–508, 629–632; 7 (February–March 1856), 166–169, 295–300.

Crane, Jacob L. "Planning Suburban Towns." *City Planning* 3 (October 1927), 263–270.

Crawford, Mary Caroline. "One Hundred Years." *The Epicure* 65 (May 1931), 45–52.

Creese, Walter L. *The Search for Environment: The Garden City: Before and After*. New Haven: Yale Univ. Press, 1966.

Crothers, Samuel McChord. "A Social Survey of the Literary Slums." *Atlantic Monthly* 140 (September 1927), 318–327.

Cruger, Mary. *How She Did It: or, Comfort on $150 a Year*. New York: Appleton, 1888.

"Culture of Sumach." *American Agriculturist* 2 (October 16, 1843), 239–240.

Curtiss, Philip. "They Are Moving to the Country." *Harper's* 171 (June 1935), 67–79.

Cushing, John D. "Town Commons of New England, 1640–1840." *Old-Time New England* 50 (1961), 86–94.

Cutting, Mary Stewart. *The Suburban Whirl*. New York: McClure, 1907.

Danhof, Clarence H. *Change in Agriculture: The Northern United States, 1820–1870*. Cambridge: Harvard Univ. Press, 1969.

Daniels, Howard. "Villa Parks." *Horticulturist* 13 (November 1858), 495–496.

Darby, William. *A Tour from the City of New York, to Detroit* [1819]. Chicago: Quadrangle, 1962.

Davenport, F. Garvin. "The Sanitation Revolution in Illinois, 1870–1890." *Journal of the Illinois State Historical Society* 66 (Autumn 1973), 306–326.

Davidson, Donald. *The Attack on Leviathan: Regionalism and Nationalism in the United States* [1938]. Gloucester, Mass.: Peter Smith, 1962.

Davies, Jane B. "Llewellyn Park in West Orange, New Jersey." *Antiques* 107 (January 1975), 142–158.

Davis, Alexander Jackson. *Rural Residences* [1838], ed. Jane B. Davies. New York: DaCapo, 1980.

Davis, R. H. "Our Suburban Friends." *Harper's* 89 (June 1894), 155–157.

Day, Sherman. *Historical Collections of the State of Pennsylvania*. Philadelphia: Gorton, 1843.

"Day in Westchester County." *American Agriculturist* 10 (January 1851), 31–32.

Dearborn, Henry Alexander Scammel. *Address Delivered before the Massachusetts Horticultural Society on the Celebration of their First Anniversary*. Boston: Burlington, 1833.

Dearborn, Ned. "Bird Houses and How to Build Them." *Craftsman* 27 (November 1914), 216–220.

"Deleterious Effects of Brick-yards." *Farmer's Cabinet* 11 (December 1846), 151–152.

"Democratic Principle." *The United States Magazine and Democratic Review* 1 (October–December 1837), 1–15.

"Design for a Partially Enclosed Veranda." *Horticulturist* 7 (September 1857), 423–424.

"Design for a Suburban Cottage." *The Horticulturist* 3 (May 1849), 520–522.

"Desperate Plight of New York." *Century* 62 (October 1901), 951–954.

"Destroy Your Weeds." *Farmer's Cabinet* 4 (August 1839), 34.

"Development of Character." *American Agriculturist* 1 (June 1842), 80.

Diggs, Annie L. "An English Garden City." *Cosmopolitan* 35 (June 1903), 190–195.

Doolittle, A. E. "The Cost of a Home in Suburban Baltimore." *Suburban Life* 12 (June 1911), 411.

"Domestic Architecture." *The New-England Magazine* 2 (January 1832), 30–36.

Douglass, Theodora. "Summer Use of the Screen." *Suburban Life* 12 (August 1911), 108.

Downing, Andrew Jackson. *The Architecture of Country Houses*. New York: Appleton, 1850.

———. "Multiplication of Horticultural Societies." *Horticulturist* 2 (July 1847), 9–11.

———. *Rural Essays*. New York: Putnam, 1853.

———. *A Treatise on the Theory and Practice of Landscape Gardening*, 6th ed., ed. Henry Winthrop Sargent. New York: Moore, 1859.

Drake, Samuel Adams. *Historic Fields and Mansions of Middlesex*. Boston: Osgood, 1874.

"Dress." *The New-England Magazine* 2 (June 1832), 452–453.

Durand, L. "Grounds for Farm Houses." *Horticulturist* 7 (May 1857), 56–68.

Dwight, H. G. "Gardens and Gardeners." *Atlantic Monthly* 110 (July 1912), 61–68.

Dwight, Timothy. *Greenfield Hill.* New York: Childs & Swain, 1794.

———. "Greenfield Hill" [excerpt], *American Monthly Magazine* 1 (June 1829), 162–163.

———. *Travels in New England and New York,* ed. Barbara Miller Solomon [1822]. Cambridge: Harvard Univ. Press, 1969.

Eaton, Florence Taft. "Equipping the Toolhouse." *House Beautiful* 59 (June 1926), 801, 838.

Eberlein, Harold Donaldson, and Cortlandt Van Dyke Hubbard. *Portrait of a Colonial City: Philadelphia, 1670–1838.* Philadelphia: Lippincott, n.d.

Ebner, Michael H. " 'In the Suburbs of Town' : Chicago's North Shore to 1871." *Chicago History* 11 (Summer 1982), 66–77.

"Economic Cultivation." *The Plough, the Loom, and the Anvil* 8 (July 1855), 21.

"Editor's Easy Chair." *Harper's New Monthly Magazine* 8 (June 1853), 129–130.

"Effects of the Fire upon Real Estate." *Lakeside Monthly* 8 (October 1872), 260–264.

Egleston, Nathaniel Hillyer. *Villages and Village Life, with Hints for Their Improvement.* New York: Harper, 1878.

Ehrlich, Heyward. "The 'Mysteries' of Philadelphia: Lippard's *Quaker City* and 'Urban' Gothic." *ESQ: A Journal of the American Renaissance* 18 (January 1972), 50–59.

"Eight Houses for Modern Living." *Life* 5 (September 26, 1938), 45–67.

Elliott, R. F. "Paint for Buildings." *Western Horticultural Review* 2 (May 1852), 381.

Embury, Aymar. "Co-Operative Building." *House Beautiful* 33 (March 1916), 116–118.

Emerson, Ralph Waldo. *Early Lectures,* ed. Robert E. Spiller et al. Cambridge: Harvard Univ. Press, 1972.

"Environs of Cincinnati." *Western Horticultural Review* 2 (June 1852), 399–400.

Evans, John. *History of All Christian Sects . . . Revised by an American Editor.* New York: Burgess, 1844.

"Exhortation." *Farmer's Cabinet* 4 (July, 1840), 380.

Fahey, John. *The Inland Empire: Unfolding Years, 1879–1929.* Seattle: Univ. of Washington Press. 1986.

Faragher, John Mack. *Sugar Creek: Life on the Illinois Prairie.* New Haven: Yale Univ. Press, 1986.

"Farm Houses." *American Journal of Agriculture and Science* 9 (November 1847), 286.

"Farm of G. G. Howland, Esq." *American Agriculturist* 2 (October 1843), 196–198.

"Farmer Snug and Farmer Slack." *American Agriculturist* 10 (December 1851), 366–367.

"Farmer and Storekeeper." *Rural Repository* 7 (August 14, 1830), 47.

"Farming and Gardening on Long Island." *American Agriculturist* 2 (September 1843), 162–163.

"Farming Life in New England." *Atlantic Monthly* 2 (August 1858), 334–341.

"Farms, Farm Houses, Water." *New England Farmer* 1 (June 7, 1823), 353–354.

Farrington, E. I. "Poultry-Yard Patriotism." *Countryside* 24 (June 1917), 316.

Fawcett, Waldon. "Roland Park, Baltimore County, Maryland: A Representative American Suburb." *House and Garden* 3 (April 1903), 174–196.

———. "Suburban Life in America." *Cosmopolitan* 35 (July 1903), 308–316.

Fellmann, Jerome. "Pre-Building Growth Patterns of Chicago." *Annals of the Association of American Geographers* 47 (March 1957), 59–82.

Ferris, G. T. "Suburban." *Harper's Weekly* 36 (January 9, 1892), 30–31.

Field, Henry. "Shenandoah: The Best Type of Iowa's Small Towns." *Suburban Life* 8 (January 1910), 12–13.

"Fire." *New England Farmer* 3 (November 5, 1824), 120.

Fisher, Herbert W. "Ten Commandments of Health." *Country Life* 20 (August 15, 1911), 25–26.

Fisher, Sidney. *A Philadelphia Perspective . . . Diary,* ed. Nicholas B. Wainwright. Philadelphia: Historical Society of Pennsylvania, 1967.

Fitzgerald, F. Scott. *The Great Gatsby* [1925]. New York: Scribner's, 1953.

Flagg, Wilson. "The Birches." *Magazine of Horticulture* 23 (February 1857), 62–66.

———. "The Cherries." *Magazine of Horticulture* 23 (March 1857), 131–135.

———. "The Elm." *Magazine of Horticulture* 23 (January 1857). 27–32.

———. "The Field and the Garden." *Atlantic Monthly* 28 (September 1871), 268–271.

———. *Halcyon Days.* Boston: Estes and Lauriat, 1881.

———. "Landscape." *Magazine of Horticulture* 23 (September–October 1857), 389–395, 438–444.

———. "The Maples." *Magazine of Horticulture* 23 (September 1853), 403–407.

———. "The Oak." *Magazine of Horticulture* 23 (June 1857), 265–269.

———. "The Old and the New." *Magazine of Horticulture* 26 (December 1860), 534–540.

———. "The Poplar." *Magazine of Horticulture* 23 (April, 1857), 170–175.

———. "Spontaneity." *Magazine of Horticulture* 26 (November 1860), 484–491.

———. "Treatment of Landscape." *Magazine of Horticulture* 26 (July 1860), 293–298.

———. *Year Among the Trees: or, The Woods and By-Ways of New England.* Boston: Estes and Lauriat, 1881.

Fleming, Donald. "The Roots of the New Conservation Movement." *Perspectives in American History* 7 (1972), 7–94.

Fletcher, Henry J. "The Doom of the Small Town." *The Forum* 19 (April 1895), 214–222.

"Floral Dictionary." *New England Farmer* 12 (August 21, 1833), 48.

"The Flower Forget-Me-Not." *Rural Repository* 3 (May 12, 1827), 198.

"Flower Gardens." *Annual Register of Rural Affairs* 1 (1856), 35–37.

"The Flower Girl." *Rural Repository* 3 (January 6, 1827), 125.

"Forest Hills Gardens." *American City* 4 (March 1911), 135–136.

"Forest Hills Gardens Sold." *Survey* 48 (May 13, 1922), 257.

Forster, W. "An American in Cheshire." *Cheshire Round* 1 (Autumn 1966), 188–194.

Fowler, John. *Journal of a Tour in the State of New York in the Year 1830.* London: Whittaker, 1831.

Frary, I. T. "Suburban Landscape Planning in Cleveland." *Architectural Record* 21 (April 1918), 371–384.

Frederick, Christine. "Is Suburban Living a Delusion?" *Outlook* 148 (February 22, 1928), 290–291, 313.

French, J. H. *Gazetteer of the State of New York.* Syracuse: Smith, 1860.

Freneau, Philip. *Poems,* ed. Harry Hayden Clark. New York: Hafner, 1968.

Fritts, Frank, and Ralph W. Gwinn. *Fifth Avenue to Farm: A Biological Approach to the Problem of the Survival of our Civilization.* New York: Harper, 1938.

"Frontispiece." *Antiques* 2 (August 1922), 56.

Fryer, Judith. *Felicitous Space: The Imaginative Structures of Edith Wharton and Willa Cather.* Chapel Hill: Univ. of North Carolina Press, 1986.

Gage, Thomas. *History of Rowley.* Boston: Andrews, 1840.

"Garden City Platted by Russell Sage Foundation." *Survey* 25 (November 26, 1910), 309–310.

"Garden in the House." *Craftsman* 28 (July 1915), 389–395.

"Gardening Clothes for the Woman with the Hoe." *Suburban Life* 12 (March 1911), 165.

Garland, Hamlin. *A Son of the Middle Border.* New York: Macmillan, 1917.

"Gas in the Next War." *World's Work* 57 (December 1928), 128–129.

Gaunt, W. "A Modern Utopia? Berlin—The New Germany—The New Movement." *Creative Art* 5 (December 1929), 859–865.

Gavignaud, Genevieve. *La Révolution rurale: essai a partir du cas américain.* Paris: Horvath, 1986.

Gay, Peter. *A Loss of Mastery: Puritan Historians in Colonial America.* New York: Random House, 1968.

Gaylor, Frank W. "If You Can't Get Beef, Eat Poultry." *Craftsman* 27 (December 1914), 326–330.

Geselbracht, Raymond H. "The Ghosts of Andrew Wyeth: The Meaning of Death in the Transcendental Myth of America." *New England Quarterly* 47 (March 1974), 13–29.

Gillespie, Harriet Sisson. "The House One Woman Built for Another." *Countryside* 24 (February 1917), 74–76.

Gilman, Charlotte Perkins. "The Passing of the Home in Great American Cities." *Cosmopolitan* 38 (December 1904), 137–147.

Girdner, John. *Newyorkitis*. New York: Grafton, 1901.

Githens, Alfred Morton. "The Farmhouse Reclaimed." *House and Garden* 12 (June 1910), 216–218, xviii; 13 (July 1910), 14–18.

Glaab, Charles N. *A History of Urban America*. New York: Macmillan, 1967.

"Glance at the Suburbs." *Rural Repository* 8 (February 25, 1832), 156–157.

Glazier, Willard. *Peculiarities of American Cities*. Philadelphia: Hubbard, 1884.

Gloag, John. "Wood or Metal?" *Creative Arts* 4 (January 1929), 49–50.

Godley, John Robert. *Letters from America*. London: Murray, 1844.

"Good and Bad Farming." *Farmer's Cabinet* 12 (August 1847), 29–30.

Goodman, Paul. "Ethics and Enterprise: The Values of the Boston Elite, 1800–1860." *American Quarterly* 18 (Fall 1966), 437–451.

Goodwin, G. D. "Commuter's Wife." *Good Housekeeping* 49 (October 1909), 362–366.

Gookins, S. B. "Culture of Rural Taste." *Horticultural Review* 4 (March [?] 1854), 104–111.

Gordon, Thomas F. *Gazetteer of the State of New York*. Philadelphia: author, 1836.

———. *History of New Jersey*. Trenton: Fenton, 1834.

Goss, Charles Frederic. *Cincinnati: The Queen City, 1788–1912*. Chicago: Clarke, 1912.

Gowans, Alan. *The Comfortable House: North American Suburban Architecture, 1890–1930*. Cambridge: MIT Press, 1986.

Graves, Louis. "A 'Model Village' Run on Business Principles." *Building Progress* 1 (July 1911), 210–215.

———. "A 'Model Village' Under Way." *Building Progress* 2 (January 1912), 18–24.

Gray, J. C. "The New American Orchardist." *North American Review* 47 (October 1838), 423–451.

Gray, John C. "Review of *Sylva Americana*." *North American Review* 44 (April 1837), 334–361.

Greeley, Horace. *What I Know of Farming*. New York: Carleton, 1871.

Greenwood, Francis W. P. *A Sermon on the Death of John Lowell*. Boston: Little and Brown, 1840.

Greve, Charles Theodore. *Centennial History of Cincinnati*. Chicago: Biographical Publishing, 1904.

Grey, Elmer. "The New Suburb of the Pacific Coast." *Scribner's* 52 (July 1912), 36–51.

Griffith, Ernest S. *A History of American City Government: The Conspicuous Failure, 1870–1900*. New York: Praeger, 1974.

Griffith, Ira S. "Handy Man About the House." *Suburban Life* 10 (October 1910), 390.

"Growth of Cities in the United States." *Harper's* 7 (July 1853), 171–175.

Haberman, Ian S. *The Van Sweringens of Cleveland: The Biography of an Empire*. Cleveland: Western Reserve Historical Society, 1979.

Hale, Sarah Josepha. *Flora's Interpreter and Fortuna Flora* [1832[, rev. ed. Boston: Mussey, 1852.

"Half an Acre." *American Agriculturist* 16 (January, 1857), 14–15.

Haliburton, Thomas Chandler. *Nature and Human Nature*. London: Hurst & Blackett, 1855.

Hall, Sarah. "Reminiscences of Philadelphia." *The Philadelphia Book: or, Specimens of Metropolitan Literature*, pp. 278–287. Philadelphia: Key and Biddle, 1836.

Halttunen, Karen. *Confidence Men and Painted Women: A Study of Middle-Class Culture in America, 1830–1870*. New Haven: Yale Univ. Press, 1982.

Hancock, William. *An Emigrant's Five Years in the Free States of America.* London: Newby, 1860.

Handlin, Oscar. *The Uprooted.* Boston: Little, Brown, 1951.

Harland, Marion. "Home-Made Efficiency." *Countryside* 24 (June 1917), 317–318.

Harmond, Richard. "Progress and Flight: An Interpretation of the American Cycle Craze of the 1890s." *Journal of Social History* 5 (1971/1972), 235–257.

Harold, John. "Cultivation of Asparagus for the New York Market." *Report of the Commissioner of Patents for the Year 1861, Agriculture.* Washington, D. C., 1862.

Harris, Neil. *The Artist in American Society: The Formative Years, 1790–1860.* New York: George Braziller, 1966.

Hart, Liddell. "Would Another War End Civilization?" *Harper's* 170 (February 1935), 313–322.

Hartt, Mary Bronson. "Beautifying the Ugly Things." *World's Work* 9 (February 1905), 5859–5868.

Hatfield, T. D. "The Long-Lived Hardy Evergreens." *Country Life* 12 (January 1907), 308.

Hawes, Louis. *Presences of Nature: British Landscape, 1780–1830.* New Haven: Yale Univ. Press, 1982.

Hawthorne, Nathaniel. *English Note-Books.* Boston: Osgood, 1871.
———. *Our Old Home* [1863]. Boston: Houghton, 1898.
———. *The Scarlet Letter* [1850]. Boston: Houghton, 1883.
———. *Twice-Told Tales* [1851]. Boston: Houghton, 1882.

Haxton, Fred. "Why People Left the City." *Suburban Life* 12 (April 1911), 266.

Hayden, Dolores. *The Grand Domestic Revolution: A History of Feminist Designs for American Homes, Neighborhoods, and Cities.* Cambridge: MIT Press, 1981.

Hazard, Lucy Lockwood. *The Frontier in American Literature.* New York: Barnes & Noble, 1941.

Henretta, James A. "Families and Farms: Mentalite in Pre-Industrial America." *William and Mary Quarterly* 35, 3d ser. (January 1978), 3–32.

The Heritage of the Shakers. Cleveland: Van Sweringen Co., 1923.

Hentz, Caroline Lee. *Lovell's Folly: A Novel.* Cincinnati: Hubbard, 1833.

"Hick's Hardy Evergreens." *Countryside* 23 (September 1916), 146.

"Higher Values and Profits Through Modernization." *National Real Estate Journal* 36 (April 20, 1935), 17–30.

"Hill Dryer Co." *Suburban Life* 3 (October 1906), 196.

"History and Incidents of the Plague in New Orleans." *Harper's Monthly* 7 (November 1853), 797–806.

Hitchcock, A. P. "The Joys of Being a Farmer." *Country Life* 20 (July 1, 1911), 46–52.

Hodgins, Eric. *Mr. Blandings Builds His Dream House.* New York: Simon and Schuster, 1946.

Holly, Henry Hudson. *Country Seats.* New York: Appleton, 1863.
———. "Modern Dwellings: Their Construction, Decoration, and Future." *Harper's Monthly* 52 (May 1876), 855–867.

Home Book of the Picturesque. New York: Putnam, n.d.

Hooker, Thomas. *The Application of Redemption: The Ninth and Tenth Books.* London: Peter Cole, 1659.

Hoopes, James. *Van Wyck Brooks: In Search of American Culture.* Amherst: Univ. of Massachusetts Press, 1977.

"Horticulture." *American Quarterly Review* 21 (June 1837), 364–378.

Hoskins, W. G. "An Elizabethan Provincial Town: Leicester." *Studies in Social History: A Tribute to G. M. Trevelyan,* ed. J. H. Plumb. London: Longmans, 1955.

Hovey, C. M. "Our Ornamental Trees." *Magazine of Horticulture* 23 (March 1857), 135–137.
———. "The Virginia Fringe Tree." *Magazine of Horticulture* 23 (January 1857), 33–35.

"How to Build a Greenhouse." *Ladies' Home Journal* 7 (July 1890), 24–25.

"How to Cool a Hot Porch." *House Beautiful* 19 (May 1906), 38; (June 1906), 28.

"How to Protect Yourself When Buying a Home." *American Magazine* 85 (June 1918), 120–122.

Howard, Horton. *An Improved System of Botanic Medicine.* Columbus: author, 1832.

Howard, Joseph. *Life of Henry Ward Beecher.* Philadelphia: Hubbard, 1887.

Howard, L. O. "The Menacing Mosquito." *Country Life* 20 (August 15, 1911), 29–30.

Howe, Frederick C. *The City: The Hope of Democracy.* New York: Scribner's, 1906.

———. "Dusseldorf: A City of Tomorrow." *Hampton's Magazine* 25 (December 1910), 697–709.

———. "The Garden Cities of England." *Scribner's* 52 (July 1912), 1–19.

———. "The German and the American City." *Scribner's* 49 (April 1911), 485–492.

———. "Industrial Villages in America." *Garden City* 1 (July 1906), 142.

———. "A Way Toward the Model City." *Harper's* 27 (July 1913), 186–197.

Howe, John R., Jr. *The Changing Political Thought of John Adams.* Princeton Univ. Press, 1966.

Howe, Samuel. "Town Planning on a Large Scale." *House Beautiful* 36 (October 1914), 130–136.

Howells, William Dean. *A Hazard of New Fortunes.* New York: Harper, 1889.

———. *Suburban Sketches* [1898]. Freeport, New York: Books for Libraries Press, 1969.

Hoyt, Helen. "The Haystack Loaves." *Countryside* 24 (July 1917), 367.

Hoyt, Homer. *One Hundred Years of Land Values in Chicago.* Chicago: Univ. of Illinois Press, 1933.

———. *The Structure and Growth of Residential Neighborhoods in American Cities.* Washington: Government Printing Office, 1939.

Hubbard, E. "Commuter Country, 1837." *Cheshire Round* 1 (Autumn 1966), 185–187, 194.

Hunter, Ethel A. "Relics of an Independent Way of Life: The Ten-Footers of New England." *The New England Galaxy*, ed. Roger Parks. Chester, Conn.: Globe, 1980.

Hurd, Richard M. *Principles of City Planning.* New York: Record & Guide, 1903.

Hutchinson, Woods. "How Doth the Little Bug Fly." *Country Life* 20 (August 15, 1911), 31–32.

Hutton, Laurence. "Henry Cuyler Bunner." *The Bookman* 3 (July 1896), 398–402.

"Improving and Planting Grounds." *Register of Rural Affairs for 1855* 1 (1855), 32–42.

"Improving Old Houses." *Register of Rural Affairs* 1 (1856), 29–31.

"In Praise of the Eighteenth Century." *Atlantic* 86 (November 1900), 717–718.

"In Praise of the Lumber Garret." *American Home Magazine* 1 (January 1897), 14.

"Industrial Experiment at South Manchester." *Harper's* 45 (November 1872), 838–853.

"Influence of Poetry on the Cultivation and Appreciation of Flowers." *Yearbook of Agriculture for 1855–1856.* Philadelphia: Childs and Peterson, 1856.

"Insulting Women in the Streets." *The New York Times* 2 (May 27, 1858), 6.

Jackson, Kenneth. *The Crabgrass Frontier: The Suburbanization of the United States.* New York: Oxford, 1985.

James, Henry. *The American Scene.* New York: Harper, 1907.

Jaques, George. "Landscape Gardening in New-England." *Horticulturist* 7 (January 1852), 33–37.

Jensen, Gerard E. *The Life and Letters of Henry Cuyler Bunner.* Durham: Duke Univ. Press, 1939.

Johnson, Henry C. *North Chicago: Its Advantages, Resources, and Probable Future.* Chicago: Johnson, 1873.

Johnson, Ruth P. "Tree Seats and Balconies." *Suburban Life* 4 (April 1907), 205–206.

Johnstone, Paul H. "Turnips and Romanticism." *Agricultural History* 12 (July 1938), 224–255.

Jordan, William G. "What Do Our Children Know? A Challenge to Education." *Collier's* 71 (January 27, 1923), 9.

Josephson, Matthew. "The Frontier and Literature." *New Republic* 68 (September 2, 1931), 77–78.

"Joys of City Life." *Life* 75 (March 4, 1920), 408.

"Judge Quincy's Farm." *New England Farmer* 1 (August 3, 1822), 2–3.

Junius. "Remarks on Rural Scenery: The Cottage Garden." *American Gardener's Magazine* 1 (March 1835), 104–105.

———. "Remarks on Rural Scenery: The Thatched Cottage." *American Gardener's Magazine* 2 (May 1836), 210–212.

Kahn, Ely Jacques. "The Province of Decoration in Modern Design." *Creative Art* 5 (December 1929), 885–886.

Kaplan, Barry J. "Andrew H. Green and the Creation of a Planning Rationale: The Formation of Greater New York City, 1865–1890." *Urbanism Past and Present* 8 (Summer 1979), 32–34.

Kaplan, Wendy. "R. T. H. Halsey: An Ideology of Collecting American Decorative Arts." *Winterthur Portfolio* 17 (Spring 1982), 43–53.

Kazin, Alfred. *On Native Ground: A Study of American Prose Literature from 1890 to the Present.* Garden City, N.Y.: Doubleday, 1956.

Keats, John. *The Crack in the Picture Window.* Boston: Houghton, 1957.

Keese, John. *The Floral Keepsake for 1850.* New York: Leavitt, 1850.

Kenny, D. J. *Illustrated Cincinnati.* Cincinnati: Clarke, 1875.

Ketcham, William. "The Manures Used upon Long-Island." *New York State Agricultural Society Transactions* 3 (1843), 462–466.

Kirkland, Caroline, ed. *Chicago Yesterdays: A Sheaf of Reminiscences.* Chicago: Daughaday, 1919.

[Kirkland, Caroline.] "Illinois in Spring Time: With a Look at Chicago." *Atlantic* 2 (September 1858), 475–488.

Klaber, John T. "The Garden City of Hellerav: A German Housing Development." *Architectural Record* 35 (February 1914), 151–161.

Knevels, Mary Eastwood. "What the Suburban-Dweller May Learn from a Model Town." *American Homes and Gardens* 12 (February 1915), 38–45.

Knight, Richard Payne. *The Landscape.* London: Bulmer, 1794.

"Kohler of Kohler." *American Home* 3 (June 1930), 351; (September 1930), 540; (October 1930), 71.

"Kohler Village: Every Inch and Every Brick Planned from Beginning." *National Real Estage Journal* 26 (October 19, 1925), 33–37.

Kolodny, Annette. *The Land Before Her: Fantasy and Experience of the American Frontiers, 1630–1860.* Chapel Hill: Univ. of North Carolina Press, 1984.

Kouwenhoven, John A. *Made in America: The Arts in Modern Civilization.* Garden City, N.Y.: Doubleday, 1948.

Krim, Arthur J. "Graphic Landscapes of Massachusetts, 1835–1845." Paper presented at New England College English Association, April 7, 1979.

Lady's Almanac for 1854. Boston: Jewett, 1853.

Lady's Almanac for 1861. Boston: Damrell & Moore, 1860.

Lagerberg, Lars. *New Jersey Architecture: Colonial and Federal.* Springfield, Mass.: Whittum, 1956.

"Landscape-Gardening." *The Crayon* 4 (August 1857), 248.

Lang, Daniel. "Los Alamos." *New Yorker* 24 (April 17, 1948), 76–89.

Langland, William. *Piers Plowman* [1550], ed. Arthur Burrell. London: Dent, 1919.

"Large and Small Farms." *Farmer's Cabinet* 4 (July 1840), 381.

"Laying Out Farms." *Register of Rural Affairs* 3 (1857), 309–314.

Lee, Eliza Buckminster. *Sketches of a New England Village in the Last Century.* Boston: Munroe, 1838.

Lee, Gerald Stanley. "The Dominance of the Crowd." *Atlantic* 86 (December 1900), 754–761.

"Legends of Trees." *Horticulturist* 7 (September 1857), 406–409.

Leggett, Benjamin F. *Out-Door Poems.* New York: Raeburn, 1906.

Lemon, James T. "Early Americans and Their Social Environment." *Journal of Historical Geography* 6 (April 1980), 115–131.

Leuchtenburg, William E. *The Perils of Prosperity, 1914–1932*. Chicago: Univ. of Chicago Press, 1958.

Lewis, G. P. "Long Island Farming." *American Agriculturist* 6 (September, December 1847), 281–372.

Lewis, Sinclair. *Babbitt*. New York: Harcourt, 1924.

Lewis, W. L. "Poison Gas and Pacifists." *Independent* 115 (September 12, 1925), 289–291.

"Life Houses." *Life* 5 (December 12, 1938), 36–38.

Lincoln, Almira H [Phelps]. *Familiar Lectures on Botany* [1829]. New York: Huntington, 1841.

Lincoln, Enoch. *The Village*. Portland: Little, 1816.

Lincoln, Joseph C. *Cap'n Eri: A Story of the Coast*. New York: Burt, 1904.

"Lines Written on Prospect Hill." *Rural Repository* 3 (June 10, 1826), 8.

Lippard, George. *The Monks of Monk Hall* [1844]. New York: Odyssey, 1970.

"Liquid Manure." *New England Farmer* 1 (September 7, 1822), 44.

"Llewellyn Park." *Every Saturday* 3 (September 2, 1871), 227.

Lockwood, Alice G. B. *Gardens of Colony and State*. New York: Scribner's, 1931.

London, Jack. "The Story of an Eye Witness." *Collier's* 37 (May 5, 1906), 22–26.

"Long Island Farming." *American Agriculturist* 6 (September 1847), 278–279.

"Look to Your Weeds." *Farmer's Cabinet* 4 (September 1839), 65.

Lossing, Benson J. "Arlington House: The Seat of G. W. P. Curtis, Esq." *Harper's* 7 (September 1853), 433–454.

Lowenthal, Max. "The Case of the Missouri Pacific." *Harper's* 170 (December 1934), 87–98.

Luitwieler, C. S. "An Old Settler." *Photo-Era* 5 (August 1911), 29.

McComb, Samuel. "Nervousness—A National Menace." *Everybody's Magazine* 22 (February 1910), 258–264.

McCrea, A. E. "Color Harmony and Discord." *Suburban Life* 4 (May 1907), 311–312.

McCullough, David. *Brooklyn—And How It Got that Way*. New York: Dial, 1983.

Macdonald, A. B. "Home District Beautiful." *Ladies' Home Journal* 38 (February 1921), 12–13.

McFarland, J. Horace. "My Growing Garden." *Surburban Life* 21 (August 1915), 64–66, 98.

Mackenzie, Alexander Slidell. *The American In England*. London: Bentley, 1836.

McLaughlin, James. "Transplanting Large Trees." *Suburban Life* 21 (November 1915), 273, 280.

McLeod, Ward. "Planting to the Best Advantage." *Suburban Life* 4 (April 1907), 222–224.

McManus, Otile. "The Madding Crowd Is Us." *Boston Globe Magazine* 231 (November 30, 1986), 18–19, 92–96.

Manning, Warren H. "The History of Village Improvement in the United States." *Craftsman* 5 (February 1904), 423–435.

———. "A National Plan Study Brief." *Landscape Architecture* 13 (July 1923), 2–24.

———. *Suggestions for Beautifying the Home, Village, and Roadway*. Philadelphia: American Civic Association, 1910.

"Map of the Property of the Shaker Heights Improvement Company." Cleveland: Van Sweringen Co., 1914.

March, Ada. "Fences in Towns and Villages." *American Homes and Gardens* 5 (March 1908), 93.

Marchand, Roland. *Advertising the American Dream: Making Way for Modernity, 1920 to 1940*. Berkeley: Univ. of California Press, 1985.

Marks, Bayly Ellen. "Rural Response to Urban Penetration: Baltimore and St. Mary's County, Maryland, 1790–1840." *Journal of Historical Geography* 8 (April 1982), 113–127.

Marsh, Margaret Sammartino. "Suburbanization and the Search for Community: Residential Decentralization in Philadelphia, 1880 to 1900." *Pennsylvania History* 44 (April 1977), 99–116.

Martyn, Payne. "The Era of the Motor Boat." *Country Life* 12 (June 1907), 187–189, 230.

Martyn, S. T. [Mrs.]. "How to Make a Happy Home." *The Ladies' Wreath* 9 (1847), 221–226.

Marx, Leo. *The Machine in the Garden: Technology and the Pastoral Ideal in America*. New York: Oxford, 1964.

Masotti, Louis, and Jeffrey Haddon, eds. *Urbanization of the Suburbs*. Beverly Hills: Sage, 1973.

Mather, Cotton. *Magnalia Christi Americana; or, The Ecclesiastical History of New-England* [1702]. Hartford: Silas Andrus, 1855.

Mather, William G. "Littleton: The Story of an American Village." *Harper's* 170 (January 1935), 199–208.

Mathews, H. W. "Montclair the Beautiful." *Suburban Life* 4 (May 1907), 267–271.

———. "Mount Vernon—A Suburban City." *Suburban Life* 5 (July 1907), 16–18.

Maxwell, A. M. *A Run Through the United States During the Autumn of 1840*. London: Colburn, 1841.

Maxwell, M. M. "Lack of Privacy in the American Home." *Living Age* 269 (May 20 1911), 451–456.

Maxwell, Sidney D. *The Suburbs of Cincinnati*. Cincinnati: Stevens, 1870.

May, Charles C. "Forest Hills Gardens from the Town Planning Viewpoint." *Architecture* 34 (August 1916), 161–181.

———. "Indian Hill: An Industrial Village at Worcester, Massachusetts." *Architectural Record* 41 (January 1917), 20–35.

Mays, James O'Donald. *Mr. Hawthorne Goes to England: The Adventures of a Reluctant Diplomat*. Ringwood, Eng.: New Forest Leaves, 1983.

Mead, Sidney E. *The Lively Experiment: The Shaping of Christianity in America*. New York: Harper & Row, 1963.

"The Mechanick." *Rural Repository* 6 (June 20, 1829), 15.

Melville, Herman. *Great Short Works*, ed. Warner Berthoff. New York: Harper and Row, 1970.

———. *Redburn: His First Voyage* [1849]. Evanston: Northwestern Univ. Press, 1969.

Meyer, William E., Jr. "The American Religion of Vision." *Christian Century* 100 (November 16, 1983), 1045–1047.

"Middle Class Threatened." Quincy [Mass.] *Patriot Ledger* 150 (December 10, 1986), 51.

Milgram, Stanley. "The Experience of Living in Cities." *Science* 167 (March 13, 1970), 1461–1468.

Miller, Perry. *Errand into the Wilderness* [1956]. New York: Harper, 1964.

———. *Orthodoxy in Massachusetts, 1630–1650* [1933]. New York: Harper, 1970.

Miller, Roger, and Joseph Siry. "The Emerging Suburb: West Philadelphia, 1850–1880." *Pennsylvania History* 47 (April 1980), 99–145.

Minton, Arthur. "Names of Real Estate Developments." *Names* 7 (September 1959), 129–153; (December 1959), 235–255; 9 (March 1961), 6–36.

"Mission of Country Life Magazines." *Suburban Life* 1 (August 1905).

"Mistakes of Suburbans." Cambridge [Mass.] *Chronicle* 9 (September 9, 1854), 2.

Mitchell, Cornelius B. "Trees in City Streets." *Municipal Affairs* 111 (December 1899), 691–693.

Mitchell, Donald G. *My Farm of Edgewood: A Country Book*. New York: Scribner, 1863.

———. "The Farmer's Homestead and Its Relation to Farm Thrift." *Agriculture of Massachusetts* 25 (1877), 131–141.

"Modern Farmer." *Farmer's Cabinet* 12 (September, 1847), 47–48.

Monchow, Helen Corbin. *Seventy Years of Real Estate Subdividing in the Region of Chicago*. Evanston: Northwestern Univ. Press, 1939.

———. *The Use of Deed Restriction in Subdivision Development*. Chicago: Institute for Research, 1928.

Monroe, James P. "Elias Phinney." *Proceedings of the Lexington Historical Society* 2 (April 1890), 65–84.

Moore, Charles C. "Materials for Landscape Art in America." *Atlantic* 64 (November 1889), 670–681.

"Moral Influence of Gardening." *Western Horticultural Review* 1 (November 1850), 103–104.

Morgan, Edmund S. *The Puritan Dilemma: The Story of John Winthrop.* Boston: Little, Brown, 1958.

Morrow, Lance. "Downsizing the American Dream." *Time* 42 (October 5, 1981), 95–96.

Morse, Frances Clary. *Furniture of the Olden Time.* New York: Macmillan, 1902.

"Mosquito Window Screens." *Year-Book of Agriculture for 1855 and 1856.* Philadelphia: Childs & Peterson, 1856.

Mowbray, J. P. *A Journey to Nature.* New York: Doubleday, 1901.

"Mr. Willis's Prose." *American Monthly Magazine* 2 (October 1836), 347–356.

"Mrs. Sage Gives Church." *New York Times* 64 (October 7, 1915), 4.

Muir, Richard. *The English Village.* New York: Thames & Hudson, 1980.

Muirhead, James F. "Some Recent Books on the United States." *Atlantic* 100 (October 1907), 553–568.

Mullen, John R. "American Perceptions of German City Planning at the Turn of the Century." *Urbanism Past and Present* 3 (Winter 1976–77), 5–15.

Mumford, Lewis. "The Economics of Contemporary Decoration." *Creative Art* 4 (January 1929), xix-xxii.

———. *The Golden Day: A Study in American Experience and Culture.* New York: Boni & Liveright, 1926.

———. *Green Memories: The Story of Geddes Mumford.* New York: Harcourt, 1947.

———. "The Intolerable City: Must It Keep on Growing?" *Harper's* 152 (February 1926), 283–293.

———. *Sticks and Stones: A Study of American Architecture and Civilization.* New York: Boni & Liveright, 1924.

Nash, Roderick. *Wilderness and the American Mind.* New Haven: Yale Univ. Press, 1967.

Nashe, Thomas. "Christ's Teares over Jerusalem" [1593]. In *Works.* London: Bullen, 1904.

"Nature as a Landscape Garden." *Craftsman* 28 (June 1915), 255–262.

Nelson, H. L. "The Cheneys' Village at South Manchester, Connecticut." *Harper's Weekly* 34 (February 1, 1890), 87–88.

Neufeldt, Leonard N. "Henry David Thoreau's Political Economy," *New England Quarterly* 57 (September 1984), 359–383.

"New American Orchardist." *North American Review* (May 1838), 447–449.

"New Homes of New York: A Study of Flats." *Scribner's* 8 (May 1874), 63–74.

"New Shelter from Poison Gas Tested in France." *Popular Science* 38 (October 1932), 121.

"New Word: 'Democracy.' " *Craftsman* 27 (January 1915), 451.

"New York Central Park." *Magazine of Horticulture* 26 (December 1860), 529–534.

"New York Revisited." *Harper's Weekly* 55 (July 8, 1911), 11.

Newcomb, Rexford. *The Colonial and Federal House: How to Build an Authentic Colonial House.* Philadelphia: Lippincott, 1933.

"Niagara." *Harper's* 7 (August 1853), 289–305.

Nichols, J. C. "Housing and the Real Estate Problem." *Annals of the American Academy of Political and Social Science* 51 (January 1914), 132–139.

———. "Suburban Subdivisions with Community Features." *American City* 31 (October 1924), 335–338.

Northrop, Birdsley Grant. "The Work of Village Improvement Societies." *Forum* 19 (March 1895), 95–104.

"Notes on Some of the Nurseries and Private Gardens in the Neighborhood of New York" *Magazine of Horticulture* 3 (April 1837), 121–129.

Nutting, Wallace. *Wallace Nutting's Biography*. Framingham, Mass.: Old America, 1936.

———. *Massachusetts Beautiful*. Framingham, Mass.: Old America, 1922.

———. *Pennsylvania Beautiful*. Framingham, Mass.: Old America, 1924.

———. *Photographic Art Secrets*. New York: Dodd, Mead, 1927.

Nygren, Edward J. et al. *Views and Visions: American Landscape Before 1830*. Washington, D.C.: Corcoran Gallery of Art, 1986.

Oberholtzer, Ellis Paxson. *Philadelphia: A History of the City and Its People*. Philadelphia: Clarke, n.d.

Olmsted, Frederick Law, Sr. "Riverside, Illinois." *Landscape Architecture* 21 (July 1931), 257–291.

———. *Riverside: Village in a Park*. Riverside, Ill.: Frederick Law Olmsted Society, 1970.

———. "Village Improvement." *Atlantic* 95 (June 1905), 798–803.

———. *Walks and Talks of an American Farmer in England* [1859], ed. Alex L. Murray. Ann Arbor: Univ. of Michigan Press, n.d.

Olson, Mancur. *The Logic of Collective Action: Public Goods and the Theory of Groups*. Cambridge, Mass.: Harvard Univ. Press, 1965.

"Ornamental Planting." *Register of Rural Affairs for 1856* 2 (1856), 237–239.

"Our Bookshop." *Country Life* 20 (September 15, 1911), 8.

"Our Neglected Poets: William Martin Johnson." *United States Magazine and Democratic Republic* 1 (February 1838), 293–306.

Our Suburbs: A Resume of Their Origins. Chicago: Chicago Times, 1873.

Packard, Winthrop. "Developing a Suburban Colony." *Suburban Life* 9 (January 1905), 7–11.

"Page of Shingled-All-Over Houses." *Suburban Life* 3 (October 1906), 181.

Palfrey, John Gorham. *History of New England*. Boston: Little, Brown, 1876.

Parkman, Francis. *The Book of Roses*. Boston: Talton, 1866.

"Parks Versus Villages." *Horticulturist* 6 (April 1856), 153–155.

Parrington, Vernon Louis. *Main Currents in American Thought*. New York: Harcourt, Brace, 1930.

Parry, B. E. "Study for a Modern Suburban Development." *American City* 31 (August 1924), 146–148.

Partridge, William. "To Our Farmers Who Obtain Manure from the City of New York." *American Agriculturist* 1 (December 1842), 281–282.

Peabody, W. B. O. "American Forest Trees." *North American Review* 35 (October 1832), 399–433.

———. "Rural Architecture in America." *North American Review* 56 (January 1843), 1–17.

Peaceful Shaker Village. Cleveland: Van Sweringen Co., 1927.

Pease, F. A. *Shaker Country Estates and Adjacent Territory* [map]. Cleveland: Pease, n.d.

———. *Shaker Heights* [map]. Cleveland: Pease, 1922.

———. *Shaker Heights for Sale* [map]. Cleveland: Pease, 1922.

Peets, Elbert. "Street Trees in the Built-Up Districts of Large Cities." *Landscape Architecture* 6 (October 1915), 15–31.

Periam, Jonathan and A. H. Baker. *The American Farmer's Pictorial Cyclopedia of Livestock and Complete Livestock Doctor, Embracing Horse, Cattle, Swine, Sheep, and Poultry*. New York: Thompson, 1884.

Perrin, Noel. *Second Person Rural: More Essays of a Sometime Farmer*. Boston: Godine, 1980.

———. *Third Person Rural: Further Essays of a Sometime Farmer*. Boston: Godine, 1983.

Peterson, Elmer T., ed. *Cities Are Abnormal*. Norman: Univ. of Oklahoma Press, 1946.

———. *Forward to the Land*. Norman: Univ. of Oklahoma Press, 1942.

Philadelphia in 1824 [map]. Philadelphia: Carey & Lea, 1824.

Philadelphia in 1830 [map]. Philadelphia: Carey, 1830.

"Pictures to the Editors." *Life* 5 (August 15, 1938), 68.

"The Picturesque in Floriculture." *Magazine of Horticulture* 4 (July 1838), 241–243.

"Piermont." *American Agriculturist* 16 (March 1857), 56.

Pierson, David Lawrence. *History of the Oranges to 1921*. New York: Lewis, 1922.

Pierson, William H., Jr. *American Buildings and Their Architects: Technology and the Picturesque, the Corporate, and the Early Gothic Styles*. Garden City, New York: Doubleday, 1978.

"Pitchfork." *Farmer's Almanac . . . 1840*. Boston: Jenks & Palmer, 1839.

"Planet Jr. Garden Implements." *Countryside* 24 (May 1917), 281.

Platt, Colin. *The English Medieval Town*. New York: David McKay, 1976.

Pocock, J. G. A. "Virtue and Commerce in the Eighteenth Century." *Journal of Interdisciplinary History* 3 (Summer 1972), 119–134.

Poems of Home Life. New York: American Tract Society, ca. 1850.

"Poetry and Profit of City Life." *Prairie Farmer* 10 (January[?] 1850), 18–19.

Pomfret, John. *Poems upon Several Occasions*. London: Cook, 1736.

Pope, Alexander. *Poems*, ed. John Butt. London: Methuen, 1963.

"Porch Shades." *Countryside* 22 (June 1916), 372.

"Port Jefferson: Belle Terre." *Country Life* 15 (April 1909), 574–575.

"Portrait of an Anti-Book Farmer." *Farmer's Cabinet* 12 (December 15, 1847), 154.

Posadas, Barbara M. "A Home in the Country: Suburbanization in Jefferson Township, 1870–1889." *Chicago History* 7 (Fall 1978), 134–149.

Powell, Edward Payson. *Hedges, Windbreaks, Shelters, and Live Fences*. New York: Orange Judd, 1900.

"In Praise of the Lumber Garret." *American Home Magazine* 1 (January 1897), 14.

"President of the Massachusetts Horticultural Society." *Horticulturist* 3 (July 1848), 14–18.

Price, Uvedale. *Essay on the Picturesque*. London: Robson, 1794.

"Privacy." *Harper's Weekly* 49 (January 14, 1905), 46.

"Problem of Pressures in Planning." *Architectural Record* 95 (January 1944), 87–92.

"Proposed Remedy for Stealing Fruit." *Western Horticultural Review* 1 (January 1881), 168.

Quarles, E. A. "Protection of Birds at Forest Hills Gardens." *New York Times* 63 (May 10, 1914), sec. 4, p. 6.

Questions and Answers Regarding Shaker Heights Village. Cleveland: Green-Cadwallader-Long, 1910.

"Railroad Station at Chestnut Hill." *Garden and Forest* 2 (April 3, 1889), 159–160, 163.

Ramsey, Victoria Post. *Olmsted in Chicago*. Chicago: Donnelley, 1972.

Rath, E. J. *The Nervous Wreck*. New York: Grosset & Dunlap, 1923.

———. *Too Much Efficiency*. New York: Watt, 1917.

Rawson, Marion Nicholl. *Forever the Farm*. New York: Dutton, 1939.

Raymond, Arthur I. "A Study in Contrasts." *Suburban Life* 3 (November 1906), 219–220, 245, 246.

"Realtor Experts Give Pointers on Successful Home Building." *National Real Estate Journal* 3 (February 1935), 42–44.

"Recent Houses at Forest Hills Gardens." *Brickbuilder* 25 (May 1916), 139–142.

Reinhardt, Elizabeth W. and Anne A. Grady. "Asher Benjamin in East Lexington, Massachusetts." *Old-Time New England* 67 (Winter–Spring 1977), 23–35.

"Residence of John R. Chapin, Esq." *American Agriculturist* 16 (April 1857), 80.

"Resor's Greenhouse." *Western Horticultural Review* 1 (January 1851), frontispiece.

Richards, T. Addison. "Lake George." *Harper's* 7 (July 1853), 161–170.

———. "The Susquehanna." *Harper's* 7 (October 1853), 613–622.

"Right and Wrong Way of Gardening." *House Beautiful* 46 (July 1919), 38.

Riley, Phil M. "Running the Home Like a Business." *Country Life* 20 (September 15, 1911), 19–22, 66, 68, 70.

Ripley, Hubert G. "The Village That Ought To Be." *House Beautiful* 51 (March 1922), 193–196.

Riverside Improvement Co. *Riverside in 1871: With a Description of Its Improvements.* Chicago, 1871.

Robbins, Mary Caroline. "Village Improvement Societies." *Atlantic* 79 (February 1897), 212–222.

Robert, Brian K. *Village Plans.* Aylesbury: Shire, 1982.

Roberts, Kenneth L. *Antiquamania.* Garden City, N.Y.: Doubleday, 1928.

Robie, Virginia. *The Quest of the Quaint.* Boston: Little, Brown, 1916.

Robinson, Solon. "Day in Westchester County." *American Agriculturist* 10 (January 1851), 31–32.

———. "The Farmer's Errors." *Report of the Massachusetts Board of Agriculture* 3 (1856), 347–362.

Rockwell, F. F. "The War Garden." *Countryside* 24 (July, 1917), 368–369.

"Rockwood." *Western Horticultural Review* 1 (March 1851), 284–287.

"Rolup Screens." *Vanity Fair* 8 (March 1922), 110; (April 1922), 106.

Rosanthal, Leon S. *A History of Philadelphia's University City.* Philadelphia: Univ. of Pennsylvania Press, 1963.

Rose, Anne C. *Transcendentalism as a Social Movement, 1830–1850.* New Haven: Yale Univ. Press, 1981.

Rosenberg, Charles E. *The Cholera Years: The United States in 1832, 1849, and 1866.* Chicago: Univ. of Chicago Press, 1962.

Rosenthal, Michael. *Constable: The Painter and His Landscape.* New Haven: Yale Univ. Press, 1983.

Ross, Marjorie Drake. *The Book of Boston: The Federal Period, 1775 to 1837.* New York: Hastings, 1961.

Rourke, Constance. *American Humor: A Study of the National Character.* Garden City, N.Y.: Doubleday, 1931.

———. *The Roots of American Culture and Other Essays,* ed. Van Wyck Brooks. New York: Harcourt, 1942.

Rowley, Trevor. *Villages in the Landscape.* London: Dent, 1978.

Rubin, Joan Shelley. *Constance Rourke and American Culture.* Chapel Hill: Univ. of North Carolina Press, 1980.

Ruggles, Thomas. "Picturesque Farming." *Annals of Agriculture and Other Useful Arts* 9 (1788), 1–15.

"*Rural Hours:* By a Lady" [review]. *The Horticulturist* 5 (November 1850), 230–232.

"Rural Objects in England and America." *Putnam's* 7 (July 1855), 32–40.

"Rural Scenery: The Thatched Cottage." *American Gardener's Magazine* 2 (May 1836), 210–212.

Rush, Leonard. "An American at Rock Park." *Cheshire Life* 32 (October 1966), 70–73.

Sadler, William S. "The Suburban and the City Child." *Suburban Life* 10 (February 1910), 66.

Sage Foundation Homes Co. *Declaration of Restrictions.* New York, 1911.

———. *Forest Hills Gardens.* New York, 1909.

———. *Forest Hills Gardens: Preliminary Information.* New York, 1911.

———. *Forest Hills Inn.* New York, 1914.

———. *A Forward Movement in Suburban Development.* New York, 1910.

St. John, Adrian. "Will Gas Destroy Populations in the New War?" *Literary Digest* 17 (March 3, 1934), 117.

Saint-Maur, Kate V. "Housekeeping Methods for Country Women." *Country Life* 20 (September 15, 1911), 23–25.

Salerno, Luigi. "The Picturesque." *Encyclopedia of World Art,* XI, 335–342. New York: McGraw-Hill, 1966.

Sangster, Margaret E. "The Suburban Resident." *Collier's* 26 (March 4, 1901), 20.

Sargent, D. A. "Exercise and Longevity." *North American Review* 164 (May 1897), 556–560.

"Satisfaction of Good Tools." *Country Life* 19 (December [mid-month] 1910), cxxxiii.

Sayers, E. "Notes and Observations on Gardens and Nurseries in the Vicinity of Newark." *Magazine of Horticulture* 3 (September 1837), 321–329.

Saylor, Henry H. "Personality in a Country Home." *House and Garden* 13 (September 1910), 140–144.

"Scarlet Oaks Cottage." *Western Horticultural Review* 1 (December 1850), frontispiece.

Schalk, Harry G. "Planning Roland Park." *Journal of the Society of Architectural Historians* 35 (December 1976), 285–292.

Schauman, Sally, and Carolyn Adams. *An Assessment Procedure for Countryside Landscapes.* Seattle: Univ. of Washington Department of Landscape Architecture, 1982.

Schmitt, Peter J. *Back to Nature: The Arcadian Myth in Urban America.* New York: Oxford, 1969.

Schneider, J. Herbert. "A Country Lane." *Photo-Era* 54 (June 1930), 320.

Schott, Henry. "A City's Fight for Beauty." *World's Work* 11 (February 1906), 7191.

Schultze-Naumburg, Paul. *Dorfer und Kolonien.* Munchen: Callwey, 1908.

Schwartz, Janet. "The Poet and the Pastoral in the Naming of Suburbia." *Names* 28 (September 1980), 231–255.

"Science of Agriculture and Book Farming." *New England Farmer* 1 (August 10, 1822), 14–15.

Scott ["Rev. Dr."]. *Influence of Great Cities.* San Francisco: Whitton, 1854.

Scoville, Samuel. *Everyday Adventures.* Boston: Atlantic, 1920.

Sears, George Washington. *Woodcraft.* New York: Forest and Stream, 1884.

Seaton, Beverly. "Idylls of Agriculture; or, Nineteenth-Century Success Stories of Farming and Gardening." *Agricultural History* 55 (January 1981), 21–30.

Sedgwick, A. G. "Village Improvement." *The Nation* 19 (September 1874), 149–150.

Seymour, E. L. D. "Economy and the Vegetable Garden." *Country Life* 20 (September 15, 1911), 27–29, 70, 72.

Shackleton, Robert, and Elizabeth Shackleton. *The Charm of the Antique.* New York: Hearst, 1914.

———. *The Quest of the Colonial.* New York: Century, 1907.

The Shaker Heights Subdivision of Shaker Heights. Cleveland: Shaker Heights Improvement Co., 1914.

Shaker Village Standards. Cleveland: Van Sweringen Co., 1925.

Sharp, Dallas Lore. "The Commuter and the 'Modern Conveniences.' " *Atlantic* 106 (October 1910), 554–564.

———. *The Hills of Hingham.* Boston: Houghton, 1916.

———. *The Lay of the Land.* Boston: Houghton, 1922.

Sheahan, J. W. "Chicago." *Scribner's* 10 (September 1875), 528–551.

Sherman, Rexford B. "Daniel Webster: Gentleman Farmer." *Agricultural History* 53 (April 1979), 475–487.

"Shiftless Farmer." *New England Farmer* 10 (May 23, 1832), 357–358.

Shores, Robert J. "Plea for Privacy." *Forum* 51 (March 1914), 425–428.

Simpson, George W. "Enclosing the Laundry Yard." *Suburban Life* 3 (September 1906), 136.

Singer, Mark. "Funny Money." *New Yorker* 61 (April 22, 1985), 51–103.

Singleton, Esther. *The Collecting of Antiques.* New York: Macmillan, 1937.

"Six Samples of Back-Jersey Farmers." *American Agriculturist* 6 (December 1847), 370–371.

Slater, T. R. "Family, Society, and the Ornamental Villa on the Fringes of English Country Towns." *Journal of Historical Geography* 4 (April 1978), 129–144.

"Small Carriage House and Stable." *Annual Register of Rural Affairs* 2 (1856), 190–191.

Smith, Carl. "Urban Disorder and the Shape of Belief: The San Francisco Earthquake and Fire." *Yale Review* 74 (Autumn 1984), 79–95.

Smith, F. A. Cushing. "The Glory of Shaker Village." *American Landscape Architect* 1 (July 1929), 21–35.

Smith, Nora Archibald. "A Country Catechism." *Countryside* 24 (March 1917), 136.

Smith, R. A. *Philadelphia as It Is In 1852.* Philadelphia: Lindsay, 1852.

Smith, R. Morris. "A Suburban Country Residence." *Horticulturist* 6 (April 1856), 182–184.

Smith, Wendell. *Overbrook Farms: A Suburb Deluxe.* Philadelphia: Smith, 1905.

Solomon, Barbara Miller. *Ancestors and Immigrants: A Changing New England Tradition* [1956]. Chicago: Univ. of Chicago Press, 1972.

Solotaroff, William. "The City's Duty to Its Trees." *American City* 4 (March 1911), 131–134.

"Some Inexpensive Country Homes." *Scientific American* 75 (December 5, 1896), 75.

"Some Recollections of a Village." *The New-England Magazine* 2 (March 1832), 192–196.

Spafford, Horatio Gates. *A Gazetteer of the State of New-York.* Albany: Packard, 1824.

"Speaking of Antiques." *Antiques* 2 (July 1922), 8–9.

Speed, John Gilner. "Right of Privacy." *North American Review* 163 (July 1896), 64–74.

Stanley Rule and Level Plant. *How to Work with Tools and Wood: For the Home Workshop.* New Britain, Conn.: Stanley Rule and Level Plant, 1927.

Steed, W. "The Future of Warfare." *Nineteenth Century* 116 (August 1934), 129–140.

Stetson, Sarah P. "William Hamilton and His 'Woodlands.'" *Pennsylvania Magazine of History and Biography* 73 (January 1949), 26–27.

Stickley, Gustav. "The Craftsman Movement: Its Origin and Growth." *Craftsman* 25 (October 1913), 17–26.

———. "Most Valuable of All Arts." *Craftsman* 28 (September 1915), 527–531, 615.

Stilgoe, John R. *Common Landscape of America, 1580 to 1845.* New Haven: Yale Univ. Press, 1982.

———. "Hobgoblin in Suburbia: Origins of Contemporary American Place Consciousness." *Landscape Architecture* 73 (November 1983), 54–61.

———. *Metropolitan Corridor: Railroads and the American Scene.* New Haven: Yale Univ. Press, 1983.

———. "Popular Photography, Scenery Values, and Visual Assessment." *Landscape Journal* 3 (Autumn 1984), 111–122.

———. "Privacy and Energy-Efficient Residential Site Design: An Example of Context." *Journal of Architectural Education* 37 (Spring/Summer 1984), 20–25.

———. "Smiling Scenes." *Views and Visions: American Landscape Before 1830,* ed. Edward J. Nygren. Washington, D.C.: Corcoran Gallery of Art, 1986.

———. "Suburbanites Forever: The American Dream Endures." *Landscape Architecture* 72 (May 1982), 88–93.

———. "The Suburbs." *American Heritage* 35 (February–March 1984), 21–36.

———. "Town Common and Village Green in New England, 1620 to 1981." In *On Common Ground,* ed. Ronald Lee Fleming and Lauri A. Halderman. Harvard, Mass.: Harvard Common Press, 1982.

———. "Treasured Wastes: Spaces and Memory." *Places* 4 (Summer 1987), 64–74.

Stillinger, Elizabeth. *The Antiquers.* New York: Knopf, 1980.

"Stock on Long Island." *American Agriculturist* 2 (October 1843), 194–196.

Stourzh, Gerald. *Alexander Hamilton and the Idea of Republican Government.* Stanford: Stanford Univ. Press, 1970.

Stowe, Harriet Beecher. *The Minister's Wooing* [1859]. Ridgewood, N.J.: Gregg Press, 1968.

Strong, George Templeton. *Diary*, ed. Allan Nevins and Milton Halsey Thomas. New York: Macmillan, 1952.

"Study in Architectural Alchemy." *Craftsman* 28 (June 1915), 284–292.

"Study the Beautiful in Nature." *Western Horticultural Review* 1 (August 1851), 505–507.

Stuyvesant, Jared. "Why You Should Have A Workshop and How." *House and Garden* 18 (December 1910), 352–353, 378, 380, 382.

"Suburban Cottage at Boston, Mass." *Scientific American* 77 (August 28, 1897), 134.

"Suburban Cottages Versus Flats." *Independent* 62 (March 28, 1907), 748–749.

"Suburban Gardening." *The Horticulturist* 7 (October 1852), 447–448.

"Suburban Prices." *Good Housekeeping* 49 (November 1909), 588–593.

"Suburban Seventies." *Annals of the American Academy of Political and Social Science* 422 (1975).

"Suburban Woman and Her Neighborhood Clubs." *Suburban Life* 12 (September 1911), 166.

"Summer Windows." *Ladies' Home Journal* 7 (June 1890), 4.

"Supposed Effects of the Gases of Brick-Kilns." *American Agriculturist* 6 (March 1847), 83–84.

Susman, Warren. "The Useless Past: American Intellectuals and the Frontier Thesis, 1910 to 1930." *Bucknell Review* 11 (March 1963), 1–20.

Swift, Ethel Longworth. "In Defense of Suburbia." *Outlook* 148 (April 4, 1928), 543–544, 558.

Swift, Samuel. "Llewellyn Park." *House and Garden* 3 (June 1906), 326–335.

Talmadge, T. Dewitt. "Under My Study Lamp." *Ladies' Home Journal* 7 (April 1890), 9.

Taylor, Albert D. "Care and Preservation of Street Trees." *Good Roads* 9 (December 1908), 409–413.

Taylor, Christopher. *Village and Farmstead*. London: George Phillip, 1983.

Taylor, Graham. *Satellite Cities: A Study of Industrial Suburbs*. New York: Appleton, 1915.

Thomas, John L. "Romantic Reform in America, 1815–1865." *American Quarterly* 17 (Winter 1965), 656–681.

Thompson, Flora McDonald. "The Servant Question." *Cosmopolitan* 28 (March 1908), 521–528.

Thompson, Warren S. "Future of the Large City." *American Mercury* 20 (July 1930), 327–337.

———. "On Living in Cities." *American Mercury* 20 (June 1930), 192–201.

Thoreau, Henry David. *Miscellanies*. Boston: Houghton, 1895.

———. *Journal*, ed. Bradford Torrey. Boston: Houghton, 1906.

Thornton, Tamara Plakins. "Between Generations: Boston Agricultural Reform and the Aging of New England, 1815 to 1830." *New England Quarterly* 59 (June 1986), 189–211.

———. "Cultivating the American Character." *Orion Nature Quarterly* 4 (Spring 1985), 10–19.

———. "The Moral Dimensions of Horticulture in Antebellum America." *New England Quarterly* 57 (March 1984), 3–24.

Tichi, Cecilia. *New World, New Earth: Environmental Reform in American Literature from the Puritans through Whitman*. New Haven: Yale University Press, 1979.

Tocqueville, Alexis de. *Democracy in America* [1848], trans. George Lawrence, ed. J. P. Mayer. New York: Doubleday, 1969.

Tompkins, D. A. "Working People's Homes." *Cassier's Magazine* 23 (April 1903), 600–614.

Torrey, Bradford. "My Real Estate." *Atlantic* 58 (October 1886), 496–502.

"Town and Country; or, Which Is Best." *Horticulturist* 8 (June 1858), 249–250.

"Town of Kohler, Wisconsin: A Model Industrial Development." *Architecture* 5 (April 1925), 149–154.

Trotter, Thomas. *A View of the Nervous Temperament*. London: Longman, 1807.

True, John Preston. "Beatitudes of a Suburbanite." *Atlantic* 102 (October 1908), 552–555.

Tryon, Lilliam Hart. "Reflections of a Housewife." *House Beautiful* 37 (May 1915), 169–170.

Tuckerman, H. T. "An Essay on Flowers." *Horticulturist* 5 (July 1850), 33–40.

Twain, Mark. *Adventures of Huckleberry Finn* [1885], ed. Leo Marx. Indianapolis: Bobbs-Merrill, 1967.

"Twenty Miles Out: Indiscretions of a Commuter's Wife." *House Beautiful* 57 (January–June, 1925), 62, 158, 274, 406, 566, 702.

"Two Pictures." *American Agriculturist* 16 (March 1857), 60.

"Two Young Men." *American Magazine* 83 (March 1917), 50–51.

Underwood, Loring. "A Garden to Live In." *Suburban Life* 4 (March 1907), 117–118, 164.

Urry, William. *Canterbury Under the Angevin Kings.* London: Athlone, 1967.

"Value of Arts." *Craftsman* 28 (September 1915), 528.

Veblen, Thorstein. "The Country Town." *Freeman* 7 (July 11, 1923), 417–420; (July 18, 1923), 440–443.

Veiller, Lawrence. "Industrial Housing Developments in America." *Architectural Record* 43 (March 1918), 231–257.

"Villa of Mr. Halsey." *American Agriculturist* 4 (September 1845), 298–299.

"Villa of Mr. Sargent." *American Agriculturist* 10 (December 1851), 362–363.

Village Builder. New York: Bicknell, 1872.

"Village Teacher: Favorite Occupation." *Rural Magazine and Literary Evening Fireside* 1 (September 1820), 323–325.

"Village Teacher: One Morning." *Rural Magazine and Literary Evening Fireside* 1 (November 1820), 403–407.

Villard, H. S. and R. S. Allen. "Poison Gas, 1915 to 1926." *Nation* 124 (January 12, 1927), 32–33.

"Visits to Country Places: Around Baltimore." *Horticulturist* 7 (May 1857), 206–208.

Wade, Richard. *Chicago: Growth of a Metropolis.* Chicago: Univ. of Chicago Press, 1969.

Wales, John G. "Holliston." Boston: Wales, 1831.

Walker, Amasa. "The Farmer's Wants." *Report of the Massachusetts Board of Agriculture* 3 (1856), 336–346.

Walker, George Leon. *Thomas Hooker: Preacher, Founder, Democrat.* New York: Dodd, Mead, 1891.

Walker, John Brisben. "The Wonders of New York." *Cosmopolitan* 36 (December 1903), 143.

Walling, Henry F. "Braintree." Boston: Wallin, 1856.

———. "Weymouth." Boston: Walling, 1853.

Ward, Hilda. "The Automobile in the Suburbs from a Woman's Point of View." *Suburban Life* 5 (November 1907), 269–271.

Ware, John F. W. *Home Life: What It Is, and What It Needs.* Boston: Spencer, 1868.

Waring, George E., Jr. *Village Improvement and Farm Villages.* Boston: Osgood, 1877.

Warner, Sam Bass, Jr. "The Liberal City." *Design Quarterly* 129 (Summer 1985), 32–41.

———. *Streetcar Suburbs: The Process of Growth in Boston, 1870 to 1900.* Cambridge, Mass.: Harvard Univ. Press, 1962.

"Waste Places Around Villages, Farms, Etc." *American Agriculturist* 16 (June 1857), 131.

Waterman, Catharine H. *Flora's Lexicon: An Interpretation of the Language and Sentiment of Flowers.* Philadelphia: Hooker & Claxton, 1839.

Watson, John Fanning. *Annals of Philadelphia.* Philadelphia: Carey, 1845.

Weaver, John C. and Michael J. Doucet. "Material Culture and the North American House: The Era of the Common Man, 1870–1920." *Journal of American History* 72 (December 1985), 560–587.

Webster, Richard J. *Philadelphia Preserved.* Philadelphia: Temple Univ. Press, 1976.

Wells, Benjamin W. "Henry Cuyler Bunner." *Sewanee Review* 5 (January 1897), 1–16.

Wells, H. G. *The War in the Air.* London: Bell, 1908.

Weiss, Marc. *The Rise of the Community Builders.* New York: Columbia Univ. Press, 1987.

Wertenbaker, Thomas J. *The First Americans, 1607–1690.* New York: Macmillan, 1927.

Wheeler, Everett P. "The Unofficial Government of Cities." *Atlantic* 85 (March 1900), 370–376.

"Which *Life* House Is Nearest You?" *Life* 5 (December 26, 1938), 60.

White, E. B. "Here Is New York" [1949]. *Perspectives USA* 4 (Summer 1953), 26–45.

White, B. R. *The English Separatist Tradition: From the Marian Martyrs to the Pilgrim Fathers.* New York: Oxford Univ. Press, 1971.

Whitehill, Walter Muir. "Francis Parkman as Horticulturist." *Arnoldia* 33 (May/June, 1973), 169–183.

Whiting, Frederick A. "What an Enterprising Improvement Society Can Do When It Tries." *Suburban Life* 4 (February 1907), 70.

Whitman, Roger. *First Aid for the Ailing House.* New York: McGraw-Hill, 1934.

"Why Is a Suburb?" *Countryside* 24 (July 1917), 370.

Wiebe, Robert H. *The Search for Order, 1877–1920.* New York: Hill & Wang, 1967.

"Wild Scenes Near Home." *American Monthly Magazine* 2 (November 1836), 469–498.

Wilder, H. J. "Agriculture in the Coal Regions of Southwestern Pennsylvania." *Yearbook of Agriculture for 1909.* Washington, D.C.: Government Printing Office, 1910.

Wilder, Marshall Pinckney. "Horticulture of Boston and Vicinity." *Memorial History of Boston,* ed. Justin Winsor. Boston: Osgood, 1881.

Williams, M. J. "Wood in the Garden Picture." *Garden and Home Beautiful* 45 (May 1927), 261–262.

Williams, Raymond. *The Country and the City.* London: Chatto and Windus, 1973.

Willis, Nathaniel Parker. *American Scenery Illustrated.* London: George Virtue, 1840.

———. Hurry-Graphs; or, Sketches of Scenery, *Celebrities, and Society.* Auburn, New York: Alden, 1853.

———. *Out-Doors at Idlewild; or, The Shaping of a Home on the Banks of the Hudson.* New York: Scribner, 1855.

———. *Rural Letters.* New York: Baker and Scribner, 1849.

Wilson, Charles Morrow. *The Landscape of Rural Poverty: Corn Bread and Creek Water.* New York: Holt, 1940.

Wilson, Daniel Munro. *Where American Independence Began.* Boston: Houghton, 1904.

Wilson, Edmund. "Wanted: A City of the Spirit." *Vanity Fair* 21 (January 1924), 63, 94.

Wilson, Perry. "The New Market." *National Real Estate Journal* 36 (January 1935), 34–35.

Wilson, Richard Guy. "Idealism and the Origin of the First American Suburb: Llewellyn Park, New Jersey." *American Art Journal* 11 (October 1979), 79–90.

Wilson, Warren H. "Social Life in the Country." *Annals of the American Academy of Political and Social Science* 40 (March 1912), 119–216.

Winslow, Helen M. "Buying the Supplies for a Suburban Home." *Suburban Life* 3 (December 1906), 221, 249.

"Woman's Poultry." *Suburban Life* 10 (June 1910), 379.

Wood, Charles B. "Powelton: An Unresearched Building by William Strickland." *Pennsylvania Magazine of History and Biography* 91 (April 1967), 145–163.

Wood, Eugene. "Why Pay Rent?" *Everybody's Magazine* 22 (June 1910), 765–774.

Wood, Gordon S. *The Creation of the American Republic, 1776–1787.* Chapel Hill: Univ. of North Carolina Press, 1969.

Wood, Joseph S. "Elaboration of a Settlement System: The New England Village in the Federal Period." *Journal of Historical Geography* 10 (October 1984), 331–356.

———. "Village and Community in Early Colonial New England." *Journal of Historical Geography* 8 (October 1982), 333–346.

"Wood Office Furniture." *Fortune* 2 (November 1930), 19.

Woodward, Margaret. "Suburban Woman and Her Children." *Suburban Life* 12 (August 1911), 107.

Woolworth, Clara. "That Matter of Wiring Your Home." *American Cookery* 30 (November 1925), 263–266.

Wordsworth, William. *A Description of the Scenery of the Lakes in the North of England.* London: Longman, 1822.

"World of New York." *Putnam's Monthly Magazine* 7 (June 1856), 659–668.

Wright, Gwendolyn. *Building the Dream: A Social History of Housing in America.* New York: Pantheon, 1981.

Wright, Richardson. *Truly Rural: Adventures in Getting Back to Earth.* Boston: Houghton, 1922.

Wyckoff, W. A. "With Iowa Farmers." *Scribner's* 29 (May 1901), 525–536.

Yeoman. "Old Colony Memorial," *New England Farmer* 1 (January 18, 1822), 198.

Yeomans, Edward. "The Suburb De Luxe." *Atlantic* 125 (January 1920), 105–107.

Young, Thomas P. "Long Island Farming and the Expense of Reclaiming Marshlands." *American Journal of Agriculture and Science* 9 (January 1847), 45–47.

Zelinsky, Wilbur. "By Their Names You Shall Know Them: A Toponymic Approach to the American Land and Ethos." *New York Folklore* 8 (Summer 1982), 85–96.

———. "The Pennsylvania Town: An Overdue Geographical Account," *Geographical Review* 67 (April 1977), 127–147.

Ziff, Larzer. *The Career of John Cotton: Puritanism and the American Experience.* Princeton: Princeton Univ. Press, 1962.

———. *Puritanism in America: New Culture in a New World.* New York: Viking, 1973.

INDEX

Cowley, Malcolm, 298–99
Cozzens, Frederick B., 168–70
Crothers, Samuel McChord, 296–98
Cruger, Mary, 306–08
Curtiss, Philip, 9
Cushing Island, 259
Cutting, Mary Stewart, 64

Daniels, Howard, 52
Davidson, Donald, 295
Davis, Alexander, 53–54
Dearborn, Henry Alexander Scammell, 109
delivery men. *See* express shipment
Deutsche Werkstatten, 256
Diggs, Annie L., 258
dogs, 168
do-it-yourself, 262–67; patriotism of, 268
Downing, Andrew Jackson, 32, 93, 102–03, 110, 118, 201, 272; on villages, 86–87
dynamite, in cities, 280
Dwight, Timothy, 78–79, 87–92

earthquakes, 280
East Hampton, Long Island, 79, 81
Eaton, Florence Taft, 266
Emerson, Ralph Waldo, 31, 38
"environs," 9
express shipment, 208–10

farming, difficulties of, 69–77; part-time, 166
Fawcett, Waldon, 259, 260
Federalism, 93–95; in architecture, 94–95
feminists, 235
feudal landscape, 28
Field, Henry, 296
fire, 84–85, 280
firestorm, 280
Fisher, Sidney, 131–33, 151–52
Flagg, Wilson, 114–19, 186–90, 201
floral alphabetizing, 36–37
floriculture, 32–33, 118–20
Forest Hills Gardens, 225–38, 260, 271; building materials, 232–33; as picture, 232; restrictions, 228–30
Frederick, Christine, 288–89
freedom of movement, 7
Freneau, Philip, 79
frontier, 3–5

Galveston fire, 280
garden cities, 253–56
gazetteers, 80–81
Geneseo, New York, 151–52
Germantown, 132–33
geranium fad, 119–20
Glazier, Willard, 60–64
Gloag, John, 299
Godley, John Robert, 186
Goldsmith, Oliver, 78
Graves, Louis, 230–32
Greeley, Horace, 123
Grey, Elmer, 271–72
ground zero, 301

Hale, Sarah Josepha, 36
Hall, Sarah, 121
Hamilton, William, 135–36
hardware advertising, 267
Harland, Marion, 266
Haskell, Llewellyn S., 52–55
Hawthorne, Nathaniel, 9, 28–30, 36, 49
Hazard, Lucy Lockwood, 295
hedges, 198–202
Hellerav, 253–56
Holly, Henry Hudson, xi, 118, 272
homes, urban, 31
Hooker, Thomas, 10
horticulture, 107–22
Horton, Howard, 34–35
houses, restored, 290–95
household repair, 266–67; and women, 266
Howe, Frederick C., 256
Howells, William Dean, 153, 175–76, 209
Howland, G. G., 111
Huxtable, Ada Louise, 303

Indian Hill, Massachusetts, 256–58
insects, 16

James, Henry, 190, 281
Jacques, George, 107, 115
Jefferson Township, Illinois, 143–45
Johnson, Henry C., 148–49
Josephson, Matthew, 4

Keese, John, 36
Kenilworth, Illinois, 194, 208–09, 220
Kirkland, Caroline, 139
Klaber, John T., 253–56
Knevels, Mary Eastwood, 233
Kohler, Wisconsin, 258

landscape aesthetics, 176, 186–88, 196, 290
Langland, William, 78
Lewis, Sinclair, 287–88
Life houses, 300
light, in houses, 102
Lincoln, Almira H., 34
Lipman, Samuel, 306
Llewellyn Park, New Jersey, 52–55
London, Jack, 280
Long Island, farming on, 75–76
Lost Generation writers, 285

Mackenzie, Alexander Slidell, 52
McCrea, A. E., 219
Manning, Warren, 212–13
manufactories, 81
manure, urban, 74
market gardening, 74–75
Mather, Cotton, 6
Maxwell, A., 129
Maxwell, Sidney D., 57–60
May, Charles C., 233, 236
Mead, Sydney E., 8
mechanics, 80, 273
Melville, Herman, 30, 102

ILLUSTRATION CREDITS

Unless otherwise noted, all illustrations are courtesy of Harvard College Library. Sources cited in shortened form here are given in full in the bibliography.

Page		
ii–iii	*Life,* Jan. 3, 1901	
3	*Saturday Evening Post,* Nov. 26, 1960	
12	*Saturday Evening Post,* Dec. 24, 1960	
14	*New Yorker,* Aug. 19, 1939	
14	Author's collection	
17	*New Yorker,* Aug. 11, 1986	
17	*House Beautiful,* May 1915	
17	*Saturday Evening Post,* Aug. 4, 1956	
19	*Picturesque America*	
26	Cooper, *Rhyme and Reason*	
26	Willis, *American Scenery*	
29, 35 (top and center)	Cooper, *Rhyme and Reason*	
35 (bottom)	Lincoln, *Familiar Lectures* (author's collection)	
40	Willis, *American Scenery*	
40	"New Homes of New York"	
41	Willis, *Out-Doors at Idlewild*	
44 (top)	"Growth of Cities"	
44 (bottom)	Willis, *American Scenery*	
46 (top)	Richards, "Susquehanna"	
46 (center)	Cooper, *Rhyme and Reason*	
46 (bottom)	Richards, "Susquehanna"	
47	James Monteith, *Youth's Manual of Geography* (New York: Barnes, 1854)	
50, 51	Collection of Jan Mazur	
58–59	*Picturesque America*	
61 (top)	"Camp Meeting"	
61 (bottom), 62, 63	Kenny, *Illustrated Cincinnati*	
65	Griffin, *Westchester*	
72 (top)	*Pictorial National Library*	
72 (center and bottom)	"Two Pictures"	
77	Periam, *Pictorial Cyclopedia*	
82 (top)	Barber, *Connecticut*	
82 (bottom), 83	Barber, *Massachusetts*	
88	Barber, *Connecticut*	
88	"Half an Acre"	
90 (top)	Barber, *New York*	
90 (bottom)	"Small Carriage House"	
91	Walling, "Braintree"	
96 (top)	"Laying Out Farms"	
96 (bottom)	"Complete Country Residence"	
100 (top)	"Residence of John R. Chapin"	
100 (bottom)	Downing, *Rural Residences*	
101 (top)	"Scarlet Oaks Cottage"	
101 (bottom)	"Piermont"	
104 (top)	*Western Horticultural Review,* March 1851	
104 (bottom), 105	Scharf, *Westchester County*	
106	"Improving Old Houses"	
108	*Horticulturist,* Aug. 1856	
108	*Western Horticultural Review,* 1854 [month unknown]	
113 (top)	Willis, *American Scenery*	
113 (bottom)	"Resor's Greenhouse"	
116 (top)	*Western Horticultural Review,* 1854 [month unknown]	
116 (bottom)	"Laying Out and Dividing Farms"	
117 (top)	"Complete Country Residence"	
117 (bottom)	"Flower Gardens"	
125	*Philadelphia in 1830*	
130	"Plan of the City of Philadelphia and Its Environs" (Philadelphia: Lindsay and Blakiston, 1852)	
134	Smith, "Suburban or Country Residence"	
141, 147	Chamberlin, *Chicago*	

150		237 (bottom)	Atterbury, "Cottage and
155 (top and			Garden"
center)	Wood, "Why Pay Rent?"	243, 248, 249	
155 (bottom)	*Life,* Aug. 15, 1901	(top)	*Shaker Village Standards*
157	Author's collection	249 (bottom)	"Map of the Property of
158 (top)	Caparn, "Parallelogram		the Shaker Heights Im-
	Park"		provement Company"
158 (bottom)	*Life,* 1906		[n.d.], Loeb Library,
160	Caparn, "Parallelogram		Harvard Graduate
	Park"		School of Design
163, 173 (top		254	"Industrial Experiment"
left)	Cozzens, "Sparrowgrass	255	Diggs, "English Garden
	Papers"		City"
173 (top right		257 (top)	Klaber, "Hellerav"
and bottom)	Coffin, *Out of Town*	257 (center and	
177	Howells, *Suburban*	bottom)	Atterbury, "Model
	Sketches		Towns"
178 (top and		261 (top)	May, "Indian Hill"
center)	Bunner, *Jersey Street*	261 (bottom)	Loeb Library, Harvard
178 (bottom)	Bunner, *Runaway Browns*		Graduate School of
181	Bunner, *Jersey Street*		Design
183 (top)	Bunner, *Runaway Browns*	263	Wood, "Why Pay Rent?"
183 (bottom),		264	*Suburban Life,* Dec. 1906
184, 185	Bunner, *Suburban Sage*	265 (top)	Stuyvesant, "Why You
187, 191 (top)	Author's collection		Should Have a Home
191 (bottom)	Solottaroff, "City's Duty"		Workshop"
193	Loeb Library, Harvard	265 (bottom)	*House and Garden,* Dec.
	Graduate School of		1910
	Design	269	Stanley Rule and Level
195 (top)	Bunner, *Suburban Sage*		Plant, *How to Work with*
195 (center and			*Tools and Wood*
bottom)	Cole, "Chicago's Most	270, 274 (top)	Grey, "New Suburbs"
	Unique Suburb"	274 (bottom)	Ward, "Automobile"
197 (top)	"Design for a Partially En-	277	London, "Story"
	closed Veranda"	278 (top)	Author's collection
197 (bottom)	Fisher, "Ten	278 (bottom),	
	Commandments"	282	London, "Story"
200 (top)	Luitwieler, "Old Settler"	284	Gaunt, "Modern Utopia"
200 (bottom)	Fisher, "Rational Scheme"	291 (top)	Shackleton, *Charm*
203 (top)	"How to Cool a Hot	291 (center and	
	Porch" [May 1906]	bottom)	Shackleton, *Quest*
203 (bottom)	Fisher, "Rational Scheme"	292 (top)	Shackleton, *Charm*
205	*Life,* March 4, 1920	292 (center and	
211 (top)	Bunner, *Runaway Browns*	bottom)	Carrick, *Next-to-Nothing*
211 (center)	Bunner, *Jersey Street*		*House*
211 (bottom)	Wood, "Why Pay Rent?"	297 (top)	"Bringing an Old New En-
218 (top)	Sanborn Map Company,		gland Home Up to
	Wellesley		Date"
	[Massachusetts]	297 (center)	Field, "Shenandoah"
218 (bottom)	*Suburban Life,* July 1915	297 (bottom)	Schneider, "Country
221, 229, 231,			Lane"
234 (top and		304	Author's collection
center), 237		305	*Saturday Evening Post,*
(top)	Loeb Library, Harvard		May 18, 1957
	Graduate School of	307 (top)	*Suburban Life,* March
	Design		1915
237 (center)	Atterbury, "Church in the	307 (bottom)	Cruger, *How She Did It*
	Gardens"		